CDO & MAPI Programming with Visual Basic

CDO & MAPI Programming with Visual Basic

Dave Grundgeiger

O'REILLY®

Beijing · Cambridge · Farnham · Köln · Paris · Sebastopol · Taipei · Tokyo

CDO & MAPI Programming with Visual Basic
by Dave Grundgeiger

Published by O'Reilly & Associates, Inc., 101 Morris Street, Sebastopol, CA 95472.

Editor: Ron Petrusha

Production Editor: Leanne Clarke Soylemez

Cover Designer: Ellie Volckhausen

Printing History:

October 2000: First Edition.

Library of Congress Cataloging-in-Publication Data

Grundgeiger, Dave.
CDO & MAPI programming with Visual Basic/Dave Grundgeiger.
p. cm.
Includes index.
ISBN 1-56592-665-X
1. Microsoft Visual BASIC. 2. BASIC (Computer program language) 3.
Object-oriented programming (Computer science) 4. Electronic mail systems. I. Title.

QA76.73.B3 G775 2000
005.13'3--dc21 00-045275

ISBN: 1-56592-665-X

[M]

To Peace

Table of Contents

Preface

I wrote this book because I was unable to find an in-depth book on MAPI and CDO for Visual Basic developers. This was perplexing to me because the need to build messaging technology into applications is not at all uncommon. Many developers, for example, find that their applications must send email messages in response to certain events. Even this simple task can be difficult to get working without a good roadmap. I wanted to write a book that would be that roadmap.

Besides teaching how to send and receive email, I wanted much more. MAPI and CDO are powerful technologies that provide the infrastructure for sophisticated collaboration and workflow applications. This book teaches you how to exploit that infrastructure.

Web applications, too, can take advantage of the power and flexibility of MAPI and CDO. Microsoft even provides a server-side helper component (the CDO Rendering Library) that turns CDO data into browser-ready HTML. Sadly, the documentation in this area is poor. This book shows you how to get this capability up and running on your web site.

Who This Book Is For

The book's primary audience is intermediate to advanced Visual Basic developers who have real-world applications to write. Beginning developers may feel lost during the technical discussions of MAPI, CDO, COM, and object models, but they still stand to gain from the sample code. I have provided numerous code listings to illustrate the concepts and capabilities discussed in the book. All of the code listings were tested within the Visual Basic development environment and copied directly from that environment into the text.

This book does not attempt to provide a complete reference for every MAPI and CDO object, property, and method call. Rather, the book approaches the topic from the point of view of a developer who has a job to do, or who wants to learn the material in a logical progression of concepts. Objects, properties, and methods are introduced as appropriate to the task under discussion.

Organization of This Book

The book contains 12 chapters and 6 appendixes:

Chapter 1, *Introduction*, gives an overview of messaging concepts. The chapter provides definitions for MAPI and CDO, presents their pros and cons, and discusses the kinds of applications that can be written to use this technology.

Chapter 2, *MAPI*, provides a thorough explanation of MAPI architecture and an introduction to the technologies based on MAPI. This chapter provides fundamental concepts that are used throughout the book.

Chapter 3, *Simple MAPI*, examines Simple MAPI, which offers a subset of MAPI functionality. Simple MAPI should be used only by programmers who are maintaining existing Simple MAPI code. Other developers can safely skip this chapter.

Chapter 4, *The MAPI ActiveX Controls*, examines the MAPI ActiveX controls that come with the Professional and Enterprise editions of Visual Basic. These controls don't expose the full functionality of MAPI (in fact, they use Simple MAPI internally), but they are sufficient for sending and receiving email with or without attachments. The controls have a shallow learning curve compared to other technologies described in this book. Jump directly to this chapter if you need to get something simple up and running quickly.

Chapter 5, *Collaboration Data Objects*, introduces CDO and lays the foundation for understanding its use. It introduces the concept of *object model* and examines the CDO object model in particular.

Chapter 6, *An Email Client Application*, gives practical instruction in using CDO to send and receive email, including email with attachments, formatted text, and embedded documents.

Chapter 7, *Enhancing the Email Client*, examines some of CDO's advanced email functionality. It also provides a detailed look at the relationship between CDO and MAPI.

Chapter 8, *Calendar Folders*, shows how to manipulate schedule information residing in MAPI folders, including how to create meetings and meeting requests programmatically.

Chapter 9, *Task Folders*, shows how to manipulate task information residing in MAPI folders, including how to create, save, send, move, and delete task items. This chapter also explains why it's difficult to access task information using CDO, and what you can (and can't) do about it.

Chapter 10, *Contacts Folders*, shows how to manipulate contact information residing in MAPI folders.

Chapter 11, *Web Applications*, shows how to use CDO and the CDO Rendering Library to create awesome web applications. The CDO Rendering Library is powerful but difficult to use and under-documented. This chapter provides detailed instructions to get your application up and running.

Chapter 12, *CDO for Windows 2000*, shows how to take advantage of this new technology. Although CDO for Windows 2000 doesn't use MAPI and is not backward-compatible with CDO, it's worth a look so that you're not left wondering what it is and how your CDO applications fit into the Windows 2000 scheme.

Appendix A, *Programming Internet Email Protocols*, examines an alternative to MAPI-based email. This appendix shows how to use the Winsock control to send and receive Internet email without using MAPI.

Appendix B, *Programming the Outlook Object Model*, examines an alternative to CDO. This appendix shows how to use the Outlook object model (a MAPI-based technology that is included with Microsoft Outlook) to send and receive email.

Appendix C, *The Outlook E-mail Security Update*, introduces this security patch from Microsoft. Installing the update reduces the threat from viruses such *Melissa* and *ILOVEYOU*, but it is likely to break code that uses CDO or the Outlook object model. This appendix gives an overview of the patch and tells how to get it.

Appendix D, *Where Am I Running?*, by Ron Petrusha, examines how to determine the platform on which an application is running. As discussed in Chapter 2, certain registry entries made by MAPI are in different locations depending on which operating system is in use. Programs that are to access these registry entries need to be able to determine the platform on which they are running.

Appendix E, *Resources for Messaging Developers*, is for when you get stuck. There are links to sites with articles and information, and to MAPI- and CDO-related discussion lists.

Appendix F, *Obtaining the Sample Code*, explains how to download this book's sample code from the O'Reilly & Associates web site.

Obtaining the Sample Code

All of the example Visual Basic source code from *CDO and MAPI Programming with Visual Basic* is freely downloadable from the O'Reilly & Associates web site at *http://vb.oreilly.com*. For details, see Appendix F.

Conventions Used in This Book

Throughout this book, we have used the following typographic conventions:

`Constant width`
: Indicates a language construct such as a language statement, a constant, or an expression. Interface names appear in constant width. Lines of code also appear in constant width, as do function and method prototypes.

Italic
: Represents intrinsic and application-defined functions, the names of system elements such as directories and files, and Internet resources such as web documents. New terms also are italicized when they are first introduced.

`Constant width italic`
: Indicates replaceable parameter names in prototypes or command syntax, and indicates variable and parameter names in body text.

How to Contact Us

We have tested and verified all the information in this book to the best of our ability, but you may find that features have changed (or even that we have made mistakes!). Please let us know about any errors you find, as well as your suggestions for future editions, by writing to:

O'Reilly & Associates, Inc.
101 Morris Street
Sebastopol, CA 95472
800-998-9938 (in the U.S. or Canada)
707-829-0515 (international/local)
707-829-0104 (fax)

You can also send messages electronically. To be put on our mailing list or to request a catalog, send email to:

nuts@oreilly.com

To ask technical questions or to comment on the book, send email to:

bookquestions@oreilly.com

For technical information on Visual Basic programming, to participate in VB discussion forums, or to acquaint yourself with O'Reilly's line of Visual Basic books, you can access the O'Reilly Visual Basic web site at:

> *http://vb.oreilly.com*

Acknowledgments

Please take a few minutes to read the names of the people who made this project a success—they've earned it, and I am humbly grateful to them all.

Thank you to Michael Bertrand and to Nicholas Wootton, two colleagues and friends who critiqued most chapters before I submitted them to my editor. You are holding a finer product because of their facility with both technology and the English language.

Thank you to Daniel J. Mitchell and to Siegfried Weber for their careful technical review of the manuscript after it was completed.

Thank you to the partners at Tara Software, Inc.: Roger Mills, Lynne Pilsner, Larry Kloepping, Garrett Peterson, and Dan Phelps. Because of their vision of a "Taliesin for developers," I'm happy when the alarm clock rings on Monday morning. Because of their flexibility, I was able to take a part-time leave to work on this book.

Thank you to the Quality Assurance team at Tara Software, Inc. These folks seemed to take genuine pleasure in supplying me with specially configured machines when I needed things that were difficult to set up on my home computer. They are the very definition of *customer service*.

Thank you again to Michael Bertrand for teaching me how to write Windows software. That was back in the days of "C SDK" programming, and it sure was fun. Mike is a tireless teacher of mathematics and programming at Madison Area Technical College in Madison, Wisconsin. His enthusiasm for coding and teaching is renowned in Madison's development community.

Thank you to my editor at O'Reilly & Associates, Inc., Ron Petrusha, who not once asked me to make a change just because our writing styles are not the same. Every change Ron suggested was right on the mark, making this a better book and me a better writer in the process. In addition, Ron graciously allowed me to reprint his article, "Where Am I Running?", in Appendix D. Thank you also to Ron's editorial assistant, Bob Herbstman, and to the production staff at O'Reilly & Associates, Inc. Thank you to Tim O'Reilly for starting a very cool publishing company.

Thank you to my mother, Amy Lynne Grundgeiger, for defining by example the words *strength*, *courage*, and *love*. Thank you to my father, Richard Grundgeiger, for uttering the one sentence that I remember above all: *People are here to help each other; that's what people do.*

Finally, thank you with great love, affection, and appreciation to the one single person who worked harder than I did for the success of this book: my friend and wife, Annemarie Newman. Annemarie has a successful professional career of her own, and the load that was placed on her by my relative absence during the past year was difficult, to say the least. Annemarie not only carried the load, but also had words of encouragement during the dark times when an author wonders if his book is any good at all, or if it will ever get done. Thank you to my children, Sasha and Nadia, for the times when they insisted that Daddy play with them instead of work on the computer.

1

Introduction

Messaging is the transmission of information using electronic means. The information transmitted can be anything: email, documents, images, meeting requests, music, purchase orders, faxes, etc., etc., etc. Anything that can be represented in digital form can be the content of a message. Usually, messaging uses *store-and-forward* technology. That means that the sender and receiver of a message don't need to be in direct contact with each other. The sender first gives the message to a messaging server. The server *stores* the message until it is able to *forward* it either to the intended recipient or to another server that will forward it to the recipient. That's the kind of messaging described in this book.

Messaging technology is used for more than just passing messages from one user to another asynchronously. There are natural extensions to this technology that support new ways of communicating and sharing information. For example, you're familiar with the concept of the *discussion list*—a use of messaging that enables groups of users to discuss topics of interest in public forums. In addition, message stores can be thought of as databases, providing a central place to store data that is not forwarded but waits for users to come view it. This is the concept behind Microsoft Exchange Server's public folders. Messaging technology is being used in new and unique ways to manage personal information of all kinds, including schedules, tasks, and contacts. By the time you reach the end of this book, you'll have learned how to tap into all of this and more in your own programs.

Messaging technology makes people more productive and efficient. Because of the asynchronous nature of email, communicators do not have to coordinate a time when they can both (or all) communicate at the same time. As mentioned, discussion lists are a great example of this. Rather than coordinating a huge meeting where everyone can contribute their opinions, discussion list members can contribute to the list and read others' communications when and where it's convenient. Messaging technology makes new things possible.

Messaging technology not only enables humans to communicate more effectively with each other, but also gives humans a new way to communicate with machines, and machines with each other. Web sites can automatically email users when content changes or notify them of events such as stock prices changing or news items appearing. Applications can automatically distribute tasks to personnel and monitor the progress of those tasks. Humans can send email directly to computers to initiate activity on those computers. Computers can email each other using email's store-and-forward paradigm to queue requests and responses among them.

Microsoft has provided an application-independent architecture for developing messaging and collaboration software. At the core of this architecture is the *Messaging Application Programming Interface (MAPI)*. It is a set of interface specifications to be used by developers of messaging-enabled client and server software. Although the term MAPI refers to this specification, in casual speech (and in writing) it is often used to refer to Microsoft's *MAPI Subsystem*, which is the core software component that must be present on a computer in order to run MAPI-based client and server software.

MAPI is a significant departure from traditional messaging systems. It is an attempt to establish open standards to allow different aspects of a messaging system to be written by different software vendors. Prior to MAPI, messaging systems typically were monolithic and proprietary. In contrast, software written to the MAPI standard is immediately compatible with all other MAPI-based software. This allows software vendors to write specific messaging components and ignore the rest. Developers of client applications, for example, needn't worry about how messages will be stored or transmitted—other components can be purchased by users to fill those needs. Looking at it from the users' point of view, this allows for mixing and matching of messaging components. ("I like *this* user interface, but I like *that* message store.")

MAPI has a few drawbacks. Because of its depth, it can be hard to learn. MAPI message storage is like a database management system. However, the way information is manipulated in MAPI message stores is not at all what programmers are used to from relational databases. In MAPI, all data—whether it's email, contacts, audio, invoices, etc.—is stored in entities called *message items*, which are like records in a database. Within each message item, data is stored in *MAPI properties*, which are like fields within a record. MAPI is very flexible in that any message item is permitted to possess any set of properties. This is like a database in which the set of fields that define a record can vary on a record-by-record basis. This is a powerful feature, but it takes some getting used to. Another drawback for Visual Basic and VBScript programmers is that MAPI is not directly callable from those languages. To access MAPI features, programmers using these languages can use Simple MAPI, the MAPI ActiveX controls, and Collaboration Data Objects

(CDO). All of these technologies are explained in this book, with particular emphasis on CDO.

MAPI has two more strikes against it. First, although it has delivered remarkably well on its promise of breaking email applications into components, this has not kept certain products from becoming dominant. For example, Microsoft Exchange Server is the dominant message store in Windows-based messaging systems. Indeed, some developers regard MAPI simply as the way to access Exchange Server. Finally, MAPI is likely to fade away over the next few years. Internet standards are in the process of replacing MAPI. Even the new version of Exchange Server (Exchange Server 2000) has dumped MAPI in favor of Internet protocols.

In its broadest usage, the term "CDO" refers to a group of messaging technologies, some of them completely unrelated to the others. However, "CDO" is also commonly used to refer to one of these technologies specifically: CDO 1.x, the Visual Basic- and VBScript-friendly "wrapper" for MAPI. That's how I use the term in this book: "CDO" means "CDO 1.x." I also touch on some of the other technologies that gather under the big CDO umbrella, but when I do, I qualify the term to differentiate it from the main topic of the book (for example, "CDO for Windows 2000").

CDO (i.e., CDO 1.x) exposes messaging functionality that is easily accessible to Visual Basic and VBScript programs. Internally, CDO calls MAPI to implement its messaging functionality. CDO is only for developers of client applications; *MAPI service providers* can't be written using CDO and therefore can't be written in Visual Basic. CDO is important because it allows Visual Basic and VBScript developers to get into the messaging game. Messaging frontends, schedulers, discussion lists, document servers, fax-back servers, workflow management systems, and much more can all be written using Visual Basic and CDO. All of these applications can be written for the Web using VBScript and CDO.

The drawback to CDO is that it does not expose all of MAPI's functionality. As already mentioned, CDO can't be used for writing MAPI service providers. This is acceptable, since Visual Basic and VBScript programmers are more likely to be interested in writing frontend application software. However, CDO is also missing some nice-to-have features for client applications. For example, CDO provides no way to add Rich Text Format (RTF) text to a message nor to read RTF from a message. This is unfortunate because users have come to expect the ability to use formatted text within messages. (Don't worry, though, I've written a helper component that will do this for you. See Chapter 6, *An Email Client Application*, for details.)

Messaging and long-distance collaboration are becoming increasingly important in our connected world. CDO gives your Visual Basic and VBScript applications the ability to participate in this phenomenon. In fact, as developers we may not be able to escape the need to include some messaging awareness in all our applications. In document-based applications, for example, users now expect to be able to email the current document to another user by selecting Send To from the File menu. These basic expectations of collaboration will continue to increase. Using MAPI and CDO to fulfill these needs is what this book is about. Solution developers have an opportunity to make their customers more efficient and productive. I sincerely hope this book helps you to achieve that goal.

2

MAPI

The Messaging Application Programming Interface (MAPI) specification was written in collaboration with more than 100 software vendors, and therefore (theoretically) it represents an industry-wide consensus on the features that should be supported by messaging platforms. Of the messaging choices available on the Microsoft Windows platforms, MAPI has the richest feature set and is the most flexible.

Although "API" is part of MAPI's name, it's not an API, or Application Programming Interface, in the way that Windows programmers usually think of that term. While many other APIs expose their capabilities through function libraries, MAPI is object-oriented. MAPI uses Microsoft's Component Object Model (COM) to provide a way to instantiate messaging objects, which in turn expose methods that can be called to manipulate those objects. I'll explain COM later in the book, when we need it to understand the structure of Collaboration Data Objects (CDO). For now, it's enough to note that MAPI uses COM features that aren't supported by Visual Basic, so it's not possible to program MAPI directly from Visual Basic. So why have a chapter on MAPI if it can't be used directly from Visual Basic? The reason is that MAPI is the foundation for many messaging technologies that *are* accessible to Visual Basic, including CDO. To fully understand CDO and other MAPI-based technologies, it is necessary to understand MAPI.

In addition to a survey of MAPI architecture, this chapter provides information about other technology choices available to Visual Basic developers.

MAPI Architecture

Figure 2-1 shows the major components in the MAPI architecture. The purpose and use of each component are described in this and following sections.

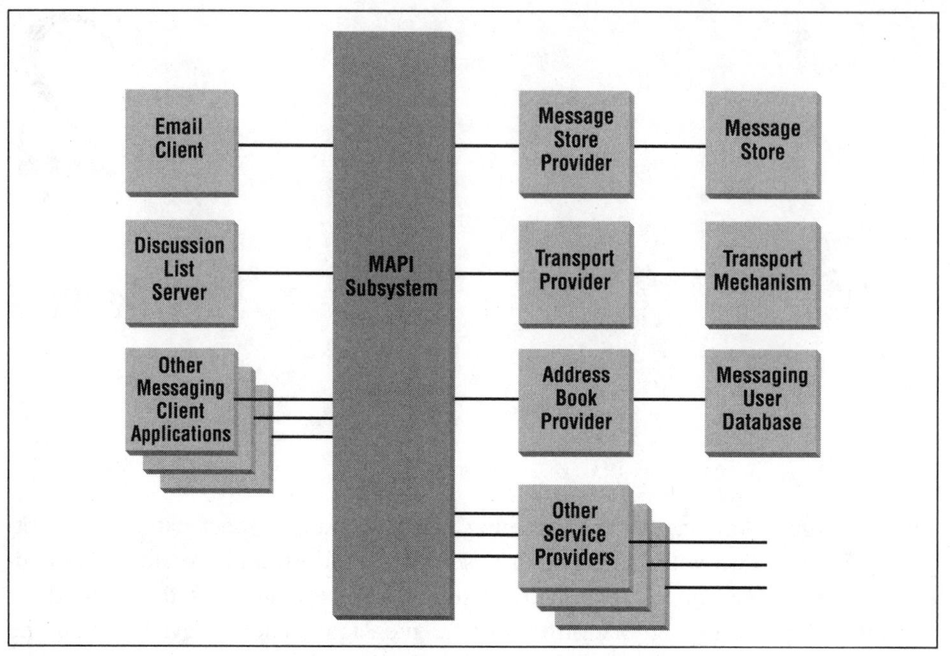

Figure 2-1. The MAPI architecture

The designers of MAPI recognized that messaging applications have certain features in common, and that these features can be factored out of the applications into separate components. These common features are:

- A front end, or *client*, to manipulate messaging objects (or present them to the user)
- A message store, to store messaging objects (typically on disk)
- A transport provider, to move messaging objects from one location to another
- An address book provider, to allow storing, retrieving, and looking up user addresses in a directory

Depending on the needs of the application, there may be more than one occurrence of any of these components. For example, a user may want to send a message to a list of other users, some via the Internet and some via fax. That user needs two transport providers: one that knows how to send messages through the Internet, and one that knows how to send faxes. The frontend need not have any knowledge of how to do either.

In "the old days," messaging applications were written from scratch to include all of this functionality in a single application. The designers of such an application would decide how messages were to be stored (perhaps in a proprietary database format), and how they were to be transmitted (perhaps via a proprietary protocol over a LAN, over a WAN, or simply between files on a mainframe computer). A shortcoming of this approach is that all users who wanted to exchange messages would have to use the same messaging application, because the storage and transport mechanisms were specific to that application.

The MAPI architecture breaks this mold. MAPI divides messaging applications into components that map to the above tasks, and it strictly defines the ways in which those components can interact. Third-party software vendors can offer prepackaged components that fit in with components written by other software vendors. Components can be added to provide access to additional transport mechanisms, message stores, or address books. For example, consider a software company that sells human resources (HR) management software. Such a system would store a variety of information about employees. To provide additional value for its customers, that company could write an *address book provider* that would be an interface between MAPI-compatible client applications (such as Microsoft Outlook) and the proprietary back-end database. By doing this, the software company allows its customers to leverage the employee databases that have already been built, rather than having to duplicate information in an email program's proprietary address book format.

MAPI is a specification, not an implementation. The implementation comes from a variety of sources, including Microsoft, third-party software vendors, and you. I'll discuss these sources as I explain each part of the architecture.

Service Providers

Service providers are the "backend" of a messaging system. Client applications make use of service providers to create, send, save, and retrieve email messages. There are three types of service providers, as listed here:

Message Store

A *message store provider* acts as the interface between some data storage system and a MAPI-based client. The mechanism that is used to actually store the data is not specified—it can be a relational database, flat file, or anything else. The MAPI specification is very flexible about the data that can be saved in a message store. A message is an object with certain properties (such as subject, text, etc.). The MAPI specification provides mechanisms for adding arbitrary properties to any given message object, thereby providing a way to represent and store any information at all. MAPI properties are discussed in more detail later in this chapter.

All outgoing messages are created in a message store before being submitted to a transport provider for dispatch.

Transport

A *transport provider* acts as the interface between some message transportation mechanism and a MAPI-based client. As is the case with message stores, the mechanism that actually moves the data is irrelevant. Only the transport provider itself needs to be aware of it.

Address Book

An *address book provider* acts as the interface between a database of user information and a MAPI-based client. Once again, the mechanism for data storage is not specified. Address book providers allow the client application to browse or look up messaging user information.

Service providers are typically supplied by third-party vendors of messaging systems. For example, Microsoft Outlook includes the service providers necessary for working with messages on a Microsoft Exchange server. Outlook also includes the transport providers necessary for sending mail over the Internet or via fax. Once these service providers are installed on a system, any MAPI-compatible client application can make use of them (including the applications you'll write using the information in this book).

When writing applications that use MAPI (which all CDO-based applications do), keep in mind that the service providers are indispensable to the application. Ask yourself whether the service providers your software needs will be on your users' machines. You can either require that your users already have a MAPI-compatible messaging client that supplies the service providers, or look into licensing the service providers from their respective vendors. (Of course, don't copy *dlls* that you aren't licensed to distribute.)

Microsoft doesn't currently provide a Visual Basic–friendly interface to the service provider-related functionality of MAPI, so it's not currently possible to write service providers in Visual Basic.

Client Applications

A client application makes some use of the services provided by the messaging system. Examples of client applications include:

- A full-featured email, calendar, and contact-management system
- A document workflow management system
- An Inbox assistant that performs custom processing of incoming messages
- A discussion list server
- A document-based application that has a Send item on its File menu

There are many other possibilities. The common element here is that data items are manipulated and moved on behalf of some user, making use of the service providers to store data, to transport data, and to find the addresses of other messaging users. A client application may or may not have a user interface, depending on the needs of the application. In addition, a client application may run on a machine typically considered to be a server (such as a web server), but we still refer to it as a client application.

This book is about writing client applications.

The MAPI Subsystem

The MAPI Subsystem is the interface between client applications and service providers. When a client application needs access to a service, it asks the MAPI Subsystem. The MAPI Subsystem then communicates with the appropriate service provider on behalf of the client application. The MAPI Subsystem is the glue that holds the service provider and client application components together.

The MAPI Spooler

The MAPI Spooler is part of the MAPI Subsystem. Its job is to move outgoing mail from message store providers to transport providers. The MAPI Spooler selects an appropriate transport provider based on the message's address type. When a message is addressed to multiple recipients having different address types, the MAPI Spooler hands a copy of the message to every appropriate transport provider. The MAPI Spooler also ensures that all outgoing messages are correctly addressed.

The MAPI Spooler is bypassed in the case of *tightly coupled* store/transport providers. A tightly coupled store/transport provider is a message store provider that also knows how to transport messages to certain address types. Microsoft Exchange is an example of such a provider.

MAPI Objects

MAPI is an object-oriented architecture. As such, it contains data structures for representing messages, folders, message stores, address books, recipients, and so on. These data structures have properties for representing an object's state and methods for performing actions. Technologies built on MAPI, such as CDO, use MAPI services by obtaining MAPI objects, setting and reading their properties, and calling their methods.

MAPI Properties

Properties represent data held by an object. For example, an object that represents a message may have a "Subject" property to hold text describing the subject of the message. Such a message object is likely to have many other properties as well. The designers of MAPI wisely recognized two facts:

- Developers might wish for properties that hadn't occurred to the designers.
- It would be inefficient to force a MAPI object to carry around properties that aren't relevant at the time. (A lot of messaging happens over dialup connections, so efficiency is of great concern.)

To address both issues, the MAPI designers devised a scheme in which the set of properties possessed by an object is dynamic. Resources (memory, disk, bandwidth, etc.) are allocated only for properties that actually have a value. This gave the designers the freedom to specify a great number of standard properties, knowing that there will be no overhead for the properties that the developer doesn't use. In addition, the MAPI designers provided a mechanism by which a developer can define *custom properties* for holding information that they didn't envision. This makes it very easy to transmit arbitrary information over email systems, as long as both sides are aware of the custom properties being used. This dynamic mechanism is accessible through CDO, and examples later in the book make use of it, so I will describe it further here.

Each standard property is identified by its own numeric identifier, called a *property tag*. A property tag is a 4-byte unsigned integer. Because Visual Basic doesn't support unsigned integers, Visual Basic sees these values as 4-byte signed integers, or in other words, as the Long datatype. Nothing is lost when converting between the unsigned and signed representations.

A property tag is typically represented as a hexadecimal number (e.g., `&H0037001E`), or as a symbolic constant defined either by MAPI (e.g., `PR_SUBJECT`) or by CDO (e.g., `CdoPR_SUBJECT`). MAPI documentation uses the MAPI symbolic constants (the ones whose names start with PR_). The MAPI-defined symbolic constants aren't recognized in Visual Basic. Instead, use the equivalents defined by CDO (the ones whose names start with CdoPR_.)

The high-order two bytes of a property tag are the *property ID*, and the low-order two bytes are the *property type*. (To determine the high-order two bytes, take the leftmost four digits of the hexadecimal representation of the property tag. The low-order two bytes are the rightmost four digits.) The property ID uniquely identifies the property, and the property type indicates the property's datatype. Property IDs are divided into ranges that indicate their use. Table 2-1 shows the property ID ranges. The range 3000 to 3FFF is divided further, as shown in Table 2-2. Don't worry about the precise meaning of each range—the ranges are shown here simply to give you an overview of how the properties are used. Finally, Table 2-3 shows the potential values for the property type.

Table 2-1. Property ID Ranges

From	To	Use of Property
0001	0BFF	MAPI-defined envelope property
0C00	0DFF	MAPI-defined per-recipient property
0E00	0FFF	MAPI-defined non-transmittable property
1000	2FFF	MAPI-defined message content property
3000	3FFF	MAPI-defined property (usually not message or recipient)
4000	57FF	Transport-defined envelope property
5800	5FFF	Transport-defined per-recipient property
6000	65FF	User-defined non-transmittable property
6600	67FF	Provider-defined internal non-transmittable property
6800	7BFF	Message class-defined content property
7C00	7FFF	Message class-defined non-transmittable property
8000	FFFE	Named property

Table 2-2. Property ID Sub-Ranges for 3000 to 3FFF Range

From	To	Use of Property
3000	33FF	Common property such as display name, entry ID
3400	35FF	Message store object
3600	36FF	Folder or address book container
3700	38FF	Attachment
3900	39FF	Address book object
3A00	3BFF	Mail user
3C00	3CFF	Distribution list
3D00	3DFF	Profile section
3E00	3FFF	Status object

Table 2-3. Property Types

MAPI-Defined Symbolic Constant (Not Available in Visual Basic)	Value	Datatype
`MV_FLAG`	4096	Multi-value flag (indicates that the property contains an array of values)
`PT_UNSPECIFIED`	0000	Type doesn't matter to caller
`PT_NULL`	0001	Null property value
`PT_I2`	0002	Signed 16-bit value
`PT_SHORT`	0002	Same as `PT_I2`
`PT_LONG`	0003	Signed 32-bit value
`PT_I4`	0003	Same as `PT_LONG`

Table 2-3. Property Types (continued)

MAPI-Defined Symbolic Constant (Not Available in Visual Basic)	Value	Datatype
PT_R4	0004	4-byte floating point
PT_FLOAT	0004	Same as PT_R4
PT_DOUBLE	0005	Floating point double
PT_R8	0005	Same as PT_DOUBLE
PT_CURRENCY	0006	Signed 64-bit integer (decimal with 4 digits right of decimal point)
PT_APPTIME	0007	Application time
PT_ERROR	000A	32-bit error value
PT_BOOLEAN	000B	16-bit Boolean (zero means False, non-zero means True)
PT_OBJECT	000C	Embedded COM object in a property
PT_I8	0014	8-byte signed integer
PT_LONGLONG	0014	Same as PT_I8
PT_STRING8	001E	Null-terminated 8-bit character string
PT_UNICODE	001F	Null-terminated Unicode string
PT_TSTRING		On Windows 95 and Windows 98 systems, this is equal to PT_STRING8. On Windows NT and Windows 2000 systems, this is equal to PT_UNICODE.
PT_MV_TSTRING		MV_FLAG + PT_TSTRING
PT_SYSTIME	0040	FILETIME 64-bit integer with number of 100ns periods since January 1, 1601
PT_CLSID	0048	GUID
PT_BINARY	0102	Uninterpreted (counted byte array) (Visual Basic code sees this not as an array, but as a string, where each character is a hexadecimal digit. Two characters taken together represent one byte from the byte array.

Armed with the information in these tables, you can make better use of the MAPI documentation in MSDN (Microsoft Developer Network). For example, Figure 2-2 shows the MSDN documentation screen for the PR_SUBJECT property tag. (Don't worry at this point about understanding everything you see in the figure.)

Example 2-1 shows three short functions that you can use to help you learn about the relationships among the property ID, the property type, and the property tag. The *PropertyIDFromTag* function takes as its argument a property tag and returns the property ID that is embedded in it. Similarly, the *PropertyTypeFromTag* function takes as its argument a property tag and returns the property type that is embedded in it. Lastly, the *MakePropertyTag* function takes two arguments—a property ID and a property type—and combines them to make a property tag.

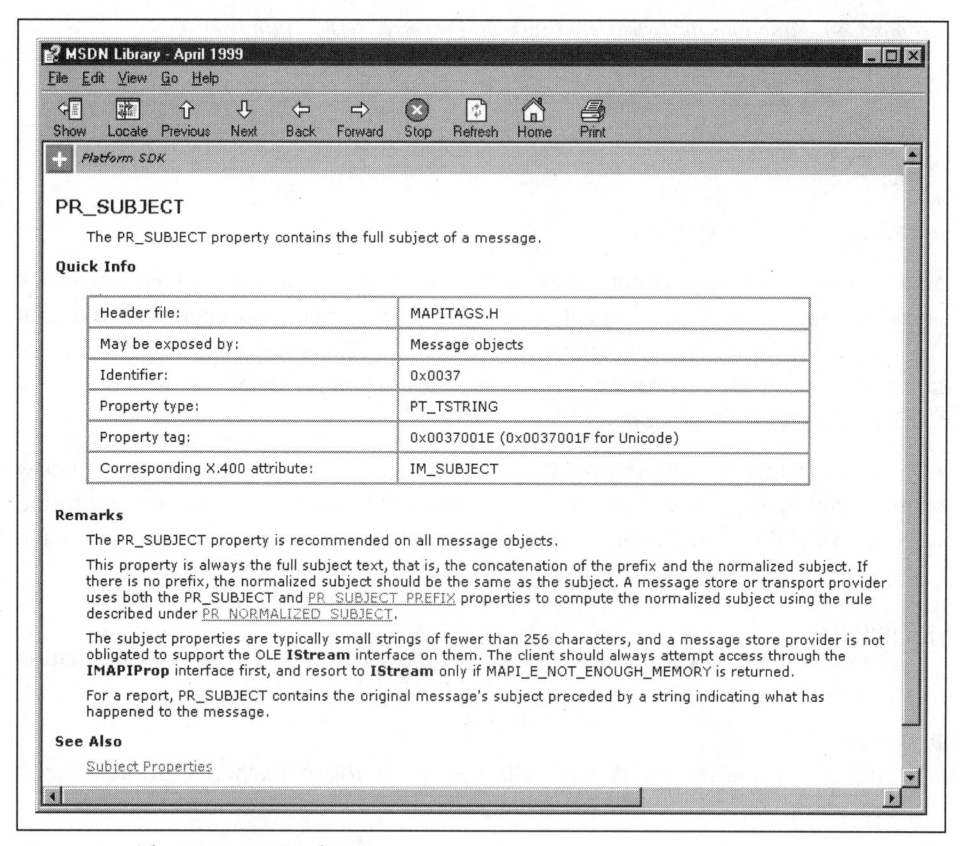

MSDN Library - April 1999

Platform SDK

PR_SUBJECT

The PR_SUBJECT property contains the full subject of a message.

Quick Info

Header file:	MAPITAGS.H
May be exposed by:	Message objects
Identifier:	0x0037
Property type:	PT_TSTRING
Property tag:	0x0037001E (0x0037001F for Unicode)
Corresponding X.400 attribute:	IM_SUBJECT

Remarks

The PR_SUBJECT property is recommended on all message objects.

This property is always the full subject text, that is, the concatenation of the prefix and the normalized subject. If there is no prefix, the normalized subject should be the same as the subject. A message store or transport provider uses both the PR_SUBJECT and PR_SUBJECT_PREFIX properties to compute the normalized subject using the rule described under PR_NORMALIZED_SUBJECT.

The subject properties are typically small strings of fewer than 256 characters, and a message store provider is not obligated to support the OLE **IStream** interface on them. The client should always attempt access through the **IMAPIProp** interface first, and resort to **IStream** only if MAPI_E_NOT_ENOUGH_MEMORY is returned.

For a report, PR_SUBJECT contains the original message's subject preceded by a string indicating what has happened to the message.

See Also

Subject Properties

Figure 2-2. The PR_SUBJECT documentation in MSDN

You'll also find in this book's sample code a function called *CdoPrTextFromCode* that takes as its parameter a property tag and returns a string indicating the property tag's symbolic constant, as defined by CDO. See Chapter 6, *An Email Client Application*, for details.

Example 2-1. Functions for Experimenting with Property Tags

```
Public Function PropertyIDFromTag(ByVal nPropertyTag As Long) As Integer

   ' Retrieve the property ID from a property tag.
   PropertyIDFromTag = nPropertyTag / 65536

End Function ' PropertyIDFromTag

Public Function PropertyTypeFromTag(ByVal nPropertyTag As Long) As Integer

   ' Retrieve the property type from a property tag.
   PropertyTypeFromTag = 65535 And nPropertyTag

End Function ' PropertyTypeFromTag
```

Example 2-1. Functions for Experimenting with Property Tags (continued)

```
Public Function MakePropertyTag(ByVal nPropertyID As Integer, _
   ByVal nPropertyType As Integer) As Long

   ' Make a property tag given the property ID and property type.
   MakePropertyTag = (65536 * nPropertyID) Or nPropertyType

End Function ' MakePropertyTag
```

MAPI allows client applications and service providers to define *named properties*. Named properties are custom properties that have a name associated with them, in the form of a 32-bit globally unique identifier (GUID) plus a character string or numeric value. Named properties are discussed in more detail in the context of CDO in Chapter 9, *Task Folders*.

If you also happen to develop in Visual C++, you may be interested to know where MAPI property tag constants are defined. The header (*.h*) files can be found in your Visual C++ installation's *Include* folder. Here is a brief description for each file:

edkmdb.h
: This file defines properties specific to the Microsoft Exchange information store provider.

emsabtag.h
: This file defines properties specific to the Microsoft Exchange address book provider.

mapitags.h
: This file defines the standard MAPI properties.

mapiwz.h
: This file defines the one custom property that is used by the Profile Setup Wizard.

msfs.h
: This file defines properties specific to the Microsoft Mail transport provider.

mspab.h
: This file defines properties specific to the Microsoft "Personal Address Book" address book provider.

mspst.h
: This file defines properties specific to the Microsoft "Personal Information Store" message store provider.

MAPI Profiles

A *MAPI profile* is configuration information that tells the MAPI Subsystem which service providers to use on behalf of the messaging user. It also usually stores additional configuration information for each service provider (such as the name of a mail server). A computer must have at least one profile set up on it in order to use messaging services through MAPI. Multiple profiles on a machine are permitted. Multiple profiles allow the user of a laptop machine, for example, to select one profile for use in the office where network resources are available, and a different profile for use on the road where email is retrieved over a dialup connection.

Profiles are set up through the Mail Control Panel applet. We'll briefly take a look at this applet and how to use it, because doing so helps to understand what a profile is and what is stored in it. The intent isn't to provide complete documentation for using the Mail applet—rather, just to get a general overview. Each of the dialog boxes in the Mail applet contains a Help button for further information.

If your system lacks a Mail applet, or if the applet appears substantially different from the one presented here, the MAPI Subsystem probably has not been installed on the computer. As will be discussed later in this chapter, under "Obtaining MAPI," MAPI is not part of the operating system but typically is obtained by installing a MAPI-compliant email client, such as Microsoft Outlook. (However, if Outlook is installed in Internet-only mode, MAPI components are not installed.)

The first dialog box shown by the Mail applet displays the configuration of the user's *default profile* (Figure 2-3). There is only one default profile on a computer. A client application can choose to use the default profile, rather than specifying a profile explicitly.

Profiles are named. The profile configuration shown in Figure 2-3 is for a profile called "MyProfile" that I have set up on my system. When I set it up, I also specified that it was to be used as the default profile. The figure shows that the MyProfile profile is set up to use the following service providers:

Internet E-mail - dg
: Primarily a transport provider but also provides address resolution for Internet-style addresses

Outlook Address Book
: An address book provider

Personal Address Book
: An address book provider

Personal Folders
: A message store provider

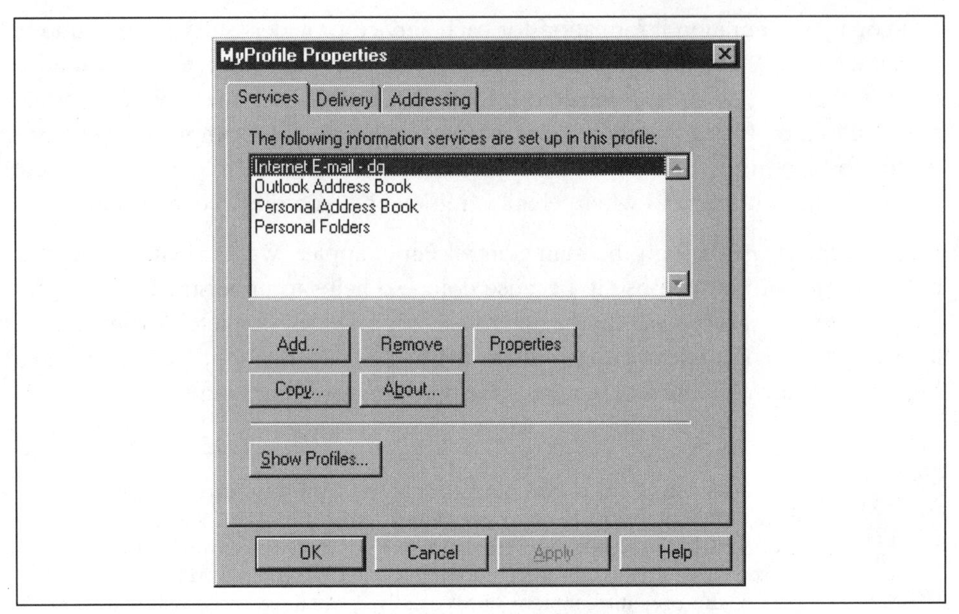

Figure 2-3. Displaying the Properties dialog box for the default profile

Figure 2-4 shows the Delivery tab of the same dialog box. The figure indicates that when new messages arrive (via the transport provider set up in this profile), the MAPI Spooler saves the messages in the "Personal Folders" message store. If a profile has multiple transport providers, incoming messages from all providers are delivered to this location. If a profile has multiple message store providers, only one of them (the one selected here) can be the one that receives new messages.

Figure 2-4. Delivery configuration for the MyProfile profile

The list box in Figure 2-4 shows the names of the transport providers set up in the profile. If more than one transport provider is capable of handling the same message type, the order of items in this list box becomes important. For example, the "Microsoft Exchange Transport" transport provider (not shown here) is capable of processing mail destined for the Internet. If a profile contains that service provider in addition to the "Internet E-mail" service provider, the one that is listed first will process messages having Internet-style addresses.

Figure 2-5 shows the Addressing tab of the MyProfile Properties dialog box. This tab deals with the address book providers contained in the profile. If the profile contains more than one address book provider, the selection in the "Show this address list first" drop-down list determines which address book is shown first when address selection dialogs are displayed to the user. The setting in the "Keep personal addresses in" drop-down list determines which address book to use by default when the user adds names. Finally, the list box in the figure controls the order in which address book providers are searched during *name resolution*. Name resolution is the process of verifying the address entered by the user on an outgoing message against addresses in the address book. Because of the address resolution process, the user can address a message just by typing in another user's display name, or even just a portion of the display name. The display name is used to find the recipient's real address in the address book, as well as other information that assists with sending the message.

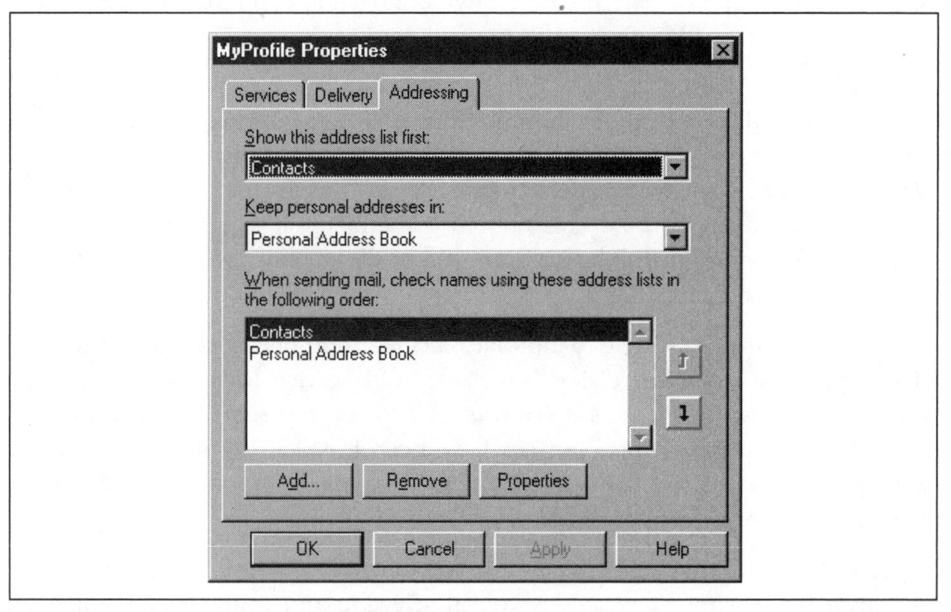

Figure 2-5. Addressing configuration for the MyProfile profile

So far we've been looking just at the default profile. To see all of the profiles on a system, click the Show Profiles button on the Services tab of the default profile's Properties dialog box. This brings up the Mail dialog box, as shown in Figure 2-6.

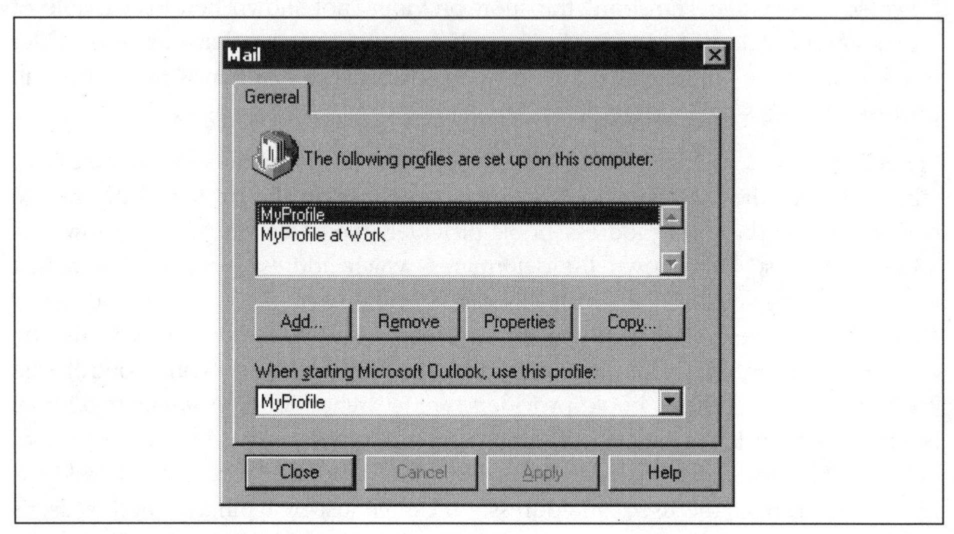

Figure 2-6. The Mail dialog box

The Mail dialog box lists the profiles set up on the computer. As shown in the figure, this computer has two profiles: "MyProfile" and "MyProfile at Work." The MyProfile profile is identified as the default profile in the drop-down list box labeled "When starting Microsoft Outlook, use this profile."

To view the settings for one of these profiles, select the desired profile and click the Properties button. This brings up a properties dialog box that is identical to the dialog box shown when the applet is first started, except that the Show Profiles button is absent (Figure 2-7). This button is absent because at this point simply closing the Properties dialog box returns you to the Mail dialog box, where additional profiles can be modified.

To add an information service to a profile, click the Add button on the Services tab of that profile's Properties dialog box. The "Add Service to Profile" dialog box appears, as shown in Figure 2-8. The set of choices you see on this dialog box depends on what information services have been installed on the computer. The subsequent setup screens are specific to each information service, and we won't go into them here.

To create a brand-new profile, click the Add button on the Mail dialog box. This invokes a setup wizard that guides you in selecting and configuring information services for the profile.

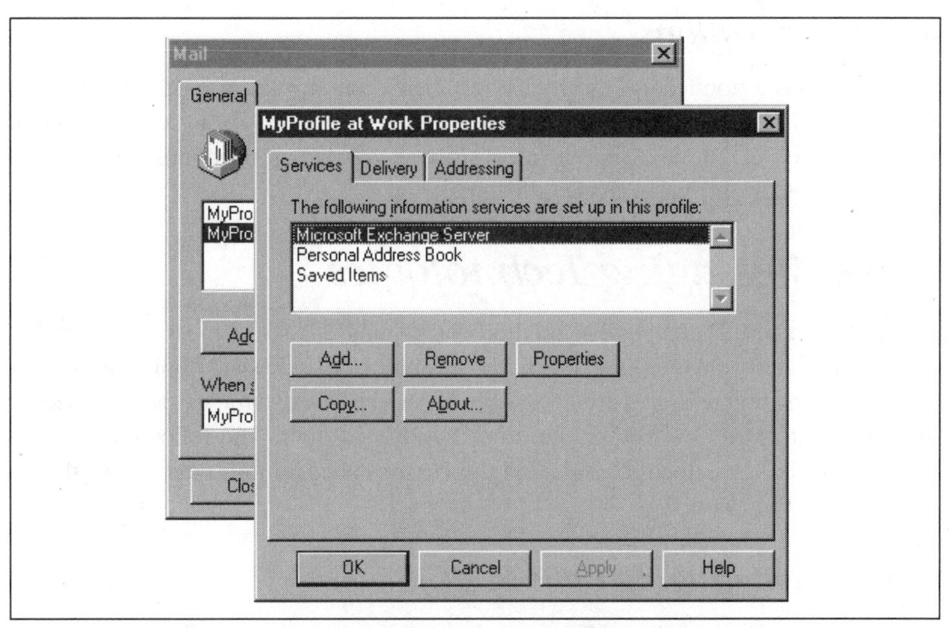

Figure 2-7. Displaying the Properties dialog box for a specific profile

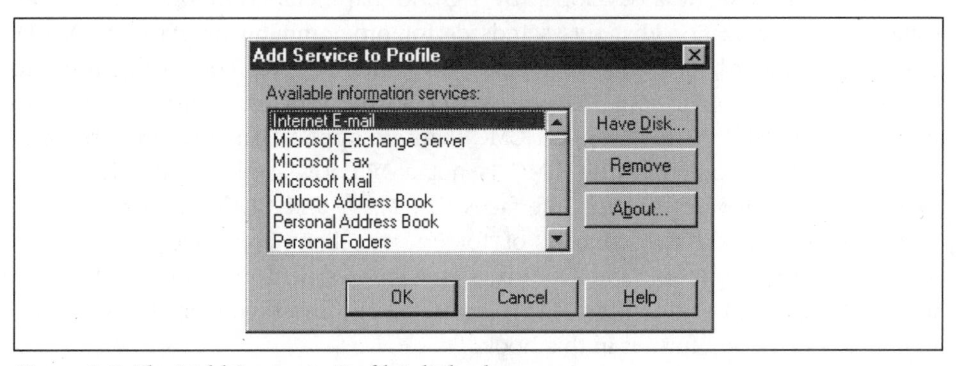

Figure 2-8. The "Add Service to Profile" dialog box

The MAPI Session

A *session* is a period of time in which MAPI services are used. To begin a session, the client application must *log on* to MAPI, at which time the client tells the MAPI Subsystem which profile to use. User authentication to service providers also happens at this time, if necessary. After a session is established, the client application can use MAPI services. When the client application is finished using MAPI services, it *logs off*, thereby ending the session. Attempting to use MAPI services without an active session results in an error. Later chapters will show precisely how to begin and terminate MAPI sessions.

MAPI Notifications

MAPI provides a notification mechanism to alert client applications of changes that occur in MAPI objects. For example, client applications may wish to update their user interface (UI) as new mail arrives. However, MAPI notifications are not currently exposed to the Visual Basic developer.

Other Messaging Technologies

MAPI is a powerful and flexible method for gaining access to messaging capability. Unfortunately, MAPI is not directly accessible to Visual Basic applications. Several messaging technologies are accessible to Visual Basic, some of them providing an interface to MAPI and others ignoring MAPI altogether. The following sections briefly describe these technologies and the circumstances under which they should (or shouldn't) be used.

Common Messaging Calls (CMC)

Common Messaging Calls (CMC) is a platform-independent API for sending and receiving email. CMC was developed by a group that included the X.400 API Association, the organization that sets standards for programming interfaces to X.400. X.400 is a standard for connecting email networks, and for connecting users to email networks. Applications that are written to the CMC standard are easier to port to other platforms that support CMC than are applications that are written to the MAPI specification because CMC is not a Windows-specific API. However, CMC does not provide the rich interfaces that MAPI and CDO do. For example, CMC doesn't support the concept of folders, so client applications only have access to the user's Inbox and Outbox. On Windows platforms, CMC is built on top of MAPI, so it benefits from MAPI's transport and message store transparency. CMC is not discussed further in this book.

Simple MAPI

Like CMC, Simple MAPI is a set of functions for accessing mail system functionality. It predates the specification that is now called "MAPI," and at the time it was released it was itself simply called "MAPI." When the specification that is now called "MAPI" was released, the old MAPI was renamed "Simple MAPI," and the new MAPI was called "Extended MAPI," or just "MAPI." Got it?

The Simple MAPI API is callable from Visual Basic and is explained in its entirety in Chapter 3, *Simple MAPI*. However, Microsoft recommends that Simple MAPI be used only to maintain code that is already written in Simple MAPI. New code should use CMC, MAPI, the MAPI ActiveX Controls, CDO, CDO for Windows 2000, or CDO for Exchange 2000.

The MAPI ActiveX Controls

As a Visual Basic programmer, you're familiar with ActiveX controls. The MAPI ActiveX controls are a Visual Basic-friendly wrapper for Simple MAPI. The Visual Basic programmer need only drop a couple of controls on a form (one MAPISession control and one MAPIMessages control), and then set properties and invoke methods to access messaging functionality. Because the controls use Simple MAPI, they are subject to the same shortcomings mentioned for that technology. The MAPI ActiveX controls are explained in Chapter 4, *The MAPI ActiveX Controls.*

CDO

CDO is a Visual Basic–friendly wrapper for MAPI. Like MAPI, it's built on COM. Unlike MAPI, it supports *Automation,* a technology that allows otherwise COM-challenged clients (such as scripting environments) to access its functionality. This mechanism is described in detail in Chapter 5, *Collaboration Data Objects.* CDO provides the richest messaging interface available to the Visual Basic programmer and should be used for most new development. The majority of this book is dedicated to discovering and taking advantage of CDO's features.

The CDO Rendering Library

The CDO Rendering Library provides the ability to display messaging objects (such as folders and email) on web pages. It is used on a web server and works in conjunction with CDO. The CDO Rendering Library is explained in Chapter 11, *Web Applications.*

The CDO for NTS Library

The CDO for NTS (Collaboration Data Objects for NT Server) library is intended to be used by web page scripts running on a web server. CDO for NTS wraps Internet mail protocols, rather than MAPI. It's useful in the case that the web page scripts don't need the full functionality of MAPI—perhaps they only need to send a simple email to an Internet email address. This allows you to avoid having to install MAPI on the web server. The nice thing about CDO for NTS is that its objects, properties, and methods are upward compatible with CDO, so it's easy to make the shift to MAPI in the future, if desired. The CDO for NTS Library is not discussed further in this book.

The Outlook Object Model

The Outlook Object Model is similar to CDO in that it provides an Automation wrapper for MAPI. For many client applications, there may not be a clear choice between CDO and the Outlook Object Model. For server-based applications, however, CDO is required. This book is primarily about CDO, but the Outlook Object Model is addressed briefly in Appendix B, *Programming the Outlook Object Model.*

Simple Mail Transport Protocol (SMTP)

Simple Mail Transport Protocol (SMTP) has been around for many years and is the primary protocol that carries email around the Internet. If you're writing an application that communicates only over the Internet, it's possible to bypass MAPI and send SMTP commands directly to a mail server on the Internet. However, don't select this approach casually. By taking MAPI out of the loop, you lose the back-end transparency that MAPI was designed to provide. Imagine spending months writing your messaging application using SMTP, only to have your boss say, "That's great, but the steering committee wants it to do faxes now, too." If you had used MAPI, or a technology based on MAPI, such a request would be trivial. In case you need it, however, Appendix A, *Programming Internet Email Protocols*, explains how to send Internet messages from Visual Basic without using MAPI.

CDO for Windows 2000

CDO for Windows 2000, formerly known as CDO 2.0, is a completely different animal from CDO. CDO for Windows 2000 wraps Internet mail protocols rather than MAPI, and it exposes a completely different set of classes, methods, and properties than does CDO. Therefore, code written for CDO has no chance of running on CDO for Windows 2000. The good news is that the two products can be used concurrently in the same application, if desired. CDO for Windows 2000 is explained in detail in Chapter 12, *CDO for Windows 2000.*

CDO for Exchange 2000

CDO for Exchange 2000, sometimes called CDO 3.0, is being billed as the next generation of CDO. It has been written from the ground up to use Internet standards rather than MAPI. CDO for Exchange 2000 is a superset of CDO for Windows 2000, so applications written to use CDO for Windows 2000 will run with CDO for Exchange 2000 without modification. In addition, Microsoft claims that CDO 1.21 applications (the kind that this book is about) can be ported easily to the new architecture. CDO for Exchange 2000 ships with Microsoft Exchange 2000 Server, which was in beta test at press time. CDO for Exchange 2000 is not discussed further in this book.

Obtaining MAPI

MAPI may or may not already be on your target users' systems. It is typically installed during the installation of a MAPI-compatible messaging application such as Microsoft Outlook.* If your application's users don't have such an application, you may want to distribute MAPI with your application. Microsoft permits this, with certain restrictions. Further information and MAPI itself are available at *http://www.microsoft.com/exchange/downloads/intro.htm*.

The download available at this URL gives you the MAPI Subsystem and some standard service providers, such as the Personal Folders message store provider and the Personal Address Book address book provider. Note well that if your application requires additional service providers, you'll have to investigate the licensing requirements of those components before distributing them with your application.

To learn how to obtain CDO, see Chapter 5.

Programmatically Discovering Whether MAPI Is Present

Application programs can examine the Windows registry to determine whether messaging components have been installed on the computer. The registry key used for this purpose is:

```
HKEY_LOCAL_MACHINE\SOFTWARE\Microsoft\Windows Messaging Subsystem
```

Table 2-4 shows the entry names to look for. A value of `"1"` for any entry means that the corresponding component is present on the computer.

Table 2-4. Registry Entries for Determining Whether Messaging Components are Installed

Messaging Component	Registry Entry Name
MAPI	"`MAPIX`"
Simple MAPI	"`MAPI`"
CMC	"`CMC`"
CDO	"`OLEMessaging`"

Your Visual Basic application has merely to check for these registry entries to determine whether specific messaging components have been installed. Unfortunately, the Visual Basic functions for registry access—*SaveSetting*, *GetSetting*,

* However, when Outlook has been installed in *Internet Mail Only (IMO)* mode, MAPI is not involved. If your system has Outlook installed in this mode, you must reinstall it in *Corporate or Workgroup (CW)* mode (that's one mode, not two) to be able to use the examples in this book. Outlook's Help → About dialog box indicates the mode that has been installed.

GetAllSettings, and *DeleteSetting*—are not flexible enough to retrieve data from arbitrary registry keys. Because checking for messaging components is potentially a useful feature, I'll explain how to access arbitrary registry keys from Visual Basic. I'll also give you a function that nicely wraps up the cumbersome stuff.

To access arbitrary registry entries, it is necessary to use the Win32 registry API functions *RegOpenKeyEx*, *RegQueryValueEx*, and *RegCloseKey*. Win32 API functions are made available to Visual Basic through Visual Basic's `Declare` statement. The `Declare` statement specifies the name of the desired function, as well as the name of the operating system or third-party *dll* that implements the function. For example, here is the `Declare` statement for the *RegOpenKeyEx* function:

```
Public Declare Function RegOpenKeyEx Lib "advapi32.dll" _
   Alias "RegOpenKeyExA" ( _
   ByVal hKey As Long, _
   ByVal lpSubKey As String, _
   ByVal ulOptions As Long, _
   ByVal samDesired As Long, _
   phkResult As Long _
) As Long
```

This `Declare` statement indicates to the Visual Basic compiler that somewhere in the Visual Basic application a call is made to the function *RegOpenKeyEx*, and that the implementation of this function can be found in the file *advapi32.dll*, but that inside the *dll* it's called *RegOpenKeyExA*. The datatype of each argument is also specified. Given this `Declare` statement, code elsewhere in the application can call the *RegOpenKeyEx* function as though it were an intrinsic Visual Basic function, as follows (don't worry about the constants `HKEY_LOCAL_MACHINE` and `KEY_QUERY_VALUE` for now—a complete example is coming up):

```
nResult = RegOpenKeyEx(HKEY_LOCAL_MACHINE, _
      "SOFTWARE\Microsoft\Windows Messaging Subsystem", _
      0, KEY_QUERY_VALUE, hKey)
```

The `Declare` statement will come in especially handy in Chapter 3, *Simple MAPI*, where you'll learn how to call messaging APIs directly. In that chapter, I'll discuss the `Declare` statement and its syntax in depth.

Example 2-2 shows a function, *IsMessagingAvailable*, that reads the system registry and returns `True` if messaging is present on the computer and `False` if not. The function takes one parameter, which is a string that identifies the messaging component in question, as given in Table 2-4. If the parameter is absent from the call, "`MAPIX`" is assumed. Note that the `Declare` statements shown in the example must be placed at *module level*, which means that they must be outside of any procedures. (If you place this code in a form or class module, you must also change the `Public` keyword to `Private`.) The constant definitions shown in the example are necessary in order for the caller to specify certain options to the API functions. The **Const** statements can appear anywhere that constant definitions are allowed (see the Visual Basic documentation), but it makes sense to keep them near the **Declare** statements. Don't be confused by the strangely named constant **ERROR_SUCCESS**. The registry functions return this constant when they are successful—it doesn't mean that an error occurred.

Example 2-2. Checking for Messaging Components on a Computer

```
' Place these declarations at the module level.
Public Const HKEY_LOCAL_MACHINE = &H80000002
Public Const KEY_QUERY_VALUE = &H1
Public Const ERROR_SUCCESS = 0&
Public Const ERROR_FILE_NOT_FOUND = 2&

Public Declare Function RegOpenKeyEx Lib "advapi32.dll" _
   Alias "RegOpenKeyExA" ( _
   ByVal hKey As Long, _
   ByVal lpSubKey As String, _
   ByVal ulOptions As Long, _
   ByVal samDesired As Long, _
   phkResult As Long _
) As Long

Public Declare Function RegQueryValueEx Lib "advapi32.dll" _
   Alias "RegQueryValueExA" ( _
   ByVal hKey As Long, _
   ByVal lpValueName As String, _
   ByVal lpReserved As Long, _
   lpType As Long, _
   lpData As Any, _
   lpcbData As Long _
) As Long

Public Declare Function RegCloseKey Lib "advapi32.dll" ( _
   ByVal hKey As Long) As Long

Public Function IsMessagingAvailable( _
   Optional strComponent As String = "MAPIX" _
) As Boolean

   ' Query the system registry to determine whether the specified
   ' messaging component is available on the system.
   '
   ' strComponent must be one of these values:
   '     "MAPIX"          ' MAPI (A.K.A. Extended MAPI)
   '     "MAPI"           ' Simple MAPI
   '     "CMC"            ' Common Messaging Calls
   '     "OLEMessaging"   ' Collaboration Data Objects
   '
   ' If strComponent is omitted, "MAPIX" is assumed.

   Dim hKey As Long             ' handle to registry key
   Dim nResult As Long          ' results from API function calls
```

Example 2-2. Checking for Messaging Components on a Computer (continued)

```
   Dim nType As Long           ' type of data read from registry
   Dim strData As String       ' data read from registry
   Dim nBufferSize As Long     ' size of data buffer

   ' Initialize data buffer.
   strData = String(2, 0)
   nBufferSize = Len(strData)

   ' Open the registry key where the entries reside.
   nResult = RegOpenKeyEx(HKEY_LOCAL_MACHINE, _
      "SOFTWARE\Microsoft\Windows Messaging Subsystem", _
      0, KEY_QUERY_VALUE, hKey)

   If nResult <> ERROR_SUCCESS Then
      Err.Raise 335, App.Title, "Could not access system registry"
   End If

   ' Read the desired entry.
   nResult = RegQueryValueEx(hKey, strComponent, 0, nType, _
      ByVal strData, nBufferSize)

   ' Done with the registry.
   RegCloseKey hKey

   ' Did we find the desired registry entry?
   If nResult = ERROR_SUCCESS Then
      ' Truncate the returned data at the terminating null.
      strData = Left(strData, InStr(strData, Chr(0)) - 1)
      ' Is MAPI present?
      IsMessagingAvailable = (strData = "1")
   ' else was the registry entry not found?
   ElseIf nResult = ERROR_FILE_NOT_FOUND Then
      IsMessagingAvailable = False
   Else ' else there was some error
      Err.Raise 335, App.Title, "Could not access system registry"
   End If

End Function ' IsMessagingAvailable
```

Programmatically Discovering Profile Names and the Default Profile

Application programs can examine the Windows registry to determine the names of the profiles set up for a user, as well as which profile is the user's default profile. The registry key used for this purpose on a Windows 9x system is:

```
HKEY_CURRENT_USER\Software\Microsoft\Windows Messaging Subsystem\Profiles
```

On Windows NT, the key is:

```
HKEY_CURRENT_USER\Software\Microsoft\WINDOWS NT\CURRENTVERSION\Windows Messaging
Subsystem\Profiles
```

Regardless of operating system, the key has a string value called `DefaultProfile` that contains the name of the user's default MAPI profile (if the user has a default profile). In addition, the key has a subkey for each profile that has been set up for the user. The name of each subkey corresponds to the name of the associated profile. Example 2-3 shows two functions for accessing this information on a Windows 9x machine. *GetDefaultProfileName* returns the user's default profile name, and *GetProfileNames* returns a string array containing the names of the user's profiles. As in Example 2-2, several registry-related constants and API functions must be declared.

Example 2-3. Obtaining Profile Names from the Windows 9x Registry

```
' Place these declarations at the module level.
Public Const HKEY_LOCAL_MACHINE = &H80000002
Public Const HKEY_CURRENT_USER = &H80000001
Public Const KEY_QUERY_VALUE = &H1
Public Const ERROR_SUCCESS = 0&
Public Const ERROR_FILE_NOT_FOUND = 2&

Public Type FILETIME
        dwLowDateTime As Long
        dwHighDateTime As Long
End Type

Public Declare Function RegOpenKeyEx Lib "advapi32.dll" _
   Alias "RegOpenKeyExA" ( _
   ByVal hKey As Long, _
   ByVal lpSubKey As String, _
   ByVal ulOptions As Long, _
   ByVal samDesired As Long, _
   phkResult As Long _
) As Long

Public Declare Function RegQueryValueEx Lib "advapi32.dll" _
   Alias "RegQueryValueExA" ( _
   ByVal hKey As Long, _
   ByVal lpValueName As String, _
   ByVal lpReserved As Long, _
   lpType As Long, _
   lpData As Any, _
   lpcbData As Long _
) As Long

Public Declare Function RegCloseKey Lib "advapi32.dll" ( _
   ByVal hKey As Long) As Long

Public Declare Function RegQueryInfoKey Lib "advapi32.dll" _
   Alias "RegQueryInfoKeyA" ( _
   ByVal hKey As Long, _
   ByVal lpClass As String, _
   lpcbClass As Long, _
   ByVal lpReserved As Long, _
```

Example 2-3. Obtaining Profile Names from the Windows 9x Registry (continued)

```
   lpcSubKeys As Long, _
   lpcbMaxSubKeyLen As Long, _
   lpcbMaxClassLen As Long, _
   lpcValues As Long, _
   lpcbMaxValueNameLen As Long, _
   lpcbMaxValueLen As Long, _
   lpcbSecurityDescriptor As Long, _
   lpftLastWriteTime As FILETIME _
) As Long

Public Declare Function RegEnumKeyEx Lib "advapi32.dll" _
   Alias "RegEnumKeyExA" ( _
   ByVal hKey As Long, _
   ByVal dwIndex As Long, _
   ByVal lpName As String, _
   lpcbName As Long, _
   ByVal lpReserved As Long, _
   ByVal lpClass As String, _
   lpcbClass As Long, _
   lpftLastWriteTime As FILETIME _
) As Long

Public Function GetDefaultProfileName() As String

   ' Returns the name of the user's default profile. If none, an empty
   ' string is returned.

   Dim hKey As Long             ' handle to registry key
   Dim nResult As Long          ' results from API function calls
   Dim nType As Long            ' type of data read from registry
   Dim strData As String        ' data read from registry
   Dim nBufferSize As Long      ' size of data buffer

   ' Initialize data buffer.
   strData = String(256, 0)
   nBufferSize = Len(strData)

   ' Open the registry key where the entry resides.
   nResult = RegOpenKeyEx(HKEY_CURRENT_USER, _
      "SOFTWARE\Microsoft\Windows Messaging Subsystem\Profiles", _
      0, KEY_QUERY_VALUE, hKey)

   If nResult <> ERROR_SUCCESS Then
      Err.Raise 335, App.Title, "Could not access system registry"
   End If

   ' Read the desired entry.
   nResult = RegQueryValueEx(hKey, "DefaultProfile", 0, nType, _
      ByVal strData, nBufferSize)

   ' Done with the registry.
   RegCloseKey hKey
```

Example 2-3. Obtaining Profile Names from the Windows 9x Registry (continued)

```
    ' Did we find the desired registry entry?
    If nResult = ERROR_SUCCESS Then
        ' Truncate the returned data at the terminating null.
        strData = Left(strData, InStr(strData, Chr(0)) - 1)
        ' Return result.
        GetDefaultProfileName = strData
    ' else was the registry entry not found?
    ElseIf nResult = ERROR_FILE_NOT_FOUND Then
        GetDefaultProfileName = ""
    Else ' else there was some error
        Err.Raise 335, App.Title, "Could not access system registry"
    End If

End Function ' GetDefaultProfileName

Public Sub GetProfileNames(ByRef astr() As String)

    ' Loads astr with the names of the profiles that have been
    ' set up for the user.

    Dim hKey As Long             ' handle to registry key
    Dim nResult As Long          ' results from API function calls
    Dim strData As String        ' data read from registry
    Dim nSubkeys As Long         ' number of subkeys
    Dim nMaxBufferSize As Long ' length of longest subkey name + 1
    Dim nBufferSize As Long      ' size of data buffer
    Dim nIndex As Long           ' for enumerating the subkeys
    Dim astrRetVal() As String ' for gathering results
    Dim ft As FILETIME           ' dummy required for registry api calls

    ' Open the registry key where the subkeys reside.
    nResult = RegOpenKeyEx(HKEY_CURRENT_USER, _
        "SOFTWARE\Microsoft\Windows Messaging Subsystem\Profiles", _
        0, KEY_QUERY_VALUE, hKey)

    If nResult <> ERROR_SUCCESS Then
        Err.Raise 335, App.Title, "Could not access system registry"
    End If

    ' Determine the number of keys to enumerate, and the size of the buffer
    ' needed for the longest subkey name.
    nResult = RegQueryInfoKey(hKey, 0, 0, 0, nSubkeys, _
        nMaxBufferSize, 0, 0, 0, 0, ft)

    ' Allocate results array.
    ReDim astrRetVal(1 To nSubkeys) As String

    ' Retrieve subkeys.
    For nIndex = 1 To nSubkeys

        ' Initialize data buffer.
        strData = String(nMaxBufferSize, 0)
```

Example 2-3. Obtaining Profile Names from the Windows 9x Registry (continued)

```
        nBufferSize = Len(strData)

        ' Get the subkey name.
        nResult = RegEnumKeyEx(hKey, nIndex - 1, strData, nBufferSize, _
           0, 0, 0, ft)

        ' Everything OK?
        If nResult = ERROR_SUCCESS Then
           ' Truncate the returned data at the terminating null.
           strData = Left(strData, InStr(strData, Chr(0)) - 1)
           ' Return result.
           astrRetVal(nIndex) = strData
        Else ' else there was some error
           Err.Raise 335, App.Title, "Could not access system registry"
        End If

   Next nIndex

   ' Done with the registry.
   RegCloseKey hKey

   ' Return the array of names.
   astr = astrRetVal

End Sub ' GetProfileNames
```

To modify the code in Example 2-3 for use on Windows NT, change the call to *RegOpenKeyEx* to reference the correct registry key, as shown here:

```
nResult = RegOpenKeyEx(HKEY_CURRENT_USER, _
   "Software\Microsoft\WINDOWS NT\CURRENTVERSION" _
   & "\Windows Messaging Subsystem\Profiles", _
   0, KEY_QUERY_VALUE, hKey)
```

See Appendix D, *Where Am I Running?*, to learn how to discover the operating system version programmatically.

Summary

In this chapter you learned about the MAPI architecture. Although MAPI isn't directly callable from Visual Basic, the MAPI architecture strongly influences the structure of the technologies that are callable from Visual Basic, most notably CDO. You learned about the handful of messaging technologies that Visual Basic developers can use. Some of these are based on MAPI, and some on Internet mail protocols. Finally, you learned how to get MAPI from Microsoft, and how to test a system programmatically for the presence of messaging components.

Now it's time to write some software. Turn the page, and I'll show you how to send and receive email using the Simple MAPI API.

3

Simple MAPI

Simple MAPI is a set of 12 functions that were created to allow developers to access Microsoft Mail post offices programmatically. At the time the API was created, it was known simply as *MAPI*. This API was later superseded by the completely different and much richer *Extended MAPI*. At that time, the old API was renamed *Simple MAPI*, and today the name MAPI by itself refers to Extended MAPI. Incidentally, Simple MAPI has been rewritten to use MAPI (i.e., Extended MAPI) internally.

There is no reason to use Simple MAPI in new development. The MAPI ActiveX controls, explained in the next chapter, are a Simple MAPI wrapper that is far easier to use than the API itself. However, Simple MAPI remains available and documented in order to support existing applications that were written to use it. This chapter explains how Simple MAPI is used from Visual Basic. If you're not maintaining Simple MAPI code, it's perfectly safe to skip this chapter.

Accessing APIs from Visual Basic

API stands for *Application Programming Interface*. In general, an API is any documented methodology for a software application to make use of functionality provided by another software application. On the Windows platforms, this exposure of functionality historically has been provided as function libraries implemented in *dll* files (although this is changing). You may be familiar with the *Windows API*—a set of operating system services exposed as functions implemented in Windows operating system *dll*s. Similarly, Simple MAPI is a set of functions implemented in a *dll*, namely, *mapi32.dll*.

If you've ever developed an ActiveX component using Visual Basic or another language, don't confuse the methods exposed by such a component with the functions that are *exported* by a *dll*. The former uses Microsoft's Component Object

Model (COM) technology, which is not involved in Simple MAPI. The latter uses a mechanism that existed before COM and is still in widespread use (although as I said, this is changing; COM is now the preferred way to expose functionality to other programs).

The Declare Statement

Visual Basic gives us a way to call functions exported by *dll*s. It requires two steps:

1. Use the `Declare` statement to make the Visual Basic compiler aware of the function that is to be called.
2. Call the function.

The `Declare` statement has two forms, depending on whether the statement declares a subroutine or a function. The form for a subroutine is:

```
[Public | Private] Declare Sub name Lib "libname" [Alias "aliasname"]
[([arglist])]
```

and the form for a function is:

```
[Public | Private] Declare Function name Lib "libname" [Alias "aliasname"]
[([arglist])] [As type]
```

Regardless of which form is used, `Declare` statements can appear only at the module level, which means that they must be outside of any procedure. The meaning of each syntax element is as follows:

`Public | Private`
: Use one of these keywords to indicate the scope of the declaration. Procedures declared with `Public` scope are visible throughout the application. Those declared with `Private` scope are visible only within the module in which the `Declare` statement appears. If neither keyword is specified, `Public` is assumed.

`name`
: This is the name of the procedure being declared, as it will be used in the Visual Basic application. This is usually the same name by which the procedure is known inside the *dll*, but it doesn't have to be. If it's not, the `Alias` clause must be present. Note that procedure names in *dll*s are case sensitive.

`libname`
: This is the name of the *dll* file, as it resides on disk. If no path is specified, the system looks for the *dll* in the following locations, in the given order:

    1. The directory from which the application loaded
    2. The current directory

3. The 32-bit Windows system directory
4. The 16-bit Windows system directory
5. The Windows directory
6. The directories that are listed in the `PATH` environment variable

`aliasname`

This is the name of the procedure exported by the *dll*, if different from the name specified for *`name`*, above. For example, if the name of the exported procedure is the same as a Visual Basic keyword, this feature permits the procedure to be known by a different name within the Visual Basic application. Similarly, if a procedure has ANSI and Unicode variants, it permits one of the variants to be called while the documented procedure name is used in code.

`arglist`

This is the list of arguments required by the exported procedure. The purpose of this list is to allow Visual Basic to perform type checking on parameters passed to the procedure.

`type`

This is the datatype of the value returned by the function.

Here is a sample `Declare` statement:

```
Public Declare Function MAPILogon Lib "MAPI32.DLL" ( _
   ByVal UIParam As Long, _
   ByVal User As String, _
   ByVal Password As String, _
   ByVal Flags As Long, _
   ByVal Reserved As Long, _
   ByRef Session As Long _
) As Long
```

This `Declare` statement instructs the Visual Basic compiler to make a function called *MAPILogon* available to the Visual Basic code. Further, the statement indicates the following facts about this function:

- The function is implemented in the library file *mapi32.dll*.
- Inside the library file, the function is known as *MAPILogon*. (The absence of an `Alias` clause indicates that the name inside the library file is the same as the one being used in the Visual Basic project.)
- The function has six parameters, of the types shown.
- The last parameter, *`Session`*, is passed by reference. That means that the *address* of a variable is to be passed in this position, not the value of the variable. This usually indicates that the called procedure writes a value to that variable as part of its operation, which indeed is the case here.
- The function returns a Long.

The API Viewer

To write a proper `Declare` statement, it is necessary to know the answers to several questions:

- What are the names of the procedures that are to be called?
- What are the names of the *dll*s that contain the implementations of the procedures?
- What are the parameters and their datatypes?
- What is the datatype of the return value?

Unlike Visual Basic procedures, API procedures are very fussy about the formats of their arguments. A developer often must spend considerable time reviewing the documentation for the procedure to be called, as well as the documentation for the `Declare` statement and Microsoft's hints for passing arguments of various types. There's usually some trial and error, too. Fortunately, Microsoft supplies `Declare` statements for all of Simple MAPI's procedures, as well as `Type` and `Const` statements for Simple MAPI's custom datatypes and constants. These statements are available by using the API Viewer utility.

To run the API Viewer, in the Visual Basic IDE choose API Viewer from the Add-Ins menu. (If API Viewer doesn't appear in the Add-Ins menu, choose Add-In Manager from the Add-Ins menu, then select VB 6 API Viewer, place a checkmark in the Loaded/Unloaded checkbox, and click the OK button. Then choose API Viewer from the Add-Ins menu.) The API Viewer appears, as shown in Figure 3-1.

To view the declarations for Simple MAPI's procedures, datatypes, and constants, choose Load Text File from the File menu. In the resulting dialog box, select *mapi32.txt* and click the Open button.

After the *mapi32.txt* file is loaded, the Available Items list box shows the names of the procedure declarations that are available. To select an appropriate declaration to be copied to a Visual Basic source file, highlight a procedure name in the Available Items list box and click the Add button. This displays a `Declare` statement in the Selected Items text box for the selected procedure (see Figure 3-2). Click the Copy button to copy this text to the Windows clipboard, then switch back to the Visual Basic IDE and paste the code into a Visual Basic module.

Datatype and constant declarations can be obtained in a similar way. In the API Type drop-down list, choose Types or Constants, then select the datatype or constant of interest in the Available Items list box, click the Copy button, and then paste into Visual Basic.

It's interesting to view the *mapi32.txt* file directly with a text editor. It turns out that this file contains the Simple MAPI-related datatype, constant, and procedure

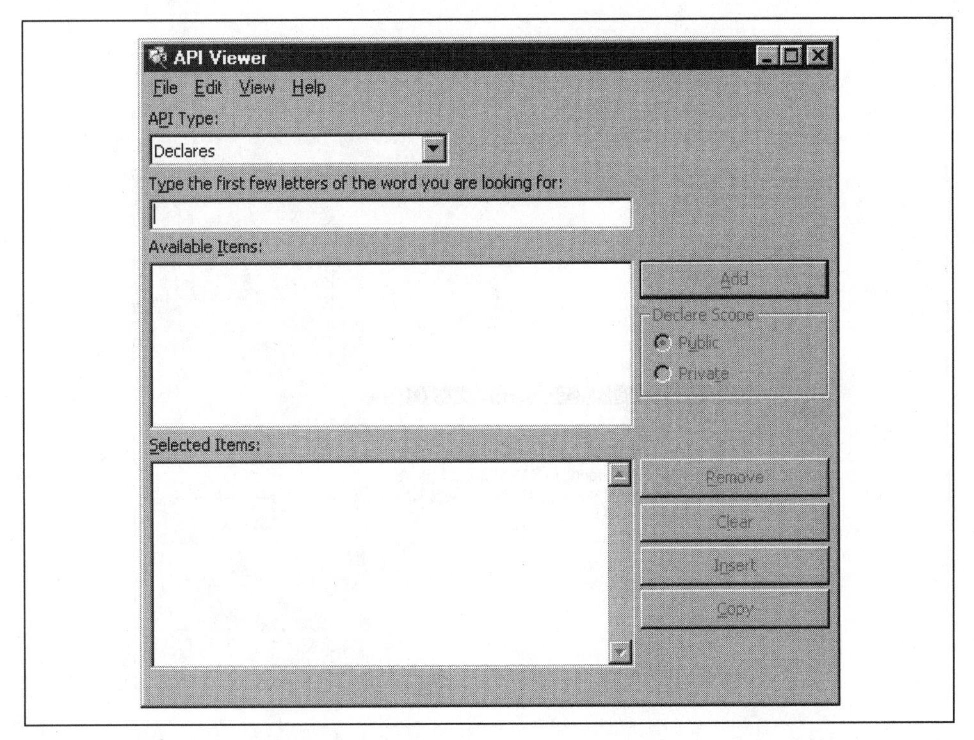

Figure 3-1. The API Viewer

declarations in standard Visual Basic syntax. Because of this, it's possible to bypass the API Viewer utility altogether and simply copy *mapi32.txt* directly into a Visual Basic project (renaming it to have a *.bas* file extension—for example, *mapi32.bas*). If this is done, it's also necessary to insert the keyword `Public` at the beginning of each `Const` statement so that the constant definitions are available to other parts of the project.

I'll touch on most of the datatypes, constants, and procedures in *mapi32.txt* as I get down to explaining the business at hand—sending and receiving email.

Establishing a Session

All technologies based on MAPI, as Simple MAPI is, require that a MAPI session be established prior to sending and receiving messages. MAPI sessions were explained in Chapter 2, *MAPI*. To establish a MAPI session using Simple MAPI, call the *MAPILogon* function, as shown here:

```
Dim nMAPISession As Long

' Initiate a MAPI session.
nRetVal = MAPILogon(0, "MyProfile", "", MAPI_NEW_SESSION, _
   0, nMAPISession)
```

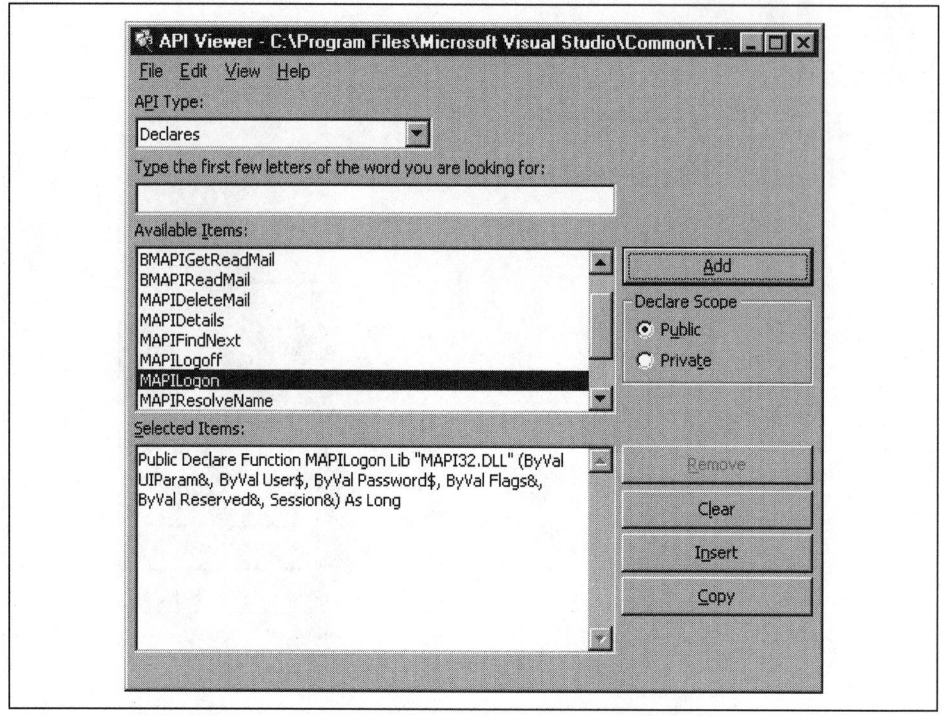

Figure 3-2. Obtaining a Declare Statement from the API Viewer

The *MAPILogon* function has several parameters. Its `Declare` statement looks like this:

```
Public Declare Function MAPILogon Lib "MAPI32.DLL" ( _
   ByVal UIParam As Long, _
   ByVal User As String, _
   ByVal Password As String, _
   ByVal Flags As Long, _
   ByVal Reserved As Long, _
   Session As Long _
) As Long
```

The parameters to the *MAPILogon* function are:

`UIParam`

The handle of the window that is to be considered the parent of any dialog boxes displayed by MAPI during logon.

Depending on the values passed in the ***`User`*** and ***`Flags`*** parameters, MAPI may need to display a logon dialog box. Pass the hWnd property of a form to make that form the parent window. Pass a 0 to indicate that any dialog boxes should be application-modal. If no dialog box is displayed during logon, *`UIParam`* is ignored.

User

This is the name of the profile that is to be used for the session. (MAPI profiles were explained in Chapter 2.) To cause MAPI to prompt the user for a profile to use, pass an empty string in the ***User*** parameter and specify the `MAPI_LOGON_UI` flag in the ***Flags*** parameter.

Password

Always pass an empty string in this parameter. If passwords are necessary, they can be specified in the profile. The ***Password*** parameter is a holdover from a time prior to Extended MAPI and is now obsolete. To avoid confusion, I'll say this again: leave the ***Password*** parameter blank. Some developers assume that the user's login password should be passed here, but that is not correct and it won't work.

Flags

In the ***Flags*** parameter, pass one or more of the following constants:

`MAPI_FORCE_DOWNLOAD`

During the logon process, MAPI should attempt to connect to the mail server(s) set up in the user's profile and retrieve any messages waiting there. The call to *MAPILogon* doesn't return until this process is complete.

`MAPI_LOGON_UI`

If MAPI is unable to logon because of incomplete or inaccurate information in the *MAPILogon* call, a dialog box should be displayed to the user to collect the information. If this flag is not specified and incomplete or inaccurate logon information is supplied to *MAPILogon*, logon fails and an error code is returned.

`MAPI_NEW_SESSION`

A new MAPI session should be established, even if an active session is already established on the computer. If this flag is not specified, *MAPILogon* attempts to find and use an already-established MAPI session. If one is found, it is used for the current application as well, even if it was logged on using a profile different from the one specified in the *MAPILogon* call. If no existing session is found, a new one is created. If the `MAPI_NEW_SESSION` flag is specified, a new session is created regardless of whether one is already established on the computer. Applications that must use a specific profile should specify this flag. Applications that don't care what profile they use, or that are intended to affect the currently logged-on user, should not specify this flag.

To specify more than one flag, use the `Or` operator to combine the flags. To specify no flags, pass 0 in this parameter.

Reserved

Not used. Pass 0 in this parameter.

Session

Passes a session handle from the *MAPILogon* function to the calling procedure. To receive the session handle, declare a variable of type Long and pass that variable to the *MAPILogon* function as the ***Session*** argument. The value of the variable prior to calling *MAPILogon* doesn't matter. Upon successful return from *MAPILogon*, the variable contains the handle for the session. This handle is used in subsequent calls to other Simple MAPI functions.

The *MAPILogon* function's return value indicates the success or failure of the call and is one of the following constants:

MAPI_E_FAILURE

An unknown error occurred.

MAPI_E_INSUFFICIENT_MEMORY

There was insufficient memory to complete the process.

MAPI_E_LOGIN_FAILURE

It was not possible to log on to the profile specified.

MAPI_E_TOO_MANY_SESSIONS

MAPI wasn't able to establish an additional session.

MAPI_E_USER_ABORT

The user cancelled the process (via a Cancel button on a MAPI-supplied dialog box).

SUCCESS_SUCCESS

The call succeeded and a session was established.

Simple MAPI functions indicate error conditions through their return values, rather than by raising errors. Well-written code should check each return value and take appropriate action. However, I've omitted such error checking from the examples in this chapter in order to focus on the demonstration of each function. I've included lists of return values in the functions' syntax discussions.

Logging Off

To terminate the MAPI session, call the *MAPILogoff* function, as shown here:

```
' Terminate the MAPI session.
' Assume that nMAPISession contains the session handle, as returned
' by the MAPILogon function.
nRetVal = MAPILogoff(nMAPISession, 0, 0, 0)
```

The *MAPILogoff* function's **Declare** statement looks like this:

```
Public Declare Function MAPILogoff Lib "MAPI32.DLL" ( _
   ByVal Session As Long, _
   ByVal UIParam As Long, _
   ByVal Flags As Long, _
   ByVal Reserved As Long _
) As Long
```

The parameters to the *MAPILogoff* function are:

Session
: The session handle that was obtained in the call to *MAPILogon.*

UIParam
: The handle of the window that is to be considered the parent of any dialog boxes displayed by MAPI during logoff. The window handle of a Visual Basic form is found in its hWnd property. Pass 0 to indicate that any dialog boxes should be application-modal.

Flags
: Not used. Pass 0 in this parameter.

Reserved
: Not used. Pass 0 in this parameter.

Sending Mail

After logging on to MAPI with the *MAPILogon* function, messages can be created and sent. The process is as follows:

1. Declare a variable of type **MAPIMessage** and set the values of its members.
2. Declare an array of **MAPIRecip** and call *MAPIResolveName* on each element.
3. If attachments are desired, declare an array of **MapiFile** and set each element appropriately. Sending attachments is covered later in this chapter.
4. Call *MAPISendMail* to send the message.

Example 3-1 shows how to send a message, assuming the *MAPILogon* function has already been called successfully.

Example 3-1. Sending a Message

```
Dim nRetVal As Long
Dim MyMessage As MAPIMessage
Dim MyRecips() As MapiRecip
Dim MyFiles() As MapiFile

' Set the subject and body text.
MyMessage.Subject = "Test message from Simple MAPI."
MyMessage.NoteText = "This is the body text of the message."
```

Example 3-1. Sending a Message (continued)

```
' Add a recipient.
MyMessage.RecipCount = 1
ReDim MyRecips(1 To MyMessage.RecipCount) As MapiRecip
nRetVal = MAPIResolveName(nMAPISession, 0, "Annemarie", 0, 0, MyRecips(1))

' Send the message.
nRetVal = MAPISendMail(nMAPISession, 0, MyMessage, MyRecips, MyFiles, 0, 0)
```

The `MAPIMessage` datatype is defined in *mapi32.txt* like this:

```
Type MAPIMessage
    Reserved As Long
    Subject As String
    NoteText As String
    MessageType As String
    DateReceived As String
    ConversationID As String
    Flags As Long
    RecipCount As Long
    FileCount As Long
End Type
```

The member elements of this datatype are:

`Reserved`
: This member is not used and must be 0.

`Subject`
: The subject of the message.

`NoteText`
: The body text of the message.

`MessageType`
: The message class of the message. Standard email messages have a message class of "`IPM.Note`". (IPM stands for *interpersonal message*—defined as a message that is sent or received by a human user, as opposed to an application.) If `MessageType` is left blank on a new message, MAPI automatically gives the message a class of "`IPM.Note`".

`DateReceived`
: On incoming messages, this is the date and time that the message was received. It is a string of the form "`YYYY/MM/DD HH:MM`" where the hours are in 24-hour format.

`ConversationID`
: On incoming messages, this string indicates the conversation thread to which the message belongs. See Chapter 4, *The MAPI ActiveX Controls*, for a discussion of conversation threads.

`Flags`

Flags that represent further information about the message. Possible values are:

`MAPI_RECEIPT_REQUESTED`

Indicates that the sender of the message is requesting a confirmation of receipt of the message. On outgoing messages, set this flag to request that the destination mail system send back a confirmation email when the message is received. On incoming messages, no special action is required—MAPI automatically sends the confirmation.

`MAPI_SENT`

This flag indicates that the message has been moved to the mail server. It is set by MAPI.

`MAPI_UNREAD`

This flag indicates that the message has not been read. This is useful on incoming messages.

When multiple flags apply, their values are combined with the **Or** operator. To check for the presence of a particular flag, use the **And** operator, like this:

```
Dim bUnread As Boolean
bUnread = MAPI_UNREAD And MyMessage.Flags
```

`RecipCount`

The number of recipients to which the message is being sent.

`FileCount`

The number of attachments. Attachments are discussed later in this chapter.

For a message to be sent, it must have one or more recipients. Recipients are set up in variables of type **MapiRecip**, and an array of such recipients is passed to the *MAPISendMail* function. The **MapiRecip** datatype is defined in *mapi32.txt* like this:

```
Type MapiRecip
    Reserved As Long
    RecipClass As Long
    Name As String
    Address As String
    EIDSize As Long
    EntryID As String
End Type
```

Its members are:

`Reserved`

This member is not used and must be 0.

`RecipClass`

This member can take the following values:

1 The recipient is a *primary recipient* (on the "To" list)

2 The recipient is a *copy recipient* (on the "Cc" list)

3 The recipient is a *blind copy recipient* (on the "Bcc" list)

mapi32.txt doesn't define symbolic constants for these values. It would be appropriate to define such constants in your own code. I won't do so in the examples here, so as not to give the impression that I'm using intrinsic symbols.

Set this member as desired for recipients of outgoing messages. Read this member on the recipients of incoming messages to determine for each recipient whether it was a primary or copy recipient (blind copy recipients aren't seen on incoming messages).

`Name`

This is the display name of the recipient.

`Address`

This is the address of the recipient, in the form "*`address_type:address`*".

`EIDSize`

This is the size of the data in the `EntryID` member, in bytes.

`EntryID`

This is a unique string that the messaging system has assigned to represent the recipient on the local computer during the current session.

To set up a variable of type **`MapiRecip`**, let the *MAPIResolveName* function do the work. *MAPIResolveName* uses a display name to find the intended recipient in the user's address book. When the recipient is found in the address book, its information is copied into the **`MAPIRecip`** variable.

Example 3-1 showed how to send a message to a single recipient. Adding more recipients requires setting the **`MAPIMessage`** variable's **`RecipCount`** member appropriately, and calling the *MAPIResolveName* function for each recipient. Example 3-2 shows how to send a message to three recipients, one of which is a copy recipient. Bold type indicates lines that differ from Example 3-1.

Example 3-2. Sending a Message to Three Recipients

```
Dim nRetVal As Long
Dim MyMessage As MAPIMessage
Dim MyRecips() As MapiRecip
Dim MyFiles() As MapiFile
```

Example 3-2. Sending a Message to Three Recipients (continued)

```
' Set the subject and body text.
MyMessage.Subject = "Test message from Simple MAPI."
MyMessage.NoteText = "This is the body text of the message."

' Add recipients.
MyMessage.RecipCount = 3
ReDim MyRecips(1 To MyMessage.RecipCount) As MapiRecip
nRetVal = MAPIResolveName(nMAPISession, 0, "Annemarie", 0, 0, MyRecips(1))
nRetVal = MAPIResolveName(nMAPISession, 0, "Dave", 0, 0, MyRecips(2))
nRetVal = MAPIResolveName(nMAPISession, 0, "Mike", 0, 0, MyRecips(3))
MyRecips(3).RecipClass = 2 ' Signifies a copy recipient

' Send the message.
nRetVal = MAPISendMail(nMAPISession, 0, MyMessage, MyRecips, MyFiles, 0, 0)
```

The *MAPIResolveName* function's `Declare` statement looks like this:

```
Public Declare Function MAPIResolveName Lib "MAPI32.DLL" _
   Alias "BMAPIResolveName" ( _
   ByVal Session As Long, _
   ByVal UIParam As Long, _
   ByVal UserName As String, _
   ByVal Flags As Long, _
   ByVal Reserved As Long, _
   Recipient As MapiRecip _
) As Long
```

The parameters are:

`Session`
: The session handle that was obtained in a previous call to *MAPILogon*. Alternatively, pass 0 to cause MAPI to log on the user and create a session that exists only for the duration of the call. If necessary, a dialog box is displayed to request further logon information from the user.

`UIParam`
: The handle of the window that is to be considered the parent of any dialog boxes displayed by MAPI during the call. The window handle of a Visual Basic form is found in its hWnd property. Pass 0 to indicate that any dialog boxes should be application-modal.

`UserName`
: The display name or email address of the messaging user to be resolved. A partial name can be passed, if desired. If the name can be resolved to more than one address book entry, MAPI's response depends on whether the `MAPI_DIALOG` flag is specified in the ***`Flags`*** parameter. If it is, MAPI displays a dialog box to request the user to decide which address book entry to use. If it isn't, the *MAPIResolveName* function returns `MAPI_E_AMBIGUOUS_RECIPIENT`.

Flags

One or more of the following values:

MAPI_AB_NOMODIFY

Indicates that if an address book dialog box is shown, the user should not be able to modify the entries in it. An address book dialog box is shown only if MAPI can't resolve the name and the **MAPI_DIALOG** flag has been specified.

MAPI_DIALOG

Indicates that if MAPI can't resolve the name, an address book dialog box should be displayed to allow the user to resolve the name.

MAPI_LOGON_UI

This flag is relevant only if 0 is passed in the ***Session*** parameter. It indicates that a logon dialog box should be displayed if MAPI needs additional logon information.

MAPI_NEW_SESSION

This flag is relevant only if 0 is passed in the ***Session*** parameter. This causes MAPI to create a new session for this call, rather than attempting to use an existing session. If there is no existing session, MAPI creates a new session regardless of whether this flag is specified.

To specify more than one flag, combine their values using the **Or** operator. To specify no flags, pass 0 in this parameter.

Reserved

Not used. Pass 0 in this parameter.

Recipient

A variable of type **MapiRecip** that will receive the data for the matched address book entry.

The return value from *MAPIResolveName* is a Long that indicates the success or failure of the function, as follows:

MAPI_E_AMBIGUOUS_RECIPIENT

The address could not be resolved.

MAPI_E_FAILURE

There was an unspecified failure.

MAPI_E_INSUFFICIENT_MEMORY

There was not enough memory to complete the function call successfully.

MAPI_E_LOGIN_FAILURE

The user could not be logged on.

MAPI_E_NOT_SUPPORTED
: The address book service provider doesn't support the attempted address resolution.

MAPI_E_USER_ABORT
: The user cancelled the operation on a MAPI-supplied dialog box.

SUCCESS_SUCCESS
: The function was successful.

After setting the message data and resolving the recipient name(s), the *MAPISendMail* function is called to submit the message to the message store, as already shown in Examples 3-1 and 3-2. The *MAPISendMail* function's `Declare` statement looks like this:

```
Public Declare Function MAPISendMail Lib "MAPI32.DLL" _
   Alias "BMAPISendMail" ( _
   ByVal Session As Long, _
   ByVal UIParam As Long, _
   Message As MAPIMessage, _
   Recipient() As MapiRecip, _
   File() As MapiFile, _
   ByVal Flags As Long, _
   ByVal Reserved As Long _
) As Long
```

Its parameters are:

`Session`
: The session handle that was obtained in a previous call to *MAPILogon*. Alternatively, pass 0 to cause MAPI to log on the user and create a session that exists only for the duration of the call. If necessary, a dialog box is displayed to request further logon information from the user.

`UIParam`
: The handle of the window that is to be considered the parent of any dialog boxes displayed by MAPI during the call. The window handle of a Visual Basic form is found in its hWnd property. Pass 0 to indicate that any dialog boxes should be application-modal.

`Message`
: The message to be sent. The datatype is `MAPIMessage`.

`Recipient`
: An array of recipients. The datatype of each element of the array is `MapiRecip`.

`File`
: An array of attachments. Attachments are discussed later in this chapter. The datatype of each element of the array is `MapiFile`.

Flags

One or more of the following values:

MAPI_DIALOG

Indicates that if necessary, MAPI should display a dialog box to prompt the user for recipients and other sending options. This flag is ignored if MAPI is able to send the message with no further information.

MAPI_LOGON_UI

This flag is relevant only if 0 is passed in the *Session* parameter. Specify this flag to indicate that a logon dialog box should be displayed if MAPI needs additional logon information.

MAPI_NEW_SESSION

This flag is relevant only if 0 is passed in the *Session* parameter. Specify this flag to cause MAPI to create a new session for this call, rather than attempting to use an existing session. If there is no existing session, MAPI creates a new session regardless of whether this flag is specified.

To specify more than one flag, combine their values using the `Or` operator. To specify no flags, pass 0 in this parameter.

Reserved

Not used. Pass 0 in this parameter.

Sending File Attachments

To add attachments to an outgoing message:

1. Prepare a variable of type `MAPIMessage` to represent the message (as already described in this chapter).
2. Set the `FileCount` member of the `MAPIMessage` variable equal to the desired number of attachments.
3. Dimension an array of `MapiFile` elements with as many elements as there are files to attach.
4. Set the member values of each array element.
5. Pass the array to the *MAPISendMail* function.

Example 3-3 shows a code fragment that sends a single file attachment to a single recipient. This code assumes that a session has already been established via a call to the *MAPILogon* function, and that the session handle is held in a variable called *nMAPISession*. The message thus sent, when viewed in Microsoft Outlook 98, is shown in Figure 3-3.

Example 3-3. Sending a File Attachment

```
Dim nRetVal As Long
Dim MyMessage As MAPIMessage
Dim MyRecips() As MapiRecip
Dim MyFiles() As MapiFile

' Set the subject and body text.
MyMessage.Subject = "Test message from Simple MAPI, with attachment."
MyMessage.NoteText = "This is the body text of the message."

' Add a recipient.
MyMessage.RecipCount = 1
ReDim MyRecips(1 To MyMessage.RecipCount) As MapiRecip
nRetVal = MAPIResolveName(nMAPISession, 0, "Annemarie", 0, 0, MyRecips(1))

' Add an attachment.
MyMessage.FileCount = 1
ReDim MyFiles(1 To MyMessage.FileCount) As MapiFile
MyFiles(1).PathName = "c:\autoexec.bat"

' Send the message.
nRetVal = MAPISendMail(nMAPISession, 0, MyMessage, MyRecips, MyFiles, 0, 0)
```

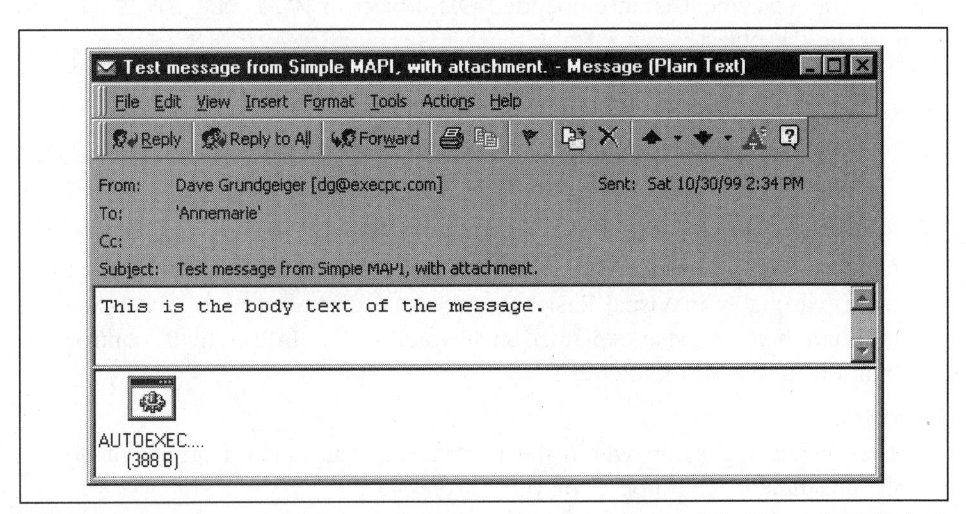

Figure 3-3. Message received from code in Example 3-3, as displayed by Microsoft Outlook 98

Note the technique used when declaring the **MapiFile** array:

```
Dim MyFiles() As MapiFile
   .
   .
   .
ReDim MyFiles(1 To MyMessage.FileCount) As MapiFile
```

The array is originally declared as a dynamic array with no elements; then, when the number of file attachments is known, the array is redeclared to be the appropriate size. The **MapiFile** datatype is declared as follows:

```
Type MapiFile
    Reserved As Long
    Flags As Long
    Position As Long
    PathName As String
    FileName As String
    FileType As String
End Type
```

The members of this type are:

`Reserved`
: This member is not used and must remain 0.

`Flags`
: The **Flags** member can take one or both of the following values:

  `MAPI_OLE`
  : The attachment is an embedded OLE object. If `MAPI_OLE_STATIC` is also set, the object is not editable (i.e., it is static). If `MAPI_OLE_STATIC` is not set, the object is editable.

  `MAPI_OLE_STATIC`
  : This flag indicates that the attachment is a non-editable (static) embedded OLE object.

  If neither flag is set (i.e., if this member contains 0), the attachment is a data file. Handling embedded OLE objects using Simple MAPI is too complex to be done reasonably in Visual Basic and won't be discussed here. The issues are the same here as those explained in Chapter 4 (the MAPI ActiveX controls are built on Simple MAPI, after all).

`Position`
: The character position within the text message at which a representation of the attachment should be displayed.

`PathName`
: The full path and filename of the attached file on the local system.

`FileName`
: The name of the file as it should be displayed in the user interface.

`FileType`
: This member is not used and must remain an empty string.

Reading Mail

Three API functions are related to reading messages. Each one handles a different aspect of the process, and all three must be used to retrieve incoming messages successfully. These functions are:

MAPIFindNext
: Iterates through the messages in the user's Inbox, returning a message ID for each message.

BMAPIReadMail
: Fetches a message to the local machine, given the message ID returned from *MAPIFindNext.*

BMAPIGetReadMail
: Reads a fetched message.

The code in Example 3-4 loops through the messages in the user's Inbox and prints the subject text of each message to the Visual Basic Immediate window. This code assumes that a session has already been established via a call to the *MAPILogon* function, and that the session handle is held in a variable called `nMAPISession`.

Example 3-4. Reading Messages

```
Dim nRetVal As Long
Dim nRetValFindNext As Long
Dim strSeedMessageID As String
Dim strMessageID As String
Dim nMsg As Long
Dim MyMessage As MAPIMessage
ReDim MyRecips(0 To 0) As MapiRecip
ReDim MyFiles(0 To 0) As MapiFile
Dim recipOriginator As MapiRecip
Dim nRecipients As Long
Dim nFiles As Long

' This tells MAPIFindNext to start with the first message.
strSeedMessageID = ""

Do ' for each message in the user's Inbox

   ' Get the next message ID.
   strMessageID = String(512, 0)
   nRetValFindNext = MAPIFindNext(nMAPISession, 0, "", _
      strSeedMessageID, 0, 0, strMessageID)

   ' if there was another message
   If nRetValFindNext = SUCCESS_SUCCESS Then

      ' Fetch message associated with the message ID.
```

Example 3-4. Reading Messages (continued)

```
      nRetVal = BMAPIReadMail(nMsg, nRecipients, nFiles, nMAPISession, 0, _
         strMessageID, MAPI_ENVELOPE_ONLY Or MAPI_PEEK, 0)
      Debug.Assert nRetVal = SUCCESS_SUCCESS

      ' Prepare the MyRecips and MyFiles arrays to receive
      ' the recipient and attachment information.
      If nRecipients > 0 Then
         ReDim MyRecips(0 To nRecipients - 1) As MapiRecip
      End If
      If nFiles > 0 Then
         ReDim MyFiles(0 To nFiles - 1) As MapiFile
      End If

      ' Read the fetched message.
      nRetVal = BMAPIGetReadMail(nMsg, MyMessage, MyRecips, MyFiles, _
         recipOriginator)
      Debug.Assert nRetVal = SUCCESS_SUCCESS

      ' Write the subject line to the immediate window.
      Debug.Print MyMessage.Subject

      ' The message ID becomes the seed for the next call to MAPIFindNext.
      strSeedMessageID = strMessageID
   End If
Loop While nRetValFindNext = SUCCESS_SUCCESS
```

The declaration of the *MAPIFindNext* function is as follows:

```
Public Declare Function MAPIFindNext Lib "MAPI32.DLL" _
   Alias "BMAPIFindNext" ( _
   ByVal Session As Long, _
   ByVal UIParam As Long, _
   MsgType As String, _
   SeedMsgID As String, _
   ByVal Flag As Long, _
   ByVal Reserved As Long, _
   MsgID As String _
) As Long
```

The parameters of this function are:

`Session`

The session handle that was obtained in a previous call to *MAPILogon*. Alternatively, pass 0 to cause MAPI to log on the user and create a session that exists only for the duration of the call. If necessary, a dialog box is displayed to request further logon information from the user.

`UIParam`

The handle of the window that is to be considered the parent of any dialog boxes displayed by MAPI during the call. The window handle of a Visual Basic form is found in its hWnd property. Pass 0 to indicate that any dialog boxes should be application-modal.

MsgType

Use the *MsgType* parameter to consider only messages that have a message class equal to *MsgType*. To find IPMs (i.e., standard user-to-user email), pass either "`IPM.Note`" or an empty string.

SeedMsgID

The *MAPIFindNext* function uses the value of this parameter to keep track of where it is in the search. To start a new search, pass an empty string in this parameter. To find subsequent messages, pass the message ID from the previous find.

Flag

One or more of the following values:

`MAPI_GUARANTEE_FIFO`

MAPIFindNext should return message IDs in order of the date and time that each message was received. Some message stores don't support this feature, in which case *MAPIFindNext* returns `MAPI_E_NOT_SUPPORTED`. Calls to *MAPIFindNext* may take longer to execute when this flag is specified.

`MAPI_NEW_SESSION`

This flag is relevant only if 0 is passed in the *Session* parameter. Specify this flag to cause MAPI to create a new session for this call, rather than attempting to use an existing session. If there is no existing session, MAPI creates a new session regardless of whether this flag is specified.

`MAPI_UNREAD_ONLY`

MAPIFindNext should find only unread messages.

To specify more than one flag, combine their values using the `Or` operator. To specify no flags, pass 0 in this parameter.

Reserved

Not used. Pass 0 in this parameter.

MsgID

A string variable to receive the message ID of the next found message. The *MAPIFindNext* function doesn't know how to allocate the space it needs in a Visual Basic string, so the allocation must be done in Visual Basic code prior to calling *MAPIFindNext*. In Example 3-4, the allocation is accomplished with this line:

```
strMessageID = String(512, 0)
```

This line allocates space for a string of 512 characters and initializes each character in the string to `Chr(0)`. 512 characters are sufficient for any message ID that *MAPIFindNext* can return.

MAPIFindNext returns `SUCCESS_SUCCESS` if the function is successful, or one of the following error codes if not:

`MAPI_E_FAILURE`
: An unknown error occurred.

`MAPI_E_INSUFFICIENT_MEMORY`
: There was insufficient memory to complete the process.

`MAPI_E_INVALID_MESSAGE`
: The value passed in the *`SeedMsgID`* parameter is invalid.

`MAPI_E_INVALID_SESSION`
: The value passed in the *`Session`* parameter is invalid.

`MAPI_E_NO_MESSAGES`
: There are no more messages of the requested type to return.

While the purpose of *MAPIFindNext* is to iterate through the user's Inbox, it's the job of *BMAPIReadMail* to move a specific message and its attachments from the message store to temporary storage on the user's machine. The declaration of *BMAPIReadMail* is as follows:

```
Public Declare Function BMAPIReadMail Lib "MAPI32.DLL" ( _
   lMsg As Long, _
   nRecipients As Long, _
   nFiles As Long, _
   ByVal Session As Long, _
   ByVal UIParam As Long, _
   MessageID As String, _
   ByVal Flag As Long, _
   ByVal Reserved As Long _
) As Long
```

The parameters are:

`lMsg`
: A variable of type Long to receive a numeric message ID from the *BMAPIReadMail* function. This numeric value will be used later when calling *BMAPIGetReadMail*.

`nRecipients`
: A variable of type Long to receive the count of recipients for this message.

`nFiles`
: A variable of type Long to receive the count of attachments on this message.

`Session`
: The session handle that was obtained in a previous call to *MAPILogon*. Alternatively, pass 0 to cause MAPI to log on the user and create a session that exists only for the duration of the call. If necessary, a dialog box is displayed to request further logon information from the user.

UIParam

The handle of the window that is to be considered the parent of any dialog boxes displayed by MAPI during the call. The window handle of a Visual Basic form is found in its hWnd property. Pass 0 to indicate that any dialog boxes should be application-modal.

MessageID

The message ID of the message to be read, as returned in the ***MsgID*** parameter of the *MAPIFindNext* function.

Flag

One or more of the following values:

MAPI_BODY_AS_FILE

The message's body text should be written to a temporary file, which is added as the first message attachment.

MAPI_ENVELOPE_ONLY

The *BMAPIReadMail* function should not retrieve attachments or message text. This is useful when all that is needed is to display header information, such as subject text and the date on which the message was received.

MAPI_PEEK

The *BMAPIReadMail* function should not mark the message as read.

MAPI_SUPPRESS_ATTACH

The *BMAPIReadMail* function should not fetch file attachments.

To specify more than one flag, combine their values using the `Or` operator. To specify no flags, pass 0 in this parameter.

Reserved

Not used. Pass 0 in this parameter.

BMAPIReadMail returns **SUCCESS_SUCCESS** if the call is successful, or one of the MAPI_E_ codes if not (Microsoft doesn't document the error codes that can be returned by this function).

Finally, the *BMAPIGetReadMail* function retrieves the contents of a fetched message. Here's its declaration:

```
Public Declare Function BMAPIGetReadMail Lib "MAPI32.DLL" ( _
   ByVal lMsg As Long, _
   Message As MAPIMessage, _
   Recip() As MapiRecip, _
   File() As MapiFile, _
   Originator As MapiRecip _
) As Long
```

Its parameters are:

lMsg
: The *lMsg* value received from the *BMAPIReadMail* function.

Message
: A variable of type **MAPIMessage** to receive the message data.

Recip
: A variable that has been dimensioned as an array of **MapiRecip**. The *BMAPIGetReadMail* function fills the array with information about the recipients of the message. The indexes of the array must range from zero to one less than the number of recipients. The number of recipients is obtained through the *nRecipients* parameter in the call to *BMAPIReadMail*.

File
: A variable that has been dimensioned as an array of **MapiFile**. The *BMAPIGetReadMail* function fills the array with information about the message's attachments. The indexes of the array must range from zero to one less than the number of files. The number of files is obtained through the *nFiles* parameter in the call to *BMAPIReadMail*.

Originator
: A variable of type **MapiRecip** to receive information about the user who sent the message.

BMAPIGetReadMail returns SUCCESS_SUCCESS if the call is successful, or one of the MAPI_E_ codes if not. (Microsoft doesn't document the error codes that can be returned by this function.)

After you've read a message, you may wish to delete it. This is accomplished by calling the *MAPIDeleteMail* function and passing it a message ID string, as received from the *MAPIFindNext* function. The declaration of *MAPIDeleteMail* is:

```
Public Declare Function MAPIDeleteMail Lib "MAPI32.DLL" ( _
   ByVal Session As Long, _
   ByVal UIParam As Long, _
   ByVal MsgID As String, _
   ByVal Flags As Long, _
   ByVal Reserved As Long _
) As Long
```

Its parameters are:

Session
: The session handle that was obtained in a previous call to *MAPILogon*. This parameter cannot be 0.

UIParam
: The handle of the window that is to be considered the parent of any dialog boxes displayed by MAPI during the call. The window handle of a Visual

Basic form is found in its hWnd property. Pass 0 to indicate that any dialog boxes should be application-modal.

MsgID
: The message ID of the message to be deleted, as returned in the ***MsgID*** parameter of the *MAPIFindNext* function.

Flags
: Not used. Pass 0 in this parameter.

Reserved
: Not used. Pass 0 in this parameter.

Reading File Attachments

Attachments are retrieved from the message store and copied to temporary local files automatically when messages are read. After a call to *BMAPIGetReadMail*, attachment information appears in the array passed to that function's ***File*** parameter. Have another look at the *BMAPIGetReadMail* call from Example 3-4:

```
' Read the fetched message.
nRetVal = BMAPIGetReadMail(nMsg, MyMessage, MyRecips, MyFiles, _
   recipOriginator)
```

Just prior to this call in Example 3-4, the ***MyFiles*** array was dimensioned to have as many elements as there are attachments to the email. The *BMAPIGetReadMail* call then fills each element with information about the corresponding attachment. Each element holds a **MapiFile** user-defined type, shown earlier in this chapter and repeated here:

```
Type MapiFile
    Reserved As Long
    Flags As Long
    Position As Long
    PathName As String
    FileName As String
    FileType As String
End Type
```

The usage of each member is the same as that described in the "Sending File Attachments" section earlier in this chapter.

What you do with this information depends on your application's requirements. One option would be to allow the user to copy an attachment from an email to a disk file. Because email attachments are stored as temporary files when the email is fetched, this feature can be implemented simply by calling Visual Basic's **FileCopy** statement to copy the file from its temporary location to a destination specified by the user. Assuming that **MyFiles** is defined as in Example 3-4, that *BMAPIGetReadMail* has been called as already described, that ***nIndex*** identifies the attachment to be copied, and that `strCopyTo` holds the destination path and filename, the following statement does the job:

```
FileCopy MyFiles(nIndex).PathName, strCopyTo
```

Note that the **PathName** member of the **MapiFile** type contains the full path of the file attachment, including the filename.

Another nice feature is to allow the user to open an attached document directly from an email. This is a little trickier to implement because Visual Basic doesn't have a statement for opening documents. To implement this feature, it is necessary to use the Windows API call, *ShellExecute*. The **Declare** statement for *ShellExecute* looks like this:

```
' Place this Declare statement at module level.
Public Declare Function ShellExecute Lib "shell32.dll" _
   Alias "ShellExecuteA" ( _
   ByVal hwnd As Long, _
   ByVal lpOperation As String, _
   ByVal lpFile As String, _
   ByVal lpParameters As String, _
   ByVal lpDirectory As String, _
   ByVal nShowCmd As Long _
) As Long
```

In addition to this declaration, we need to declare a constant that will be used in the call to *ShellExecute*, as shown here:

```
' Place this constant at module level too.
Public Const SW_SHOWMAXIMIZED = 3
```

To make calling *ShellExecute* straightforward, I wrote the short helper function *OpenDocument*, shown here:

```
' Place this helper function in a standard module.
Public Function OpenDocument( _
   ByVal frm As Form, _
   ByVal strFullPath As String _
) As Boolean

   ' Launch the application associated with the document specified in
   ' strFullPath, causing the application to open the document. frm is
   ' used as the parent window for any dialog boxes that must be displayed.

   ' A return value of True indicates success, False indicates failure.

   Dim nResult As Long

   nResult = ShellExecute(frm.hwnd, "Open", strFullPath, 0, 0, _
      SW_SHOWMAXIMIZED)

   OpenDocument = (nResult > 32)

End Function ' OpenDocument
```

With these declarations and the helper function, it becomes easy to open an attached document. Assuming that ***MyFiles*** is defined as in Example 3-4, that *BMAPIGetReadMail* has been called as already described, and that ***nIndex*** identifies the attachment to be opened, here's how to open the file:

```
Dim bSuccess As Boolean
bSuccess = OpenDocument(Me, MyFiles(nIndex).PathName)
```

Note that this code must be part of a Form object so that **Me** is of the proper type. If you want to put the code in a non-Form object, substitute a valid Form reference for **Me**.

Message attachments are a popular carrier for computer viruses. Consider security concerns before writing code that opens attachments.

Showing the Address Book

If you're writing an application that allows the user to enter recipients for an outgoing message, it's convenient for the user to have a way to display the address book and to select recipients directly from it. In Simple MAPI, this is done using a combination of two functions: *BMAPIAddress* and *BMAPIGetAddress. BMAPIAddress* displays the address book and records the user's selections (internally), returning a handle to the selections through an out parameter. *BMAPIGetAddress* accepts the handle as input and returns (again through an out parameter) an array of **MapiRecip** records representing the address entries selected from the address book. This array can then be passed to the *MAPISendMail* function. Example 3-5 demonstrates this process. Figure 3-4 shows the address book dialog box displayed by the MAPI system when *BMAPIAddress* is called.

Example 3-5. Showing the Address Book

```
' Assume that a MAPI session has already been established, and that
' nMAPISession holds the session handle.

Dim nRetVal As Long
Dim MyMessage As MAPIMessage
Dim MyRecips() As MapiRecip
Dim MyFiles() As MapiFile
Dim nInfo As Long
Dim nRecipients As Long

' Set the subject and body text of the message.
MyMessage.Subject = "Test message from Simple MAPI."
MyMessage.NoteText = "This is the body text of the message."
```

Example 3-5. Showing the Address Book (continued)

```
' Show the address book to allow the user to select recipients.
nRetVal = BMAPIAddress(nInfo, nMAPISession, 0, "Select Names", 4, "", _
   nRecipients, MyRecips, 0, 0)

If nRetVal = SUCCESS_SUCCESS Then
   ' Load the recipients into MyRecip().
   ReDim MyRecips(0 To nRecipients - 1)
   nRetVal = BMAPIGetAddress(nInfo, nRecipients, MyRecips)

   If nRetVal = SUCCESS_SUCCESS Then
      ' Send the message.
      MyMessage.RecipCount = nRecipients
      nRetVal = MAPISendMail(nMAPISession, 0, MyMessage, MyRecips, _
         MyFiles, 0, 0)
   End If
End If
```

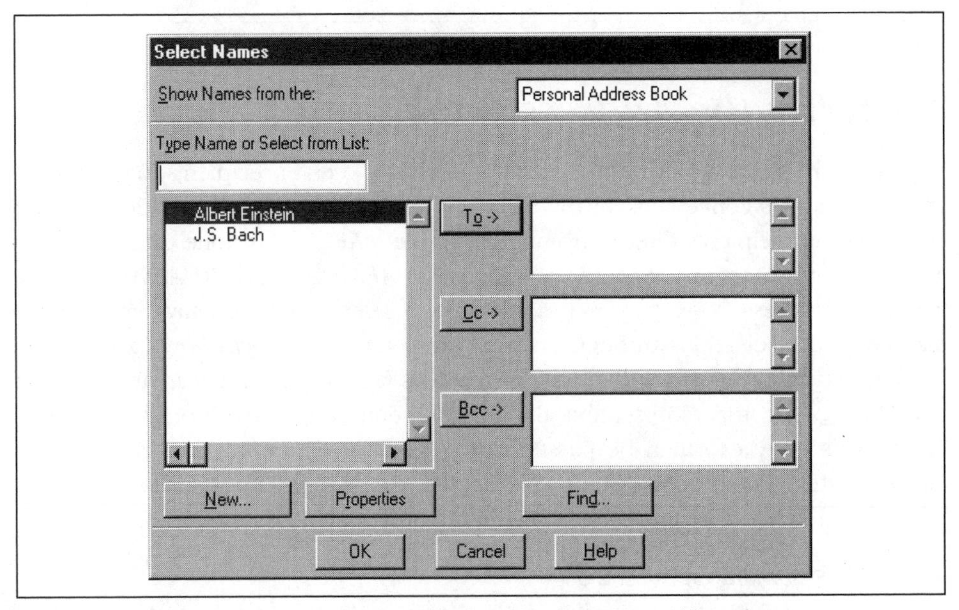

Figure 3-4. The address book dialog box displayed by the BMAPIAddress function

The declaration of *BMAPIAddress* looks like this:

```
Public Declare Function BMAPIAddress Lib "MAPI32.DLL" ( _
   lInfo As Long, _
   ByVal Session As Long, _
   ByVal UIParam As Long, _
   Caption As String, _
   ByVal nEditFields As Long, _
   Label As String, _
   nRecipients As Long, _
   Recip() As MapiRecip, _
   ByVal Flags As Long, _
```

```
    ByVal Reserved As Long _
) As Long
```

The parameters to this function are:

`lInfo`
: A variable of type Long to receive a handle that represents the selected recipients. Pass the handle thus received to the *BMAPIGetAddress* function to get the actual recipient records.

`Session`
: The session handle that was obtained in a previous call to *MAPILogon*. Alternatively, pass 0 to cause MAPI to log on the user and create a session that exists only for the duration of the call. If necessary, a dialog box is displayed to request further logon information from the user.

`UIParam`
: The handle of the window that is to be considered the parent of any dialog boxes displayed by MAPI during the call. The window handle of a Visual Basic form is found in its hWnd property. Pass 0 to indicate that any dialog boxes should be application-modal.

`Caption`
: The text that is to appear in the title bar of the address book dialog box. If an empty string is passed, the string "`Address Book`" is used.

`nEditFields`
: Controls whether users are able to select recipients in the address book dialog box, and if so, whether the recipients can be copy or blind copy recipients. Pass 0 in this parameter to specify that the user is not allowed to select recipients of any kind—that is, the user is allowed only to browse the address book (Figure 3-5). Pass 1 in this parameter to specify that the user is allowed to select primary recipients but not copy or blind copy recipients (Figure 3-6). Pass 2 in this parameter to specify that the user is allowed to select primary and copy recipients but not blind copy recipients (Figure 3-7). Pass 3 in this parameter to indicate that the user may select recipients of any kind (already shown in Figure 3-4). Pass 4 in this parameter to indicate that the user is allowed to select recipients of any type supported by the underlying mail system.

`Label`
: This parameter is ignored unless the value passed in the *`nEditFields`* parameter is 1. In the *`Label`* parameter, pass the text that is to appear on the button for selecting primary recipients in the address book dialog box. If an empty string is passed, the string "`To`" is used.

`nRecipients`
: This parameter is used both for input and for output. On the way in, pass the number of recipients contained in the *`Recip`* parameter. Upon return from the

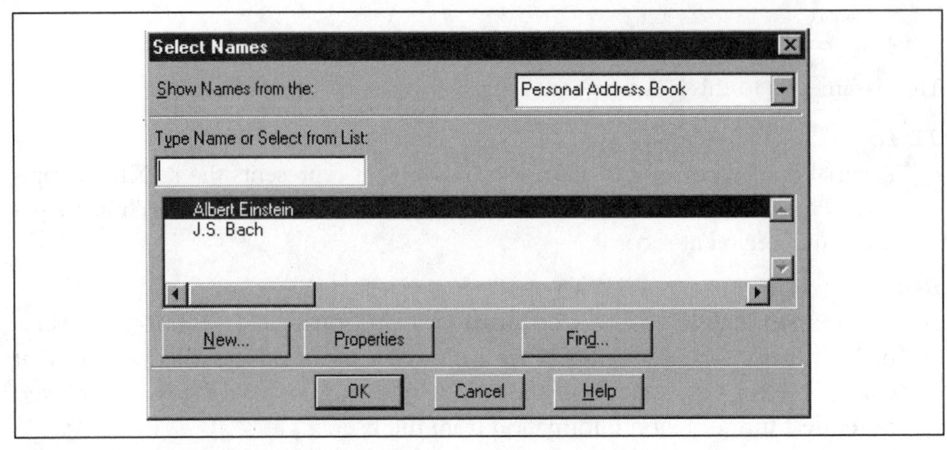

Figure 3-5. A browse-only address book

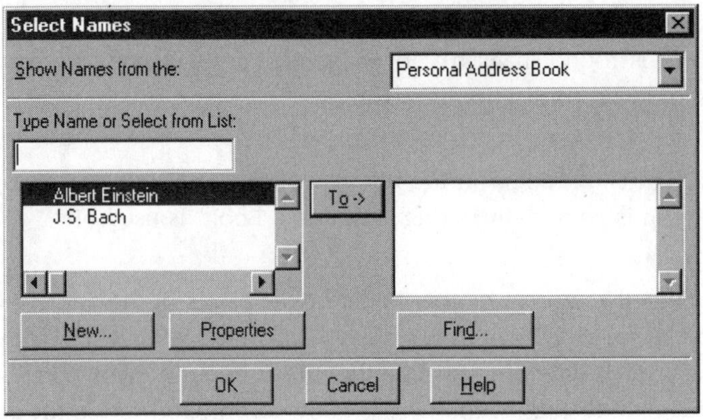

Figure 3-6. Allowing the user to select primary recipients only

function, ***nRecipients*** indicates the number of recipients selected from the address book by the user.

Recip

An array of `MapiRecip` records that are to be used to populate the address book dialog box on entry.

Flags

One or more of the following constants:

`MAPI_LOGON_UI`

This flag is relevant only if 0 is passed in the ***Session*** parameter. Specify this flag to indicate that a logon dialog box should be displayed if MAPI needs additional logon information.

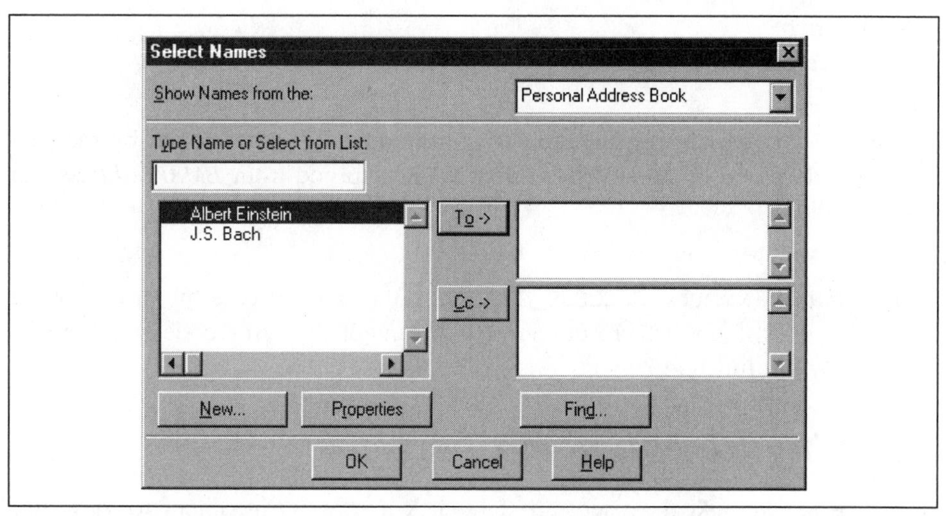

Figure 3-7. Allowing the user to select primary and copy recipients only

`MAPI_NEW_SESSION`
: This flag is relevant only if 0 is passed in the ***Session*** parameter. Specify this flag to cause MAPI to create a new session for this call, rather than attempting to use an existing session. If there is no existing session, MAPI creates a new session regardless of whether this flag is specified.

To specify more than one flag, use the `Or` operator to combine the flags. To specify no flags, pass 0 in this parameter.

Reserved
: Not used. Pass 0 in this parameter.

BMAPIAddress returns `SUCCESS_SUCCESS` if the call is successful, or one of the `MAPI_E_` codes if not. (Microsoft doesn't document the error codes that can be returned by this function.)

Calling *BMAPIAddress* does only half the job. After this call completes, it is necessary to call *BMAPIGetAddress* to load an array with `MapiRecip` records representing the address entries selected by the user. The declaration of *BMAPIGetAddress* looks like this:

```
Public Declare Function BMAPIGetAddress Lib "MAPI32.DLL" ( _
   ByVal lInfo As Long, _
   ByVal nRecipients As Long, _
   Recipients() As MapiRecip _
) As Long
```

Its parameters are:

lInfo
: The ***lInfo*** value received from *BMAPIAddress*.

nRecipients
The *nRecipients* value received from *BMAPIAddress*.

Recipients
An array of MapiRecip records. This array must be dimensioned by the calling code based on the *nRecipients* value returned from *BMAPIAddress*. For example:

```
ReDim MyRecips(0 To nRecipients - 1)
```

BMAPIGetAddress returns SUCCESS_SUCCESS if the call is successful, or one of the MAPI_E_ codes if not. (Microsoft doesn't document the error codes that can be returned by this function.)

Showing Recipient Properties

In Microsoft Outlook, the user can right-click a message recipient to view that recipient's properties. Simple MAPI provides this feature through the *MAPIDetails* function. *MAPIDetails* causes MAPI to invoke the underlying address book provider's address entry dialog box. This allows the user to display and modify the address entry properties associated with a specified recipient. Here's a sample call to this function:

```
nRetVal = MAPIDetails(nMAPISession, 0, MyRecip, 0, 0)
```

The *MapiRecip* variable that is passed to *MAPIDetails* could be from one of the elements in the recipients array of an incoming message. A sample address entry properties dialog box is shown in Figure 3-8.

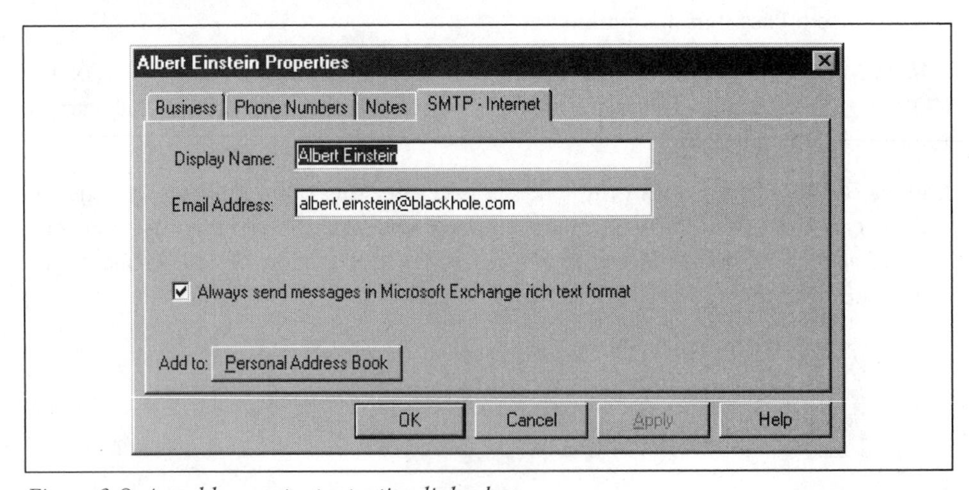

Figure 3-8. An address entry properties dialog box

MAPIDetails is declared as follows:

```
Public Declare Function MAPIDetails Lib "MAPI32.DLL" Alias "BMAPIDetails" ( _
   ByVal Session As Long, _
   ByVal UIParam As Long, _
   Recipient As MapiRecip, _
   ByVal Flags As Long, _
   ByVal Reserved As Long _
) As Long
```

Its parameters are:

Session
: The session handle that was obtained in a previous call to *MAPILogon*. Alternatively, pass 0 to cause MAPI to log on the user and create a session that exists only for the duration of the call. If necessary, a dialog box is displayed to request further logon information from the user.

UIParam
: The handle of the window that is to be considered the parent of any dialog boxes displayed by MAPI during the call. The window handle of a Visual Basic form is found in its hWnd property. Pass 0 to indicate that any dialog boxes should be application-modal.

MapiRecip
: The recipient whose properties are to be shown.

Flags
: One or more of the following constants:

  MAPI_AB_NOMODIFY
  : The user is not allowed to modify the address book entry. There is no guarantee that this request will be honored.

  MAPI_LOGON_UI
  : This flag is relevant only if 0 is passed in the *Session* parameter. Specify this flag to indicate that a logon dialog box should be displayed if MAPI needs additional logon information.

  MAPI_NEW_SESSION
  : This flag is relevant only if 0 is passed in the *Session* parameter. Specify this flag to cause MAPI to create a new session for this call, rather than attempting to use an existing session. If there is no existing session, then MAPI creates a new session regardless of whether this flag is specified.

  To specify more than one flag, use the `Or` operator to combine the flags. To specify no flags, pass 0 in this parameter.

Reserved
: Not used. Pass 0 in this parameter.

The *MAPIDetails* function returns SUCCESS_SUCCESS if it is successful, or one of the following error codes if not:

MAPI_E_AMBIGUOUS_RECIPIENT
: The specified recipient couldn't be resolved to a unique address book entry.

MAPI_E_FAILURE
: An unknown error occurred.

MAPI_E_INSUFFICIENT_MEMORY
: There was insufficient memory to complete the process.

MAPI_E_INVALID_RECIPS
: The specified recipient is unknown.

MAPI_E_LOGIN_FAILURE
: It was not possible to log on to the profile specified.

MAPI_E_NOT_SUPPORTED
: The underlying message system couldn't satisfy the request to display an address entry properties dialog box.

MAPI_E_USER_ABORT
: The user clicked the Cancel button on the address entry properties dialog box.

Microsoft's Helper Functions

Some of the Simple MAPI functions are a little cumbersome to call, to say the least. In particular, it seems a bit excessive to have to call both *BMAPIReadMail* and *BMAPIGetReadMail* simply to retrieve a list of messages. Similarly, why should we have to call both *BMAPIAddress* and *BMAPIGetAddress* to display the address book and retrieve the list of selected address entries? To help make things a little easier, Microsoft has provided a couple of helper functions in Knowledge Base article Q163216, *Updated Mapivb32.bas for Simple MAPI on 32-Bit Platforms.* (Search for this article on the Microsoft Developer Network [MSDN] web site at *http://msdn.microsoft.com.*) The article provides *MAPIReadMail,* which wraps *BMAPIReadMail* and *BMAPIGetReadMail,* and *MAPIAddress,* which wraps *BMAPIAddress* and *BMAPIGetAddress.*

Here is the syntax for the *MAPIReadMail* function:

```
Function MAPIReadMail(Session As Long, UIParam As Long, MessageID As String, Flags
As Long, Reserved As Long, Message As MAPIMessage, Orig As MapiRecip, RecipsOut()
As MapiRecip, FilesOut() As MapiFile) As Long
```

The parameters are:

Session
: The session handle that was obtained in a previous call to *MAPILogon.* Alternatively, pass 0 to cause MAPI to log on the user and create a session that

exists only for the duration of the call. If necessary, a dialog box is displayed to request further logon information from the user.

UIParam

The handle of the window that is to be considered the parent of any dialog boxes displayed by MAPI during the call. The window handle of a Visual Basic form is found in its hWnd property. Pass 0 to indicate that any dialog boxes should be application-modal.

MessageID

The message ID of the message to be read, as returned in the *MsgID* parameter of the *MAPIFindNext* function.

Flags

One or more of the following values:

MAPI_BODY_AS_FILE

The message's body text should be written to a temporary file, which is added as the first message attachment.

MAPI_ENVELOPE_ONLY

The *BMAPIReadMail* function should not retrieve attachments or message text. This is useful when all that is needed is to display header information, such as subject text and the date that the message was received.

MAPI_PEEK

The *BMAPIReadMail* function should not mark the message as read.

MAPI_SUPPRESS_ATTACH

The *BMAPIReadMail* function should not fetch file attachments.

To specify more than one flag, combine their values using the `Or` operator. To specify no flags, pass 0 in this parameter.

Reserved

Not used. Pass 0 in this parameter.

Message

A variable of type **MAPIMessage** to receive the message data.

Orig

A variable of type **MapiRecip** to receive information about the user who sent the message.

RecipsOut

A variable that has been dimensioned as an array of **MapiRecip**. The *MAPIReadMail* function fills the array with information about the recipients of the message. The array is redimensioned as necessary to accommodate the number of recipients associated with the message.

`FilesOut`
: A variable that has been dimensioned as an array of **`MapiFile`**. The *MAPIReadMail* function fills the array with information about the message's attachments. The array is redimensioned as necessary to accommodate the number of attachments associated with the message.

The *MAPIReadMail* function returns one of the following constants:

`MAPI_E_ATTACHMENT_WRITE_FAILURE`
: An attachment couldn't be written to disk. This can be caused by not having sufficient directory permissions to create a file.

`MAPI_E_DISK_FULL`
: There was insufficient disk space to complete the process.

`MAPI_E_FAILURE`
: An unknown error occurred.

`MAPI_E_INSUFFICIENT_MEMORY`
: There was insufficient memory to complete the process.

`MAPI_E_INVALID_MESSAGE`
: The value passed in the *`MessageID`* parameter is invalid.

`MAPI_E_INVALID_SESSION`
: The value passed in the *`Session`* parameter is invalid.

`MAPI_E_TOO_MANY_FILES`
: The message could not be read because there were too many attachments.

`MAPI_E_TOO_MANY_RECIPIENTS`
: The message could not be read because there were too many recipients.

`SUCCESS_SUCCESS`
: The message was read successfully.

Example 3-6 shows how to use the *MAPIReadMail* function. The example is functionally identical to Example 3-4, which loops through the messages in the user's Inbox and prints the subject text of each message to the Visual Basic Immediate window. The only difference in Example 3-6 is that *BMAPIReadMail* and *BMAPIGetReadMail* have been replaced by *MAPIReadMail.*

Example 3-6. Reading Messages Using the MAPIReadMail Helper Function

```
Dim nRetVal As Long
Dim nRetValFindNext As Long
Dim strSeedMessageID As String
Dim strMessageID As String
Dim nMsg As Long
Dim MyMessage As MAPIMessage
ReDim MyRecips(0 To 0) As MapiRecip
```

Example 3-6. Reading Messages Using the MAPIReadMail Helper Function (continued)

```
ReDim MyFiles(0 To 0) As MapiFile
Dim recipOriginator As MapiRecip

' This tells MAPIFindNext to start with the first message.
strSeedMessageID = ""

Do ' for each message in the user's Inbox

   ' Get the next message ID.
   strMessageID = String(512, 0)
   nRetValFindNext = MAPIFindNext(nMAPISession, 0, "", _
      strSeedMessageID, 0, 0, strMessageID)

   ' if there was another message
   If nRetValFindNext = SUCCESS_SUCCESS Then

      ' Fetch message associated with the message ID.
      nRetVal = MAPIReadMail(nMAPISession, 0, strMessageID, _
         MAPI_ENVELOPE_ONLY Or MAPI_PEEK, 0, MyMessage, recipOriginator, _
         MyRecips, MyFiles)
      Debug.Assert nRetVal = SUCCESS_SUCCESS

      ' Write the subject line to the immediate window.
      Debug.Print MyMessage.Subject

      ' The message ID becomes the seed for the next call to MAPIFindNext.
      strSeedMessageID = strMessageID
   End If
Loop While nRetValFindNext = SUCCESS_SUCCESS
```

The *MAPIAddress* function combines the *BMAPIAddress* and *BMAPIGetAddress* functions to allow the caller to display the address book and obtain an array of **MapiRecip** records representing the address entries selected from the address book. The syntax for the *MAPIAddress* function is:

```
Function MAPIAddress(Session As Long, UIParam As Long, Caption As String,
nEditFields As Long, Label As String, nRecipients As Long, Recips() As MapiRecip,
Flags As Long, Reserved As Long) As Long
```

The parameters are:

Session
: The session handle that was obtained in a previous call to *MAPILogon*. Alternatively, pass 0 to cause MAPI to log on the user and create a session that exists only for the duration of the call. If necessary, a dialog box is displayed to request further logon information from the user.

UIParam
: The handle of the window that is to be considered the parent of any dialog boxes displayed by MAPI during the call. The window handle of a Visual

Basic form is found in its hWnd property. Pass 0 to indicate that any dialog boxes should be application-modal.

Caption

The text that is to appear in the title bar of the address book dialog box. If an empty string is passed, the string "`Address Book`" is used.

nEditFields

Controls whether users are able to select recipients in the address book dialog box, and if so, whether the recipients can be copy or blind copy recipients. Pass 0 in this parameter to specify that the user is not allowed to select recipients of any kind—that is, the user is allowed only to browse the address book (Figure 3-5). Pass 1 in this parameter to specify that the user is allowed to select primary recipients but not copy or blind copy recipients (Figure 3-6). Pass 2 in this parameter to specify that the user is allowed to select primary and copy recipients but not blind copy recipients (Figure 3-7). Pass 3 in this parameter to indicate that the user may select recipients of any kind (Figure 3-4). Pass 4 in this parameter to indicate that the user is allowed to select recipients of any type supported by the underlying mail system.

Label

This parameter is ignored unless the value passed in the *nEditFields* parameter is 1. In the *Label* parameter, pass the text that is to appear on the button for selecting primary recipients in the address book dialog box. If an empty string is passed, the string "`To`" is used.

nRecipients

This parameter is used for both input and output. On the way in, pass the number of recipients contained in the *Recip* parameter. Upon return from the function, *nRecipients* indicates the number of recipients selected from the address book by the user.

Recips

This parameter is used both for input and for output. On entry, pass an array of `MapiRecip` records representing recipients that are to be selected initially in the address book dialog box. On return, this array contains the recipients selected by the user. The array is redimensioned as necessary to be large enough to hold the user's selections.

Flags

One or more of the following constants:

`MAPI_LOGON_UI`

This flag is relevant only if 0 is passed in the *Session* parameter. Specify this flag to indicate that a logon dialog box should be displayed if MAPI needs additional logon information.

`MAPI_NEW_SESSION`

This flag is relevant only if 0 is passed in the ***`Session`*** parameter. Specify this flag to cause MAPI to create a new session for this call, rather than attempting to use an existing session. If there is no existing session, MAPI creates a new session regardless of whether this flag is specified.

To specify more than one flag, use the `Or` operator to combine the flags. To specify no flags, pass 0 in this parameter.

`Reserved`

Not used. Pass 0 in this parameter.

The *MAPIAddress* function returns one of the following constants:

`MAPI_E_FAILURE`

An unknown error occurred.

`MAPI_E_INSUFFICIENT_MEMORY`

There was insufficient memory to complete the process.

`MAPI_E_INVALID_EDITFIELDS`

The value passed in the ***`nEditFields`*** parameter was invalid.

`MAPI_E_INVALID_RECIPS`

Either the ***`Recips`*** parameter was not a valid array, or one or more of the recipient records in the array was invalid.

`MAPI_E_INVALID_SESSION`

The value passed in the ***`Session`*** parameter was invalid.

`MAPI_E_LOGIN_FAILURE`

It was not possible to log on to the profile specified.

`MAPI_E_NOT_SUPPORTED`

This is an error that bubbles up from the address book service provider. Unfortunately, there's no way to tell precisely what is not supported. This is the only error condition under which recipients might be returned.

`MAPI_E_USER_ABORT`

The user cancelled the process (via the Cancel button on a MAPI-supplied dialog box).

`SUCCESS_SUCCESS`

The function was successful.

Example 3-7 shows how to use the *MAPIAddress* function. The example is functionally identical to Example 3-5, which invokes the address book dialog box and then sends a message to the selected recipient(s). The only difference in Example 3-7 is that *BMAPIAddress* and *BMAPIGetAddress* have been replaced by *MAPIAddress*.

Example 3-7. Showing the Address Book Using the MAPIAddress Helper Function

```
' Assume that a MAPI session has already been established, and that
' nMAPISession holds the session handle.

Dim nRetVal As Long
Dim MyMessage As MAPIMessage
Dim MyRecips() As MapiRecip
Dim MyFiles() As MapiFile
Dim nRecipients As Long

' Set the subject and body text of the message.
MyMessage.Subject = "Test message from Simple MAPI."
MyMessage.NoteText = "This is the body text of the message."

' Show the address book to allow the user to select recipients.
nRetVal = MAPIAddress(nMAPISession, 0, "Select Names", 4, "", _
   nRecipients, MyRecips, 0, 0)

If nRetVal = SUCCESS_SUCCESS Then
   ' Send the message.
   MyMessage.RecipCount = nRecipients
   nRetVal = MAPISendMail(nMAPISession, 0, MyMessage, MyRecips, _
      MyFiles, 0, 0)
End If
```

Summary

In this chapter, you learned about Simple MAPI, the precursor to MAPI. You learned how to use the `Declare` statement to gain access to this API (and others) and how to use the API to read and send messages, with or without attachments. You also learned a couple of nice extras, such as showing the address book.

In the next chapter, you'll see a technology that is built on Simple MAPI—the MAPI ActiveX controls. If you're looking for a quick start in messaging from Visual Basic, read on.

4

The MAPI ActiveX Controls

ActiveX controls are a great way for Visual Basic programmers to reuse functionality written by other programmers. Using the Messaging Application Programming Interface (MAPI) ActiveX controls, a Visual Basic programmer can create mail-enabled code in less than five minutes. The controls encapsulate the know-how of dealing with the underlying mail system, leaving the programmer free to focus on business requirements.

The downside is that the MAPI controls don't expose MAPI's full functionality. For example, MAPI has rich features for creating and accessing multiple folders, but the MAPI controls are able to access only the Inbox folder. Similarly, MAPI makes it easy to define custom fields on message items, but the MAPI controls are unable to access custom fields. This lack of depth comes from the fact that the MAPI controls are built on Simple MAPI. Simple MAPI was introduced in Chapter 1, *Introduction.*

If you need a rich interface to MAPI, skip ahead to Chapter 5, *Collaboration Data Objects.* However, if you need to work with legacy code that uses the MAPI controls, or if you just need a quick way to send emails programmatically, read on.

Getting Started

The remainder of this chapter assumes that you're familiar with ActiveX controls in general—that is, you know how to add a control to a form, how to set and read properties in code and at design time, and how to call methods.

The MAPI controls are included in the Professional and Enterprise editions of Visual Basic. The Learning Edition doesn't include them. Microsoft doesn't sell the controls individually, and it's not legal to get them from a friend, so Learning Edition owners must upgrade if they want to use these controls.

Of course, before the MAPI controls can be used, your computer must have MAPI installed, it must have message store, address book, and transport providers installed, and a MAPI profile must be set up. Chapter 2, *MAPI*, discussed these requirements at length. The best test that your computer is set up correctly for messaging application development is to ensure that you can send and receive emails using an existing commercial MAPI-compliant email application, such as Microsoft Outlook.

By default, the MAPI controls do not appear in your Toolbox. To add them to the Toolbox for your project, choose Components from the Project menu. The Components dialog box appears, as shown in Figure 4-1.

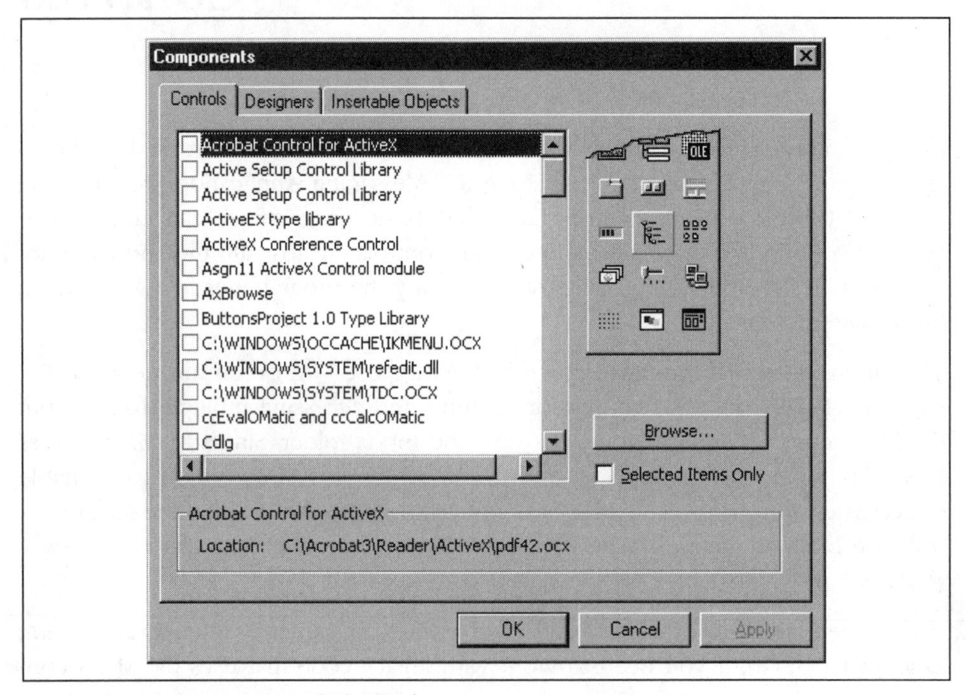

Figure 4-1. The Components dialog box

Scroll down the list of components until you find Microsoft MAPI Controls 6.0. Select the checkbox if it's not selected already, then click OK. After doing so, you'll see the two MAPI controls in your Toolbox. (If you don't see the Toolbox at all, choose View → Toolbox from the Visual Basic menu.) The tool icons are shown in Figure 4-2.

Once the Toolbox has the MAPI controls, the controls can be added to a form. Typically, one of each is added to one of the forms in a project. The MAPI controls are invisible at runtime, so it doesn't matter where they're placed. Once they've been added to a form, they can be referred to in code to manipulate messages.

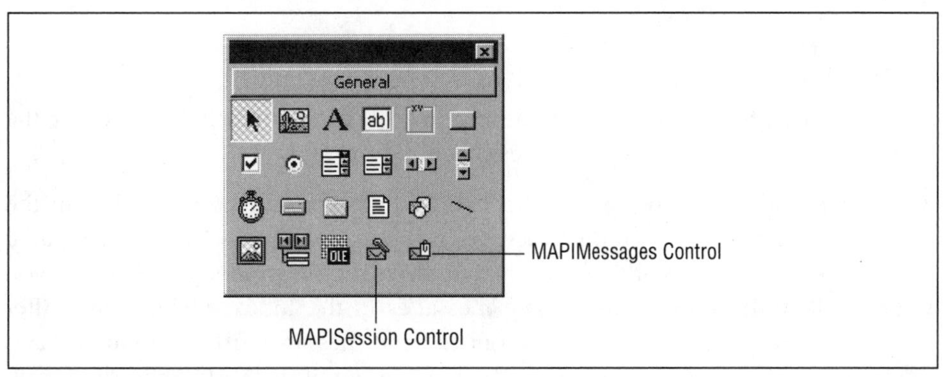

Figure 4-2. A Toolbox with MAPI controls

Let's look briefly at each control, and then we'll dive into sending and receiving messages.

The MAPISession Control

The MAPISession control is used for signing onto and off of the MAPI Subsystem. Your program must sign onto the MAPI Subsystem before it can work with messages. Signing on establishes a MAPI session; signing off releases the session.

During sign on, your program tells MAPI which profile to use during the session. MAPI accesses the profile to discover which mail services (message store, address book, and transport providers) to load. Again, refer to Chapter 2 for more information on profiles and service providers. Once signed on, you can use the MAPIMessages control to work with messages in the MAPI Inbox.

To sign on, set the MAPISession control's UserName property to the name of the profile you want to use, then call the SignOn method, as shown here:

```
With MAPISession1
    .UserName = "MyProfile"
    .SignOn
End With
```

I've left the Password property blank because the profile itself specifies any username and password needed to authenticate to the underlying service providers. Older mail systems, such as Microsoft Mail, didn't use profiles—they required the username and password to be set directly in the MAPISession control.

Given the MAPISession control's default values, the previous code is equivalent to:

```
With MAPISession1
    .DownLoadMail = True
    .LogonUI = True
    .NewSession = False
    .Password = ""
```

```
    .UserName = "MyProfile"
    .SignOn
End With
```

It's likely that you'll want to adjust these property settings to achieve precisely the effects you're looking for, so I'll address each in turn.

The DownLoadMail property tells the MAPI subsystem to retrieve mail from the mail server during the sign-on process. This forces your modem to dial out if you're using dialup networking. You may wish to set this property to `False` if you want to allow the user to manipulate messages in the Inbox while offline. After working offline, you can force a dial out to send messages from the Outbox and to receive new messages. This is done by logging out of the MAPI Subsystem (calling the SignOff method), then setting the DownLoadMail property to `True`, then logging back into the MAPI subsystem (calling the SignOn method). This is the only way to empty the Outbox programmatically of messages that were "sent" while offline. Note also that some service providers (e.g., Microsoft Exchange Server) allow you to specify a schedule for automatically downloading new mail from the mail server (and uploading sent mail). This is configured in the profile.

The DownLoadMail property's name may be misleading. You might think it controls whether a copy of each message is left on the mail server. This isn't the case. The service provider configuration in the profile determines whether retrieved messages are deleted from the mail server. To view a service provider's property page, run the Mail applet in the Control Panel, highlight the service you'd like to view, and click Properties. For example, on the property page for Microsoft Exchange Server, you'll find a checkbox labeled "Enable offline use." (See Figure 4-3.) If this is checked, the Exchange service provider automatically deletes messages from the mail server after they've been copied to your local computer. Similarly, on the property page for the Internet E-mail service provider, you'll find a checkbox labeled "Leave a copy of messages on server." (See Figure 4-4.)

The LogonUI property controls whether a dialog box is displayed to the user during sign-on in the event of a sign-on failure. If the profile name is properly specified in the UserName property and there is no problem signing on, no dialog box is displayed, regardless of the setting of this property. If there is some problem signing on—for example, if an invalid profile is specified—the LogonUI property is checked. If its value is `True`, the MAPI subsystem displays a dialog box presenting a list of valid profile names from which the user must choose. The user can either select from the list and continue, or choose Cancel. If the user chooses Cancel, a `mapLoginFail` error is raised in your code. (Note that "`mapLoginFail`" in the previous sentence isn't a typo. This constant and others used by the MAPI ActiveX controls begin with "`map`", not "`mapi`".) If there was a problem signing on, and the LogonUI property contains `False`, in that case too a `mapLoginFail` error is raised in your code.

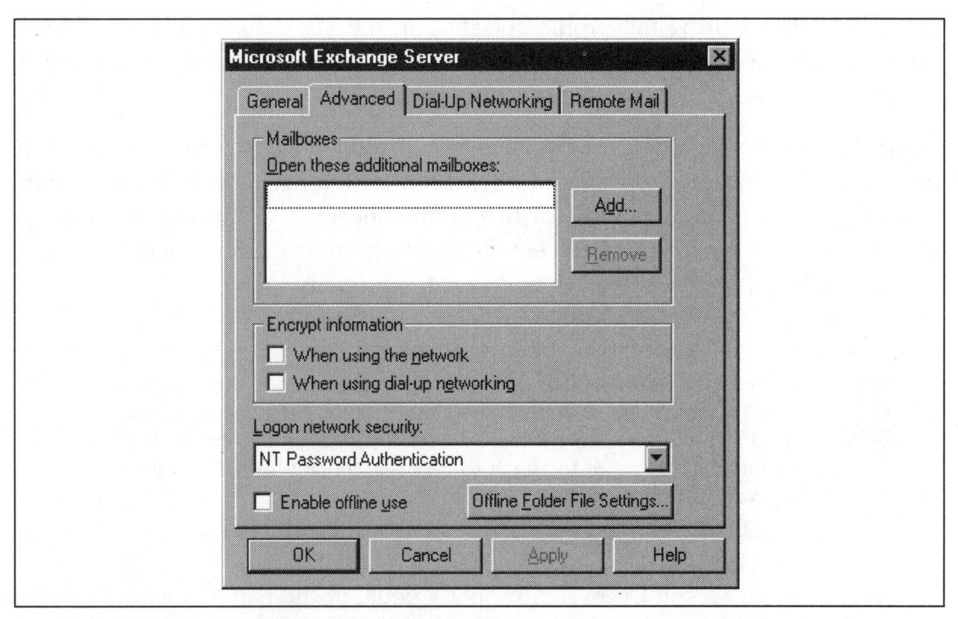

Figure 4-3. The Microsoft Exchange Server service provider property page, showing the "Enable offline use" checkbox

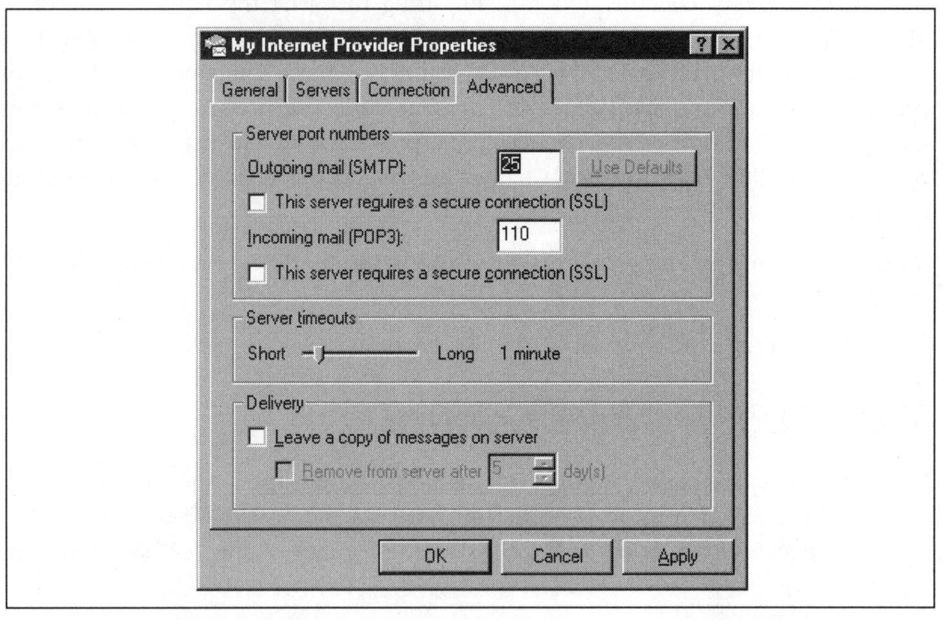

Figure 4-4. The Internet E-mail service provider property page, showing the "Leave a copy of messages on server" checkbox

The NewSession property of the MAPISession control determines whether SignOn uses a new or existing MAPI session. If the property is set to `True`, a new MAPI session is created using the profile specified in the UserName property. If UserName is blank or invalid, either an error occurs (if LogonUI=`False`), or the user is prompted to select a valid profile (if LogonUI=`True`).

If the NewSession property is set to `False`, its default value, the MAPISession control attempts to locate an existing MAPI session on the machine. If found, it signs on using that session, regardless of the profile specified in the UserName property. If there is currently no MAPI session active on the machine, a new one is created using the profile specified in the UserName property.

The problem with signing on to an existing session is that you don't know which profile is being used. Applications that need to use a specific profile should set the NewSession property to `True`. Applications that just want to attach to a profile already in use should set the NewSession property to `False`.

Your code should set the UserName property equal to the name of a MAPI profile set up on the user's system, or leave it blank. If you leave it blank, the mail system prompts the user to select from the list of profiles set up on the system. If the UserName property contains a non-blank string that isn't the name of a profile, MAPI displays an error message, then shows the list of valid profiles from which to choose. Be aware that the Choose Profile dialog box has a Cancel button, which, if pressed, raises a `mapLoginFail` error in your code. Be prepared to handle this error. Note also that the MAPI controls don't provide a way to get a list of profiles programmatically. (However, see Chapter 2 for a way to read profile names from the system registry.)

When you're finished using MAPI, sign off using the MAPISession control's SignOff method:

```
MAPISession1.SignOff
```

The MAPIMessages Control

The MAPIMessages control is used to manipulate messages. After signing on to MAPI using the MAPISession control, you must set the SessionID property of the MAPIMessages control equal to the SessionID property of the MAPISession control, like this:

```
MAPIMessages1.SessionID = MAPISession1.SessionID
```

After doing so, you can compose and manipulate messages until you call the SignOff method of the MAPISession control.

The MAPI controls access only a user's Inbox. No other folders are available, not even other message folders such as Sent Items or Deleted Items, nor any nested folders that have been created inside or nested within the Inbox.

Structure of the MAPIMessages Control

The MAPIMessages control has properties related directly to *messages* (e.g., MsgSubject, MsgNoteText), properties related to *attachments* (e.g., AttachmentName, AttachmentType), and properties related to *recipients* (e.g., RecipDisplayName, RecipType). These three categories are important because each property in each group actually references an array of values. The mechanism for accessing these values is similar in all three cases.

Consider the message-related properties. It's clear that an Inbox may have more than one message. When reading the MsgNoteText property, for example, there must be a way to tell the control which message to access. The MsgIndex property has been provided for this purpose. All of the properties that reference messages retrieve their values from the message that is indicated by the current value of MsgIndex. This is referred to as the *currently indexed message*. The total number of messages is given by the MsgCount property. MsgIndex is zero-based, so its value can range from 0 through `(MsgCount - 1)`. It is an error to set the MsgIndex property to a value higher than `MsgCount - 1`. To give an example, the following code loops through all messages, adding each message's subject line to a list box named *`lstSubjects`* (the Fetch method will be discussed later):

```
Dim nMsgIndex As Long

lstSubjects.Clear
MAPIMessages1.Fetch
For nMsgIndex = 0 To MAPIMessages1.MsgCount - 1
   MAPIMessages1.MsgIndex = nMsgIndex ' set the current message
   lstSubjects.AddItem MAPIMessages1.MsgSubject
   lstSubjects.ItemData(lstSubjects.NewIndex) = nMsgIndex
Next nMsgIndex
```

Similarly, attachment-related properties are relative to the *currently indexed attachment*, as specified in the AttachmentIndex property. The number of attachments is given by the AttachmentCount property. Recipient-related fields are relative to the RecipIndex property, with the number of recipients given by the RecipCount property. Note that AttachmentIndex and RecipIndex, like MsgIndex, are zero-based. Note also that attachments and recipients are relative not only to AttachmentIndex and RecipIndex, respectively, but also to the currently indexed message. (In other words, attachments and recipients are accessed using a two-dimensional array, whereas messages are accessed using a one-dimensional array.)

Therefore, to refer to a specific attachment, for example, first set the MsgIndex property to select the desired message, then set the AttachmentIndex property to select a specific attachment on that message. Given a message index *nMsg*, and an attachment index *nAttachment*, this code retrieves the given attachment's display name:

```
MAPIMessages1.MsgIndex = nMsg
MAPIMessages1.AttachmentIndex = nAttachment
strName = MAPIMessages1.AttachmentName
```

Example 4-1 further demonstrates the use of these indices by displaying (in Visual Basic's Immediate window) summary information for all messages, recipients, and attachments fetched by the MAPIMessages control.

Example 4-1. Looping Through Messages, Recipients, and Attachments

```
Private Sub DebugPrintMessagesRecipientsAttachments()

   ' Demonstrate the MsgIndex, RecipIndex, and AttachmentIndex
   ' properties by looping through all messages, all recipients,
   ' and all attachments, printing information about each to the
   ' debug window.

   ' Loop control variables.
   Dim nMsg As Long
   Dim nRecip As Long
   Dim nAttachment As Long

   ' Sign on.
   With MAPISession1
      .DownLoadMail = False
      .LogonUI = True
      .NewSession = True
      .Password = ""
      .UserName = "MyProfile"
      .SignOn
   End With

   ' Associate MAPIMessages control with current session.
   MAPIMessages1.SessionID = MAPISession1.SessionID

   ' Fetch messages.
   MAPIMessages1.Fetch

   ' This outer loop cycles through all messages.
   For nMsg = 0 To MAPIMessages1.MsgCount - 1

      ' Set the control's message index. Subsequent access to the
      ' control's properties will reference this specific message.
      MAPIMessages1.MsgIndex = nMsg

      ' Print info about this message.
      Debug.Print "Message #"; Trim(CStr(nMsg)); ": "; _
         MAPIMessages1.MsgSubject
```

Example 4-1. Looping Through Messages, Recipients, and Attachments (continued)

```
        ' Now show all recipients for this specific message.
        For nRecip = 0 To MAPIMessages1.RecipCount - 1

            ' Set the control's recipient index. Subsequent access to
            ' the control's properties will reference this specific
            ' recipient on the currently indexed message (the one
            ' specificed by .MsgIndex).
            MAPIMessages1.RecipIndex = nRecip

            ' Print info about this recipient. Indent the info to show
            ' its relationship to the message info printed earlier.
            Debug.Print "    Recipient #"; Trim(CStr(nRecip)); ": "; _
                MAPIMessages1.RecipDisplayName

        Next nRecip

        ' Now show all attachments for this specific message.
        For nAttachment = 0 To MAPIMessages1.AttachmentCount - 1

            ' Set the control's attachment index. Subsequent access to
            ' the control's properties will reference this specific
            ' attachment on the currently indexed message (the one
            ' specified by .MsgIndex).
            MAPIMessages1.AttachmentIndex = nAttachment

            ' Print info about this attachment. Indent the info to show
            ' its relationship to the message info printed earlier.
            Debug.Print "    Attachment #"; Trim(CStr(nAttachment)); _
                ": "; MAPIMessages1.AttachmentName

        Next nAttachment

    Next nMsg

    ' All done. Sign off.
    MAPISession1.SignOff

End Sub ' DebugPrintMessagesRecipientsAttachments
```

Sending Mail

Sending a text message programmatically is simple. Assuming that you've already signed on with the MAPISession control and that you've set the MAPIMessages control's SessionID property equal to the MAPISession control's SessionID property, the following code does the job:

```
With MAPIMessages1
    .Compose
    .MsgSubject = "This is the subject."
    .MsgNoteText = "This is the message body."
    .RecipIndex = 0
```

```
    .RecipDisplayName = "Dave"
    .Send
End With
```

Calling the MAPIMessages control's Compose method tells the control that you are about to set some properties for a new outgoing message. Unlike incoming messages, there can never be more than one outgoing message at a time. The value of the MsgIndex property for the outgoing message is –1.

The MsgSubject and MsgNoteText properties are self-explanatory, being the subject and body portions of the message, respectively.

Unlike composing a message, there is no explicit method to call for adding a recipient, and the RecipIndex property is never –1. The number of recipients is controlled by how you set the RecipIndex property. In the code shown previously, the act of setting RecipIndex to 0 automatically causes RecipCount to become 1. RecipCount is always automatically one greater than the highest value to which you have set RecipIndex. You never set RecipCount directly. The previously shown code can be modified to send to two recipients as follows:

```
With MAPIMessages1
    .SessionID = MAPISession1.SessionID
    .Compose
    .MsgSubject = "This is the subject."
    .MsgNoteText = "This is the message body."
    .RecipIndex = 0
    .RecipDisplayName = "Dave"
    .RecipIndex = 1
    .RecipDisplayName = "Annemarie"
    .Send
End With
```

The second recipient was added by incrementing RecipIndex and setting RecipDisplayName to a new name. Note that you can't assign a variant string array to RecipDisplayName to reduce coding; the control's type library identifies this property as a String, so if you try to assign anything else, Visual Basic generates a Type Mismatch error.

The MAPIMessages control also supports a RecipAddress property, which allows you to specify a recipient's email address. But in the previous code fragment, I used the RecipDisplayName property instead. The reason is that MAPI requires all recipients of a message to go through *address resolution*, and it uses the display name for this purpose. Address resolution is the process of comparing an email address in string form to the recipients stored in the user's address books. When a matching entry is found, the system associates the address book entry with the message. When the message ultimately is sent, the system reads critical information from the address book entry, such as the address, which transport provider to use, and whether to send to that address in Microsoft Exchange Rich Text Format

(RTF). Again, this matching is based on the recipient's display name, not his or her address.

If the value in RecipDisplayName is in a format that indicates that it is itself a valid address, the system creates a temporary address book entry to associate with the message, a so-called *one-off* recipient. For example, strings of the form *user@company.com* are valid Simple Mail Transport Protocol (SMTP) addresses, allowing you to write something like this:

```
With MAPIMessages1
    .SessionID = MAPISession1.SessionID
    .Compose
    .MsgSubject = "This is the subject."
    .MsgNoteText = "This is the message body."
    .RecipIndex = 0
    .RecipDisplayName = "jsmith@FictitiousCompany.com"
    .Send
End With
```

When the Send method is called, MAPI attempts to resolve the name *jsmith@FictitiousCompany.com*. During this process, MAPI discovers that this is a valid format for SMTP email addresses, so a one-off recipient is created and associated with the message. Note that even if there is already an address book entry with that address, that entry will not be matched during the address resolution process. To match an existing entry, the display name must be used.

If MAPI can't resolve a name, or if the name resolves to more than one address, the MAPIMessages control raises an error. If the name can't be resolved at all, the control raises a `mapUnknownRecipient` error. In the case of resolving to more than one name, the control raises a `mapAmbiguousRecipient` error.

You can force more sophisticated behavior by explicitly calling the control's ResolveName method. This method resolves the name of the currently indexed recipient only. (Again, the currently indexed recipient is defined by the value of the MsgIndex and the RecipIndex properties.) If the address is not found or is ambiguous, the control does one of two things, depending on how you've set the AddressResolveUI property. If this property is set to `False`, the control behaves as described in the previous paragraph (i.e., it raises an error). However, if the AddressResolveUI property is set to `True`, the control triggers the address book's address resolution dialog box, allowing the user to choose an appropriate address.

The address resolution dialog box may contain a Cancel button which, if pressed, causes a `mapUserAbort` error to be raised in your code. Be prepared to handle this error if you allow the address resolution dialog box to be shown. Example 4-2 shows one way such an error handler could be written.

Example 4-2. Handling the mapUserAbort Error During Address Resolution

```
Private Sub Send()

   ' This procedure assumes that a message is being composed, that the
   ' recipients have already been set, and that all that needs to be done
   ' at this point is to resolve the recipient names and send the message.

   ' This procedure could be called in response to the user clicking a
   ' Send button on a form.

   Dim nRecip As Long

   On Error GoTo ErrorHandler

   For nRecip = 0 To MAPIMessages1.RecipCount - 1
      MAPIMessages1.RecipIndex = nRecip
      MAPIMessages1.ResolveName
   Next nRecip

   MAPIMessages1.Send

   Exit Sub

ErrorHandler:

   ' Did the user press Cancel on the address resolution dialog box?
   ' If so, just exit without sending the email. However, if a different
   ' error occurred, then re-raise that error so that it can be handled
   ' by the calling procedure.
   If Err.Number <> mapUserAbort Then
      Err.Raise Err.Number
   End If

End Sub ' Send
```

If it's successful, the ResolveName method uses the RecipDisplayName property and sets the RecipAddress property equal to the email address of the recipient. Further, if the recipient's display name (as configured in the user's address book) is different from or more complete than the name in RecipDisplayName, the ResolveName method sets RecipDisplayName to the name as it is stored in the address book.

To delete a recipient from the current message, call the Delete method, passing the `mapRecipientDelete` constant, as in the following code fragment:

```
' Delete current recipient.
MAPIMessages1.Delete mapRecipientDelete
```

This statement deletes the recipient in the position defined by the RecipIndex property in the message defined by the MsgIndex property, and it decrements the indices of the recipients that followed the deleted recipient in the recipient set. It also decrements the RecipIndex property if the deleted recipient was the last one in the recipient set.

MAPI distinguishes between primary, copy, and blind copy recipients. When you add recipients to your outgoing message, they are flagged by default as primary. You can change the type of a given recipient (which is defined, again, by the value of the RecipIndex property) by setting the RecipType property. To set the current recipient to be a copy recipient, set the RecipType property to `mapCcList`. For a blind copy recipient, set the RecipType property to `mapBccList`. The default value is `mapToList`. When messages are sent, the receiving parties can see the primary and copy recipients but not the blind copy recipients.

Calling the Send method instructs MAPI to send the message to the mail server for distribution. Note that the Send method does not set the MsgSent property to `True`. That only happens when the message has actually been moved to the mail server.

The Send method has an optional parameter that you'll find useful when you want to present the user with a standard message composition dialog box. Rather than developing the dialog box yourself, you can simply pass a value of `True` as an argument to the Send method. This way, it takes only two lines of code to allow the user to enter and send a standard email message:

```
MAPIMessages1.Compose
MAPIMessages1.Send True
```

The resulting dialog box is shown in Figure 4-5.

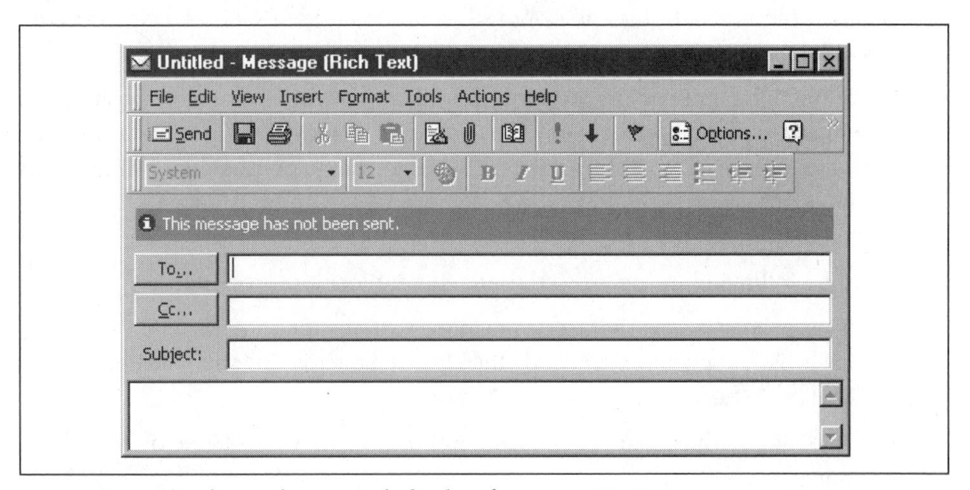

Figure 4-5. Using the mail system's dialog box for composing a message

If your code sets other properties prior to calling `Send True`, those settings are reflected in the dialog box shown to the user. For example, you may wish to set a recipient and a subject programmatically, allowing the user simply to enter the message text. However, while the dialog box is shown, the user can make any changes he or she likes. If you need total control over what the user enters, you'll need to create your own dialog box.

If the user cancels the dialog box, a `mapUserAbort` error is raised in your code. Your code should trap and handle this error.

Sending File Attachments

Sending a file as an attachment is easy. To add attachments to an outgoing message:

1. Set the AttachmentIndex property of the MAPIMessages control appropriately (0 for the first attachment, 1 for the second attachment, etc.).
2. Set the AttachmentPathName property to the fully qualified path of the file you would like to send. This is the path of the file as it exists on the sending system. This path is not communicated to the receiving mail client.
3. Set the AttachmentName property to a short name for the file. This is typically the filename and extension of the file, but it can be any string. The receiving mail client uses this string to name the file on the receiving system, so setting it to a reasonable filename and extension, such as `"MyResume.doc"`, is helpful.
4. Set the AttachmentType property to `mapData`, which indicates that the attached file is a data file (as opposed to an embedded OLE object, to be discussed shortly).
5. Set the AttachmentPosition property to indicate at which character position the attachment should appear. Some mail clients display a representation of the file within the body of the message at the character position indicated by AttachmentPosition. (However, some ignore this value and display the attachments separately.)

   Note the following in regard to the AttachmentPosition property:

   - This property is zero-based, meaning that the first character in the message is at position 0, and the last character in the message is at `Len(MAPIMessages1.MsgNoteText) - 1`.
   - It is not permissible for AttachmentPosition to be outside of the above range.
   - It is not permissible to have two attachments at the same position.
   - The Microsoft documentation states that the character at the indicated position is lost. This is not correct. The message text is unchanged by the

inclusion of attachments. How the attachments are displayed is up to the receiving mail client. Microsoft Outlook 98, for example, displays an icon representing the attachment within the text body, immediately before the character corresponding to the attachment's AttachmentPosition.

6. Repeat Steps 1 through 5 as needed for additional attachments.

If you change your mind about an attachment and want to delete it, you can do so by calling the MAPIMessages control's Delete method, passing an argument of `mapAttachmentDelete`. This deletes the currently indexed attachment (that is, the attachment at the position defined by the AttachmentIndex property in the message defined by the MsgIndex property), decrements the AttachmentCount property, and, if the deleted attachment was the last attachment in the set, decrements the AttachmentIndex property. Note that when deleting an attachment from a message in the compose buffer, the actual attachment file is not deleted from the user's system.

Example 4-3 shows sending two files from start to finish, including signing onto and off of MAPI. The attachment-specific code is in boldface. The received message is shown in Figure 4-6.

Example 4-3. Sending Two Files as Attachments

```
' Set up the MAPI session control and sign on.
With MAPISession1
   .DownLoadMail = False
   .LogonUI = True
   .NewSession = True
   .Password = ""
   .UserName = "MyProfile"
   .SignOn
End With

' Set up the MAPIMessages control and send the message.
With MAPIMessages1

   ' Hook the MAPIMessages control to the MAPI session.
   .SessionID = MAPISession1.SessionID

   ' Start a new message.
   .Compose
   .MsgSubject = "Here are my files."
   .MsgNoteText = "Attached are config.sys and autoexec.bat." _
      & Chr(13) & "  " ' Leave space for attachments.

   ' Set the recipient.
   .RecipIndex = 0
   .RecipType = 1
   .RecipDisplayName = "Dave"
   .ResolveName
```

Example 4-3. Sending Two Files as Attachments (continued)

```
    ' Set up the attachments.
    .AttachmentIndex = 0
    .AttachmentPathName = "c:\config.sys"
    .AttachmentName = "config.sys"
    .AttachmentType = mapData
    .AttachmentPosition = Len(MAPIMessages1.MsgNoteText) - 2

    .AttachmentIndex = 1
    .AttachmentPathName = "c:\autoexec.bat"
    .AttachmentName = "autoexec.bat"
    .AttachmentType = mapData
    .AttachmentPosition = Len(MAPIMessages1.MsgNoteText) - 1

    ' Send the message.
    .Send

End With

' Close the MAPI session.
MAPISession1.SignOff
```

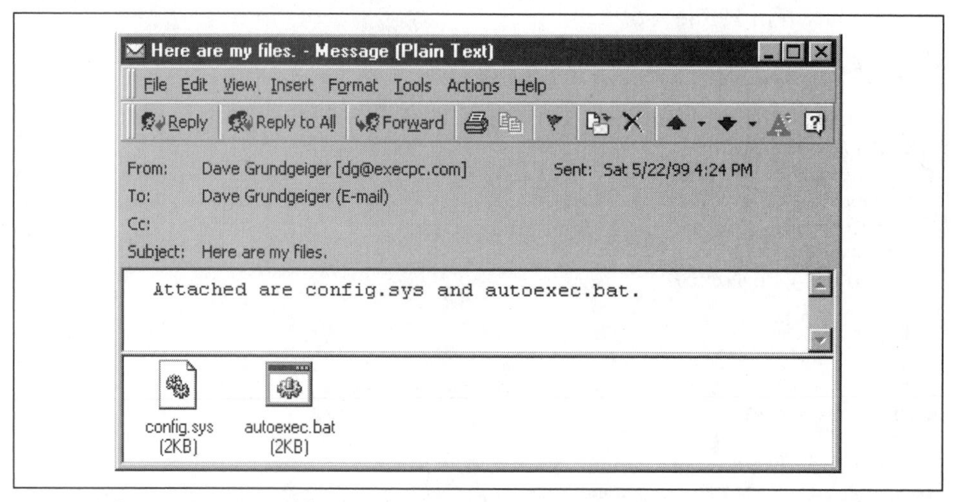

Figure 4-6. Message received from code in Example 4-3, as displayed by Microsoft Outlook 98

Sending Embedded OLE Objects

It's technically possible, but difficult, to send an *embedded OLE attachment* using the MAPI controls. (OLE is a mechanism that allows users to create and edit documents containing items or "objects" created by multiple applications. In the context of sending email, an embedded OLE attachment is an OLE object—for example, a range of cells from a spreadsheet—that is transmitted along with the message. A general discussion of OLE is not within the scope of this book; consult Microsoft documentation for further information about this technology.)

If you need to send embedded OLE attachments, you're better off using Collaboration Data Objects (CDO). However, I'll explain briefly how it could be done with the MAPI controls.

As explained in the previous section, sending a file attachment requires setting the AttachmentType property of the MAPIMessages control to `mapData`. There are two other legal values for this property: `mapEOLE` and `mapSOLE`. Either value can be used to send an OLE object. The difference is that `mapEOLE` is for an "editable" OLE object, and `mapSOLE` is for a "static" (i.e., non-editable) OLE object.

On the receiving end, the mail client displays the OLE object within the body of the message. If the AttachmentType property was set to `mapEOLE`, the user can double-click the object to begin editing it. For this to work, the user must have software on his or her system that knows how to edit the kind of object that was sent. For example, if you send an OLE object that contains a range of cells from a Microsoft Excel spreadsheet, the receiving user must have Excel in order to edit the object. However, it is not necessary to have Excel simply to view the object. (OLE objects carry inside them a static visual representation of their data.)

To attach the OLE object to an outgoing message, you must *serialize* the object into a file, and set the AttachmentPathName property of the MAPIMessages control to the fully qualified path of the file. Serialization is the process of copying an object's state to some kind of sequential storage device, such as a file. Copying to a non-volatile storage device, such as a file, is also known as *persisting* the object. The final step is to set the AttachmentName property of the MAPIMessages control equal to the name of the object's class—for example, "`Excel.Sheet`".

The hard part of all this, of course, is serializing the OLE object. The MAPI controls provide no facility for doing this, so you're forced to call into the Windows API. While I won't go into details, the basic idea is to open the file as an OLE stream and pass the `IStream` interface pointer to the *OleSaveAsStream* API. As I mentioned before, if you're going to these lengths, you're better off making the jump to CDO.

Reading Mail

Reading mail is a two-step process. First, the MAPIMessages control's Fetch method retrieves messages from the Inbox into the control's *read buffer*. Then messages are read by setting and reading the control's properties. These properties will be discussed shortly, after the Fetch method is described.

The Fetch method has no parameters. Rather, its behavior is modified by the settings of some of the properties of the MAPIMessages control.

The FetchUnreadOnly property is a Boolean flag that, if set to `True`, causes a subsequent call to Fetch to retrieve only those messages that haven't been read (i.e., the MsgRead property is `False`). If the FetchUnreadOnly property is `False`, its default value, the next call to Fetch retrieves all messages from the Inbox.

The FetchSorted property is a Boolean flag that, if set to `True`, causes a subsequent call to Fetch to sort the retrieved messages according to the order in which they were received. If the FetchSorted property is `False`, its default value, the messages are sorted according to the order specified by the Inbox. The MAPI controls don't provide a way to modify the Inbox sort order.

The FetchMessageType property is a string that allows you to fetch messages that belong to a certain message class. When this property contains a zero-length string (as it does by default), messages are retrieved without regard to their message class. However, when this property has some other value, a subsequent Fetch retrieves only those messages whose MsgType property matches the value in FetchMessageType. For more information on how to use message classes, see the discussion of the MsgType property and of message classes in the "Advanced Features" section later in this chapter.

If there is mail on the mail server that hasn't been downloaded to the Inbox, the Fetch method will not retrieve it. The purpose of the Fetch method is to retrieve a set of messages from the Inbox into the MAPIMessages control's read buffer. This is not the same thing as downloading messages from the mail server to the Inbox. For users on a LAN, this distinction may be academic; messages are generally moved from the mail server to the user's Inbox in real time, so the Fetch method always retrieves all current messages. However, users connecting over dialup networking are very aware of the difference. Messages sit on the mail server until the user explicitly dials in and retrieves them. In Microsoft Outlook, for example, this message transfer is accomplished by selecting "Send and Receive" from Outlook's toolbar. Using the MAPI controls, the same effect is achieved by setting the MAPISession control's DownLoadMail property to `True` prior to calling its SignOn method. This causes the sign-on process to connect to the mail server and download new messages to the Inbox.

After calling the Fetch method, and prior to reading any message-related properties, the MAPIMessages control must be told which message to access. As already mentioned, this is the purpose of the MsgIndex property. For a lengthier discussion of how the MsgIndex property works, see "Structure of the MAPIMessages Control," earlier in this chapter.

Once the MsgIndex property has been set, the other message-related properties are read to retrieve the information for that specific message. These properties include:

MsgSubject
: Contains the subject text.

MsgNoteText
: Contains the body text.

MsgOrigDisplayName
: Retrieves the display name of the message sender.

MsgOrigAddress
: Retrieves the sender's email address.

MsgRead
: Indicates whether a message has been read. This property is set to `True` when MsgNoteText or any of the attachment properties is read. You might use this information to mark unread messages in the user interface of your application, allowing the user to see which messages remain unread. Unfortunately, this property is read-only, so you can't provide the user with the nice feature of being able to change this flag.

MsgDateReceived
: Contains the date on which the message was received. This property is a string in "YYYY/MM/DD HH:MM" format. You can easily convert it to a standard date type using Visual Basic's *CDate* function:

```
Dim dtMsgReceived As Date

dtMsgReceived = CDate(MAPIMessages1.MsgDateReceived)
```

You can then use Visual Basic's *Format* function to output the date in any format you like. Note that if an unsent message is saved in the Inbox, the MsgDateReceived property is blank, which causes *CDate* to raise a "Type mismatch" error (error number 13). Your code should explicitly trap and handle this error.

MsgReceiptRequested
: A Boolean value that indicates whether the sender requested a return email to show that the message was received.

The mail system handles the return receipt for you—your code doesn't need to do a thing, so you're not likely to use this property.

MsgSent
: Indicates whether the message has been sent to the mail server for distribution.

This property is set to `True` by the mail system when the message has been moved onto the mail server. When you're reading messages, this property is likely to be `True` on virtually all of them. The only time you'll find it to be `False` is when an unsent message has been saved in the Inbox. This can happen, for instance, by calling the MAPIMessages control's Save method. It can also happen if another mail client is used to copy an unsent message from the Outbox to the Inbox. The Save method is discussed later in this chapter, under "Miscellanea."

MsgConversationID
Helps track conversation threads. For more information and some caveats regarding conversation threads, see the discussion on conversation threads later in this chapter, under "Advanced Topics."

MsgID
A 64-character string used by the mail system to identify the message in the message store. It's not at all useful to your client application.

Once you've read a message, you may wish to delete it. This is accomplished by calling the MAPIMessages control's Delete method with an argument of `mapMessageDelete`:

```
' Delete the currently-indexed message.
MAPIMessages1.Delete mapMessageDelete
```

Note that this *does not* move the message into the user's Deleted Items folder—it really and truly deletes the message. The MAPI controls don't provide the ability to move messages between folders.

Let's turn our attention now to a message's list of recipients. When reading received messages, read the recipient-related properties to find out to whom each message was sent. In addition, you can tell whether each recipient was a primary recipient (on the "To" list), or a copy recipient (on the "Cc" list). However, recipients that were on the sender's blind copy list do not appear at all in the received message (that's the point, after all).

Before reading recipient-related properties, first set the MsgIndex property to indicate which message to read, then set the RecipIndex property to indicate which recipient to access on that message. The RecipIndex property is a zero-based index that can range from 0 to one less than the value contained in the RecipCount property. See "Structure of the MAPIMessages Control," earlier in this chapter, for a more detailed discussion of how these properties work.

To discover whether a given recipient is a primary or copy recipient, check the setting of the RecipType property. This is an integer value that equals `mapToList` for primary recipients, and `mapCcList` for copy recipients.

The email address of the recipient is found in the RecipAddress property, and the friendly display name of the recipient is found in RecipDisplayName. See "Advanced Features," later in this chapter, to learn how to display a properties dialog box for a given recipient.

Reading File Attachments

When reading messages with attachments, the attachment-related properties are used in much the same way as they are when sending messages with attachments. The difference, of course, is that you're reading the properties rather than setting them. Before reading the attachment-related properties, first set the MsgIndex property to indicate which message to read, then read the AttachmentCount property to determine if the message has any attachments. If it does (i.e., if AttachmentCount is greater than 0), set the AttachmentIndex property to refer to a specific attachment. The AttachmentIndex property is a zero-based index that can range from 0 to one less than the value contained in the AttachmentCount property. See "Structure of the MAPIMessages Control," earlier in this chapter, for a more detailed discussion of how these properties work.

After setting the AttachmentIndex property, you're ready to read the attachment information. All attachments are saved by the mail system as files in a temporary folder, regardless of whether the attachment is actually a binary file or an embedded OLE object. This is because embedded OLE objects are saved as files prior to being sent. As discussed earlier in this chapter, working with embedded OLE objects using the MAPI controls is exceedingly laborious, so it won't be discussed further here. For a little detail on how it works, see "Sending Embedded OLE Objects," earlier in this chapter. This section considers only file attachments.

The full pathname of an attached file is found in the AttachmentPathName property of the MAPIMessages control. Again, this path points to a temporary folder on the local machine. This file may be deleted on a subsequent call to Fetch, so if you need to use it or keep it, copy it to another location first. The procedure in Example 4-4 copies a given attachment from its temporary location to a specified directory.

Example 4-4. Copying an Attached File from Its Temporary Location

```
Private Sub CopyAttachment(ByVal nMsg As Long, _
   ByVal nAttachment As Long, ByVal strCopyToDir As String)

   ' To be more robust, and/or to provide tracking of behavior, nMsg
   ' and nAttachment should be checked here to make sure they're in
   ' the right ranges. Likewise, strCopyTo should be checked to ensure
   ' that it is a proper path specification. I've omitted these checks
   ' here for clarity.
```

Example 4-4. Copying an Attached File from Its Temporary Location (continued)

```
   Dim strCopyToFile As String

   ' Construct the fully qualified destination filename.
   If Right(strCopyToDir, 1) = "\" Then
      strCopyToFile = strCopyToDir & MAPIMessages1.AttachmentName
   Else
      strCopyToFile = strCopyToDir & "\" & MAPIMessages1.AttachmentName
   End If

   ' Which message do we want?
   MAPIMessages1.MsgIndex = nMsg

   ' And which attachment?
   MAPIMessages1.AttachmentIndex = nAttachment

   ' Copy the attached file.
   FileCopy MAPIMessages1.AttachmentPathName, strCopyToFile

End Sub ' CopyAttachment
```

The AttachmentName property is the attachment's filename without the path. This name should be used if you're displaying the attachment's filename to the user.

The type of attachment is given by the AttachmentType property. This is an integer property that has only three legal values: `mapData`, to indicate that the attachment is a file; `mapEOLE`, to indicate that the attachment is an editable embedded OLE object; and `mapSOLE`, to indicate that the attachment is a static (i.e., non-editable) OLE object.

Under discussion here are attachments with an AttachmentType of `mapData`. However, just because an attachment has a type of `mapData` doesn't mean that it's not an embedded object. How can this be? The attachment types `mapEOLE` and `mapSOLE` are for attachments created by Simple MAPI, which is what you're using if you program with the MAPI controls. However, most email clients use "regular" MAPI. These clients don't serialize embedded objects in the same way Simple MAPI programs do. Rather, they save embedded objects into ActiveX compound files. The MAPI controls provide no way to read objects stored in compound files, so if you're writing a mail client that needs to deal with such objects, you'll need to use CDO.

The AttachmentPosition property is a suggestion from the sender on where to display the attachment in relation to the message body text. This property is a long integer that is a zero-based character index into the message body text. Some mail clients choose to ignore this value and display all attachments in a separate window.

Showing the Address Book

If you're writing an application that allows the user to enter recipients for an outgoing message, it's convenient for the user to have a way to display the address book and to select recipients directly from it. The MAPIMessages control makes this easy. Before continuing, however, note what the MAPI controls can't do with the address book. The controls can't programmatically manipulate the address book in any way. There isn't even a way to enumerate the entries in the address book.

Now let's talk about what the controls *can* do. The Show method of the MAPIMessages control, when called with no argument or with the argument set to `False`, displays the user's address book. The UI is provided for you by the system. If you've programmatically set any recipients prior to showing the address book, these recipients will be shown as selected in the address book dialog box. Similarly, new selections or deletions made by the user in the address book dialog box are reflected in the MAPIMessages control's recipient list immediately upon returning from the Show method.

By default, the address book allows the user to select only primary recipients, not copy or blind copy recipients. To change this behavior, set the AddressEditFieldCount property prior to calling the Show method. The default value is 1. Setting this property to 0 causes the address book dialog box to disallow any selections at all. That is, the user is only allowed to browse the address book. Setting this property to 2 allows the user to select primary and copy recipients but not blind copy recipients. Setting it to 3 allows the user to select all three kinds. Finally, setting the property to 4 allows the user to select only those kinds of recipients supported by the underlying mail system.

If there are already recipients in the MAPIMessages control's recipients list at the time the Show method is called, the value found in the AddressEditFieldCount property is upgraded to at least the minimum number required by the recipient set. For example, if the recipient set already includes a blind copy recipient at the time of the call to the Show method, the address book dialog box will appear as though AddressEditFieldCount had been set to 3, even if it actually held a lesser value. Note that the AddressEditFieldCount property itself is not changed.

If you like, you can customize the caption of the "To" button on the address book dialog box. This might be useful if your application needs the user to select a list of addresses for something other than sending a message, and you don't want the selection button to say "To." To do this, set the AddressEditFieldCount property to

1, and the AddressLabel property to your desired caption. There is no way to customize the labels on the Cc and Bcc buttons. The AddressLabel property is ignored if AddressEditFieldCount is set to anything other than 1, or if the recipient list already contains copy or blind copy recipients. To put this another way, if you want to customize the text on the "To" button, you have to dispense with allowing the user to use the address book to select copy and blind copy recipients.

The final address book-related property is AddressModifiable. The Microsoft documentation states that if this property is set to `False`, the user is not allowed to modify the personal address book. However, I found that regardless of how I set this property, I was always able to modify the address book.

Advanced Features

The MAPI controls do offer some features beyond simply sending and receiving messages. These features are the message class, requesting a receipt, tracking a conversation thread, and displaying a recipient's properties.

The Message Class

All MAPI messages have a *message class*, which is a string that broadly differentiates types of messages. The MsgType property of the MAPIMessages control gives you access to the message class. The most common message class is `IPM.Note`, which signifies a generic email message. If you leave the MsgType property blank when composing a message, MAPI automatically gives the message a class of `IPM.Note`.

A common use of message classes is to tell the receiving mail client that a custom form should be used when displaying the message. For example, if you've created a custom form in Outlook, Outlook uses that form when displaying any message with a message class of `IPM.Note.`*`FormName`* (where *`FormName`* is the name you gave to the form). Be aware that if the receiving mail client doesn't recognize the message class, it will likely complain to the user, who may not know what the problem is.

To send a message using a custom message class, you must be sending to a recipient that is capable of receiving messages in Microsoft Exchange RTF, and the recipient's address book entry must indicate this fact, as shown in Figure 4-7.

If you are writing an application that reads and responds to messages only of a certain class, you may want to set the FetchMsgType property prior to calling the Fetch method. By setting this property equal to the desired class, you ensure that you fetch only messages of that class.

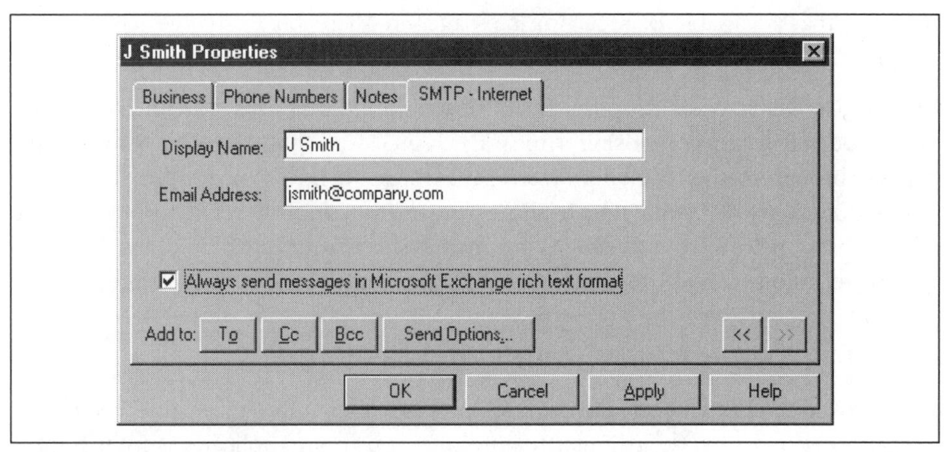

Figure 4-7. Setting Microsoft Exchange RTF for an email address

Requesting a Receipt

To be notified when your sent message has been read by a recipient, set the MsgReceiptRequested property to `True`. The mail system on the target computer replies automatically to such messages to let you know when the user has received the message.

You can also read the value of this property on a received message to determine if the sender requested a receipt. However, you do not need to generate the receipt yourself—MAPI does that for you. Also, you won't ever find this MAPI-generated outgoing message in your Outbox or Sent Items folders. MAPI simply sends the receipt message on its way.

The Conversation ID

The MsgConversationID property of the MAPIMessages control can be used to keep track of a *conversation thread*. A conversation thread is a set of messages made up of an original message plus the replies to that message.

The Microsoft documentation for this property states that new messages are assigned an ID by the message system. This is true when sending new mail using the MAPI controls, but new mail sent by other means may not generate a conversation ID. The conversation ID for new mail generated by Microsoft Outlook 98, for example, is blank. This means that you can't count on all messages having a conversation ID.

In addition, the conversation ID may get lost in transit. For example, messages sent via the Internet lose their conversation ID value, unless you are sending to a recipient that is capable of receiving messages in Microsoft Exchange RTF and the recipient's address book entry indicates this fact, as shown in Figure 4-7.

The MsgConversationID property is a string, and although it's possible to set this value yourself when composing a message, you'll find that the value you set isn't carried through to the receiving system, regardless of how you send it. Therefore, you should leave it blank, which allows the mail system to set it for you. When you reply to or forward a message, the mail system automatically copies the original conversation ID into the conversation ID property of the new message.

Showing Properties of a Message Recipient

In Microsoft Outlook, you can right-click a recipient and view that recipient's properties. You can code a similar feature into your own applications by using the MAPIMessages control's Show method, with an argument of `True`. This causes the mail system to display its properties dialog box for the currently indexed recipient. The user can make changes in this dialog box if desired and if the user has sufficient security rights to do so. (The user may not have rights to modify the Global Address List [GAL], for example.) If the user cancels this dialog box, a `mapUserAbort` error is raised in your code.

Miscellanea

The MAPI controls provide some helper methods that you don't strictly need but may find convenient when implementing certain common tasks. These are the Forward, Reply, ReplyAll, and Copy methods of the MAPIMessages control. These methods all copy the currently indexed message to the compose buffer, setting the MsgIndex property to –1. The Reply and ReplyAll methods set the recipient list appropriately and also add "RE:" to the beginning of the subject text. The Forward method clears the recipient list and adds "FW:" to the beginning of the subject text. The Copy method simply copies all properties over to the compose buffer. These methods do nothing to the message body, so if you want neat effects such as indenting the original message, you'll have to do it programmatically.

The MAPIMessages control has a method called Save, which copies the message currently in the compose buffer to the Inbox. One way to use this is to allow the user to quit the application while in the middle of composing a message. The application could later resume by locating the message in the Inbox and calling the MAPIMessages control's Copy method to copy the message back to the compose buffer. The Copy method doesn't delete the message from the Inbox, so after sending the composed message, the application would need to go back to the Inbox, find the previously saved message, and delete it.

Assessing the MAPI Controls

Whether to use the MAPI controls in your messaging project depends on the project itself. The controls have the lowest learning curve of all of the MAPI access methodologies (although CDO is not far behind). However, they don't expose anywhere near the level of functionality as does CDO. The inability to access folders other than the Inbox is a particularly glaring lack. If your application will never need to do more than send simple text messages and/or read text messages from the Inbox, go ahead and use these controls. Otherwise, you'll likely want to use CDO.

Summary

This chapter taught you how to use the MAPI ActiveX controls, Microsoft's ActiveX wrapper for Simple MAPI. You saw how to send and receive messages, including file attachments; how to set and read recipient lists; and how to work with the address book.

Chapter 5 delves into the mysteries of CDO. If you like the ActiveX controls, you'll love CDO. CDO wraps true MAPI, giving you the power to do industrial-strength messaging in your Visual Basic applications.

5

Collaboration Data Objects

Collaboration Data Objects (CDO) are the modern way for Visual Basic programmers to create professional, messaging-enabled applications. CDO provides a rich interface to the messaging API in the form of an *object model*—a programming concept that should be especially familiar to Visual Basic programmers. An object model is a (programming) language-independent way for programs to expose objects to other programs. One object model that you may be familiar with is ActiveX Data Objects (ADO), for accessing data in OLE DB data sources. You may also have used Visual Basic to control another application (such as Microsoft Word) through *Automation*. This is another example of using an object model.

CDO is the focus of the remainder of this book. This chapter emphasizes a strong understanding of fundamental CDO concepts, including discussion of Microsoft's Component Object Model (COM) and the benefit of using *software components* versus writing applications from scratch. This leads to a discussion of object models in general and the CDO object model in particular. The general discussion of COM and object models is included here because a firm understanding of these topics leads to a much better understanding of how the CDO object model works and how it relates to MAPI. Developers who have a very strong understanding of COM and of object models can safely skip the first two sections of this chapter. For developers who do not have a firm grasp of COM, it is certainly possible to use CDO without understanding the foundation upon which it stands. However, having an awareness of this foundation will help you understand why CDO is structured the way it is and how to take advantage of that structure in your Visual Basic programs. Discussion of this foundation begins with COM, because COM's architecture fundamentally shapes the way CDO's functionality is accessed.

Finally, recall from previous chapters that MAPI, too, is built on COM. Why, then, can't Visual Basic call MAPI directly? The reason is that although Visual Basic is

COM-aware, it is not completely so. There are datatypes and other constructs defined in COM that are not reflected in Visual Basic. In contrast, CDO's use of COM does support Visual Basic (and VBScript, which knows even less about COM).

COM

COM is about object-oriented programming. Object-oriented programming is about thinking of programming tasks in terms of real-world objects to be represented and of the activities that can be performed on or by those objects. A banking program, for instance, could be broken down in terms of *accounts*, *customers*, *transactions*, etc. Each kind of object has a set of *properties* that constitute the object's *state*, as well as a set of *methods* that are subroutines and functions that manipulate an object's state or perform some other action. One reason that this way of programming is useful is that it allows programmers to *encapsulate* knowledge of an object's implementation within the object itself, thus hiding implementation details for this object from other parts of the program. This supports the powerful idea of software components—building applications from prewritten modules, rather than writing everything from scratch.

When talking about object-oriented programming, it's useful to make a distinction between an object *class* and an object *instance*. *Child* is an example of a class, while my daughter Sasha is an example of an instance of the Child class. My daughter Nadia is also an instance of the Child class. The set of properties and methods an instance possesses is determined by the definition of the class—all instances of a particular class possess the same set of properties and methods. However, the values of the properties can be different for each instance. Sasha and Nadia, for example, clearly have different values in their respective Name properties. In a computer program, a class takes up no storage space. It's a definition only, from which object instances may or may not be created. Once an instance is created, it requires storage space to hold the property values for that instance. Creating an instance of a class is also known as *instantiating* an object.

Unfortunately, programmers use the term "object" by itself sometimes to mean "class," and sometimes to mean "an instance of a class," though the latter is probably the more common usage. Be aware of this blurring of meaning as you read and talk about object-oriented programming. It's helpful to make the distinction strongly in your own mind, and think about which meaning is intended whenever you run across the word.

Some programming languages have syntactical constructs that make object-oriented programming more natural. One such language is C++. This language provides elements for defining classes, creating instances of classes, and accessing individual properties and methods on specific instances. However, until recently, such languages have provided object orientation at the source level only. That is, if I have a friend who has a class defined using C++, the only way I can use that class definition is to include the C++ source file in my project. This implies that my project too must be written in C++, and that I must have access to the class definition's source code. In this scenario, there is no way to pass object instances between programs written in different languages.

COM at its core is a standard for sharing object instances between programs, without regard to the language in which each program, or the object itself, was written. In contrast to C++, COM provides object orientation at the binary (runtime) level. COM defines a standard, called *type libraries*, for sharing class definitions without having to share source code. Type libraries are stored in *.exe*, *.dll*, or *.tlb* files. Any development environment that is COM-aware can look into these standard files and make use of their class definitions. Regardless of the language the class developer used to define the classes, the developer's COM-aware development environment at some point compiled the definitions into the standard type library format. This makes the class definitions language-independent. The Windows Registry keeps a list of type library file locations for easy reference in the subkeys of `HKEY_CLASSES_ROOT\TYPELIB`.

In the Visual Basic development environment, a type library is accessed by *setting a reference* to it. This is done in the References dialog box, which is reached by selecting Project → References from the Visual Basic menu. Figure 5-1 shows the References dialog box.

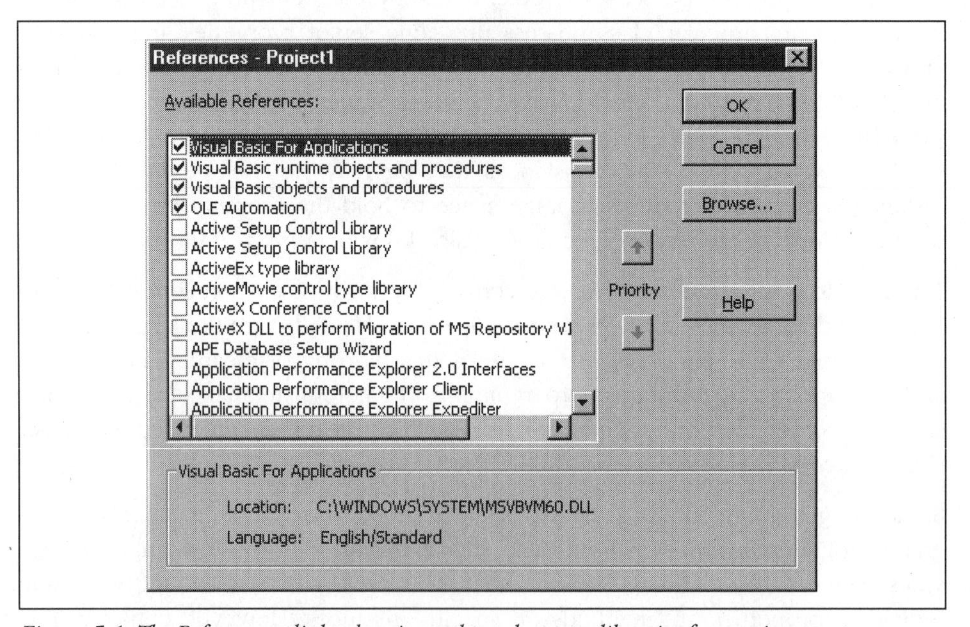

Figure 5-1. The References dialog box is used to select type libraries for use in your program

Visual Basic builds the list of available references by looking in the Windows Registry for information about type libraries. Each item in the list corresponds to a single type library, which can contain many class definitions. When you select an item on the list and click OK, Visual Basic reads the associated type library and makes its definitions available to you, the programmer. You can view these definitions yourself by using Visual Basic's Object Browser. The Object Browser is viewed by selecting View → Object Browser from the Visual Basic menu, or by pressing F2. The Object Browser is shown in Figure 5-2.

The Object Browser displays the classes available in your project, as well as their properties, methods, *events*, and constants. The concept of events is well known to every Visual Basic programmer. In COM terms, an event is a way for an instantiated object to call back to your code to report certain conditions or to pass data.

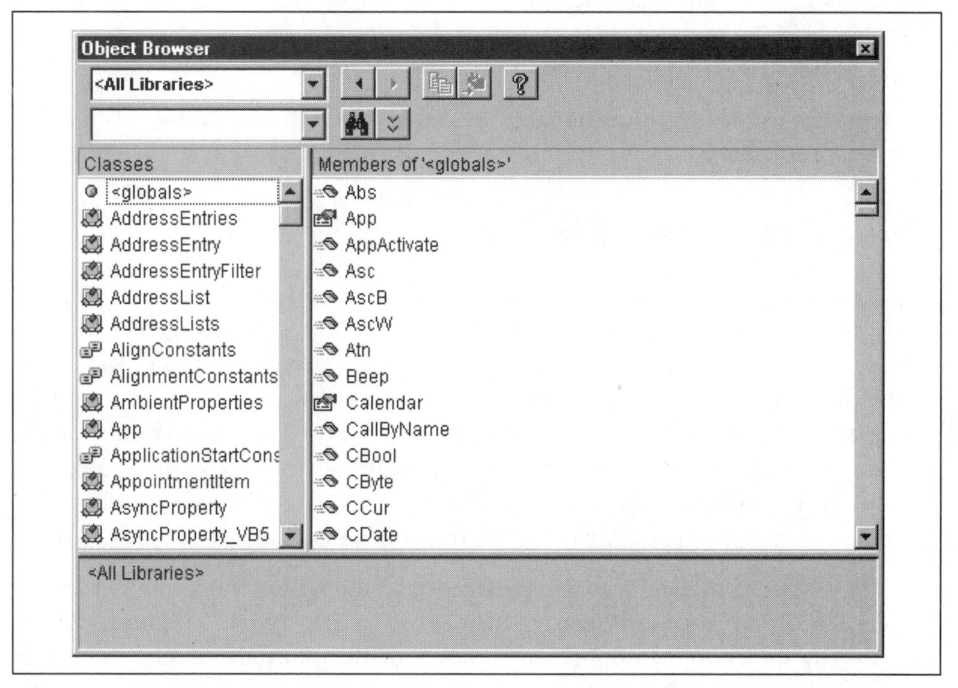

Figure 5-2. The Object Browser displays the classes, properties, methods, events, and constants available to your program

Object Models

An object model is a hierarchy of COM classes. It's a hierarchy because some classes are subordinate to or contained within others. The relationships among classes in the hierarchy are often represented by an object model diagram. An object model for accessing databases might have a Table class, which might have as one of its properties a reference to an instance of a Fields class, which in turn would maintain multiple references, each to an instance of a Field class. This portion of the object model might be represented in diagram form as shown in Figure 5-3.

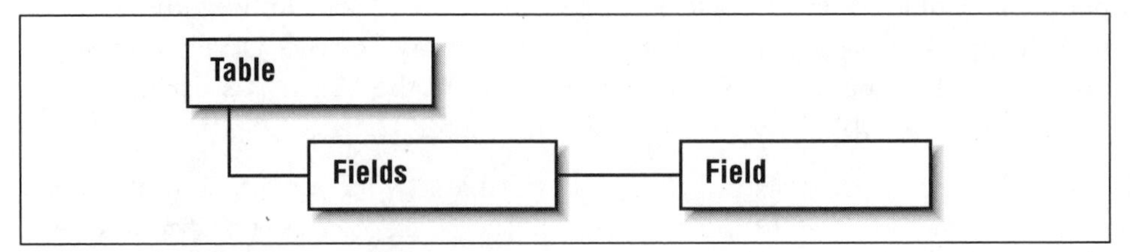

Figure 5-3. A portion of a typical object model diagram

The Fields class in this example commonly would be referred to as a *collection* class, because its purpose is to maintain a collection of objects (in this case, objects of class Field). Collection classes are common in typical object models.

This concept of making functionality available through object models is also known as Automation.

The CDO Object Model

The CDO object model contains 23 classes. These classes are defined in the type library contained in the file *cdo.dll.* This type library also contains the declarations of these classes' numerous properties, methods, and constants. (CDO objects don't expose any events.) The remainder of this chapter examines the relationships among the CDO classes, and briefly describes the most important of their methods, etc. Throughout the remainder of the book, these features will be examined in detail. It should be noted that *cdo.dll* contains more than just the type library for CDO; it also contains the executable code that implements CDO's features.

The first order of business is to set a reference to the CDO type library. From the Visual Basic menu, choose Project → References to display the References dialog box (already shown in Figure 5-1). Scroll down the list of available references until you find "Microsoft CDO *version number* Library," where *version number* should be 1.x in order to work with the samples in this book. Select this item if it's not already selected, and click OK.

If you don't find "Microsoft CDO 1.21 Library" in your list of available references, either you don't have *cdo.dll* on your system or it hasn't been registered (i.e., the location of this file hasn't been noted in the Windows Registry). Search your local hard drive(s) for *cdo.dll*. If you find it, return to the References dialog box and click Browse. Browse to *cdo.dll* and click Open, then click OK. This registers the type library and sets a reference to it in your project at the same time.

If *cdo.dll* is not on your system, or if you have an old version, you should obtain the current version of CDO. You can get *cdo.dll* by installing Microsoft Outlook 98 or higher, or Microsoft Exchange Server version 5.0 or higher. CDO also can be downloaded directly from Microsoft at *http://microsoft.com/exchange/downloads/CDO.htm*.

Once you have set a reference to CDO, you can view its classes, etc., in the Object Browser. Refer again to Figure 5-2. In the Object Browser, click the drop-down list that shows <All Libraries>. In the drop-down list, select MAPI. This limits the display to only those declarations found in the CDO type library. CDO classes and *enumerations* (named sets of constants) are shown in the "Classes" list box on the left, and members of each such item are shown in the "Members of" list box on the right. Members of classes are properties, methods, and events; members of enumerations are named constants. The Classes list box also contains an item called <Globals>. Clicking this item displays all of the items in the type library that are flagged as *global*. That means they can be used in your client code without any qualification. For example, the constant `CdoWednesday` can be used directly in your code as follows:

```
' objRecurrencePattern previously Dim'ed and Set.
objRecurrencePattern.DayOfWeekMask = CdoWednesday
```

This is equivalent to:

```
' objRecurrencePattern previously Dim'ed and Set.
objRecurrencePattern.DayOfWeekMask = CdoDaysOfWeek.CdoWednesday
```

The CDO object model diagram is shown in Figures 5-4 and 5-5. In the remainder of this section, I'll discuss the major CDO objects and their role in the object model.

The Session Object

As shown in Figures 5-4 and 5-5, the Session object is highest in the CDO object hierarchy. Use this object to establish a MAPI session and as a handle to get at your other MAPI objects. All objects in the hierarchy have a reference back to the Session object.

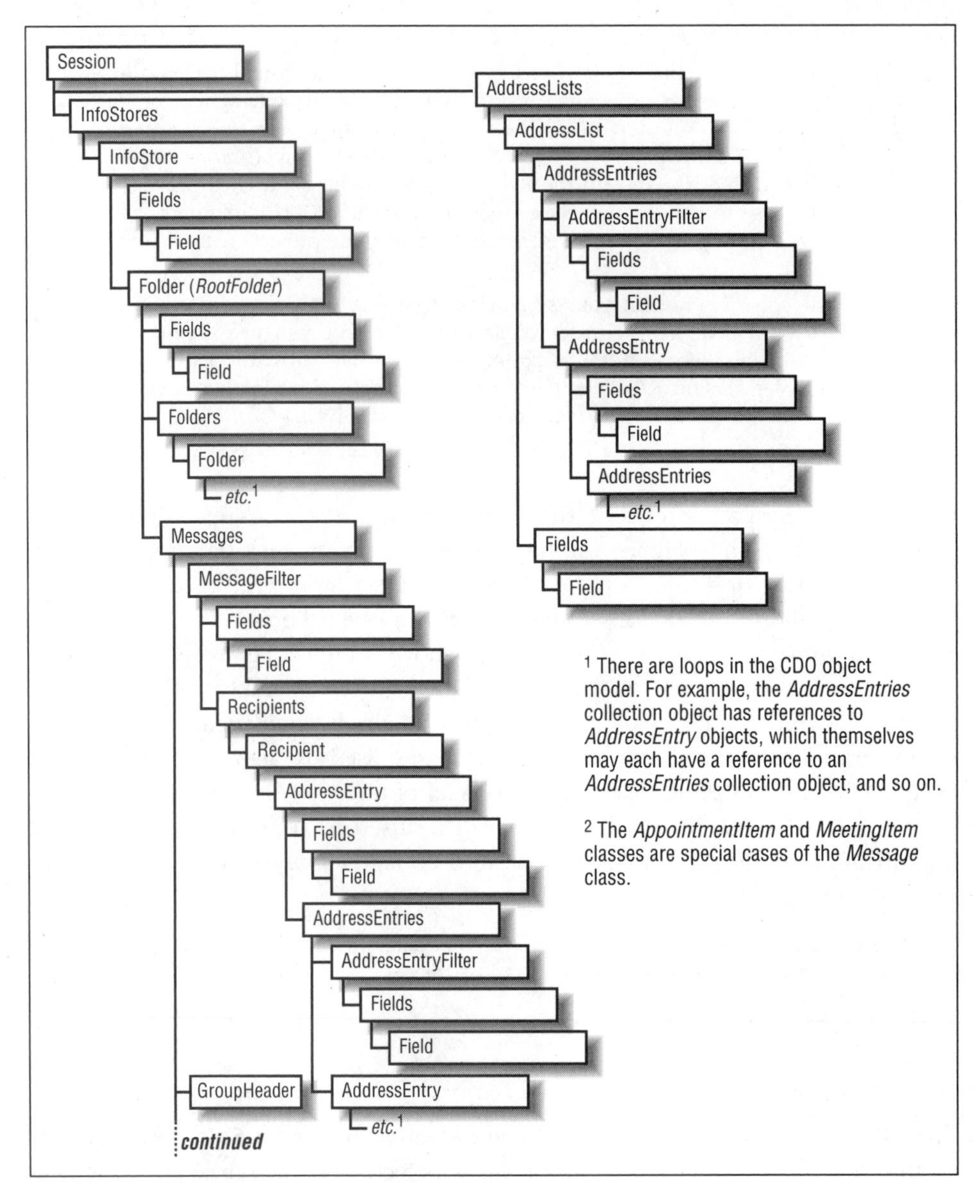

Figure 5-4. The CDO object model (continued in Figure 5-5)

Because the Session object is likely to be accessed from many places in your code, you'll want to define it in a location that is visible throughout your application. One reasonable choice is to declare it as **Public** in a standard module called *Globals.bas*, like so:

```
Public gCdoSession As MAPI.Session
```

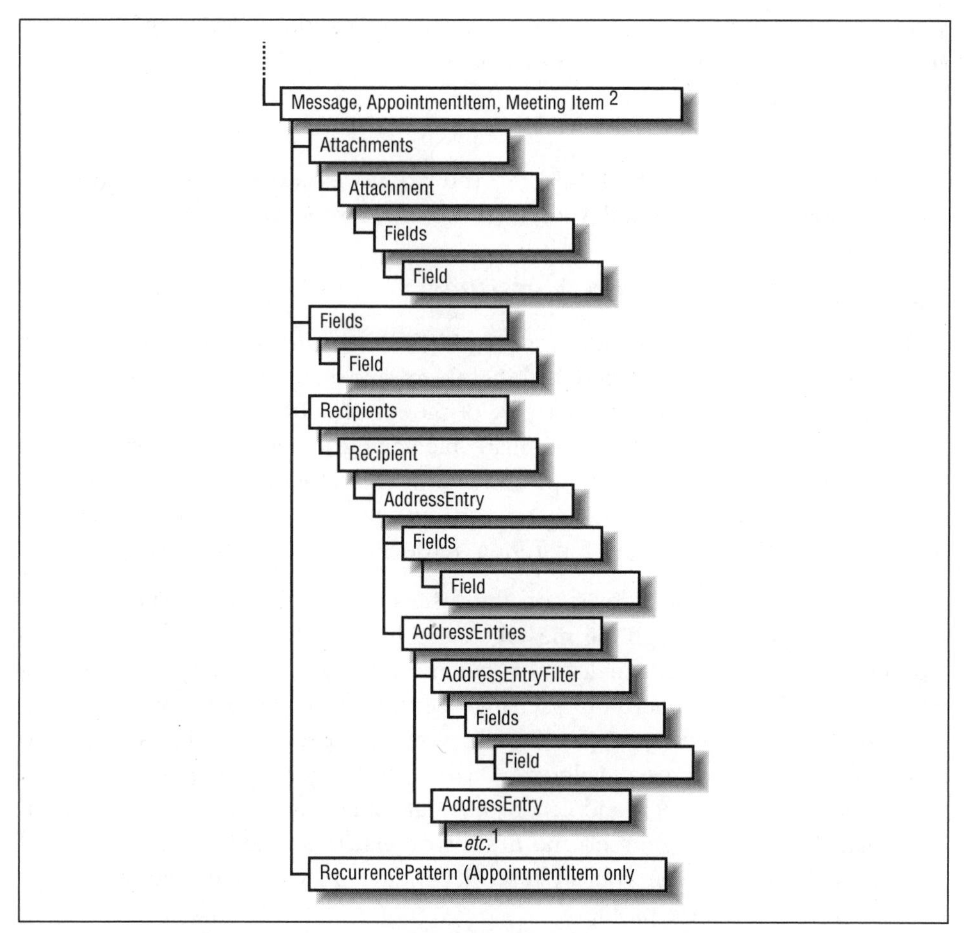

Figure 5-5. The CDO object model (continued from Figure 5-4)

The above line declares a reference to a Session object but doesn't actually instantiate an object. That means that *gCdoSession* is capable of referring to an object of this type but doesn't yet. When you're ready to access MAPI, instantiate a Session object, and log on by calling its Logon method:

```
Set gCdoSession = New MAPI.Session
gCdoSession.Logon
```

The Session object's Logon method has a number of optional parameters for selecting which profile to use and other options. These parameters will be examined in Chapter 6, *An Email Client Application.*

When finished accessing MAPI information, call the Session object's Logoff method and release the reference to the Session object, as in the following code fragment:

```
gCdoSession.Logoff
Set gCdoSession = Nothing
```

Next in the hierarchy are the InfoStores and AddressLists objects, which are simply collections of InfoStore and AddressList objects, respectively.

InfoStores, Folders, and Messages

An InfoStore object is your connection to a MAPI *message store*. Message stores are databases of messages, arranged within folders and subfolders. Where do message stores come from? They're not part of the MAPI subsystem. Rather, they are installed as part of some MAPI-compliant messaging system. On the system I'm using to write this book, for example, I have installed Outlook 98. This gave me, among other things, the message store provider that knows how to communicate with Microsoft Exchange Server for storing, retrieving, and sending messages.

Using CDO, we can get a list of the user's message stores. The code in Example 5-1 iterates through the message stores configured on the logged-in profile, adding their names to a list box named *lstInfoStores*. On my system, where my profile uses Microsoft Exchange Server, the code in Example 5-1 produces the output shown in Figure 5-6. As you can see, my profile is set up to access two message stores: "Mailbox - Dave Grundgeiger," and "Public Folders." The former holds my Inbox and other personal folders, and the latter holds folders that are shared among myself and my coworkers. The code in Example 5-1 will produce a different list on your system, depending on what message stores you have set up in your MAPI profile.

Example 5-1. Displaying Message Store Names in a List Box

```
Dim CdoInfoStores As MAPI.InfoStores
Dim CdoInfoStore As MAPI.InfoStore

Set CdoInfoStores = gCdoSession.InfoStores

lstInfoStores.Clear
For Each CdoInfoStore In CdoInfoStores
   ' Add the name of the InfoStore to the list box.
   lstInfoStores.AddItem CdoInfoStore.Name
   ' Associate the InfoStore index with this list item, so that it's
   ' easy to retrieve the index later (and thus the InfoStore).
   lstInfoStores.ItemData(lstInfoStores.NewIndex) = CdoInfoStore.Index
Next CdoInfoStore
```

The purpose of a message store is to store messages. In MAPI, messages are arranged into folders, much like files are arranged into file folders in the Windows

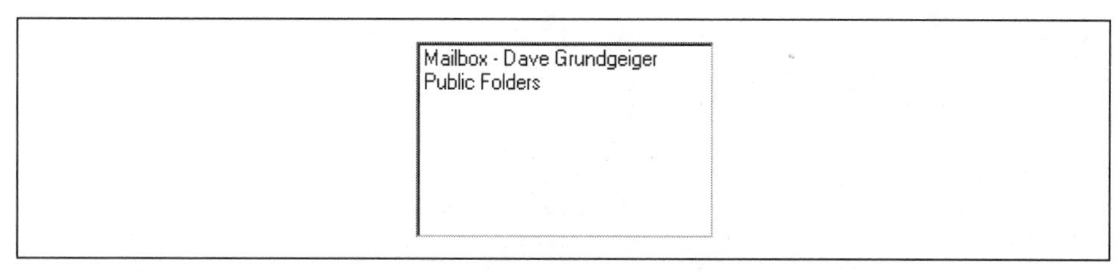

Figure 5-6. Typical message stores listed as the result of executing the code in Example 5-1 on a system with Microsoft Exchange Server configured in the MAPI profile

file system. Similar to file system folders, MAPI folders are arranged in a tree, where folders are allowed to contain not only messages, but also subfolders. To support the concept of folders-within-folders, each CDO Folder object maintains a reference to a Folders collection object. Each Folder in the collection may itself have a reference to yet another Folders collection object, and so on. At the top of the hierarchy is a Folder object which serves as a *root folder*. The root folder doesn't hold messages; it simply holds the top-level Folders collection. A reference to the root folder is stored in the InfoStore object's RootFolder property. Therefore, given the InfoStore object, it is possible to navigate programmatically through all of the folders in the message store. These relationships are illustrated in the object model diagram in Figures 5-4 and 5-5.

To store messages, CDO Folder objects maintain a reference to a Messages collection object. Each item in this collection is a Message object, which represents a single MAPI message in the given folder.

Address Books and Addresses

The other collection maintained by the Session object is the AddressLists collection. Each AddressList object represents a MAPI address book. As with message stores, address books are not part of MAPI—they are installed as part of some MAPI-compliant messaging system. The code in Example 5-2 iterates through the address books configured on the logged-in profile, adding their names to a list box named `lstAddressLists`. The output is shown in Figure 5-7.

If you run the code in Example 5-2 on your system, you will likely see a different list. Although my profile has only one address book set up, MAPI allows for many address books to be set up in a single profile.

Example 5-2. Displaying Address Book Names in a List Box

```
Dim CdoAddressLists As MAPI.AddressLists
Dim CdoAddressList As MAPI.AddressList

Set CdoAddressLists = gCdoSession.AddressLists

lstAddressLists.Clear
```

Example 5-2. Displaying Address Book Names in a List Box (continued)

```
For Each CdoAddressList In CdoAddressLists
   ' Add the name of the AddressList to the list box.
   lstAddressLists.AddItem CdoAddressList.Name
   ' Associate the AddressList index with this list item, so that it's
   ' easy to retrieve the index later (and thus the AddressList).
   lstAddressLists.ItemData(lstAddressLists.NewIndex) = _
                  CdoAddressList.Index
Next CdoAddressList
```

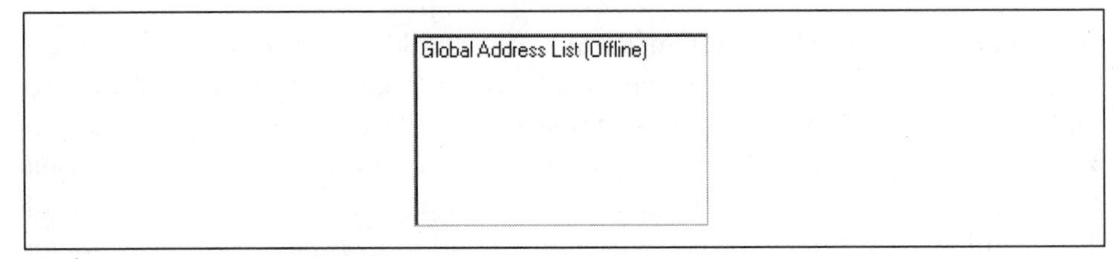

Figure 5-7. Typical address book listed as the result of executing the code in Example 5-2 on a system with Microsoft Exchange Server configured in the MAPI profile

Each AddressList object in the Session object's AddressList collection represents an installed address book. For example, you might have the Outlook Contacts and the Personal Address Book (PAB) providers both configured on the same MAPI profile. In that case you would have two AddressList objects in the AddressLists collection.

Each AddressList object has an AddressEntries collection, which has an AddressEntry object for each address in the address book. An individual AddressEntry object may represent an actual email address, or it may represent a *distribution list*, which is a named group of addresses. A distribution list allows the user to send a message to everyone in a group simply by specifying the name of the distribution list as a recipient. If the AddressEntry object represents a distribution list, it has a reference to an AddressEntries collection, which in turn contains the AddressEntry objects for the addresses on the distribution list. Distribution lists can be nested, so these secondary AddressEntry objects may themselves have references to further AddressEntries collections, and so on. Refer again to Figures 5-4 and 5-5 to see the relationships among these objects.

Miscellaneous Objects

The Messages and AddressEntries collection objects each have a filter object, MessageFilter and AddressEntryFilter, respectively. These objects allow you to specify search criteria that limit the collections to only those objects that satisfy the criteria.

The RecurrencePattern object appears only within an AppointmentItem object. It will be discussed in Chapter 8, *Calendar Folders*.

And finally, throughout Figures 5-4 and 5-5 are occurrences of the Field object and its corresponding collection object, Fields. Most CDO objects have Fields collections to assist in accessing MAPI properties. Recall from Chapter 2, *MAPI*, that MAPI properties are the mechanism by which data is associated with MAPI objects. For example, the body text of a message is stored in the `PR_BODY` property of a MAPI message object. Because CDO is a VB-friendly wrapper around MAPI, it must provide a way to access all properties of the wrapped MAPI objects. For the most popular properties, CDO provides its own properties as part of the wrapper object. For example, the CDO Message object has the Text property, which sets or reads the `PR_BODY` property of the underlying MAPI message object. Recognizing that it would be inefficient to provide a CDO object property for every possible MAPI property, and recognizing further that MAPI allows for custom programmer-defined properties, it's clear that a generic mechanism is needed to allow CDO objects to access any and all underlying MAPI properties. The Field object is that mechanism. It's used only when there is no intrinsic CDO object property that exposes the MAPI property of interest.

Consider the following code fragment for reading the body text of a message:

```
' CdoMessage previously dimmed and set.
Dim strText As String

strText = CdoMessage.Text
```

The next code fragment is identical in function but uses the Message object's Fields collection to retrieve the same value:

```
' CdoMessage previously dimmed and set.
Dim CdoFields As MAPI.Fields
Dim CdoField As MAPI.Field
Dim strText As String

Set CdoFields = CdoMessage.Fields
Set CdoField = CdoFields.Item(CdoPR_BODY)
strText = CdoField.Value
```

Given that the CDO Message object has an intrinsic Text property, there would never be any reason to access a message's body text using the code in the second fragment. However, some MAPI properties are not reflected in CDO object properties, making the Fields collection the only way to access those properties. For example, MAPI folders have a comment property, `PR_COMMENT`, that can be used to store a comment about the purpose or contents of the folder. However, the CDO Folder object does not expose this property. The only way to access the property is to use the Fields collection, as shown in this code fragment:

```
' CdoMessage previously dimmed and set.
Dim CdoFields As MAPI.Fields
Dim CdoField As MAPI.Field
```

```
Dim strComment As String

Set CdoFields = CdoMessage.Fields
Set CdoField = CdoFields.Item(CdoPR_COMMENT)
strComment = CdoField.Value
```

This concludes our whirlwind tour of the CDO object model. We'll visit each object again as we get down to the business of writing messaging-enabled software throughout the rest of this book.

Accessing CDO Online Help

The Visual Basic development environment comes with Microsoft Developer Network (MSDN), the medium through which development tools help is provided to developers. MSDN contains a complete reference for all CDO objects, methods, properties, and constants. In addition, many code samples demonstrate specific programming tasks. Unfortunately, however, there are no tutorials. Start the MSDN program and use the tree in the Contents tab to navigate to Platform SDK → Messaging and Collaboration Services → CDO 1.2.1.

If you don't have MSDN installed on your system, you can browse the online version at *http://msdn.microsoft.com.*

CDO Licensing

CDO is distributable with your application, with certain conditions. Review the information at *http://microsoft.com/exchange/downloads/CDO.htm* if you will be distributing an application that uses CDO.

Where to Go from Here

Using CDO, you can build a variety of sophisticated messaging and workflow applications. CDO is complete enough to enable you to write a full-featured personal information management system to rival Microsoft Outlook, for instance. Although replacing Outlook may not be your goal, you can use this power and flexibility in your own business solutions. For example, you may want your program to send an email to a designated contact person in response to a specific event. You may want to add a Send item to your program's File menu to allow the user to email the open document to another user. You may want to write a mailing list discussion group application. You'll learn how to do all this and more in the remainder of this book.

Summary

In this chapter you gained on overview of CDO and COM, the technology upon which CDO is built. You saw the CDO object model, learned the purpose of each object, and learned how the objects fit together. You learned how to obtain CDO if you don't have it already and how to access online help for CDO. Finally, you got a taste for the kinds of applications that can be built using this technology.

In the next chapter, you'll see a real-world messaging-enabled application using CDO.

6

An Email Client Application

A generic email client application provides familiar ground for learning about MAPI's capabilities. Today's email clients have rich feature sets that exercise every corner of MAPI. It's enjoyable and educational to duplicate such functionality in an email client application of one's own. That's what this chapter and Chapter 7, *Enhancing the Email Client*, are about, and the lessons learned along the way apply to a broad array of messaging applications.

This chapter teaches you the basics of using Collaboration Data Objects (CDO) to send and receive messages that include plain and formatted text, file attachments, and embedded objects. Chapter 7 discusses more advanced message handling techniques.

The Sample Application

The sample code for Messenger 2000, a Visual Basic/CDO email client application, can be found in *\VBMsg\Samples\Chapter6\Messenger* (if you installed the samples to their default location). See Appendix F, *Obtaining the Sample Code*, for more information. The sample demonstrates the features described in this chapter. Figure 6-1 shows Messenger 2000's main screen.

The code is divided into seven modules:

`Globals` *(Globals.bas)*
: This standard module contains helper functions, the declaration of the single Session object used throughout the program, and the application's *Sub Main*.

`frmMain` *(frmMain.frm)*
: This form module presents an Explorer-style interface similar to that found in Microsoft Outlook. The form contains a TreeView control for browsing the

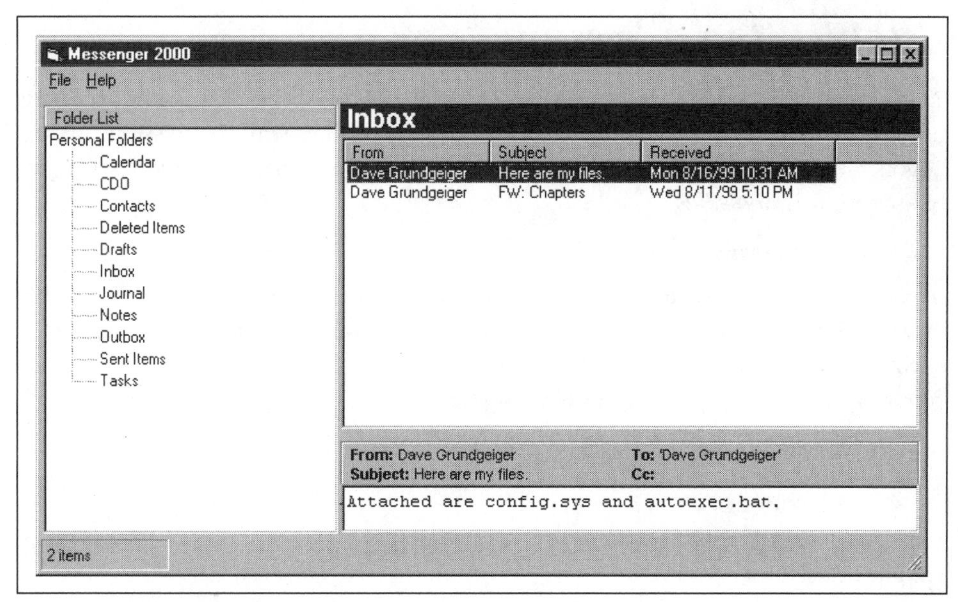

Figure 6-1. Messenger 2000, a sample CDO application

message store's folder hierarchy, a ListView control for viewing the list of messages contained in a selected folder, and a RichTextBox control for viewing the contents of a selected message.

`frmRead` *`(frmRead.frm)`*
: This form module displays the text and attachments of a selected message. Menu items are provided for manipulating the message, including saving the attachments to files.

`frmCompose` *`(frmCompose.frm)`*
: This form module allows the user to create and send a message, including attachments if desired.

`frmChooseAttachmentType` *`(frmChooseAttachmentType.frm)`*
: This form module is called by *`frmCompose`* to ask the user to select the type of attachment that is to be created (file, file link, embedded OLE object, or embedded message).

`frmAbout` *`(frmAbout.frm)`*
: This form module implements the application's About box.

`frmSplash` *`(frmSplash.frm)`*
: This form module implements the application's splash screen.

When creating your own messaging applications, remember to set a reference to the CDO library, as explained in Chapter 5, *Collaboration Data Objects*.

Establishing a Session

The first step in working with MAPI, regardless of which access methodology is used, is to establish a MAPI session. In CDO, this is done with the Session object's Logon method. The sample application declares a single Session object with global scope in *Globals.bas*:

```
Public gCdoSession As MAPI.Session
```

If you're relatively new to Visual Basic, recall that this declaration doesn't actually create a Session object, it merely declares a variable that is capable of referring to such an object. The object itself is created by this code in subroutine *tmrOpenCdoSession_Timer*, found in `frmMain`:

```
' Instantiate a new session object and logon.
Set gCdoSession = New MAPI.Session
gCdoSession.Logon
```

The Logon method accepts a number of parameters, all of which are optional. Here is the syntax:

```
CdoSession.Logon([ProfileName][, ProfilePassword][, ShowDialog][, NewSession]
[, ParentWindow][, NoMail][, ProfileInfo])
```

The parameters are:

`ProfileName`
: A string that specifies the name of the profile to use for the MAPI session. To cause the MAPI subsystem to prompt the user for the profile name, set this parameter to an empty string and set the *`ShowDialog`* parameter to `True`. These are the default settings for these parameters, so omitting them both has the same effect. Alternatively, the user's profile names and default profile name can be read from the registry, as explained in Chapter 2, *MAPI*. The *`ProfileName`* parameter is ignored if the *`ProfileInfo`* parameter is supplied.

`ProfilePassword`
: A string that specifies the password for the mail system, if necessary. This is a holdover from older mail systems; in modern MAPI development, this parameter is left empty because the profile itself specifies any username and password needed to authenticate to the underlying service providers.

`ShowDialog`
: A Boolean that determines how the MAPI subsystem behaves when *`ProfileName`* is empty or invalid. If *`ShowDialog`* is set to `True` (and *`ProfileName`* is empty or invalid), a dialog box is displayed to retrieve the necessary information (see Figure 6-2). If *`ShowDialog`* is set to `False` (and *`ProfileName`* is empty or invalid), a `CdoE_LOGON_FAILED` error is raised. The *`ShowDialog`* parameter is ignored if the session can be established without further information. The default value is `True`.

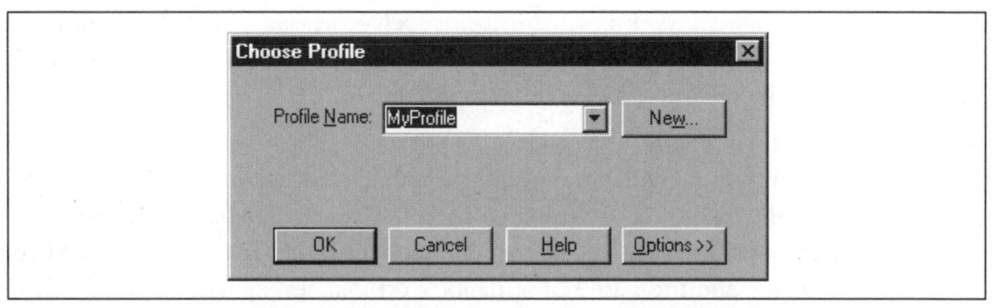

Figure 6-2. The Choose Profile dialog box is displayed automatically when the Logon method has insufficient information and the ShowDialog parameter is set to True

`NewSession`

A Boolean that determines whether the Logon method uses a new or existing MAPI session. If *`NewSession`* is set to `True`, a new MAPI session is created using the profile specified in *`ProfileName`*. If *`NewSession`* is `False`, the system attempts to locate an existing *shareable* MAPI session on the machine. If found, it signs onto that session, regardless of the profile specified in the *`ProfileName`* parameter. This might be useful, for example, for writing a utility that is expected to affect whichever profile is currently in use. If no shareable MAPI session is active on the machine, a new session is created using the profile specified in the *`ProfileName`* parameter. Applications that access MAPI directly through the API can choose to establish shareable or non-shareable sessions. CDO applications can log on through these shareable connections but can't themselves establish shareable connections—all sessions created by the Logon method are non-shareable. The default value for the *`NewSession`* parameter is `True`.

`ParentWindow`

A Long that identifies the window to be used as the parent window for any dialog boxes shown during logon. Set this parameter equal to the hWnd property of a form to make that form the parent window. Set it to 0, the default, to indicate that any dialog boxes should be application-modal, or to –1 to indicate that the currently active window should be used as the parent window. This parameter is ignored if *`ShowDialog`* is `False`.

`NoMail`

A Boolean that indicates whether the MAPI spooler should remain unaware of the session's existence. Set this parameter to `True` to indicate that the spooler should not be aware of the session. In this case, no messages can be sent or received within the session, except by a tightly coupled store and transport pair. (Tightly coupled store and transport pairs were discussed in Chapter 2. Note that Microsoft Exchange Server is a tightly coupled store and transport pair.) This might be useful for a program that only needs to browse the available message stores but not send or receive messages. Set this parameter to `False`, the default, to indicate that the session should be registered with the spooler, thereby enabling message transport.

ProfileInfo

The Logon method provides the ability to create and use a temporary profile, but only if the client is connecting to a Microsoft Exchange Server. The *ProfileInfo* parameter is a string that contains the name of a Microsoft Exchange server and the name of a mailbox on that server. The Logon method creates a temporary profile using this information. The profile is supposed to be deleted immediately upon successful logon or upon logon failure. In practice, however, temporary profiles aren't always deleted and have to be deleted manually. This appears to be a bug, but it is not yet documented by Microsoft. If this parameter is supplied, the *ProfileName* parameter is ignored.

There are two different ways to form this string, depending on whether the desired session is to be *authenticated* or *anonymous*. An authenticated session connects to a specific mailbox on the server and must have privileges to do so. An anonymous session allows anyone to connect to the server. The rights of an anonymous user to read and create messages are customizable within Exchange Server.

For an authenticated session, the *ProfileInfo* string is formatted as *<server name><linefeed><mailbox name>*, as in this example:

```
strProfileInfo = "MyServer" & vbLf & "daveg"
gCdoSession.Logon ProfileInfo:=strProfileInfo
```

For an anonymous session, the *ProfileInfo* string is formatted as *<server distinguished name><linefeed><linefeed>*`"anon"`. The *<server distinguished name>* is of the form `/o=`*<enterprise>*`/ou=`*<site>*`/cn=Configuration/cn=Servers/cn=`*<server>*. At minimum, the string must contain `cn=`*<server>*. If it doesn't, a `CdoE_INVALID_PARAMETER` error is raised. The administrator of the Exchange Server should be able to provide you with appropriate values for *<enterprise>*, *<site>*, and *<server>*.

Be aware that there is a bug in the MAPI logon and logoff procedures that CDO calls from the Session object's Logon and Logoff methods. A small amount of memory that is allocated during logon is not released during logoff. Programs that log on and off many times (perhaps thousands) might experience symptoms such as corrupt message properties, crashing, and, of course, low available memory. The only solution is to terminate the process periodically to reclaim the lost memory. This bug is documented in Microsoft's Knowledge Base article Q215463, "BUG: MAPILogonEx Memory Leak."

Handling Errors

The code that calls the Logon method should be prepared to handle the errors that might be raised. There are three error situations:

1. `CdoE_USER_CANCEL`

   This error is raised when the user cancels a MAPI-provided logon dialog box, such as the one shown in Figure 6-2. A reasonable approach upon receiving this error would be to exit the application without further messages to the user. This approach mimics the behavior of Microsoft Outlook. This is also the approach taken by this chapter's sample application.

2. `CdoE_LOGON_FAILED`

   This error is raised when CDO is unable to establish a MAPI session. The source of the problem could be in either the parameters to the Logon method call or the MAPI configuration on the client machine. In a production environment, an appropriate response would be first to notify the user that there is a problem establishing a connection to the messaging system, then to exit the application. That's what the sample application does. If this error is received during development, check the syntax of the call to the Logon method.

3. All other errors

   Any other errors will be caused by bugs in the client code or even in MAPI or the service providers. In a production environment, handle these errors as you do all other unexpected errors. For example, write them to a log and exit gracefully. The sample application again raises the error to the calling environment.

Sending Mail

After the application has successfully established a MAPI session, it can send a message. Sending a text-only message is trivial. Sending attachments and rich text is somewhat harder and is discussed later in this chapter.

Example 6-1 shows code that logs on to MAPI, sends a simple text message, and logs back off.

Example 6-1. Sending a Text Message

```
Dim CdoSession As MAPI.Session
Dim CdoFolder As MAPI.Folder
Dim CdoMessages As MAPI.Messages
Dim CdoMessage As MAPI.Message
Dim CdoRecipients As MAPI.Recipients
Dim CdoRecipient As MAPI.Recipient
```

Example 6-1. Sending a Text Message (continued)

```
' Establish a MAPI session.
Set CdoSession = New MAPI.Session
CdoSession.Logon "MyProfile"

' We must have a folder in which to create the outgoing message.
Set CdoFolder = CdoSession.Outbox

' Get the folder's messages collection, so that we can create
' a new message in it.
Set CdoMessages = CdoFolder.Messages

' Create the new message.
Set CdoMessage = CdoMessages.Add

' Set the message content.
CdoMessage.Subject = "This is the message subject."
CdoMessage.Text = "This is the message text."

' Get the message's recipients collection, so that we can
' add a recipient to it.
Set CdoRecipients = CdoMessage.Recipients

' Add a recipient.
Set CdoRecipient = CdoRecipients.Add

' Select an address.
CdoRecipient.Name = "William Gates"
CdoRecipient.Resolve

' Send the message.
CdoMessage.Send
```

Assuming that a MAPI session has already been established, creating and sending a message involves these steps:

1. Obtain a Folder object in which to create the new message. MAPI requires all outgoing messages to be created within some folder in the message store's folder hierarchy. When we created an outgoing message using the MAPI controls in Chapter 4, *The MAPI ActiveX Controls*, the MAPI controls automatically used the default Outbox folder for this purpose. A CDO application can create a new message in any Folder object it likes, but the Outbox folder is the usual choice. Example 6-1 uses the Outbox folder. In Chapter 7 you'll learn how to navigate the folder tree to find and use specific CDO folders.

2. Call the Add method of the Folder object's Messages collection. The syntax for the Add method is:

   ```
   Set CdoMessage = CdoMessages.Add([Subject][, Text][, Type][, Importance])
   ```

   The method returns a reference to the newly created Message object. The method's parameters are:

`Subject`
: This is an optional Variant/String that sets the initial value of the new Message object's Subject property. The default is an empty string.

`Text`
: This is an optional Variant/String that sets the initial value of the new Message object's Text property. The default is an empty string.

`Type`
: This is an optional Variant/String that sets the initial value of the new Message object's Type property. The default is "`IPM.Note`".

`Importance`
: This is an optional Variant/Long that sets the initial value of the new Message object's Importance property. The default is `CdoNormal`.

All of the parameters are optional. Rather than specifying arguments, the caller may choose instead to set the corresponding properties on the newly created Message object, as was done in Example 6-1. There is no technical advantage to either technique—it's a matter of preference and style.

3. Set properties of the new Message object. Of particular interest are the Subject and Text properties, if they weren't specified in the Add method call. The properties that can be set on an outgoing message are:

Categories
: This is a string array whose contents are application-defined. The idea is that this is a list of keywords that apply to the message. Accessing the values stored in this property is somewhat tricky and must be done as follows.

  To assign an entire array of strings to this property, the array must be declared as an array of strings. For example:

```
' CdoMessage previously Dim'ed and Set.

Dim astr(2) As String

astr(1) = "FirstKeyword"
astr(2) = "SecondKeyword"

CdoMessage.Categories = astr
```

  However, to assign the Categories property back to an array, the array must be declared as Variant, and it must be dynamic (that is, in the `Dim` statement the parentheses must be empty). For example:

```
' CdoMessage previously Dim'ed and Set.

Dim avnt() As Variant
Dim n As Long
```

```
avnt = CdoMessage.Categories
For n = LBound(avnt) To UBound(avnt)
   Debug.Print avnt(n)
Next n
```

Note that the assignment fails with a type mismatch error if the Categories property doesn't contain data. The following code fragment checks for this condition:

```
' CdoMessage previously Dim'ed and Set.

Dim vnt As Variant
Dim n As Long

vnt = CdoMessage.Categories
If IsArray(vnt) Then
   For n = LBound(vnt) To UBound(vnt)
      Debug.Print vnt(n)
   Next n
End If
```

This code fragment is different from the previous one in that no array is declared at all. Rather, a simple Variant is used, which receives the value of the Categories property. If no categories have been set, the assignment to *vnt* leaves it containing the value **Empty**. Because **Empty** is not an array, the following `If` block is skipped. However, if data is in the Categories property, the assignment to *vnt* leaves it containing the array of values, and the `If` block is executed. (Variants can contain arrays, even if they haven't been declared as arrays.)

To read the individual array elements in the Categories property directly, a double set of parentheses must be used, like this:

```
strKeyword = CdoMessage.Categories()(1)
```

This syntax is necessary to accommodate CDO's handling of property parameters. Similar syntax is used to assign directly to an individual array element:

```
CdoMessage.Categories()(3) = "Keyword"
```

However, this isn't very useful. For this to work, the Categories property must already contain an array with enough elements to accommodate the new value, and the only way to achieve that is to assign a string array to the Categories property as already shown. If this isn't done, a subscript-out-of-range error occurs.

ConversationIndex and ConversationTopic

Many collaboration applications use the concept of the *conversation thread*. A conversation thread is a series of messages and replies all relating to a specific topic. An application sets the ConversationTopic property of a message to indicate to which conversation thread the message belongs. The ConversationTopic property is a string, and its value is application-specific. Often the message subject is used as the conversation topic. A message that is the start of a new conversation thread should receive a new conversation topic. A message that is a reply to a previous message should have its ConversationTopic property set equal to that of the original message.

The ConversationIndex property is a message's sequence number within the message's conversation thread. It is a hexadecimal number expressed as a string of hexadecimal digits. To set the ConversationIndex property of a new message, use the CreateConversationIndex method of the Session object to obtain an appropriate value. The syntax of the CreateConversationIndex method is:

```
strNewIndex = CdoSession.CreateConversationIndex([ParentIndex])
```

The method's one parameter, ***`ParentIndex`***, is the conversation index of a received message for which a reply is being generated. To generate a conversation index for the first message in a conversation thread, omit the *`ParentIndex`* parameter.

DeliveryReceipt

A Boolean value that, if `True`, indicates that a notification message is requested when the message is delivered. The default is `False`.

Importance

This property indicates the message sender's opinion of the importance of the message. It is a Long that can be set to `CdoLow`, `CdoNormal`, or `CdoHigh`. The default is `CdoNormal`.

ReadReceipt

A Boolean value that, if `True`, indicates that a notification message is requested when the message is read. The default is `False`.

Sensitivity

This property indicates the confidentiality of the message. It is a Long that can be set to (in order of increasing confidentiality) `CdoNoSensitivity`, `CdoPersonal`, `CdoPrivate`, or `CdoConfidential`.

Subject

A string indicating the subject of the message. The default is an empty string.

Text

A string containing the body text of the message. The default is an empty string.

Type

A string that indicates the MAPI *message class* of the message. The message class indicates the type of message, such as email, appointment item, task item, contact item, etc. The default is "`IPM.Note`", which indicates a standard email. Other message classes will be seen throughout the remainder of this book. An application is also free to set the message class to an arbitrary string for messages that are to be used only by that application.

4. For each intended recipient:

   a. Call the Add method of the Message object's Recipients collection to create a new Recipient object. The syntax for the Recipients collection's Add method is:

```
Set CdoRecipient = CdoRecipients.Add([Name][, Address][, Type]
[, EntryID])
```

   The method returns a reference to the newly created Recipient object. The method's parameters are:

   `Name`
   : A Variant/String that sets the initial value of the new Recipient object's Name property. This parameter is ignored if the *`EntryID`* parameter is provided. The default is an empty string.

   `Address`
   : A Variant/String that sets the initial value of the new Recipient object's Address property. This parameter is ignored if the *`EntryID`* parameter is provided. The default is an empty string.

   `Type`
   : A Variant/Long that sets the initial value of the new Recipient object's Type property. The default is `CdoTo`.

   `EntryID`
   : A Variant/String that specifies a recipient by giving the ID of an existing AddressEntry object. Such an ID is obtained from the ID property of the AddressEntry object. Use this property only when you have an existing AddressEntry object representing a user to whom you'd like to send the message. AddressEntry objects can be obtained from the recipient lists of other messages or from an address book.

   b. Set the Name property of the Recipient object to the display name of the intended recipient, as it appears in the address book.

   c. Call the Resolve method of the Recipient object. This causes MAPI to search the user's address book(s) for the appropriate address entry. Once found, the address entry is associated with the message, and the Recipient object's Address property is set to the *full address* of the recipient. The full address is the concatenation of the address type and the address itself (for example, `"SMTP:jsmith@company.com"`). The syntax of the Resolve method is:

```
CdoRecipient.Resolve([ShowDialog])
```

The method's one parameter, ***ShowDialog***, is optional. ***ShowDialog*** is a Boolean that, if `True`, indicates that a Check Names dialog box should be shown when a recipient's name can't be resolved. This occurs when the Recipient object's Name property holds a value that either doesn't match any names in the user's address book, or matches more than one name. Note that this dialog box has a Cancel button on it that, if pressed, raises a `CdoE_USER_CANCEL` error in the calling code. Be aware also that the Resolve method raises a `CdoE_NOT_FOUND` error if ***ShowDialog*** is `False` and the name can't be resolved.

It is permissible to set the Address property directly (bypassing the Resolve method) if the full address of the recipient is already known. However, bypassing the Resolve method doesn't allow an existing address entry to be used. Rather, a *one-off* (temporary) address entry is created for the purpose of sending the message. Without matching to an existing address entry, the transport provider has to make certain default assumptions about the recipient. For example, Internet addresses are assumed not to be able to receive rich text. In general, it is recommended to use the display name of an existing address entry. This assumes that the display name is unique, which might not be the case. How you handle this depends on the type of application you're writing. If you're writing an application that sends to specific addresses for which you control the address book entries, it's within your power to make the display names unique in the address book. On the other hand, if you're writing an application that allows the user to enter addresses, it's probably OK to live with the address resolution dialog box that MAPI pops up when attempting to resolve non-unique display names.

It is often the case with Internet mail that the user knows the Internet mail address but does not have the recipient entered into her address book. In this case, the application can assign the Internet mail address to the Recipient object's Name property and call the Resolve method. The system recognizes the Name property as being in Internet mail address format, and creates the appropriate one-off address entry.

d. Set the Recipient object's Type property, if desired (not shown in Example 6-1). MAPI allows each recipient to be designated as a primary, copy, or blind copy recipient. Set the Type property to `CdoTo` (the default) for a primary recipient, `CdoCc` for a copy recipient, and `CdoBcc` for a blind copy recipient.

5. Call the Message object's Send method. The syntax of the Send method is:

```
CdoMessage.Send([SaveCopy][, ShowDialog][, ParentWindow])
```

The parameters are:

SaveCopy
: A Variant/Boolean that indicates whether to save a copy of the sent message in the user's SentItems folder. The default is `True`.

ShowDialog
: A Variant/Boolean that indicates whether to display a Send Message dialog box to the user prior to sending the message. The Send Message is the standard dialog box used for composing a new message, so this gives the user an opportunity to change recipients or message text prior to sending the message. The default is `False`.

ParentWindow
: A Variant/Long that identifies the window to be used as the parent of the Send Message dialog box if *ShowDialog* is `True`. Set this parameter equal to the hWnd property of a form to make that form the parent window. Set it to 0, the default, to indicate that the Send Message dialog box should be application-modal. This parameter is ignored if *ShowDialog* is `False`.

Sending File Attachments

MAPI defines four types of attachments: file, reference to a file, OLE object, and embedded message.

CDO handles all four types of attachments easily. To add an attachment to a message, use the Add method of the Message object's Attachments collection:

```
' (CdoMessage previously Dim'ed and Set)

Dim CdoAttachments As MAPI.Attachments
Dim CdoAttachment As MAPI.Attachment

Set CdoAttachments = CdoMessage.Attachments
Set CdoAttachment = CdoAttachments.Add(Name:="autoexec.bat", _
   Position:=-1, Type:=CdoFileData, Source:="c:\autoexec.bat")
```

The syntax of the Add method is:

```
Set CdoAttachment = CdoAttachments.Add([Name][, Position][, Type][, Source])
```

The method returns a reference to the newly created Attachment object. The method's parameters are:

Name
: The display name to be used by the receiving mail client when representing the attachment in its UI. When the attachment is a file, the name should be the filename, including its extension. The receiving mail client may default to this name when copying the data from its message store to the local file system.

(Some clients may instead default to the filename portion of the *Source* parameter.)

Position

The character position within the body of the message at which the attachment should appear. Some email client applications display a representation of the attachment within the body of the message at the character position indicated by *Position*. (However, some ignore this value and display the attachments separately.) *Position* is one-based, meaning that the first character in the message is at position 1, and the last character in the message is at `Len(`*CdoMessage*`.Text)`. To place the attachment beyond the last character of the message, set *Position* to `Len(`*CdoMessage*`.Text) + 1`. A value of –1 indicates that the attachment need not be represented within the message body. The default value is 0, which places the attachment at the beginning of the message—the same effect as setting *Position* to 1.

Type

Indicates which of the four types of attachments is to be sent. The values that can be passed in this parameter are:

`CdoFileData`

Indicates that the attachment is a data file that is to be sent along with the message. Use this type of attachment to send documents and data files.

`CdoFileLink`

Indicates that the attachment is a data file but is not to be sent along with the message. Rather, a link to the file is sent with the message. The link is used by the receiving email client application to find the original file. This implies that the file must be accessible to both the sender and the receiver. Use this type of attachment to send links to documents and data files.

`CdoOle`

Indicates that the attachment is an OLE embedded object. Use this type of attachment to cause the contents of a document to appear embedded directly within the email.

`CdoEmbeddedMessage`

Indicates that the attachment is itself a MAPI message. Use this type of attachment to include a message entirely within another message.

The default value for the *Type* parameter is `CdoFileData`, which is the type of attachment discussed in this section. The remaining three types are discussed in subsequent sections.

Source

Specifies the location of the attachment data. Its use differs depending on the value of the *Type* parameter, as shown in Table 6-1.

Table 6-1. Use of the Source Parameter

Value of Type Parameter	Use of Source Parameter
`CdoFileData`	Set to the full path and filename of the file to be attached. For example, "`C:\My Documents\Monthly Expenses.xls`".
`CdoFileLink`	Set to the full Universal Naming Convention (UNC) path and filename of the file to be linked. For example, "`\\daveg\c2\My Documents\Monthly Expenses.xls`".
`CdoOle`	Set to the full path and filename of an OLE *docfile*. For example, "`C:\My Documents\Monthly Expenses.xls`".
`CdoEmbeddedMessage`	Set to the unique identifier of the message to be embedded. This is the identifier obtained from a Message object's ID property. (However, when *reading* the Source property of an Attachment object, the value read is not a message identifier but is a reference to the embedded Message object itself.)

Sending File References

If the sender and receiver have access to a common file system (perhaps they're on the same LAN), it's not necessary to transport a file's contents with the message; it will suffice simply to specify the file's path and filename. The `CdoFileLink` attachment type is used for this purpose. For example:

```
' (CdoMessage previously Dim'ed and Set)

Dim CdoAttachments As MAPI.Attachments
Dim CdoAttachment As MAPI.Attachment

Set CdoAttachments = CdoMessage.Attachments
Set CdoAttachment = CdoAttachments.Add(Name:="autoexec.bat", _
   Position:=-1, Type:=CdoFileLink, _
   Source:="\\daveg\c2\autoexec.bat")
```

Note that the ***`Source`*** parameter specifies the path in UNC format.

Be aware that there is a difference between a file reference as defined by MAPI and a *shortcut* as defined by the 32-bit Windows operating systems. In Windows, a shortcut is a file, having a *.lnk* extension, that provides a link to another file. Shortcut files, just like other files, can be sent as attachments to email messages, thereby providing another means of sending a file reference rather than the file itself. The shortcut must link to a file that is accessible to the receiving system. To send a shortcut file, specify the ***`Type`*** parameter as `CdoFileData`, and set the ***`Name`*** and ***`Source`*** parameters based on the *.lnk* file.

Sending OLE Objects

MAPI supports embedding one document inside another, a concept known as *OLE* in Windows parlance. The document to be embedded in the message must have been previously saved as an OLE *docfile* (see sidebar). To attach it to a message, specify the parameters to the Attachment collection's Add method as follows:

1. Set the ***Type*** parameter to `CdoOle`.
2. Set the ***Source*** parameter to the full path and filename of the *docfile.*
3. Set the ***Position*** parameter to the character position within the message text at which the receiving mail client should render the object.
4. Set the ***Name*** parameter to an empty string, or omit it from the parameter list.

Compound Documents, OLE Structured Storage, and DocFiles

In the early 1990s, Microsoft developed a technology called *Object Linking and Embedding* (OLE). The goal of this technology was to enable users to create *compound documents*—documents that could contain other documents, even if the contained and container documents were created by applications that knew nothing of each other. This was all in support of Microsoft's view that users preferred to think in terms of documents rather than applications.

One problem that had to be overcome was how to save such a compound document to disk without creating a separate file for each embedded document. Microsoft's solution is *OLE Structured Storage.* OLE Structured Storage is a specification that treats a file as a filesystem unto itself, conceptually having its own internal folders and files. To avoid confusion, Microsoft invented new names to talk about the structure within these files. A virtual folder within such a file is called a *storage*, and a virtual file within such a file is called a *stream.* This arrangement allows a container application to create a file, save its own data to one or more storages or streams within the file, then ask the application responsible for a contained document to save the contained document's data into a storage or stream within the same file. Of course, for all of this to work, the two applications have to be written with OLE in mind. Documents that have been stored in this manner are sometimes referred to as *docfiles.* The *.xls* files created by Microsoft Excel and *.doc* files created by Microsoft Word are examples of *docfiles.*

Visual Basic doesn't have a way to create *docfiles* directly. However, it can be used to automate OLE-aware applications, such as Word or Excel, for the purpose of creating documents and saving them to disk. Documents thus created can be embedded in MAPI messages as described in this section. For information on how to use Visual Basic and Automation to control an application, see the documentation for the application that is to be controlled.

Here is an example of how to attach a *docfile* to a message:

```
' (CdoMessage previously Dim'ed and Set)

Dim CdoAttachments As MAPI.Attachments
Dim CdoAttachment As MAPI.Attachment

CdoMessage.Subject = "Sales Figures"
CdoMessage.Text = "Here are the sales figures:" & vbCr & vbCr

Set CdoAttachments = CdoMessage.Attachments
Set CdoAttachment = CdoAttachments.Add( _
   Position:=Len(CdoMessage.Text) + 1, _
   Type:=CdoOle, Source:="c:\sales.xls")
```

The carriage returns in the code (`vbCr`), in combination with the specification of the *`Position`* parameter in the call to Add, serve to provide a visual separation between the text and the embedded spreadsheet. Figure 6-3 shows the received message, as displayed in Microsoft Outlook.

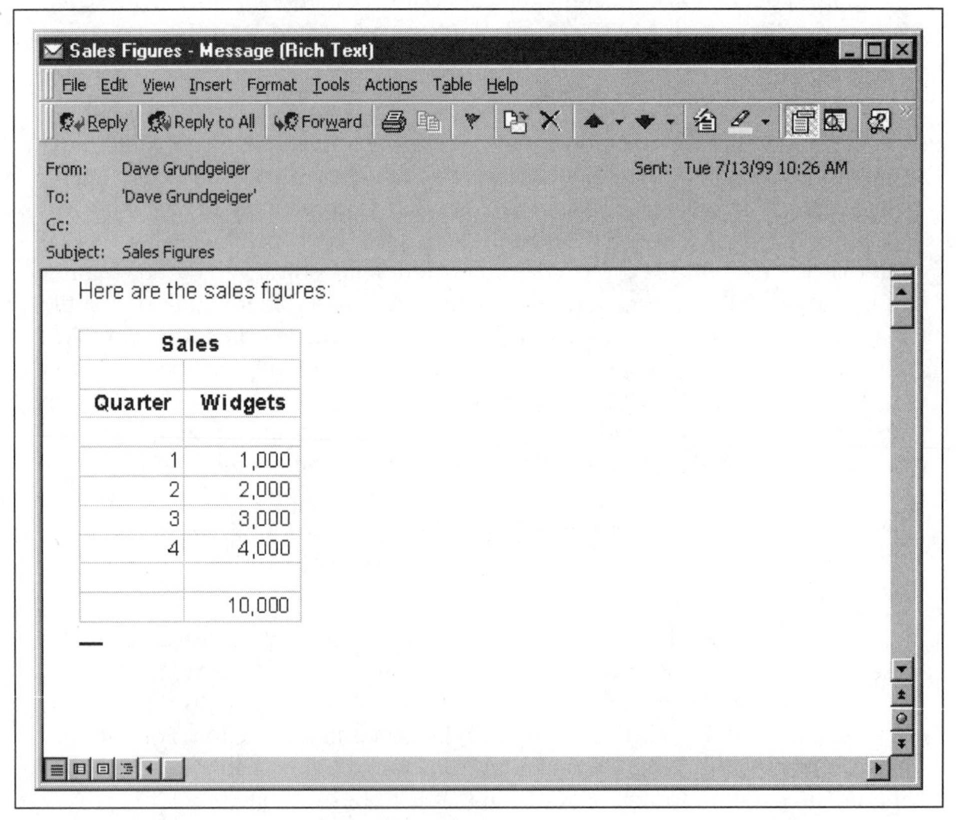

Figure 6-3. A message with an embedded object

Note in Figure 6-3 that the embedded data itself appears within the body of the message. This is in contrast to a file attachment, where, at most, an icon representing the attachment appears in the message body.

In order for the receiving client to handle this kind of OLE attachment properly, it must be aware of OLE, which is a Microsoft Windows-specific technology. Further, the recipient must exist in the sender's address book and must be flagged there as being able to receive messages in Rich Text Format (RTF). Figure 6-4 shows a sample recipient properties dialog box with the RTF option checked.

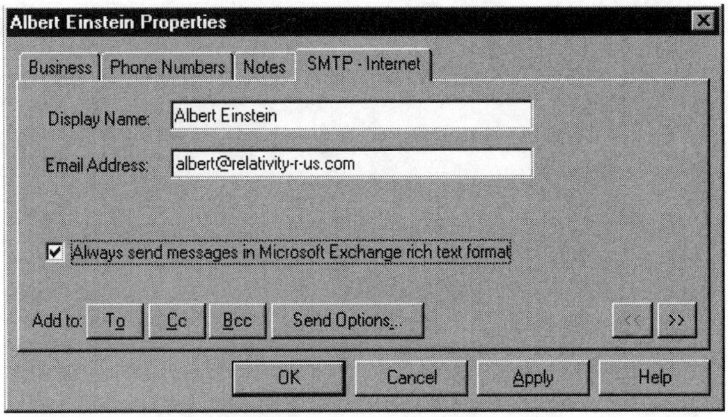

Figure 6-4. Setting Microsoft Exchange RTF for an email address

Sending Embedded Messages

Messages can be attached to other messages. You may have seen an example of this when a mail server sends you a non-delivery report and embeds a copy of your original email.

To attach a message to an outgoing message, in the call to the Attachments collection's Add method, set the *`Type`* parameter to **`CdoEmbeddedMessage`**. Set the *`Source`* parameter to the message ID of the message to be embedded. The message ID can be retrieved from the ID property of a Message object. The value assigned to the Add method's *`Name`* parameter will be used by the receiving system to label the representation of the embedded message in the UI. A good choice for this parameter is the subject of the embedded message. The *`Position`* parameter has its usual meaning.

The code looks like this:

```
' (CdoMessage and CdoMessage2 previously Dim'ed and Set)

Dim CdoAttachments As MAPI.Attachments
Dim CdoAttachment As MAPI.Attachment
```

```
CdoMessage.Subject = "Embedding a Message"
CdoMessage.Text = "There should be a message here:" _
   & vbCr & vbCr

Set CdoAttachments = CdoMessage.Attachments
Set CdoAttachment = CdoAttachments.Add( _
   Name:=CdoMessage2.Subject, _
   Position:=Len(CdoMessage.Text) + 1, _
   Type:=CdoEmbeddedMessage, Source:=CdoMessage2.ID)
```

Figure 6-5 shows the received message, as displayed by Microsoft Outlook.

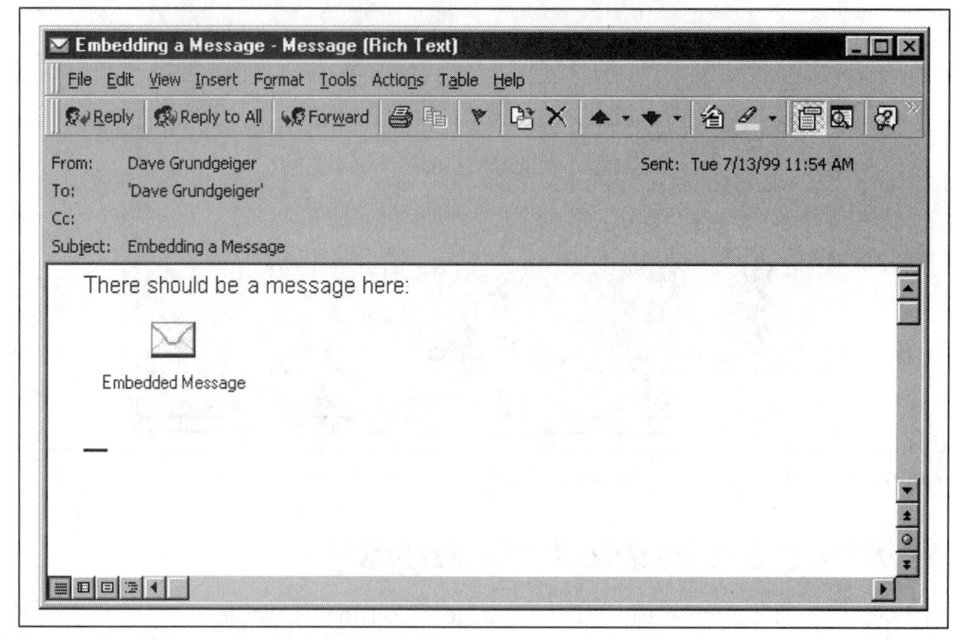

Figure 6-5. A message with an embedded message

Reading Mail

Assuming that a MAPI session has been established, reading mail is comprised of the following steps.

1. Traverse the CDO object hierarchy to find a message of interest.
2. Read the Message object's properties to retrieve message information.

As explained in Chapter 5, message stores are databases that store messages. The user's MAPI profile controls which message stores are available to the user. In CDO, a message store is represented by an InfoStore object. The Session object has an InfoStores collection, which in turn has one InfoStore object for each message store set up in the user's profile. To discover what message stores exist for a user, iterate through the InfoStores collection. You'll see an example of this in a moment.

Within each message store is a folder tree. To represent this in CDO, each InfoStore object has a RootFolder property, which contains a reference to a Folder object that acts as the root of the folder tree for that message store. The root Folder object doesn't contain messages—only additional folders. The Folders property of the root Folder object references a collection of more Folder objects, each of which can contain a reference to another Folders collection as well as a reference to a Messages collection. The Messages collection has one Message object for each message in the folder. In this way, the MAPI folder hierarchy can be traversed using the CDO object hierarchy.

Example 6-2, taken from this chapter's sample application, shows how to traverse the hierarchy. The example starts with the InfoStores collection found in the Session object and traverses the folder tree that is under each message store. It uses this process to populate a TreeView control in order to show the message stores and folders that are found. The code assumes that there is a global Session object, *gCdoSession*, and that its Logon method has been called successfully to establish a MAPI session.

Example 6-2. Loading a TreeView Control with InfoStore and Folder Objects

```
Private Sub LoadFolderList()

   Dim CdoInfoStores As MAPI.InfoStores
   Dim CdoInfoStore As MAPI.InfoStore
   Dim strKey As String
   Dim strMsg As String

   On Error GoTo ErrorHandler

   Set CdoInfoStores = gCdoSession.InfoStores

   tvFolders.Nodes.Clear

   For Each CdoInfoStore In CdoInfoStores
      strKey = "I" & CdoInfoStore.ID
      tvFolders.Nodes.Add Key:=strKey, Text:=CdoInfoStore.Name
      LoadFolder strKey, CdoInfoStore.RootFolder
   Next CdoInfoStore

   Exit Sub

ErrorHandler:

   If Err.Number = CdoE_FAILONEPROVIDER Then
      strMsg = "Unable to open your default email folders." _
         & "The information store could not be opened."
      MsgBox strMsg, vbCritical + vbOKOnly, App.Title
      Unload Me
   Else
      Err.Raise Err.Number
```

Example 6-2. Loading a TreeView Control with InfoStore and Folder Objects (continued)

```
   End If

End Sub ' LoadFolderList

Private Sub LoadFolder(ByVal strKey As String, ByRef fld As MAPI.Folder)

   ' Load one folder in the tree.

   Dim fldChild As MAPI.Folder
   Dim strKeyChild As String

   For Each fldChild In fld.Folders
      strKeyChild = "F" & fldChild.ID
      tvFolders.Nodes.Add relative:=strKey, relationship:=tvwChild, _
         Key:=strKeyChild, Text:=fldChild.Name
      LoadFolder strKeyChild, fldChild
   Next fldChild

End Sub ' LoadFolder
```

Example 6-2 includes two procedures: *LoadFolderList* and *LoadFolder*. In Messenger 2000, *LoadFolderList* is called immediately upon establishing a MAPI session.

LoadFolderList obtains an InfoStores collection from the global Session object and, for each InfoStore object in the collection, adds a node to the TreeView control. The *LoadFolder* procedure is then called to load the root folder. *LoadFolder* is recursive, so this single call loads the entire folder tree for the given message store.

Note the *Key* parameter of the Add method of the TreeView control's Nodes collection. The sample code sets this to be the concatenation of a single letter plus the CDO object's ID property. The letter used for nodes that represent InfoStore objects is "I." For Folder objects it is "F." This is a design decision on my part to facilitate later retrieval of CDO objects when the user clicks one of the nodes in the TreeView control. Example 6-3 shows how this works. When the user clicks a node in the TreeView control, the Click event handler retrieves the key from the selected node. If the first character is an "F," the user has clicked a folder name, and the item list should be refreshed with the items in the selected folder. The remainder of the key is the ID of the desired folder, which can be passed to the Session object's GetFolder method to get an actual Folder object.

Example 6-3. Loading the Item List in Response to a Click on the Folder List

```
Private Sub tvFolders_Click()

   Dim strKey As String
   Dim strFolderID As String

   strKey = tvFolders.SelectedItem.Key
   If Left(strKey, 1) = "F" Then
      strFolderID = Mid(strKey, 2)
```

Example 6-3. Loading the Item List in Response to a Click on the Folder List (continued)

```
      LoadItems strFolderID
   End If

End Sub ' tvFolders_Click

Private Sub LoadItems(ByVal strFolderID As String)

   ' Load the items list with info about the messages in the
   ' given folder.

   Dim CdoFolder As MAPI.Folder
   Dim CdoMessages As MAPI.Messages
   Dim CdoMessage As MAPI.Message
   Dim strKey As String
   Dim strRecipients As String
   Dim Item As ListItem
   Dim subitem As ListSubItem

   Set CdoFolder = gCdoSession.GetFolder(strFolderID)
   lblFolderName.Caption = " " & CdoFolder.Name
   Set CdoMessages = CdoFolder.Messages

   lvItems.ListItems.Clear

   sb.Panels.Item(1).Text = Trim(CStr(CdoMessages.Count)) & " items"

   On Error Resume Next
   CdoMessages.Sort CdoDescending, CdoPR_MESSAGE_DELIVERY_TIME
   On Error GoTo 0

   For Each CdoMessage In CdoMessages
      With CdoMessage
         strKey = "M" & .ID
         strRecipients = gRecipientListString(.Recipients)
         Set Item = lvItems.ListItems.Add(Key:=strKey, _
            Text:=gGetSenderSafe(CdoMessage))
         Item.ListSubItems.Add Text:=.Subject
         Item.ListSubItems.Add Text:=gGetDateReceivedSafe(CdoMessage)
         ' Make the text bold if the message is unread.
         If .Unread Then
            Item.Bold = True
            For Each subitem In Item.ListSubItems
               subitem.Bold = True
            Next subitem
         End If
      End With
   Next CdoMessage

End Sub ' LoadItems

Public Function gGetSenderSafe(ByRef CdoMessage As MAPI.Message) _
   As String
```

Example 6-3. Loading the Item List in Response to a Click on the Folder List (continued)

```
   On Error GoTo ErrorHandler

   gGetSenderSafe = CdoMessage.Sender

   Exit Function

ErrorHandler:

   gGetSenderSafe = ""

End Function ' gGetSenderSafe

Public Function gGetDateReceivedSafe( _
   ByRef CdoMessage As MAPI.Message) As String

   Dim dtTimeReceived As Date

   On Error GoTo ErrorHandler

   dtTimeReceived = CDate(CdoMessage.TimeReceived)
   gGetDateReceivedSafe = Format(dtTimeReceived, _
      "ddd m/d/yy h:mm AMPM")

   Exit Function

ErrorHandler:

   gGetDateReceivedSafe = ""

End Function ' gGetDateReceivedSafe
```

The *LoadItems* procedure in Example 6-3 loads a ListView control with messages found in the given folder. The Message objects in a Folder object's Messages collection are not guaranteed to be in any particular order, so the *LoadItems* procedure calls the Messages collection's Sort method to sort the messages by descending date order:

```
CdoMessages.Sort CdoDescending, CdoPR_MESSAGE_DELIVERY_TIME
```

The syntax of the Sort method is:

```
CdoMessages.Sort([SortOrder][, PropID])
```

The parameters are:

SortOrder

This is an optional Variant/Long that specifies the order in which to sort the messages in the collection. The values it can take are:

`CdoAscending`

Sort in ascending order. This is the default.

`CdoDescending`
: Sort in descending order.

`CdoNone`
: Don't sort. Use this value to cancel a previous sort.

`PropID`
: This is an optional Variant/Long that specifies the ID of the MAPI property on which to sort. MAPI properties were discussed in Chapter 2. The default is the *`PropID`* that was specified in the previous call to Sort. If Sort has not previously been called on the Messages collection during the current MAPI session, the default is `CdoPR_MESSAGE_DELIVERY_TIME`.

Some message store providers may not be able to perform the sort requested. In that case, a `CdoE_TOO_COMPLEX` error is raised. Be sure to handle this error if your code uses the Sort method. The code in Example 6-3 handles this error by ignoring it with `On Error Resume Next` (on the assumption that if the message store can't sort the messages, the best course of action is simply to display the messages unsorted).

The *gGetSenderSafe* and *gGetDateReceivedSafe* procedures in Example 6-3 keep the *LoadItems* procedure from receiving an error if the message doesn't have one or both of these properties. *gGetDateReceivedSafe* also reformats the date string.

When the user clicks an item in the form's ListView control, the ListView's ItemClick event handler reads the key from the selected item, passing the message ID to a procedure that fills a message preview window. The code is shown in Example 6-4.

Example 6-4. Loading the Message Preview in Response to a Click on the Item List

```
Private Sub lvItems_ItemClick(ByVal Item As MSComctlLib.ListItem)

   Dim strKey As String
   Dim strID As String

   Set Item = lvItems.SelectedItem
   strKey = Item.Key
   If Left(strKey, 1) = "M" Then
      strID = Mid(strKey, 2)
      LoadItemPreview strID
   End If

End Sub

Private Function LoadItemPreview(ByVal strMessageID As String)
```

Example 6-4. Loading the Message Preview in Response to a Click on the Item List (continued)

```
   Dim CdoMessage As MAPI.Message
   Dim strText As String

   Set CdoMessage = gCdoSession.GetMessage(strMessageID)

   With CdoMessage
      txtFrom.Text = .Sender
      txtTo.Text = gRecipientListString(.Recipients, CdoTo)
      txtSubject.Text = .Subject
      txtCc.Text = gRecipientListString(.Recipients, CdoCc)

      strText = gGetRtfTextSafe(CdoMessage)
      If strText <> "" Then
         rtxtItemPreview.TextRTF = strText
      Else
         rtxtItemPreview.Font.Bold = False
         rtxtItemPreview.Font.Charset = 0
         rtxtItemPreview.Font.Italic = False
         rtxtItemPreview.Font.Name = "Courier New"
         rtxtItemPreview.Font.Size = 10
         rtxtItemPreview.Font.Strikethrough = False
         rtxtItemPreview.Font.Underline = False
         rtxtItemPreview.Font.Weight = 400
         rtxtItemPreview.Text = .Text
      End If

   End With

End Function ' LoadItemPreview
```

The code in Example 6-4 loads a RichTextBox control with the body text of the given message, using rich text if rich text is available in the message; otherwise, plain text is used. The *gGetRtfTextSafe* procedure call shown in this example is discussed later in this chapter, in the "Formatted Text" section.

Reading File Attachments

Once the code has a reference to a Message object, it's easy to iterate through the object's Attachments collection to read its attachments. The Attachment object's properties of interest are Name, Position, Type, and Source. These properties are similar in use to the like-named parameters of the Attachments collection's Add method, discussed earlier in this chapter.

Attachments with their Type property equal to `CdoFileData` are file attachments. The Name property of file attachments indicates the display name that should be shown when rendering a representation of the attachment in the client UI. It is also a suggested filename to be used if the file is to be saved to disk (discussed shortly). The Position property is an index into the text of the message. It is the character position at which the attachment representation should be rendered. The Source property is the full path and filename of the file on the sender's system, not useful to the receiver.

When a message with file attachments arrives, the attachments are stored in the recipient's message store. To copy a file attachment to the recipient's local file system, the client software must call the Attachment object's WriteToFile method. The syntax of the WriteToFile method is:

```
CdoAttachment.WriteToFile(FileName)
```

The `FileName` parameter is a Variant/String that specifies the full path and filename of the file to be created. If the file already exists, it is overwritten without warning.

Example 6-5 shows a code segment that displays a common dialog box to prompt the user for a filename. The code assumes that it is running in a form that has a Common Dialog control named `dlg`. The initial value displayed in the dialog box is taken from the Name property of the Attachment object.

Example 6-5. Prompting the User for a File in Which to Save a File Attachment

```
Private Sub SaveFileAttachment( _
   ByRef CdoAttachment As MAPI.Attachment)

   On Error GoTo ErrorHandler

   dlg.CancelError = True
   dlg.DialogTitle = "Save Attachment As"
   dlg.FileName = CdoAttachment.Name
   dlg.Filter = "All Files (*.*)|*.*"
   dlg.Flags = cdlOFNExplorer Or cdlOFNHideReadOnly _
      Or cdlOFNLongNames
   dlg.ShowSave

   ' Save the file.
   CdoAttachment.WriteToFile dlg.FileName

   Exit Sub

ErrorHandler:

   ' The user may have pressed the Cancel button in the
   ' Save dialog box.
   If Err.Number <> cdlCancel Then
      Err.Raise Err.Number
   End If

End Sub ' SaveFileAttachment
```

In Chapter 3, *Simple MAPI*, I presented a method for opening an attached document that had been saved to disk. The same method applies here. See the discussion of the Windows *ShellExecute* API call and of my *OpenDocument* function in the "Reading File Attachments" section of that chapter.

Reading File References

Attachment objects with a Type property of `CdoFileLink` are similar to file attachments, except that the file is not included with the message. Rather, it is stored at the location specified in the Attachment object's Source property. Because the file is already on disk, there is no need to call the WriteToFile method. In fact, it is an error to do so. If the receiving email client software wishes to manipulate the attachment, it can do so as it would any file. For example, the file could be copied to the local machine like this:

```
' CdoAttachment already Dim'ed and set.

FileCopy CdoAttachment.Source, "C:\My Documents\" & CdoAttachment.Name
```

When an attachment is a file reference, the full path and filename are specified in UNC format in the Source property of the Attachment object. By convention, the Name property should contain the filename without the path, but this is up to the sender. If you absolutely must have the filename as it currently exists on disk, you must parse the value found in the Source property.

Reading OLE Objects

Attachment objects with a Type property of `CdoOle` are embedded OLE objects. The Attachment object's Position property identifies where in the message to render the OLE object. The Name and Source properties are not used.

To handle an embedded OLE object, first extract the object from the message store into a *docfile* using the Attachment object's WriteToFile method. The next step depends on the effect desired. One likely possibility is to display the object in a RichTextBox control. The RichTextBox control makes this easy with its OLEObjects collection. Merely calling this collection's Add method, passing it the name of the *docfile*, inserts the OLE object at the current insertion point. Here's the actual code:

```
' CdoAttachment and strFilePath already Dim'ed and assigned.
' rtxtBody is a RichTextBox control on the form.

CdoAttachment.WriteToFile strFilePath
rtxtBody.SelStart = CdoAttachment.Position - 1
rtxtBody.OLEObjects.Add Source:=strFilePath
```

Three lines to extract an embedded document (of any kind) from an email, and display it to the user. *Three lines.*

Reading Embedded Messages

An Attachment object that represents an embedded message has a Type property of `CdoEmbeddedMessage`, and its Source property is a reference to the embedded Message object. Note that this is different from how the Source property is used when sending an embedded message. When sending, the Source property is set to the ID of the message to be embedded. When receiving, the Source property contains the message object itself. To retrieve the embedded message, simply assign the Source property to a Message object variable:

```
' CdoAttachment already Dim'ed and set.

Dim CdoInnerMessage As MAPI.Message

If CdoAttachment.Type = CdoEmbeddedMessage Then
   Set CdoInnerMessage = CdoAttachment.Source
End If
```

Forwarding and Replying to Mail

Message objects contain methods that make forwarding and replying to email easy. The Forward method returns a new Message object that is a copy of the original, with a couple of exceptions. The Recipients collection and Text property of the message are not copied. The recipients aren't copied because it is assumed that a forwarded message will be sent to a different set of recipients than was the original. The message text often should be modified as well, to indent or quote the original text, for example. The Microsoft documentation is careful to note that this behavior of the Text property is for the current implementation (CDO version 1.21), implying that this could change, so don't rely on the Text property of the new message being empty.

Example 6-6 shows how the Text property might be handled on a forwarded message. The example shows a function, *CreateForward*, that takes a Message object, calls its Forward method to obtain another Message object, and sets the new Message object's Text property to contain the following:

- The text passed in to *CreateForward*
- The TimeSent property of the original message
- The name of the sender of the original message
- The indented text of the original message

The new Message object is then returned from the function for further processing. To indent the text, the *CreateForward* function calls the *IndentText* function, also shown in the example, which in turn calls the *WrapText* function, shown last in the example. Together, *IndentText* and *WrapText* break the text into lines and add an indent string ("> ") to the beginning of each line.

Example 6-6. Handling the Message Text on Forwarded Messages

```
Public Function CreateForward( _
   ByVal CdoMessage As MAPI.Message, _
   Optional ByVal strText As String = "" _
) As MAPI.Message

   ' Return a Message object to be used for forwarding the given message.
   ' The text of the original message is indented, labeled with the original
   ' sender's name and message date, appended to the given text, and set as
   ' the body text of the new message.

   Dim CdoMessageForward As MAPI.Message
   Dim CdoAddressEntry As MAPI.AddressEntry
   Dim strSenderName As String
   Dim dtTimeSent As Date

   ' Create the forward message.
   Set CdoMessageForward = CdoMessage.Forward

   ' Find the name of the sender.
   Set CdoAddressEntry = CdoMessage.Sender
   strSenderName = CdoAddressEntry.Name

   ' Find the date of the original message.
   dtTimeSent = CdoMessage.TimeSent

   ' Create the text of the new message.
   CdoMessageForward.Text = _
      strText & vbCrLf & vbCrLf _
      & "On " & Format(dtTimeSent, "Long Date") & ", " _
      & strSenderName & " wrote:" & vbCrLf & vbCrLf _
      & IndentText(CdoMessage.Text)

   Set CreateForward = CdoMessageForward

   Set CdoAddressEntry = Nothing
   Set CdoMessageForward = Nothing

End Function ' CreateForward

Public Function IndentText(ByVal strText As String) As String

   Dim strTextReply As String
   Dim nStart As Long

   strTextReply = ""
   nStart = 1
   Do While nStart <= Len(strText)
      strTextReply = strTextReply & "> " & WrapText(strText, nStart, 80) _
         & vbCrLf
   Loop
```

Example 6-6. Handling the Message Text on Forwarded Messages (continued)

```
   IndentText = strTextReply

End Function ' IndentText

Public Function WrapText( _
   ByVal strText As String, _
   ByRef nStart As Long, _
   ByVal nMaxLineLength As Long _
) As String

   ' The WrapText function breaks the given text string into lines
   ' equal to or less than the given length.

   ' WrapText is called once per line. On the first call to WrapText,
   ' pass nStart as 1. The WrapText function will return the first
   ' line of text and set nStart to the character position that begins
   ' the next line of text. Call WrapText continually, each time passing
   ' in the nStart received from the previous call. Stop calling WrapText
   ' when nStart is greater than the length of strText.

   Dim nPosCrLf As Long
   Dim nLineLength As Long

   ' Sanity check.
   If (nStart < 1) Or (nStart > Len(strText)) Then
      WrapText = ""
      Exit Function
   End If

   ' Is the text already broken by CR/LF?
   nPosCrLf = InStr(nStart, strText, vbCrLf)
   If (nPosCrLf > 0) Then
      nLineLength = nPosCrLf - nStart
      If nLineLength < nMaxLineLength Then
         WrapText = Mid(strText, nStart, nLineLength)
         nStart = nStart + nLineLength + Len(vbCrLf)
         Exit Function
      End If
   End If

   ' Else is the remaining text short enough?
   nLineLength = Len(strText) - nStart + 1
   If nLineLength <= nMaxLineLength Then
      WrapText = Mid(strText, nStart, nLineLength)
      nStart = nStart + nLineLength
      Exit Function
   End If

   ' Else just take the next nMaxLineLength characters or less, trying
   ' to make the break at a space character.
   nLineLength = nMaxLineLength
   Do While (nLineLength > 0) And _
```

Example 6-6. Handling the Message Text on Forwarded Messages (continued)

```
         (Mid(strText, nStart + nLineLength, 1) <> " ")
         nLineLength = nLineLength - 1
      Loop
      ' If nLineLength = 0, then there were no spaces, so just grab a lineful
      ' of characters.
      If nLineLength = 0 Then
         nLineLength = nMaxLineLength
      End If

      WrapText = Mid(strText, nStart, nLineLength)

      ' Set up nStart for next time.
      nStart = nStart + nLineLength

      ' Ignore spaces between words when there is a line break.
      Do While (nStart <= Len(strText)) And _
         (Mid(strText, nStart, 1) = " ")
         nStart = nStart + 1
      Loop

End Function ' WrapText
```

The Message object's Reply method is similar to its Forward method. However, it does populate the new message's Recipients collection with a single recipient, taken from the original message's Sender property. The Reply method, like the Forward method, doesn't copy the Text property (the code in Example 6-6 could be adapted for this purpose). In addition, the Reply method doesn't copy any attachments from the original message (presumably the original sender already has the attachments).

The ReplyAll method is the same as the Reply method, except that the Recipients collection of the new message is populated appropriately from the original message's Recipients collection and Sender property.

Formatted Text

Formatted text is text that can specify its own attributes, such as typeface, style, size, and color, and perhaps other features, such as paragraph spacing, bullets, and numbering. Text that is not formatted is called *plain text*. MAPI supports both plain text and formatted text.

Programs that wish to exchange formatted text must agree on how the formatting information is to be communicated between them. MAPI clients typically use Microsoft's RTF specification for this purpose. RTF encodes formatting information as plain-text keywords mixed in with the actual text of the message. For example, a formatted sentence such as, "I like to use *different* **styles**," can be encoded into plain text as:

```
{\rtf1\ansi\ansicpg1252\deff0\deftab720{\fonttbl{\f0\fswiss MS Sans Serif;}{\f1\
froman\fcharset2 Symbol;}{\f2\froman Times New Roman;}{\f3\fswiss MS Sans
Serif;}}{\colortbl\red0\green0\blue0;}\deflang1033\pard\plain\f2\fs20 I like to
use \plain\f2\fs20\i different\plain\f2\fs20  \plain\f2\fs20\b styles\plain\f2\
fs20 ,\plain\f3\fs17 \par }
```

(The line breaks in this example are for printing this book only. The actual RTF for this example contained no line breaks.)

It isn't necessary to learn RTF in order to use it in a messaging application. Visual Basic provides a very flexible RichTextBox control. The RichTextBox control has all the features of a standard TextBox control, plus the ability to work with formatted text. The control has methods for selecting portions of the text and applying formatting to the selected text. Once formatting has been applied, the control's TextRTF property can be read to retrieve the RTF that corresponds to the control's text, formatting and all. Similarly, an RTF string retrieved elsewhere, perhaps from a mail message, can be assigned to the TextRTF property, and the control displays the properly formatted text.

This isn't a tutorial on the RichTextBox control, so I won't go further into its many features. Instead, having noted that there is a way to acquire and display formatted text, I'll focus on how to use MAPI to send and receive RTF-encoded mail messages. (See O'Reilly's *Visual Basic Controls in a Nutshell*, by Evan S. Dictor, for documentation of the RichTextBox control, among many others.)

It would be nice if the Message object had a TextRTF property, but in fact CDO provides no RTF support. At the MAPI level, RTF is transmitted in the `PR_RTF_COMPRESSED` property (MAPI properties were discussed in Chapter 2). A Visual Basic program can access this property through the Message object's Fields collection:

```
' CdoMessage previously Dim'ed and set.

Dim CdoFields As MAPI.Fields
Dim CdoField As MAPI.Field
Dim strCompressedRTF As String

Set CdoFields = CdoMessage.Fields
Set CdoField = CdoFields.Item(CdoPR_RTF_COMPRESSED)
strCompressedRTF = CdoField.Value
```

However, the string thus retrieved is in an undocumented compressed format. MAPI provides functions for converting from and to this compressed format, but their use from Visual Basic is prohibitively difficult. To use them, it is necessary to write a helper component in C++.

I've provided such a component in this book's sample code, in the folder *\VBMsg\Samples\CdoHelper*. The complete source code is provided, in case you want to tinker with the implementation. The compiled component is also provided, ready to be used.

To use the CDO helper component from Visual Basic, set a reference to *O'Reilly CDO Helper 1.0* in Visual Basic's References dialog. (This assumes that the component has been registered on your system, as described in Appendix F.) Example 6-7 shows a procedure that uses the CDO Helper 1.0 component to retrieve RTF text from a Message object. The example is taken from the Messenger 2000 sample application.

Example 6-7. Using the CdoHelper Component's GetTextRTF Method

```
Public Function gGetRtfTextSafe(ByRef CdoMessage As MAPI.Message) _
   As String

   On Error GoTo ErrorHandler

   Dim MessageHelper As CdoHelper.MessageHelper
   Set MessageHelper = New CdoHelper.MessageHelper
   gGetRtfTextSafe = MessageHelper.GetTextRTF(CdoMessage)
   Set MessageHelper = Nothing

   Exit Function

ErrorHandler:

   gGetRtfTextSafe = ""

End Function ' gGetRtfTextSafe
```

The GetTextRTF method of the MessageHelper object returns a string containing the RTF text from the message, if any. If the message does not contain RTF-encoded text, the GetTextRTF method raises the `CdoE_NOT_FOUND` error. The procedure in the example handles this error by returning an empty string. Elsewhere in the Messenger 2000 application, this empty string is a signal that the message in question has no RTF text, and that the message's plain text should be read instead (from the Message object's Text property).

The MessageHelper object also provides a function called HasTextRTF, which provides a Boolean result indicating whether the given message contains RTF:

```
bHasTextRTF = MessageHelper.HasTextRTF(CdoMessage)
```

Finally, to set a message's RTF text, invoke the MessageHelper object's SetTextRTF method, as shown in this code fragment:

```
' CdoMessage previously Dim'ed and Set.
' strTextRTF previously Dim'ed and assigned.
```

```
Dim MessageHelper As CdoHelper.MessageHelper

Set MessageHelper = New CdoHelper.MessageHelper
MessageHelper.SetTextRTF CdoMessage, strTextRTF
Set MessageHelper = Nothing
```

Showing the Address Book

If you're writing an application that allows the user to enter recipients for an outgoing message, it's convenient for the user to have a way to display the address book, and to select recipients directly from the address book. In CDO, this is done by calling the Session object's AddressBook method. The syntax of the AddressBook method is:

```
Set CdoRecipients = CdoSession.AddressBook([Recipients][, Title][, OneAddress]
[, ForceResolution][, RecipLists][, ToLabel][, CcLabel][, BccLabel][,
ParentWindow])
```

Note that all of the parameters are optional. Here is how each is used:

`Recipients`
: A Recipients collection object that is used to populate the addresses in the dialog box. The user can then select additional addresses and/or deselect addresses that were previously selected. If the parameter is omitted, the displayed dialog box doesn't have any recipients selected initially.

`Title`
: A string that is used as the dialog box's caption. The default value is an empty string.

`OneAddress`
: When this Boolean parameter is set to `True`, the user is permitted to select at most a single recipient. When it is `False` (the default), the user is allowed to select multiple recipients.

`ForceResolution`
: When this Boolean parameter is set to `True`, the AddressBook method attempts to resolve all names prior to returning. If it has trouble doing so, it displays an address resolution dialog box to the user, as shown in Figure 6-6. If this parameter is set to `False`, the AddressBook method does not attempt to resolve the addresses entered by the user. Note that the Microsoft documentation states that the default value for this parameter is `True`. However, when I tested this with CDO 1.21, it was necessary to pass `True` in this parameter to cause the behavior.

`RecipLists`
: Typically, each recipient of a message is designated as a primary, copy, or blind copy recipient. In the address list dialog box, these three possibilities are

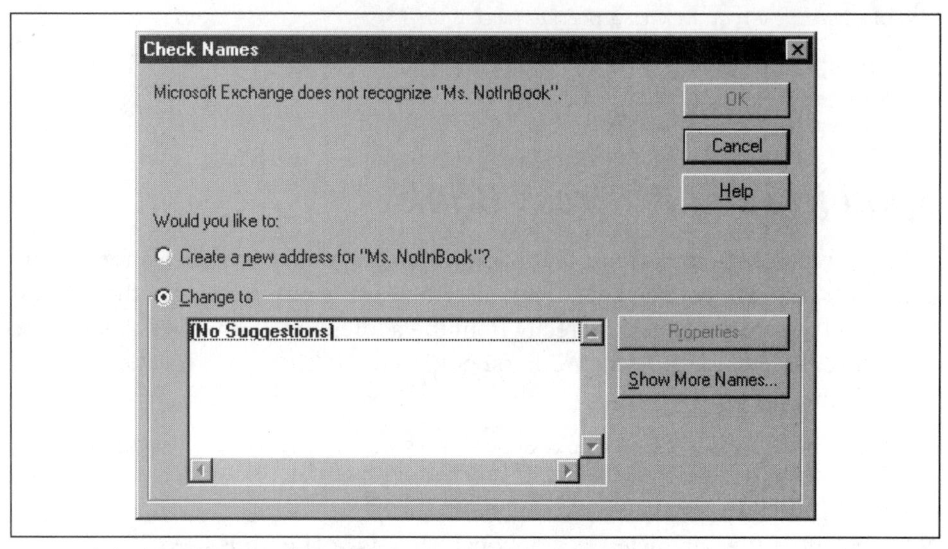

Figure 6-6. The address resolution dialog box

represented by three different list boxes containing recipient names. Refer to Figure 6-7, shown later in this section. The list box next to the "To" button is for recipients that are to be primary recipients. Similarly, the list boxes next to the "Cc" and "Bcc" buttons are for recipients that are to be copy and blind copy recipients, respectively. The ***RecipLists*** parameter controls how many of these list boxes (and associated buttons) are visible. When ***RecipLists*** is 0, none of the three boxes is shown. This allows the user to browse the address book but doesn't provide any way to select recipients. When ***RecipLists*** is 1, only the primary recipient list box and button are shown. When ***RecipLists*** is 2, the primary and copy recipient list boxes and buttons are shown, and when ***RecipLists*** is 3, all three are shown. A ***RecipLists*** value of –1 also causes all three boxes to be shown, makes ***ForceResolution*** `False`, and sets the ***ToLabel***, ***CcLabel***, and ***BccLabel*** parameters to their default values.

ToLabel, CcLabel, and BccLabel

Each of these three string parameters allows a custom caption to be applied to the corresponding button. This is in contrast to the MAPI controls, discussed in Chapter 4, which allow you to customize only the "To" button. The default values for these three parameters are "`To:`", "`Cc:`", and "`Bcc:`", respectively.

ParentWindow

This Long parameter should be set to the handle of the window that is to be the parent of the address book dialog box. If no value is specified, the address book dialog box is application-modal—that is, all other windows in the application are disabled until the address book dialog box is dismissed. If, however, a value is specified for the ***ParentWindow*** parameter, the dialog box is modal to the specified window, meaning that the specified window is disabled until the dialog box is dismissed, but other windows in the application remain enabled. Set this parameter equal to the hWnd property of a form to make that form the parent of the dialog box.

Example 6-8 shows how the Messenger 2000 sample application uses the AddressBook method. In this example, it is assumed that there is a module-level Message object variable called ***mCdoMessage*** and a global Session object variable called ***gCdoSession***. The resulting display is shown in Figure 6-7.

Example 6-8. Displaying the Address Book

```
Private Sub ShowAddressBook()

   On Error GoTo ErrorHandler

   mCdoMessage.Recipients = gCdoSession.AddressBook( _
      Recipients:=mCdoMessage.Recipients, Title:="Select Names", _
      RecipLists:=3)

   Exit Sub

ErrorHandler:

   If Err.Number <> CdoE_USER_CANCEL Then
      Err.Raise Err.Number
   End If

End Sub ' ShowAddressBook
```

Notice that the Session object's AddressBook method takes a Recipients collection as a parameter and also returns a Recipients collection. The AddressBook method uses the passed-in Recipients collection to populate the addresses in the dialog box. The user can then select additional addresses and/or deselect addresses that were previously selected. When the user clicks the OK button, the AddressBook method returns a Recipients collection object representing the new collection of selected recipients. The code in Example 6-8 is typical in that it passes in the Recipients collection of a Message object, and then assigns the returned Recipients collection back into the same Message object. Example 6-8 also shows how to handle the `CdoE_USER_CANCEL` error, which is raised if the user clicks the Cancel button on the address book dialog box.

Summary

This chapter covered the basics of sending and reading email messages, including file attachments of all kinds. In addition, you learned how to send and read for-

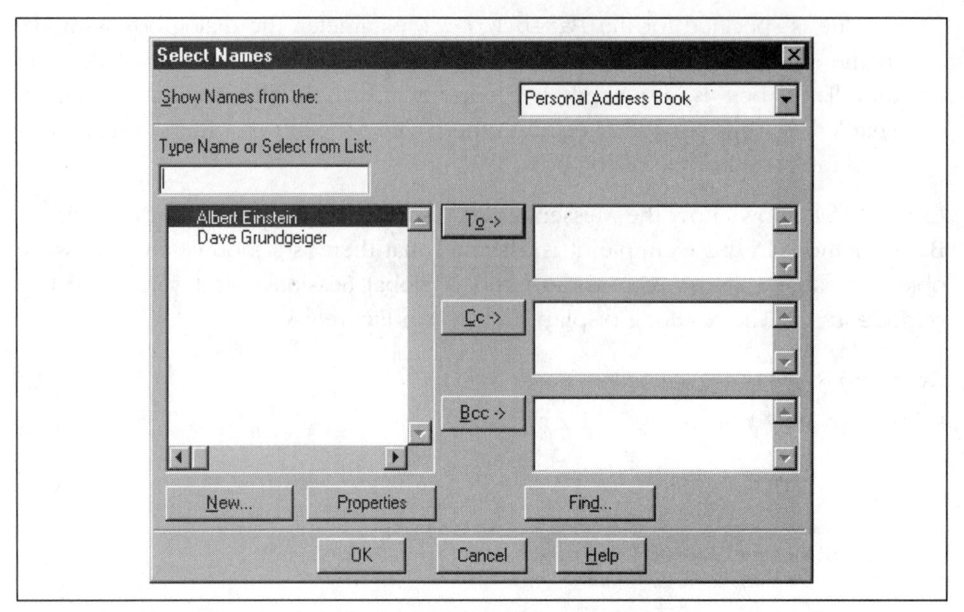

Figure 6-7. The address book dialog box displayed as a result of running the code in Example 6-8

matted text, a feature not supplied by CDO, and how to present an address book to the user.

Chapter 7 will reveal the secrets behind the most advanced features found in modern email clients.

7

Enhancing the Email Client

The previous chapter discussed the basics of sending and receiving email messages. The techniques given there are enough to complete a wide variety of email tasks—perhaps most that you're likely to run into. However, if you're writing a complete email client application or if your messaging application requires exceptional control over email, you'll need more. This chapter rounds out the discussion of CDO capabilities as they apply to email. With the information in this chapter, you'll have complete control over the email experience.

How CDO Wraps MAPI Objects

Your understanding of CDO behavior will be heightened greatly if you remember the following: *CDO objects and MAPI objects are not the same thing.*

MAPI objects are COM objects exposed by the MAPI Subsystem and third-party software designed to be MAPI-compliant. Although they are COM objects, MAPI objects are not easily accessible through Visual Basic, and they are not accessible at all through scripting languages. Therefore, CDO was invented to be the bridge from these languages to MAPI. CDO exposes COM objects, but these COM objects are of the right nature to be accessible through both Visual Basic and scripting languages. CDO is built on top of MAPI, as illustrated in Figure 7-1, which means that when you instantiate a CDO object, that CDO object is accessing a MAPI object behind the scenes to do the real work.

This can occasionally result in surprising behavior. For example, an application may wish to determine whether two object references—say, *CdoMessage1* and *CdoMessage2*—refer to the same message. The following naïve implementation of such a check won't work reliably:

```
' This won't work.
If CdoMessage1 Is CdoMessage2 Then
```

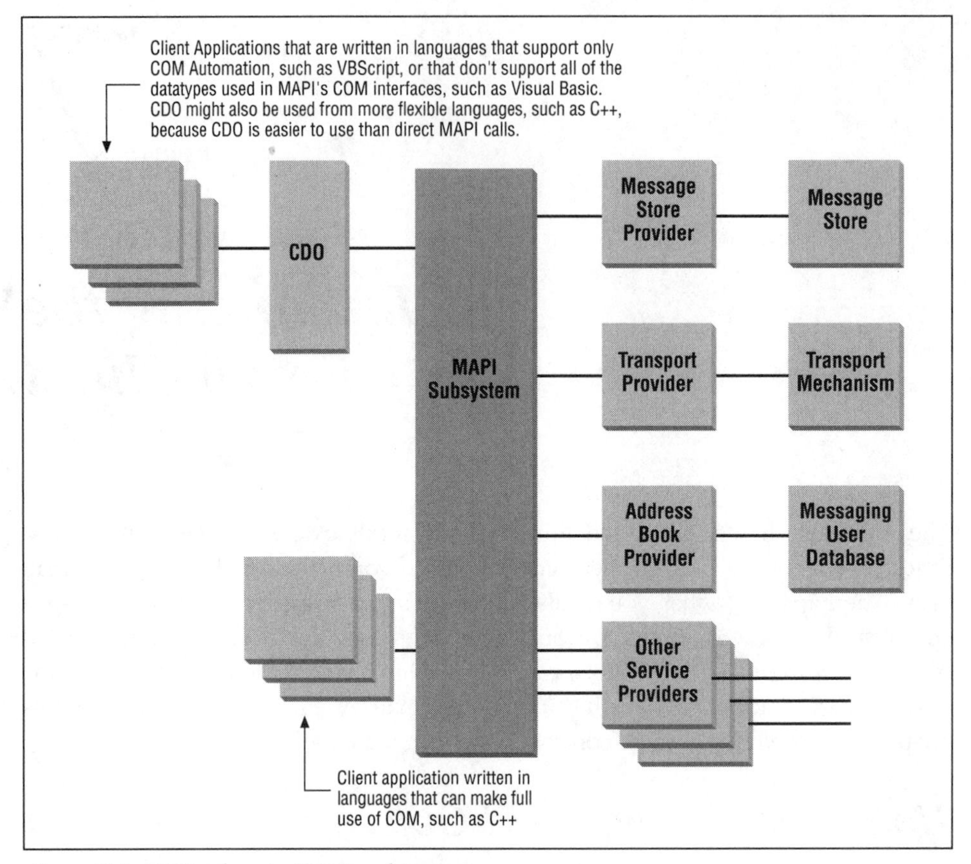

Figure 7-1. CDO's place in MAPI architecture

```
    ' Do something.
End If
```

The reason is that the two object references (*CdoMessage1* and *CdoMessage2*) may refer to different CDO Message objects, yet those CDO Message objects may both wrap the same MAPI message object. In this case, the `If` statement shown will fail (because the two references do indeed point to different objects), but we would prefer for the statement to succeed (because the two objects wrap the same MAPI object). To handle this situation, most CDO objects implement the IsSameAs method. The syntax of the IsSameAs method is:

```
bResult = CdoObject1.IsSameAs(CdoObject2)
```

The IsSameAs method returns `True` if *CdoObject1* and *CdoObject2* refer to the same CDO object or if they refer to different CDO objects that in turn wrap the same MAPI object. Here is an example of using the IsSameAs method of the CDO Message object:

```
If CdoMessage1.IsSameAs(CdoMessage2) Then
   Debug.Print "The variables reference the same MAPI message."
```

```
Else
   Debug.Print "The variables reference different MAPI messages."
End If
```

The CDO objects that implement the IsSameAs method are AddressEntry, AddressEntryFilter, AddressList, AppointmentItem, Attachment, Folder, InfoStore, MeetingItem, Message, MessageFilter, and Recipient.

Another aspect to this business of CDO objects wrapping MAPI objects is that CDO objects are ephemeral—they are created only when needed to give access to underlying MAPI objects, and they are destroyed immediately after their use. Although the syntax of the CDO hierarchy implies that there is a tree filled with bunches of CDO object instances that exist regardless of whether we traverse them, this is not the case. Consider the meaning of this Visual Basic statement:

```
Debug.Print CdoSession.Inbox.Messages.Item(1).Subject
```

This line *appears* to do the following:

1. Use the CDO Session object to find the CDO Inbox Folder object.
2. Use the CDO Inbox Folder object to find the CDO Messages collection within that object.
3. Use the CDO Messages collection to find the first CDO Message object in the collection.
4. Use the CDO Message object to read the subject of the message.

However, what the line *really* does is this:

1. Use the CDO Session object to *instantiate a new* CDO Folder object that wraps the MAPI Inbox folder.
2. Use the CDO Folder object to *instantiate a new* CDO Messages collection object that represents the set of messages stored in the Inbox.
3. Use the CDO Messages collection to *instantiate a new* CDO Message object that wraps the first message in the Inbox folder.
4. Use the CDO Message object to read the subject of the message.
5. Destroy the CDO objects created by this statement.

Given this information, code such as the following is clearly very inefficient because it performs all of the above instantiating and destroying for each statement:

```
' Wrong
Debug.Print CdoSession.Inbox.Messages.Item(1).Subject
Debug.Print CdoSession.Inbox.Messages.Item(1).TimeReceived
Debug.Print CdoSession.Inbox.Messages.Item(1).Text
```

The corrected code performs each object instantiation only once:

```
With CdoSession.Inbox.Messages.Item(1)
   Debug.Print .Subject
   Debug.Print .TimeReceived
   Debug.Print .Text
End With
```

Note further that not only are you in danger of writing inefficient code, but also your code may actually not work. For example, this code does not achieve the desired result:

```
' Wrong
CdoSession.Inbox.Messages.Item(1).Subject = "My New Subject"
CdoSession.Inbox.Messages.Item(1).Update ' Save it! (Not)
```

Because each line instantiates a new (i.e., different) Message object, the call to Update is made on a Message object other than the one on which the Subject property was changed. In fact, the Message object on which the Subject property was changed is destroyed before the Update method is even called. The change, therefore, is lost. The correct way to code this is as follows:

```
With CdoSession.Inbox.Messages.Item(1)
   .Subject = "My New Subject"
   .Update ' Save it!
End With
```

One final note on this subject concerns both efficiency and ease of coding. You may have noticed that CDO object properties that hold references to other CDO objects are declared in the CDO type library as Variant. (The CDO type library and how to view it were explained in Chapter 5, *Collaboration Data Objects*.) This has two unfortunate side effects. First, it forces so-called *late binding* when properties and methods are accessed through these Variant members. Binding and its ramifications are discussed at length in the Visual Basic online help and other sources. Briefly, late binding means that the Visual Basic compiler doesn't know at compile time what an object's type is. The compiled code therefore must jump through a lot of hoops at runtime to access properties and methods of the object. The second side effect of the Variant members is that the Visual Basic IntelliSense feature doesn't work for these objects. Again, this is because the properties are declared as Variant, so Visual Basic doesn't know what type they're really supposed to be.

You can code around both of these problems by assigning the value of a property to an appropriately declared object variable before referencing any properties or methods of the object. For example, instead of this one-liner:

```
Debug.Print CdoSession.Inbox.Messages.Item(1).Subject
```

Code this longer but more robust alternative:

```
Dim CdoFolder As MAPI.Folder
Dim CdoMessages As MAPI.Messages
```

```
Dim CdoMessage As MAPI.Message

Set CdoFolder = CdoSession.Inbox
Set CdoMessages = CdoFolder.Messages
Set CdoMessage = CdoMessages.Item(1)
Debug.Print CdoMessage.Subject
```

Because each object in this code fragment is explicitly typed, the compiler catches any typographical errors.

Handling Message Items

The Message object provides methods for copying, moving, and deleting messages. An automated email client may need to move incoming helpdesk inquiries, for example, to an appropriate folder for later retrieval by the next available technician.

To move an email message from one folder to another, use the Message object's MoveTo method. Its syntax is:

```
Set CdoMessage2 = CdoMessage.MoveTo(FolderID[, StoreID])
```

The parameters are:

FolderID
: A string that identifies the folder to which the message is to be moved. A folder ID string is obtained from the ID property of a CDO Folder object. Obtaining CDO Folder objects representing specific folders is the subject of the next section.

StoreID
: This optional parameter is a string that identifies the message store containing the target folder. If omitted, CDO assumes that the target folder resides in the same message store as the folder from which the message is being moved. A message store ID is obtained from the ID property of a CDO InfoStore object.

The CDO Message object returned by the MoveTo method (shown as *CdoMessage2* in the syntax definition) references the message in its new location. The original CDO Message object (shown as *CdoMessage*) no longer references any message. Attempting to access its properties results in an error.

Here's an example of using the MoveTo method:

```
' CdoMessage and CdoFolder previously Dim'ed and Set.
Set CdoMessage = CdoMessage.MoveTo(CdoFolder.ID, CdoFolder.StoreID)
```

Note the following in this example:

- The return value from the MoveTo method is assigned right back to *CdoMessage*. This allows you to continue using *CdoMessage* to access the message.

- The target folder knows what message store contains it. The message store ID is given in the Folder object's StoreID property. This value is passed to the Message object's MoveTo method just in case the message store of the target folder is different from the one containing the original message.
- The move occurs immediately—it is not necessary to call the Message object's Update method.

A neat use of the MoveTo method is to provide an "undoable" delete, such as Microsoft Outlook does. When the user requests to delete a message item, the software could actually just move the item to another folder, usually the Deleted Items folder in the InfoStore object's RootFolder. (Note that the Delete method, discussed next, provides an easier way to move a message directly to the Deleted Items folder, but this technique of moving folders lets you pick any folder, not just the Deleted Items folder.) How to get a reference to a specific folder of interest is discussed later, in the section "Working with Folders."

To truly delete a message from the message store, use the Message object's Delete method. The syntax of the Delete method is:

```
CdoMessage.Delete([DeletedItems])
```

The method's single parameter, ***DeletedItems***, is optional. It is a Boolean that, if **True**, indicates that the message should be moved to the user's Deleted Items folder. If **False**, this parameter indicates that the message should be permanently deleted. The default is **False**.

For example, this code permanently deletes a message:

```
' CdoMessage previously Dim'ed and Set.
CdoMessage.Delete
```

This is an irreversible operation, so be sure to ask the user whether the deletion is truly desired. To move the message to the user's "Deleted Items" folder, supply the ***DeletedItems*** parameter to the Delete method call:

```
' CdoMessage and CdoFolder previously Dim'ed and Set.
CdoMessage.Delete DeletedItems:=True
```

Believe it or not, a few different versions of CDO 1.21 are running around. At least one older version of this component doesn't accept the ***DeletedItems*** parameter of the Message object's Delete method (or at least its type library claims that it doesn't). To ensure that you're working with the latest release of CDO 1.21, download CDO directly from Microsoft, as described in Chapter 5.

To copy a message, use the Message object's CopyTo method. The syntax of the CopyTo method is:

```
Set CdoMessageCopy = CdoMessage.CopyTo(FolderID[, StoreID])
```

Its parameters are:

FolderID
: A string that identifies the folder to which the message is to be copied. A folder ID string is obtained from the ID property of a CDO Folder object. Obtaining CDO Folder objects representing specific folders is the subject of the next section.

StoreID
: This optional parameter is a string that identifies the message store containing the target folder. If omitted, CDO assumes that the target folder resides in the same message store as the folder from which the message is being copied. A message store ID is obtained from the ID property of a CDO InfoStore object.

The CDO Message object returned by the CopyTo method (shown as *CdoMessageCopy* in the syntax definition) references the new message. The original CDO Message object (shown as *CdoMessage*) continues to reference the original message.

In order for the new message to appear in the target folder, the Update method must be called on the CDO Message object returned by the CopyTo method. Here's an example:

```
' CdoMessage and CdoFolder previously Dim'ed and Set.
' CdoMessageCopy previously Dim'ed.
Set CdoMessageCopy = CdoMessage.CopyTo(CdoFolder.ID, CdoFolder.StoreID)
CdoMessageCopy.Update
```

Changes made to a CDO Message object's properties aren't written to the underlying message store until either the Send or the Update method is called. The Send method was described in the previous chapter, so I'll focus on the Update method here. The syntax of the Update method is:

```
CdoMessage.Update([MakePermanent][, RefreshObject])
```

Its parameters are:

MakePermanent
: This optional Boolean parameter controls whether changes are saved to the message store. Setting this parameter to `True`, the default, indicates that changes should be saved. Setting it to `False` indicates that changes should not be saved.

RefreshObject
: This optional Boolean parameter controls whether the Message object's *property cache* is reloaded from the message store. The default is `False`.

The *RefreshObject* parameter doesn't behave as one would expect. Its name and documentation imply that passing *RefreshObject* as `True` would cause the

Message object's properties to be reset to the values contained in the underlying message store. This isn't the case. It causes the Message object's property cache to be reloaded, which isn't the same thing. Unfortunately, Microsoft doesn't precisely document the behavior of the property cache, so this parameter isn't as useful as it could have been. Instead, to refresh a Message object's properties from the message store, discarding the object's current properties, re-instantiate it from the message store. Here is a generic subroutine to refresh a Message object:

```
Sub RefreshMessageObject(ByRef CdoMessage As MAPI.Message)
   Dim CdoSession As MAPI.Session

   Set CdoSession = CdoMessage.Session
   Set CdoMessage = CdoSession.GetMessage(CdoMessage.ID, _
      CdoMessage.StoreID)
End Sub
```

Working with Folders

An email client application can perform a number of tasks with Folder objects. An obvious one is to locate a folder of interest within the folder hierarchy. The Session object maintains references to the Inbox and Outbox folders of the default InfoStore, making it easy to obtain either. However, the Session object doesn't maintain references to other common folders, so it's useful to implement a generic function for finding a folder by name. Example 7-1 shows such a function.

Example 7-1. Finding a Folder Object by Name

```
Public Function GetFolderByName( _
   ByVal CdoSession As MAPI.Session, _
   ByVal strFolderName As String, _
   Optional ByVal CdoFolderParent As MAPI.Folder = Nothing, _
   Optional ByVal bCreate As Boolean = True _
   ) As MAPI.Folder

   Dim CdoInfoStore As MAPI.InfoStore
   Dim CdoFolderRoot As MAPI.Folder
   Dim CdoFolders As MAPI.Folders
   Dim CdoFolder As MAPI.Folder
   Dim bFound As Boolean

   ' If the parent folder wasn't passed in, then use the root
   ' folder of the default InfoStore.

   If CdoFolderParent Is Nothing Then
      ' Get the Folders collection from the default InfoStore.
      Set CdoInfoStore = CdoSession.GetInfoStore
      Set CdoFolderRoot = CdoInfoStore.RootFolder
      Set CdoFolders = CdoFolderRoot.Folders
   Else
      ' Get the Folders collection from the parent folder.
```

Example 7-1. Finding a Folder Object by Name (continued)

```
      Set CdoFolders = CdoFolderParent.Folders
   End If

   ' Loop through the folders in the collection until the
   ' desired folder is found.
   bFound = False
   Set CdoFolder = CdoFolders.GetFirst
   Do While (Not bFound) And Not (CdoFolder Is Nothing)
      If CdoFolder.Name = strFolderName Then
         bFound = True
      Else
         Set CdoFolder = CdoFolders.GetNext
      End If
   Loop

   ' If not found, then create it (if caller said to).
   If (CdoFolder Is Nothing) And bCreate Then
      Set CdoFolder = CdoFolders.Add(strFolderName)
   End If

   Set GetFolderByName = CdoFolder

   ' Release our local objects.
   Set CdoFolder = Nothing
   Set CdoFolders = Nothing
   Set CdoFolderRoot = Nothing
   Set CdoInfoStore = Nothing

End Function ' GetFolderByName
```

The *GetFolderByName* function in Example 7-1 takes at a minimum a Session object and the name of a folder to find as parameters. If no other parameters are supplied, *GetFolderByName* searches the Folders collection in the root folder of the user's default InfoStore for a Folder object possessing the given name. If found, a reference to the Folder is returned to the caller. If not found, *GetFolderByName* creates a new folder with the given name and returns a reference to the newly-created Folder object to the caller.

The *GetFolderByName* function provides a couple of optional parameters that modify its behavior. The ***`CdoFolderParent`*** parameter, if supplied, instructs the function to search the Folders collection of the given parent folder, rather than the root folder of the default InfoStore. The ***`bCreate`*** parameter, if passed as `False`, instructs *GetFolderByName* not to create a folder if one isn't found. In that case, the *GetFolderByName* method returns a value of `Nothing`.

Example 7-1 also demonstrates how easy it is to create a new folder: merely call the Folders collection's Add method. The syntax of the Add method is:

```
Set CdoFolder = CdoFolders.Add(Name)
```

The Add method's single parameter is the name of the new folder. The method returns a reference to the newly created Folder object. The addition is reflected in the message store immediately, meaning that it is not necessary to call the Folder object's Update method to reflect the change.

Deleting a folder is just as easy, requiring only a call to the Folder object's Delete method. The syntax of the Delete method is:

```
CdoFolders.Delete()
```

Drawing from Example 7-1, the Drafts folder (and everything in it) can be deleted with this code:

```
' CdoSession previously Dim'ed and Set.
Dim CdoFolder As MAPI.Folder
Set CdoFolder = GetFolderByName(CdoSession, "Drafts")
CdoFolder.Delete
```

Let me repeat that this also deletes everything in the folder, including nested folders and all messages, so be careful. Give the user a chance to back out if your application is interactive.

Folders can be moved and copied to other folders, just as messages can. As with Message objects, Folder objects have MoveTo and CopyTo methods.

The syntax of the Folder object's MoveTo method is:

```
Set CdoFolder2 = CdoFolder.MoveTo(FolderID[, StoreID])
```

The parameters are:

FolderID
: A string that identifies the folder to which the folder is to be moved. A folder ID string is obtained from the ID property of a CDO Folder object.

StoreID
: This optional parameter is a string that identifies the message store containing the target folder. If omitted, CDO assumes that the target folder resides in the same message store as the folder from which the folder is being moved. A message store ID is obtained from the ID property of a CDO InfoStore object.

The CDO Folder object returned by the MoveTo method (shown as ***CdoFolder2*** in the syntax definition) references the message in its new location. The original CDO Folder object (shown as ***CdoFolder***) no longer references any folder. Attempting to access its properties results in an error.

The syntax of the Folder object's CopyTo method is:

```
Set CdoFolderCopy = CdoFolder.CopyTo(FolderID[, StoreID][, Name]
[, CopySubfolders])
```

The parameters are:

`FolderID`
: A string that identifies the folder to which the folder is to be copied. A folder ID string is obtained from the ID property of a CDO Folder object.

`StoreID`
: This optional parameter is a string that identifies the message store containing the target folder. If omitted, CDO assumes that the target folder resides in the same message store as the folder from which the folder is being moved. A message store ID is obtained from the ID property of a CDO InfoStore object.

`Name`
: This optional parameter is a string that specifies the name of the new folder. If omitted, the new folder has the same name as the original folder.

`CopySubfolders`
: This optional parameter specifies whether to copy any subfolders contained in the original folder. The default is `True`.

To rename a folder, simply assign a new value to the Folder object's Name property. The change occurs immediately, not requiring a call to the Folder object's Update method.

Folders with Special Status

Clearly, some folders in the MAPI message store hierarchy have unique status. The Inbox and Outbox folders are obvious examples. Indeed, these two folders are so important that the Session object maintains explicit references to them for easy access. Furthermore, if their names are changed, they nevertheless retain their unique functionality. I changed the name of my Inbox folder to "foo." When new messages come in, they dutifully appear in the foo folder. Why?

After a message store provider is added to a profile as the profile's default message store, MAPI does some additional magic on our behalf. The first time a process logs on to MAPI using that profile, MAPI creates several special folders that clients are guaranteed will always exist. They are:

Deleted Items
: The folder where deleted items are stored.

Inbox
: The folder where new messages are stored after having been received by a transport provider.

Outbox
: The folder where outgoing messages are stored while waiting to be serviced by a transport provider.

Sent Items
The folder where outgoing messages are stored after they've been transmitted by a transport provider.

Once MAPI creates these folders, they retain special significance regardless of how their names are changed. There is no facility for transferring the special status of one of these folders to a different folder. Deleting any of these folders programmatically is likely to make your message store provider unusable.

In addition to the special folders created by MAPI, CDO recognizes the special folders created by Microsoft Outlook (except for Outlook's Drafts folder). The special folders created by Outlook are:

Calendar
The folder where the user's appointment items are stored. Calendar folders are discussed in detail in Chapter 8, *Calendar Folders*.

Contacts
The folder where the user's contacts are stored. Contacts folders are discussed in detail in Chapter 10, *Contacts Folders*.

Drafts
The folder where unfinished emails are stored. CDO doesn't treat this as a special folder. That is, CDO doesn't provide any special functionality for manipulating this folder or its contents, as it does with the other special folders.

Journal
The folder where the user's journal entries are stored.

Notes
The folder where the user's note items are stored.

Tasks
The folder where the user's task items are stored. Task folders are discussed in detail in Chapter 9, *Task Folders*.

These folders don't have any special significance to MAPI—only to Outlook. Outlook may or may not tolerate renaming or deleting these folders, depending on the folder and on the version of Outlook.

Hidden Messages

MAPI folders are considered to have two areas for storing message objects: the standard part and the associated part. The standard part includes messages and folders that are manipulated by the average user. These are the messages and folders that we have been working with so far in this book. The associated part is for storing additional information that is not directly manipulated by the user, such as form definitions, views, rules, reply templates, and more. It is up to the individual messaging client to decide what it will store in hidden messages, and how it will be formatted.

In CDO, associated messages are accessed through a Folder object's HiddenMessages property. The HiddenMessages property returns a Messages collection object that in turn contains Message objects representing associated messages. Example 7-2 shows two utility subroutines that together show any associated messages currently in the user's default message store. The code writes its output to a text file, and then launches the Notepad program to display the output. A sample of the output is shown in Figure 7-2. The figure shows that in this user's Calendar folder (which was created by Microsoft Outlook) there are two hidden messages. The first hidden message has a subject of "LocalFreebusy". Further, this message has a message class of "`IPM.Microsoft.ScheduleData.FreeBusy`". This is intriguing, isn't it? It's tempting to reverse engineer this further in an attempt to write code that modifies the behavior of Outlook. However, because this information is undocumented, it is subject to change without notice, thereby threatening that your application won't work with future versions of Outlook. It's better to use this information to expand your understanding of messaging, without relying on it remaining unchanged for the correct functioning of your applications.

Example 7-2 uses a function called *CdoPrTextFromCode*, which returns the name of a MAPI property given its property tag value. *CdoPrTextFromCode* is Visual Basic code that I've provided in the book's sample code. You can find it in *\VBMSG\Samples\Chapter 7*, in the VB source code module *basCdoPrTextFromCode.bas*. It is quite large but not complicated—it's just one big `Select...Case` statement. A condensed version is shown in Example 7-3.

Example 7-2. Finding the Hidden Messages in the Default Message Store

```
Private Sub ShowHidden()

   ' Traverse the folders in the user's default message store, reporting on
   ' any hidden messages found.

   Dim CdoSession As MAPI.Session
   Dim CdoInfoStore As MAPI.InfoStore
   Dim CdoRootFolder As MAPI.Folder

   ' Log on to MAPI.
   Set CdoSession = New MAPI.Session
   CdoSession.Logon
```

Example 7-2. Finding the Hidden Messages in the Default Message Store (continued)

```
    ' Get the root folder of the user's default message store.
    Set CdoInfoStore = CdoSession.GetInfoStore
    Set CdoRootFolder = CdoInfoStore.RootFolder

    ' Here's where we're going to print our output.
    Open "C:\Hidden.txt" For Output As #1

    ' Start the search, beginning with the root folder.
    RecurseHidden CdoRootFolder, ""

    ' All done.
    Close #1

    ' Use Notepad to view the results.
    Shell "notepad.exe ""C:\Hidden.txt""", vbNormalFocus

    ' Cleanup, cleanup, everybody do your share!
    Set CdoRootFolder = Nothing
    Set CdoInfoStore = Nothing

    CdoSession.Logoff
    Set CdoSession = Nothing

End Sub ' ShowHidden

Private Sub RecurseHidden(ByVal CdoFolder As MAPI.Folder, _
    ByVal strIndent As String)

    ' Recursive helper subroutine used by ShowHidden. Look for hidden
    ' messages in the given folder, then do the same for subfolders.
    ' Assumes that file #1 has been opened for writing.

    Dim CdoFolders As MAPI.Folders
    Dim CdoSubFolder As MAPI.Folder
    Dim CdoMessages As MAPI.Messages
    Dim CdoMessage As MAPI.Message
    Dim CdoFields As MAPI.Fields
    Dim CdoField As MAPI.Field
    Dim CdoAttachments As MAPI.Attachments

    ' Start by printing the folder name.
    Print #1, strIndent; "----------------------------------------"
    Print #1, strIndent; "Folder Name: """; CdoFolder.Name; """"

    ' Get the hidden messages and get the subfolders.
    Set CdoMessages = CdoFolder.HiddenMessages
    Set CdoFolders = CdoFolder.Folders

    Print #1, strIndent; "Number of Hidden Messages: "; CdoMessages.Count
    Print #1, strIndent; "Number of Subfolders: "; CdoFolders.Count

    ' Loop through all of the hidden messages.
```

Example 7-2. Finding the Hidden Messages in the Default Message Store (continued)

```
For Each CdoMessage In CdoMessages
   Set CdoFields = CdoMessage.Fields
   Set CdoAttachments = CdoMessage.Attachments

   ' Print information about the message object.
   Print #1, strIndent; "---------------------------------------"
   Print #1, strIndent; "Message Subject: """; CdoMessage.Subject; """"
   Print #1, strIndent; "Text: """; CdoMessage.Text; """"
   Print #1, strIndent; "Number of attachments: "; CdoAttachments.Count
   Print #1, strIndent; "Fields Collection: ";
   If CdoFields.Count > 0 Then
      Print #1,
   Else
      Print #1, "(empty)"
   End If

   ' Now print information about all of the fields (properties) of the
   ' message.
   For Each CdoField In CdoFields

      Print #1, strIndent; "    ----------"
      Print #1, strIndent; "    Index: "; CdoField.Index
      Print #1, strIndent; "    ID:"; CdoField.ID; " ("; _
         CdoPrTextFromCode(CdoField.ID); ")"
      Print #1, strIndent; "    Name: """; CdoField.Name; """"
      Print #1, strIndent; "    Class: """; CdoField.Class; """"
      Print #1, strIndent; "    Type: ";
      On Error Resume Next
      Print #1, CdoField.Type
      If Err.Number <> 0 Then
         Print #1, "(can't print: error "; Err.Number; ", "; _
            Err.Description; ")"
      End If
      On Error GoTo 0
      Print #1, strIndent; "    Value: """; CdoField.Value; """"

   Next CdoField

Next CdoMessage

' If we have subfolders, then print a header for those.
If CdoFolders.Count > 0 Then
   Print #1, ""
   Print #1, strIndent; "Folders Collection:"
End If

' Now start over for each subfolder.
For Each CdoSubFolder In CdoFolders
   RecurseHidden CdoSubFolder, strIndent & "    "
Next CdoSubFolder

Set CdoAttachments = Nothing
```

Example 7-2. Finding the Hidden Messages in the Default Message Store (continued)

```
   Set CdoField = Nothing
   Set CdoFields = Nothing
   Set CdoMessage = Nothing
   Set CdoMessages = Nothing
   Set CdoSubFolder = Nothing
   Set CdoFolders = Nothing

End Sub ' RecurseHidden
```

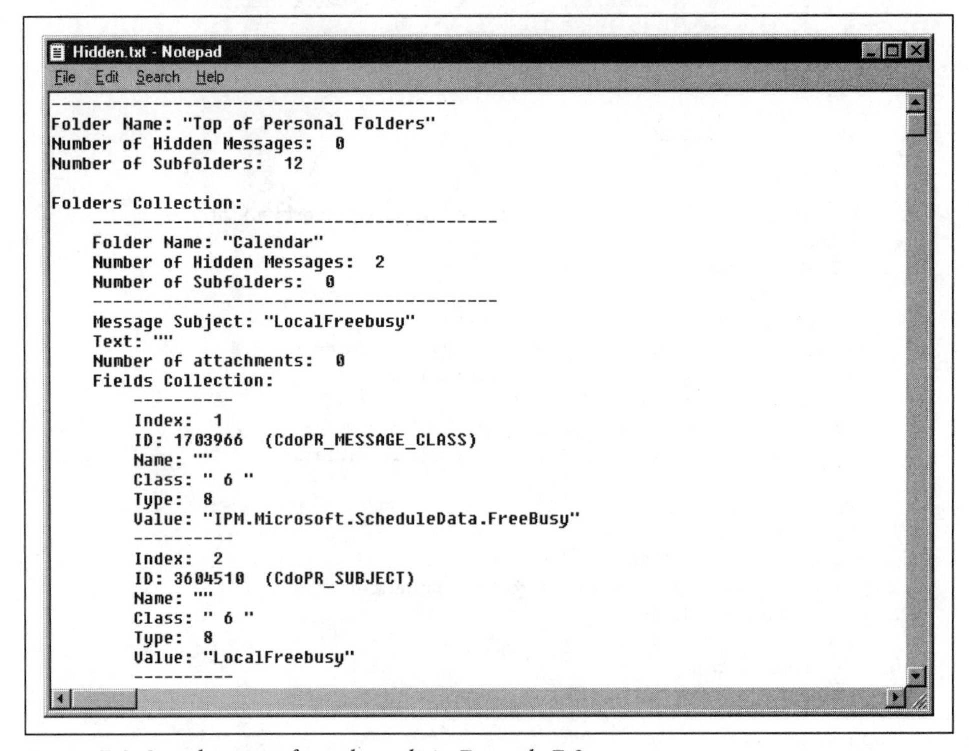

Figure 7-2. Sample output from the code in Example 7-2

Example 7-3. A Portion of CdoPrTextFromCode, a Function to Convert CDO Constants to Descriptive Text

```
Public Function CdoPrTextFromCode(ByVal CdoPropTag As MAPI.CdoPropTags) _
   As String

   ' This function returns the name of a property tag, given its numeric ID.
   ' Property tags are read from the ID property of Field objects.

   Select Case CdoPropTag
   Case CdoPR_ACKNOWLEDGEMENT_MODE:
      CdoPrTextFromCode = "CdoPR_ACKNOWLEDGEMENT_MODE"
   Case CdoPR_ALTERNATE_RECIPIENT_ALLOWED:
      CdoPrTextFromCode = "CdoPR_ALTERNATE_RECIPIENT_ALLOWED"
```

Example 7-3. A Portion of CdoPrTextFromCode, a Function to Convert CDO Constants to Descriptive Text (continued)

```
   Case CdoPR_AUTHORIZING_USERS:
      CdoPrTextFromCode = "CdoPR_AUTHORIZING_USERS"
   Case CdoPR_AUTO_FORWARD_COMMENT:
      CdoPrTextFromCode = "CdoPR_AUTO_FORWARD_COMMENT"
   Case CdoPR_AUTO_FORWARD_COMMENT_W:
      CdoPrTextFromCode = "CdoPR_AUTO_FORWARD_COMMENT_W"
   Case CdoPR_AUTO_FORWARD_COMMENT_A:
      CdoPrTextFromCode = "CdoPR_AUTO_FORWARD_COMMENT_A"
   Case CdoPR_AUTO_FORWARDED:
      CdoPrTextFromCode = "CdoPR_AUTO_FORWARDED"
   '
   ' Many, many more cases snipped for brevity in the printed listing.
   '
   Case CdoPR_INTERNET_PRECEDENCE_W:
      CdoPrTextFromCode = "CdoPR_INTERNET_PRECEDENCE_W"
   Case CdoPR_INTERNET_PRECEDENCE_A:
      CdoPrTextFromCode = "CdoPR_INTERNET_PRECEDENCE_A"
   Case CdoPR_REFERRED_BY_NAME:
      CdoPrTextFromCode = "CdoPR_REFERRED_BY_NAME"
   Case CdoPR_REFERRED_BY_NAME_W:
      CdoPrTextFromCode = "CdoPR_REFERRED_BY_NAME_W"
   Case CdoPR_REFERRED_BY_NAME_A:
      CdoPrTextFromCode = "CdoPR_REFERRED_BY_NAME_A"
   Case CdoPR_SEND_INTERNET_ENCODING:
      CdoPrTextFromCode = "CdoPR_SEND_INTERNET_ENCODING"
   Case Else
      CdoPrTextFromCode = ""
   End Select

End Function ' CdoPrTextFromCode
```

Working with Address Books

In MAPI, recipient information is stored in *address books*. A MAPI address book, much like a physical address book in which you keep your friends' names and addresses, is a place to save information about potential message recipients. Address books are implemented by *address book providers*, which are software components that plug into MAPI in order to provide this feature. MAPI-compliant email systems typically come with one or more address book providers. To see the list of address book providers on your system, run the Mail applet from the Windows Control Panel, then click the Add button on the dialog box that appears. This brings up the "Add Service to Profile" dialog box, as shown in Figure 7-3. (If you don't see this dialog box on your computer, your email system is not using MAPI. See "Obtaining MAPI" in Chapter 2, *MAPI*, for more information.) The "Add Service to Profile" dialog box shows the *information services* that can be added to a profile. An information service is an address book provider, a message store provider, a transport provider, or some combination of all three. Figure 7-3 shows two address book providers: the *Outlook Address Book*, and the *Personal Address Book*. The Outlook Address Book provider is on this list because I happen to have Microsoft Outlook installed on my system. The Personal Address Book provider is supplied by MAPI itself. Although these appear to be the only address book providers available on this system, there are actually others. In Figure 7-3, note the "Microsoft Exchange Server" information service. This information service is actually a combination of message store, transport, and address book providers that know how to communicate with Microsoft Exchange Server. Choosing this information service gives me access to the global address book that has been set up by my company's network administrator on our Exchange server.

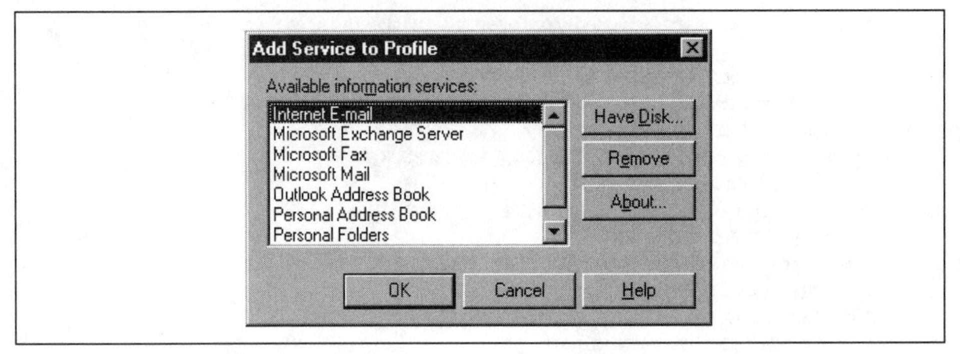

Figure 7-3. The "Add Service to Profile" dialog box

Iterating Through the Address Books

You can see from the preceding discussion that several different address books can be set up in a single profile. MAPI arranges these address books in a tree structure, with the address books all being children of a single root object. In CDO, this root object is accessed through the Session object's AddressLists collection. Figure 7-4 shows this relationship.

Each AddressList object in the AddressLists collection represents a single address book. The AddressLists collection can be iterated to examine all of the user's address books, or a particular address book can be retrieved by name, as shown here:

```
' Get the AddressList object representing the user's personal address
' book (PAB).

' CdoSession previously Dim'ed and Set.
' CdoAddressLists and CdoAddressList previously Dim'ed.

Set CdoAddressLists = CdoSession.AddressLists
Set CdoAddressList = CdoAddressLists.Item("Personal Address Book")
```

If an invalid name is specified when attempting to retrieve an AddressList object, a `CdoE_NOT_FOUND` error is raised.

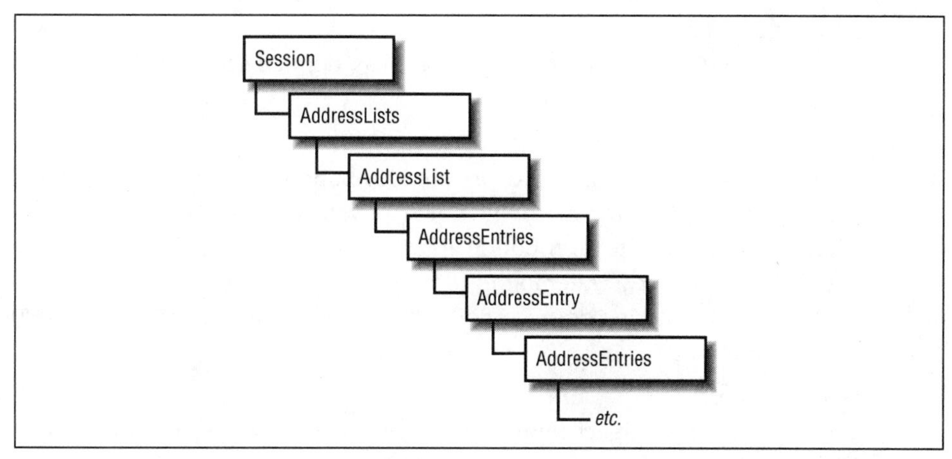

Figure 7-4. The portion of the CDO object model pertaining to the objects discussed in this section

Individual email addresses are accessed through an AddressList object's Address-Entries collection. Each AddressEntry object in the collection represents one entry in the address book.

The properties of the AddressEntry object are:

Address
: A string that specifies the address of a recipient, in whatever format is appropriate for the particular messaging system specified by the AddressEntry object's Type property. The Type property and the Address property together give the full address of the recipient, which also can be found in the Recipient object's Address property. The format of the full address is `"`***`address type`***`:`***`address`***`"`.

DisplayType
: This is a useful property that helps us deal with the fact that an AddressEntry object may actually represent something other than a single recipient's address. For example, an AddressEntry object may represent an entire distribution list. The datatype is Long. The values and their meanings are:

`CdoAgent`
: The AddressEntry represents an automated agent. In this context, an *agent* is either client or server software that handles mail delivery tasks.

`CdoDistList`
: The AddressEntry represents a *public* distribution list—one that has been set up for use by multiple users.

`CdoForum`
: The AddressEntry represents a bulletin board or public folder.

`CdoOrganization`
: The AddressEntry represents a special alias defined for a large group or organization.

`CdoPrivateDistList`
: The AddressEntry represents a *private* distribution list—one that has been set up by the user for his or her own private use. AddressEntry objects that represent private distribution lists have neither an Address property nor a Type property. Attempting to access either property when the DisplayType property is `CdoPrivateDistList` results in a `CdoE_NOT_FOUND` error being raised.

`CdoRemoteUser`
: The AddressEntry object represents a messaging user who is known to be serviced by an email server different from that servicing the logged-in user.

`CdoUser`
: The AddressEntry object represents a messaging user who is serviced by the same email server as is the logged-in user.

Fields

The Fields property holds a Fields collection, which gives access to the underlying MAPI properties applicable to the address entry.

ID

The ID property is a string that MAPI assigns to identify an object uniquely. This ID can be passed to the Session object's GetAddressEntry method to retrieve an AddressEntry object. Note that CDO does not guarantee that this ID is meaningful across MAPI sessions.

Manager

The Manager property holds a reference to an AddressEntry object that represents the user's manager in the organization. If the organization doesn't keep track of this information in the mail system, the Manager property is set to `Nothing`.

Members

If the AddressEntry object is a distribution list (that is, the value stored in the DisplayType property is `CdoDistList` or `CdoPrivateDistList`), the Members property holds an AddressEntries collection object, which represents the members of the distribution list. If the AddressEntry object is not a distribution list, the Member property is set to `Nothing`.

Name

The Name property is a string that holds the display name of the AddressEntry object.

Type

The Type property is a string (always uppercase) that specifies the type of messaging system in which the address resides. The value in this property allows MAPI to select an appropriate transport provider for message delivery. For example, a value of "`SMTP`" in this field indicates that the AddressEntry object refers to an Internet mail address. Table 7-1 shows the documented values that this property may take.

Table 7-1. Address Types

Address Type	Messaging System
3COM	3Com 3+Mail
ATT	AT&T Easylink Services
CCMAIL	Lotus cc:Mail (proposed)
COMPUSERVE	CompuServe (proposed)
EX	Microsoft Exchange Server
FAX	Fax
MAPIPDL	Personal Distribution List
MCI	MCI Mail
MHS	Novell Message Handling System
MS	Microsoft Mail Server for PC Networks
MSA	Microsoft Mail Server for AppleTalk Networks
MSFAX	Fax
MSN	The Microsoft Network
PROFS	Professional Office System
SMTP	Internet
SNADS	SNA Distributed System
TELEX	Telex (proposed)
X400	X.400 Message Handling System
X500	X.500 Directory Services

The methods of the AddressEntry object are:

Delete

Permanently removes the messaging user from the address book. If you only want to delete the recipient from a recipient list, use the Recipient object's Delete method instead.

Details

The Details method displays a dialog box with detailed information about the user represented by the AddressEntry object. Optionally, it can take as a parameter the window handle of the window that is to be the parent of the dialog box. If this parameter is not supplied, the dialog box is application-modal. Example 7-4 is a subroutine for showing the details of the sender of a given message. The resulting display is shown in Figure 7-5.

Example 7-4. Showing AddressEntry Details

```
Private Function ShowSenderDetails(ByVal CdoMessage As MAPI.Message)

   Dim CdoAddressEntry As MAPI.AddressEntry

   On Error GoTo ErrorHandler

   Set CdoAddressEntry = CdoMessage.Sender
   CdoAddressEntry.Details
   Set CdoAddressEntry = Nothing

   Exit Function

ErrorHandler:

   ' If user pressed cancel, don't treat that as an error.
   If Err.Number <> CdoE_USER_CANCEL Then
      Err.Raise Err.Number
   End If

End Function ' ShowSenderDetails
```

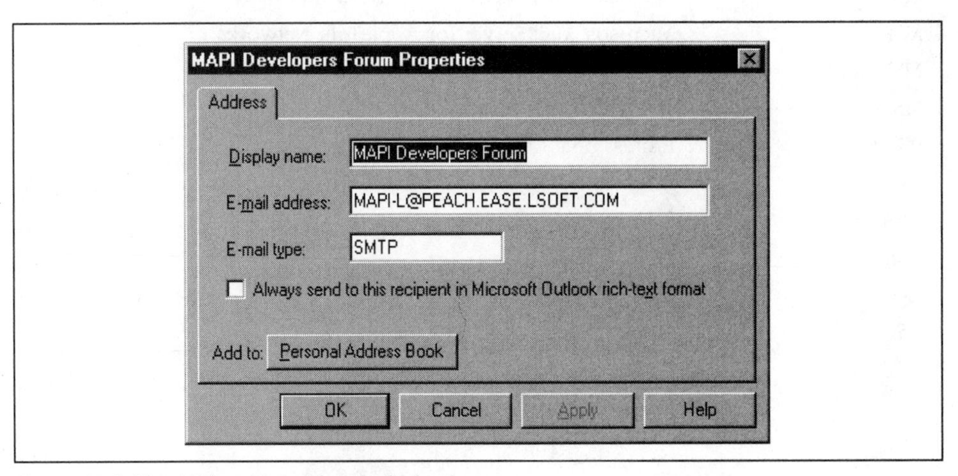

Figure 7-5. The AddressEntry details dialog box

GetFreeBusy

The GetFreeBusy method returns a string that represents the user's schedule availability for a given period of time. This method will be examined in Chapter 8, *Calendar Folders*.

IsSameAs

The IsSameAs method compares the AddressEntry object to a second AddressEntry object for equality. It's used like this:

```
' CdoAddressEntry1 and CdoAddressEntry2 previously Dim'ed and Set.

If CdoAddressEntry1.IsSameAs(CdoAddressEntry2) Then
   MsgBox "The AddressEntry objects are the same."
Else
   MsgBox "The AddressEntry objects are not the same."
End If
```

AddressEntry objects are considered to be the same if they represent the same underlying MAPI object.

Update

The Update method must be called to commit any changes made to the AddressEntry object. For example, this code fragment changes the display name of an AddressEntry object, then commits the change to permanent storage:

```
' CdoAddressEntry previously Dim'ed and Set.

CdoAddressEntry.Name = "Jane Newname"
CdoAddressEntry.Update
```

Note that such changes are relevant only if the MAPI object behind the AddressEntry object is actually an entry in an address book. For example, the following code has no effect; the Sender property of the message is unchanged.

```
' *** This code doesn't do anything. ***

' CdoMessage previously Dim'ed and Set.

Dim CdoAddressEntry As MAPI.AddressEntry

Set CdoAddressEntry = CdoMessage.Sender
CdoAddressEntry.Name = "Jane Newname"
CdoAddressEntry.Update
```

To help you visualize the address list hierarchy, Example 7-5 shows two subroutines that together print information on all users in all address books defined in a particular profile. A single call to the first subroutine, *IterateAddressLists*, accomplishes the task. The *IterateAddressLists* subroutine performs the following steps:

1. Establishes a MAPI session.
2. Obtains the top-level AddressLists collection from the Session object.
3. Opens a text file to hold the text that will be printed.
4. Iterates through all of the objects in the AddressLists collection, obtaining the AddressEntries collection from each object and passing that collection to the *RecurseAddressEntries* subroutine.

The *RecurseAddressEntries* subroutine iterates through the collection of AddressEntry objects, printing information about each object and examining it to see if it has any nested AddressEntries collections (which it would if it represented a distribution list). If an AddressEntry object has a nested AddressEntries collection, the *RecurseAddressEntries* subroutine calls itself recursively to print the nested collection's information. Sample output from this code is shown in Figure 7-6.

Example 7-5. Traversing the Address List Hierarchy

```
Public Sub IterateAddressLists()

   ' Log into MAPI and traverse the address book structure for the profile
   ' selected by the user.

   Dim CdoSession As MAPI.Session
   Dim CdoAddressLists As MAPI.AddressLists
   Dim CdoAddressList As MAPI.AddressList
   Dim CdoAddressEntries As MAPI.AddressEntries
   Dim nFileNum As Long

   ' Create a Session object and log on to MAPI.
   Set CdoSession = New MAPI.Session
   CdoSession.Logon

   ' Get the top list of address books.
   Set CdoAddressLists = CdoSession.AddressLists

   ' Here's where we're going to print our output.
   nFileNum = FreeFile
   Open "C:\AddressLists.txt" For Output As #nFileNum

   ' Each CdoAddressList represents an address book.
   For Each CdoAddressList In CdoAddressLists

      ' Print some useful information about the address book.
      Print #nFileNum, "---------------------------------------"
      Print #nFileNum, "Name: "; CdoAddressList.Name
      Print #nFileNum, "AddressEntries collection: ";

      ' Print the objects in the AddressEntries collection.
      Set CdoAddressEntries = CdoAddressList.AddressEntries
      If CdoAddressEntries.Count = 0 Then
         Print #nFileNum, "(empty)"
      Else
         Print #nFileNum, ""
         RecurseAddressEntries nFileNum, CdoAddressEntries, "    "
      End If

   Next CdoAddressList

   ' All done.
   Close #nFileNum
```

Example 7-5. Traversing the Address List Hierarchy (continued)

```
   ' Use Notepad to view the results.
   Shell "notepad.exe ""C:\AddressLists.txt""", vbNormalFocus

   Set CdoAddressEntries = Nothing
   Set CdoAddressList = Nothing
   Set CdoAddressLists = Nothing

   CdoSession.Logoff
   Set CdoSession = Nothing

End Sub ' IterateAddressLists

Private Sub RecurseAddressEntries( _
   ByVal nFileNum As Long, _
   ByVal CdoAddressEntries As MAPI.AddressEntries, _
   ByVal strIndent As String)

   ' Recursive helper subroutine used by IterateAddressLists. Output
   ' descriptive information for all of the AddressEntry objects in
   ' the given AddressEntries collection, then do the same for any
   ' nested AddressEntries collections referred to by the individual
   ' AddressEntry objects.

   ' Assumes that file #nFileNum has been opened for writing.

   Dim CdoAddressEntry As MAPI.AddressEntry
   Dim CdoAddressEntriesMembers As MAPI.AddressEntries

   For Each CdoAddressEntry In CdoAddressEntries

      Print #nFileNum, strIndent; "----------"
      Print #nFileNum, strIndent; "Name: "; CdoAddressEntry.Name
      Print #nFileNum, strIndent; "Type: "; CdoAddressEntry.Type
      Print #nFileNum, strIndent; "DisplayType: "; CdoAddressEntry.DisplayType
      Print #nFileNum, strIndent; "Address: ";
      On Error Resume Next
      Print #nFileNum, CdoAddressEntry.Address
      If Err.Number = CdoE_NOT_FOUND Then
         Print #nFileNum, "(no address)"
      End If
      On Error GoTo 0

      ' If this AddressEntry object is a distribution list, then the
      ' members of the list will be stored in the Members property.
      ' Output those members here.

      Print #nFileNum, strIndent; "Members: ";
      Set CdoAddressEntriesMembers = CdoAddressEntry.Members
      If CdoAddressEntriesMembers Is Nothing Then
         Print #nFileNum, "(none)"
      ElseIf CdoAddressEntriesMembers.Count = 0 Then
         Print #nFileNum, "(none)"
```

Example 7-5. Traversing the Address List Hierarchy (continued)

```
      Else
         Print #nFileNum, ""
         RecurseAddressEntries nFileNum, CdoAddressEntriesMembers, _
            strIndent & "   "
      End If

   Next CdoAddressEntry

   Set CdoAddressEntriesMembers = Nothing
   Set CdoAddressEntry = Nothing

End Sub ' RecurseAddressEntries
```

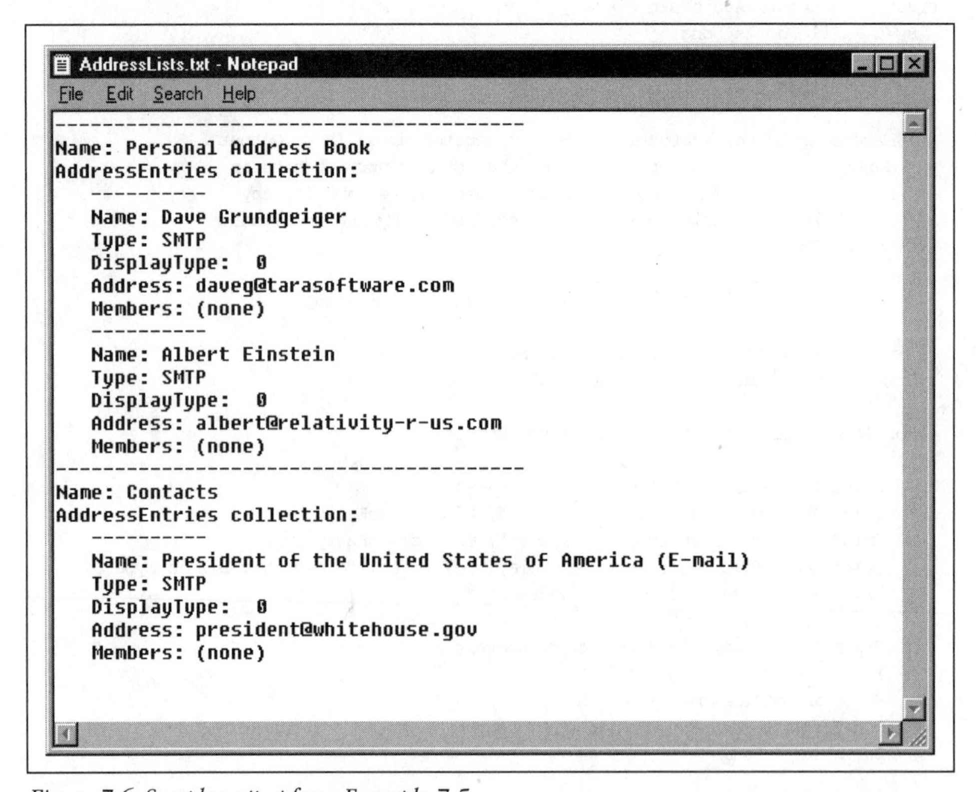

Figure 7-6. Sample output from Example 7-5

Creating and Retrieving Address Book Entries

To add a new entry to an address book:

1. Get the AddressLists collection from the Session object. Recall that the AddressLists collection represents all address books configured for the currently logged-in profile.
2. Get a particular AddressList object from the AddressLists collection.

How to Designate an Outlook Contacts Folder as a MAPI Address Book

Microsoft Outlook comes with an address book provider that can make any Outlook contacts folder (i.e., a folder that contains Contact items) appear as an address book. To use this feature, two requirements must be satisfied:

- The "Outlook Address Book" service provider must be added to the user's profile.
- The properties of the contacts folder in Outlook must be set to allow the folder to appear as an email address book.

To satisfy the first requirement, run the Mail applet from the Control Panel. This displays the properties dialog box for the user's default profile. Assuming this is the profile that is to be changed, click the Add button. The "Add Service to Profile" dialog box is displayed. Select "Outlook Address Book" and click OK. Click OK again to dismiss the profile properties dialog box. For more detailed information on working with profiles, refer to Chapter 2.

To satisfy the second requirement, in Microsoft Outlook right-click a folder that holds Contact items. This displays a context menu. From the context menu, choose Properties. This displays the Properties dialog box for the selected folder. Click the "Outlook Address Book" tab. This reveals the "Show this folder as an e-mail Address Book" check box. Check this box to cause the folder to appear as an address book. Click OK to accept the change.

3. Get the AddressEntries collection from the AddressList object.
4. Call the Add method of the AddressEntries collection to add a new address. Its syntax is:

```
Set CdoAddressEntry = CdoAddrEntries.Add(Emailtype[, Name][, Address])
```

The parameters are:

`Emailtype`
: A Variant/String that specifies the type of messaging system in which the address resides. It corresponds to the Type property of the AddressEntry object, and can take the same values (already shown in Table 7-1).

`Name`
: A Variant/String that specifies the display name for the new AddressEntry object. It corresponds to the Name property of the AddressEntry object.

`Address`
: A Variant/String that specifies the address of the new AddressEntry object. It corresponds to the Address property of the new AddressEntry object.

5. Call the Update method of the AddressEntry object returned by the Add method.

Example 7-6 illustrates these steps. This example adds a new user ("Happy Gilmore") to the Personal Address Book.

Example 7-6. Adding a New Address to an Address Book

```
Dim CdoSession As MAPI.Session
Dim CdoAddressLists As MAPI.AddressLists
Dim CdoAddressList As MAPI.AddressList
Dim CdoAddressEntries As MAPI.AddressEntries
Dim CdoAddressEntry As MAPI.AddressEntry

' Create a new session object and logon.
Set CdoSession = New MAPI.Session
CdoSession.Logon

' Get the master list of address books for this profile.
Set CdoAddressLists = CdoSession.AddressLists

' Get the user's personal address book (PAB).
Set CdoAddressList = CdoAddressLists.Item("Personal Address Book")

' Get the members of the PAB.
Set CdoAddressEntries = CdoAddressList.AddressEntries

' Add a new member.
Set CdoAddressEntry = CdoAddressEntries.Add(Emailtype:="SMTP", _
   Name:="Happy Gilmore", Address:="hgilmore@company.com")

' Commit the change.
CdoAddressEntry.Update

' Clean up.
Set CdoAddressEntry = Nothing
Set CdoAddressEntries = Nothing
Set CdoAddressList = Nothing
Set CdoAddressLists = Nothing

CdoSession.Logoff
Set CdoSession = Nothing
```

Note in Example 7-6 that the desired address book (in this case, the "Personal Address Book") is obtained simply by naming it as the index to the AddressLists collection.

Not all address books are modifiable. For example, an organization may have a global address book for use by all users. If an attempt is made to call the Add method on this address book's AddressEntries collection from a process not having sufficient privileges, a `CdoE_NO_ACCESS` error is raised. Similarly, contacts folders being used as address books can't be updated in this manner. Attempting to do so will also raise a CdoE_NO_ACCESS error. (There are ways to modify items in contacts folders. See Chapter 10, *Contacts Folders* for details.)

If an entry already exists where the name, address, and address type all equal the values supplied in the Add method, a CdoE_COLLISION error is raised.

Adding a Message Sender to an Address Book

Adding a message sender to an address book is just a special case of adding a new user to an address book. The following fragment shows the relevant code:

```
' CdoMessage previously Dim'ed and Set.
' CdoAddressEntries previously Dim'ed and Set to the AddressEntries
' collection of the address book to be updated.

Dim CdoAddressEntrySender As MAPI.AddressEntry
Dim CdoAddressEntryNew As MAPI.AddressEntry

' Get the (temporary) AddressEntry object that represents the message
' sender.
Set CdoAddressEntrySender = CdoMessage.Sender

' Add an entry to the address book, based on the sender properties.
Set CdoAddressEntryNew = CdoAddressEntries.Add( _
   Emailtype:=CdoAddressEntrySender.Type, _
   Name:=CdoAddressEntrySender.Name, _
   Address:=CdoAddressEntrySender.Address)

' Save the changes.
CdoAddressEntryNew.Update

' Clean up.
Set CdoAddressEntryNew = Nothing
Set CdoAddressEntrySender = Nothing
```

The Message Object's Sender property returns a reference to an AddressEntry object that represents the sender of the message. Although this AddressEntry object can't be added directly to an AddressEntries collection, a new AddressEntry object can be created based on the values in the sender's AddressEntry object.

Creating a Distribution List

Creating a distribution list is just like adding a new user to an address book. After all, users and distribution lists are both represented by AddressEntry objects, the distinction being made by the value of the AddressEntry object's Type property. The code in Example 7-7 logs into MAPI and creates a distribution list called "My Distribution List" in the Personal Address Book.

Example 7-7. Creating a Distribution List

```
Dim CdoSession As MAPI.Session
Dim CdoAddressLists As MAPI.AddressLists
Dim CdoAddressList As MAPI.AddressList
Dim CdoAddressEntries As MAPI.AddressEntries
Dim CdoAddressEntry As MAPI.AddressEntry

' Create a new Session object and log on.
Set CdoSession = New MAPI.Session
CdoSession.Logon

' Get the Personal Address Book's AddressEntries collection
Set CdoAddressLists = CdoSession.AddressLists
Set CdoAddressList = CdoAddressLists.Item("Personal Address Book")
Set CdoAddressEntries = CdoAddressList.AddressEntries

' Add a new entry for the distribution list.
Set CdoAddressEntry = CdoAddressEntries.Add( _
   Emailtype:="MAPIPDL", Name:="My Distribution List")

' Save the changes.
CdoAddressEntry.Update

' Clean up.
Set CdoAddressEntry = Nothing
Set CdoAddressEntries = Nothing
Set CdoAddressList = Nothing
Set CdoAddressLists = Nothing

CdoSession.Logoff
Set CdoSession = Nothing
```

Recall that when an AddressEntry object represents a distribution list, its Members property holds an AddressEntries collection which represents the members of the list. To add a new member, call the AddressEntries collection's Add method, as shown in Example 7-8.

Example 7-8. Adding a Member to a Distribution List

```
Dim CdoSession As MAPI.Session
Dim CdoAddressLists As MAPI.AddressLists
Dim CdoAddressList As MAPI.AddressList
Dim CdoAddressEntries As MAPI.AddressEntries
Dim CdoAddressEntry As MAPI.AddressEntry
Dim CdoAddressEntriesMembers As MAPI.AddressEntries
Dim CdoAddressEntryNewMember As MAPI.AddressEntry

' Create a new Session object and log on.
Set CdoSession = New MAPI.Session
CdoSession.Logon

' Get the Personal Address Book's AddressEntries collection.
Set CdoAddressLists = CdoSession.AddressLists
```

Example 7-8. Adding a Member to a Distribution List (continued)

```
Set CdoAddressList = CdoAddressLists.Item("Personal Address Book")
Set CdoAddressEntries = CdoAddressList.AddressEntries

' Get the AddressEntry for the desired distribution list.
Set CdoAddressEntry = CdoAddressEntries.Item("My Distribution List")

' Get the distribution list's members collection.
Set CdoAddressEntriesMembers = CdoAddressEntry.Members

' Add a new member to the list.
Set CdoAddressEntryNewMember = CdoAddressEntriesMembers.Add( _
   Emailtype:="SMTP", Name:="Jeanne d'Arc", Address:="jarc@orleans.fr")

' Save the changes.
CdoAddressEntryNewMember.Update

' Clean up.
Set CdoAddressEntryNewMember = Nothing
Set CdoAddressEntriesMembers = Nothing
Set CdoAddressEntry = Nothing
Set CdoAddressEntries = Nothing
Set CdoAddressList = Nothing
Set CdoAddressLists = Nothing

CdoSession.Logoff
Set CdoSession = Nothing
```

Unfortunately, CDO doesn't give us a way to associate an existing AddressEntry object with an address list. When the AddressEntries Add method is called, a brand-new AddressEntry object is created from the values supplied.

To delete a member from a distribution list, call the AddressEntry object's Delete method, as shown here:

```
CdoAddressEntryMember.Delete
```

Filters

To assist with locating specific items in Messages and AddressEntries collections, CDO provides the MessageFilter and AddressEntryFilter objects. Every Messages collection has a MessageFilter object associated with it, which can be accessed through the Messages collection's Filter property. Similarly, every AddressEntries collection has an AddressEntryFilter object associated with it, accessible through the AddressEntries collection's Filter property. By setting properties on a filter object, the associated collection retrieves only those items that fulfill the criteria thus specified. This is far more efficient than using code to read through the entire collection, examine each item to determine if it meets the criteria, and act on only the items of interest. The code in Example 7-9 processes only unread messages having a message class of "`IPM.MyMessageClass`".

Example 7-9. Constraining a Messages Collection

```
' CdoSession previously Dim'ed and Set.

Dim CdoFolder As MAPI.Folder
Dim CdoMessages As MAPI.Messages
Dim CdoMessageFilter As MAPI.MessageFilter
Dim CdoMessage As MAPI.Message

Set CdoFolder = CdoSession.Inbox
Set CdoMessages = CdoFolder.Messages
Set CdoMessageFilter = CdoMessages.Filter

' Constrain the Messages collection.
CdoMessageFilter.Type = "IPM.MyMessageClass"
CdoMessageFilter.Unread = True

For Each CdoMessage In CdoMessages
   ' Do something with the message.
Next CdoMessage

' Clean up.
Set CdoMessage = Nothing
Set CdoMessageFilter = Nothing
Set CdoMessages = Nothing
Set CdoFolder = Nothing
```

The AddressEntryFilter is used in precisely the same way. The code in Example 7-10 processes all address entries that have a display name starting with the string "Dave".

Example 7-10. Constraining an AddressEntries Collection

```
' CdoSession previously Dim'ed and Set.

Dim CdoAddressLists As MAPI.AddressLists
Dim CdoAddressList As MAPI.AddressList
Dim CdoAddressEntries As MAPI.AddressEntries
Dim CdoAddressEntryFilter As MAPI.AddressEntryFilter
Dim CdoAddressEntry As MAPI.AddressEntry

Set CdoAddressLists = CdoSession.AddressLists

For Each CdoAddressList In CdoAddressLists

   Set CdoAddressEntries = CdoAddressList.AddressEntries

   ' Constrain the address entries collection.
   Set CdoAddressEntryFilter = CdoAddressEntries.Filter
   CdoAddressEntryFilter.Name = "Dave"
```

Example 7-10. Constraining an AddressEntries Collection (continued)

```
   ' Process the "Dave" entries.
   For Each CdoAddressEntry In CdoAddressEntries
      ' Process the entry.
   Next CdoAddressEntry

Next CdoAddressList

' Clean up
Set CdoAddressEntry = Nothing
Set CdoAddressEntryFilter = Nothing
Set CdoAddressEntries = Nothing
Set CdoAddressList = Nothing
Set CdoAddressLists = Nothing
```

Summary

In this chapter, you gained a lot more detailed knowledge, not only about how CDO works with MAPI, but also about working with various CDO elements, including messages, folders, address books, and filters.

In the next chapter, you'll learn all about how calendars and schedules work, including automating scheduled tasks and getting free/busy information from other users.

8

Calendar Folders

Calendar folders store schedule information—i.e., appointments and meetings. Using CDO terminology, an *appointment* is an allocated block of time, and a *meeting* is an appointment that involves multiple people. Appointments (and therefore meetings) are stored as messages of a special type in the Messages collection of a calendar folder. A user may have more than one calendar folder, but only one of them is the default calendar folder. It is the default calendar folder that is considered to represent the user's personal schedule.

CDO provides the ability to create appointments, meetings, and *meeting requests* programmatically. (A meeting request is another special kind of message, which is used to invite other users to a meeting. Don't confuse a meeting request with the meeting itself.) Appointments and meetings are represented in CDO by AppointmentItem objects; meeting requests and responses to meeting requests are represented by MeetingItem objects. These relationships are shown in Figure 8-1.

This chapter shows how to create appointments, meetings, and meeting requests programmatically, including recurring appointments and meetings. Also explained are how to move and delete appointments, how to create recurring appointments and meetings, how to filter a calendar folder's Messages collection so that only a certain time period is seen, and how to retrieve free/busy information for other users. In short, CDO gives complete and flexible programmatic access to schedule information.

Finding the Default Calendar Folder

As mentioned, a user is permitted to have as many calendar folders as she likes, but only one of them is considered to hold her personal schedule information. This is the so-called *default calendar folder*, and CDO provides a simple way to

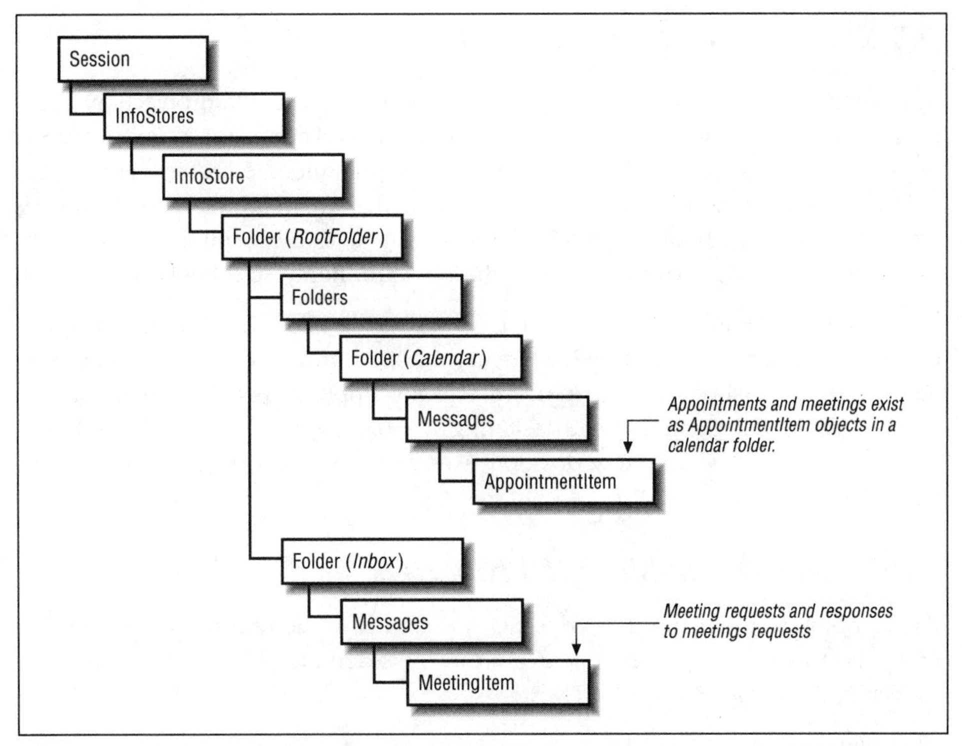

Figure 8-1. The location of AppointmentItem and MeetingItem objects in the CDO object model

get access to it. To do so, use the Session object's GetDefaultFolder method, with an argument of `CdoDefaultFolderCalendar`, as shown here:

```
' gCdoSession previously Dim'ed, Set, and logged on using valid profile.
Dim CdoFolderCalendar As MAPI.Folder

Set CdoFolderCalendar = _
   gCdoSession.GetDefaultFolder(CdoDefaultFolderCalendar)
```

When I refer to the Calendar folder (with a capital "C"), I mean the user's default calendar folder.

Microsoft documents a bug that sometimes causes the GetDefault-Folder method to fail. According to Microsoft, if a CDO application shares a profile with Outlook 98, the GetDefaultFolder raises a `CdoE_NO_SUPPORT` error when attempting to get the default calendar folder. In testing, I have found that this is not always the case, but I haven't been able to determine exactly when it occurs. If Outlook 98 and CDO applications must run on the same computer, Microsoft recommends having them use different profiles.

Appointments and Meetings

Appointments and meetings are represented by AppointmentItem objects in a calendar folder's Messages collection. The `AppointmentItem` class is said to *derive* from the `Message` class, which means that an AppointmentItem object is a special kind of Message object. Properties and methods that are valid for Message objects are also valid for AppointmentItem objects, with a few exceptions. Specifically, AppointmentItem objects don't support the Forward, Reply, and ReplyAll methods.

Because the AppointmentItem object is central to reading and creating appointments and meetings, I'll start with a discussion of its properties and methods. Subsequent sections show how to retrieve existing appointments and meetings (in "Viewing Calendar Contents" and "Filtering Appointments by StartTime and EndTime"), and how to create new ones (in "Creating an Appointment" and "Creating a Meeting").

AppointmentItem-Specific Properties

The AppointmentItem-specific properties are shown in the following list. They are in addition to the properties inherited from the `Message` class. Unless otherwise indicated, the properties are read/write:

AllDayEvent

Indicates that the appointment is an all-day or multiple-day event if set to `True`. The AllDayEvent property is not used on recurring appointments and meetings. Instead, use the corresponding property on the RecurrencePattern object. (The RecurrencePattern object is discussed later in this chapter.) The datatype of the AllDayEvent property is Boolean. The default for newly created appointments is `False`.

BusyStatus

Indicates the commitment status of the user for this appointment. The values that this property can take are:

`CdoFree`

Although the user has this appointment on her schedule, the time during this appointment is considered to be open for other appointments. This setting would be appropriate if the user wanted to be reminded of a meeting but was not attending the meeting herself.

`CdoTentative`

The user's time is tentatively committed for this appointment. This setting would be appropriate if the user is invited to a meeting, but she is not sure whether she will go.

`CdoBusy`
: The user's time is committed for this appointment.

`CdoOutOfOffice`
: The user's time is committed for this appointment that takes place away from the office.

Note that none of the values for the BusyStatus property prohibits appointments from being scheduled at the same time as each other. The value in this property is for informational purposes only. For example, if a user schedules an appointment for herself that conflicts with an existing appointment marked with `CdoBusy`, her client application may alert her to the conflict, but she is still allowed to schedule the appointment. The datatype of the BusyStatus property is Long. The default for newly created appointments is `CdoBusy`.

Duration
: Gives the duration of an appointment, in minutes. The Duration property is read-only. If an application needs to set or change the duration of an appointment, it must set the AppointmentItem object's StartTime and EndTime properties. The datatype of the Duration property is Long. The default for a newly created appointment is 30 minutes.

EndTime
: The ending date and time of the appointment. The datatype of the EndTime property is Date. The default for a newly created appointment is the current date and time plus 30 minutes.

IsRecurring
: Indicates that the appointment is recurring if set to `True`. This is a read-only property. To make an appointment recurring, use the GetRecurrencePattern method. Recurring appointments are discussed in detail later in this chapter. The datatype of the IsRecurring property is Boolean. The default for a newly created appointment is `False`.

Location
: A text description of the physical location of an appointment. The datatype of the Location property is String. The default for a newly created appointment is an empty string.

MeetingResponseStatus
: When a messaging user responds to a meeting request, the response arrives as a MeetingItem object in the Inbox of the meeting organizer. The MeetingItem object has a method, GetAssociatedAppointment, that returns the associated AppointmentItem object. When a meeting's AppointmentItem object is obtained in this way, CDO automatically sets its MeetingResponseStatus property based on the MeetingItem object that was used to obtain the AppointmentItem object. Thus the MeetingResponseStatus property of an AppointmentItem

object obtained in this way indicates the user's response to the meeting request. The values that this property can take are:

`CdoResponseNone`
: This is the value returned by the MeetingResponseStatus property on AppointmentItem objects that don't represent a meeting response.

`CdoResponseAccepted`
: The user has accepted the meeting.

`CdoResponseDeclined`
: The user has declined the meeting.

`CdoResponseTentative`
: The user has tentatively accepted the meeting.

`CdoResponseOrganized`
: This is the value returned by the MeetingResponseStatus property on AppointmentItem objects that don't represent a meeting response, when the user's email client is Microsoft Schedule+.

The datatype of the MeetingResponseStatus property is Long. The default value for a newly created appointment is `CdoResponseNone`.

MeetingStatus

Indicates whether the AppointmentItem object represents an appointment (no other users are involved) or a meeting (other users are involved). In addition, if the AppointmentItem object represents a meeting, the MeetingStatus property indicates whether the meeting request has been received by the other participants and whether the meeting has been cancelled. The values this property can take are:

`CdoNonMeeting`
: The AppointmentItem object represents an appointment, not a meeting.

`CdoMeeting`
: The AppointmentItem object represents a meeting.

`CdoMeetingCancelled`
: The meeting has been cancelled.

`CdoMeetingReceived`
: The meeting requests have been received by the other participants.

The datatype of the MeetingStatus property is Long. The default value for a newly created appointment is `CdoNonMeeting`.

Organizer

Returns an AddressEntry object representing the messaging user that created the meeting that the AppointmentItem represents. This property can't be accessed when the AppointmentItem doesn't represent a meeting (i.e., when the AppointmentItem object's MeetingStatus property is `CdoNonMeeting`). Attempting to do so raises a `CdoE_NO_SUPPORT` error. The datatype of the Organizer property is AddressEntry. This property is read-only.

ReminderMinutesBeforeStart
: Indicates the number of minutes prior to the start of an appointment that a meeting reminder should be given to the user. It's up to the client application to act on this value—CDO itself doesn't remind the user. The datatype of the ReminderMinutesBeforeStart property is Long. The default value for this property is 15.

ReminderSet
: Indicates whether a reminder is to be given to the user prior to an appointment. The datatype of the ReminderSet property is Boolean. The default value for a newly created appointment is `True`.

ReplyTime
: When a messaging user accepts a meeting request, an AppointmentItem object is created in that user's Calendar folder. The ReplyTime property of that AppointmentItem object can be used to store the date and time at which the reply was made. Note that CDO doesn't perform this task automatically—your client application must do so itself, if that behavior is desired. The datatype of the ReplyTime property is Date. There is no default value. Attempting to access the ReplyTime property before it has been set raises a `CdoE_NOT_FOUND` error.

ResponseRequested
: Indicates that the messaging user who created the meeting desires a response if set to `True`. The datatype of the ResponseRequested property is Boolean. The default value for a newly created appointment is `True`, even if the appointment does not represent a meeting.

StartTime
: The StartTime property is the starting date and time of the appointment. The datatype of the StartTime property is Date. The default for a newly created appointment is the current date and time.

AppointmentItem-Specific Methods

The following are the AppointmentItem-specific methods (they are in addition to the methods inherited from the Message class):

ClearRecurrencePattern
: Turns a recurring appointment into a nonrecurring appointment.

GetRecurrencePattern

Returns a RecurrencePattern object representing the recurrence pattern of the appointment. If the appointment is nonrecurring, calling this method turns the appointment into a recurring appointment and returns a RecurrencePattern object.

Respond

Meeting requests arrive in a messaging user's Inbox as MeetingItem objects. To respond to such requests, a MeetingItem object's GetAssociatedAppointment method is called to obtain an AppointmentItem object that represents the meeting. The Respond method is then called on the AppointmentItem object thus obtained. This in turn returns another MeetingItem object. The properties of this MeetingItem object are set as desired to indicate whether the meeting is accepted or declined, and the MeetingItem object's Send method is called to send the reply on its way to the meeting organizer. Its syntax is:

```
oMeetingItem.Respond(RespondType)
```

where *RespondType* can be `CdoResponseAccepted`, `CdoReponseDeclined`, or `CdoResponseTentative`; the meaning of these constants is described in greater detail earlier in the discussion of the MeetingResponseStatus property.

Viewing Calendar Contents

Appointment and meeting information is retrieved in one of the following four ways:

1. Iterate through the entire Messages collection of the calendar folder to process all AppointmentItem objects. The following code does this:

```
' gCdoSession previously Dim'ed, Set, and logged on.

Dim CdoFolder As MAPI.Folder
Dim CdoMessages As MAPI.Messages
Dim CdoAppointmentItem As MAPI.AppointmentItem

' Get the user's Calendar folder.
Set CdoFolder = gCdoSession.GetDefaultFolder(CdoDefaultFolderCalendar)

' Get the collection of appointments.
Set CdoMessages = CdoFolder.Messages

' Loop for each appointment.
For Each CdoAppointmentItem In CdoMessages
    '
    ' Code that does something with an AppointmentItem object
    '
Next CdoAppointmentItem
```

2. Apply a filter to the Messages collection, then iterate through the resulting members. This technique is described in the next section.

3. Invoke the GetAssociatedAppointment method of the MeetingItem object. This was discussed earlier in this chapter under "Appointments and Meetings," in the discussion of the MeetingResponseStatus property of the Appointment-Item object.
4. If the message ID of the appointment or meeting is known, invoke the Get-Message method of the Session object, as shown here:

```
' CdoSession previously Dim'ed, Set, and logged on.
' strMessageID previously Dim'ed and assigned.
Dim CdoAppointmentItem As MAPI.AppointmentItem
Set CdoAppointmentItem = CdoSession.GetMessage(strMessageID)
```

The message ID can be found in the ID property of the AppointmentItem object.

Filtering Appointments by StartTime and EndTime

By default, a calendar folder's Messages collection contains all of the user's appointments. In most applications, it's desirable to cut this down to just the appointments that fall within a certain date or time range (for example, when the application is displaying the current day's or week's appointments). This can be achieved with the MessageFilter object, available through the Messages collection's Filter property.

The MessageFilter object was introduced in Chapter 7, *Enhancing the Email Client*, and it's used here in much the same way. However, when using the Message-Filter object to filter appointments, only the start time and end time can be filtered. If an attempt is made to filter other properties, a `CdoE_TOO_COMPLEX` error is raised. Further, the MessageFilter object doesn't have explicit properties for filtering the start time and end time, so the Fields collection must be used to achieve this result. The Fields collection provides a way to access MAPI properties that aren't otherwise exposed by CDO. The Fields collection is examined in detail in Chapter 9, *Task Folders*, where it allows us to access task information. (CDO objects don't have any properties that expose task information.) For the present discussion it will suffice to note that the start and end date properties of the MessageFilter object can be set with the following code, which is taken from Example 8-1, to be shown shortly:

```
Set CdoFields = CdoMessageFilter.Fields
Set CdoField = CdoFields.Add(CdoPR_START_DATE, dtStartOnOrBefore)
Set CdoField = CdoFields.Add(CdoPR_END_DATE, dtEndOnOrAfter)
```

The two constants, `CdoPR_START_DATE` and `CdoPR_END_DATE`, are defined by CDO. They represent the MAPI properties `PR_START_DATE` and `PR_END_DATE`, which in turn represent an appointment's start and end dates, respectively. (MAPI properties were explained in Chapter 2, *MAPI*.)

Example 8-1 shows a subroutine that takes as parameters the start time and end time to filter against, applies the filter to the Messages collection in the user's default calendar folder, then prints the filtered messages to Visual Basic's Immediate window. Sample output is shown in Figure 8-2.

Example 8-1. Filtering a Collection of AppointmentItem Objects

```
Private Sub ShowAppointments(ByVal dtStartOnOrBefore As Date, _
   ByVal dtEndOnOrAfter As Date)

   ' gCdoSession previously Dim'ed, Set, and logged on with valid profile.

   Dim CdoFolder As MAPI.Folder
   Dim CdoMessages As MAPI.Messages
   Dim CdoMessageFilter As MAPI.MessageFilter
   Dim CdoFields As MAPI.Fields
   Dim CdoField As MAPI.Field
   Dim CdoAppointmentItem As MAPI.AppointmentItem

   ' Print the parameters that were passed.
   Debug.Print "dtStartOnOrBefore = #"; dtStartOnOrBefore; "#"
   Debug.Print "dtEndOnOrAfter = #"; dtEndOnOrAfter; "#"
   Debug.Print

   ' Get the user's Calendar folder.
   Set CdoFolder = gCdoSession.GetDefaultFolder(CdoDefaultFolderCalendar)

   ' Get the folder's collection of appointments.
   Set CdoMessages = CdoFolder.Messages

   ' Get the collection's MessageFilter object.
   Set CdoMessageFilter = CdoMessages.Filter

   ' Get the filter object's Fields collection, and add two fields.
   Set CdoFields = CdoMessageFilter.Fields
   Set CdoField = CdoFields.Add(CdoPR_START_DATE, dtStartOnOrBefore)
   Set CdoField = CdoFields.Add(CdoPR_END_DATE, dtEndOnOrAfter)

   ' Print the information for each appointment to Visual Basic's
   ' immediate window.
   For Each CdoAppointmentItem In CdoMessages
      Debug.Print "----------"
      Debug.Print "Subject = """; CdoAppointmentItem.Subject; """"
      Debug.Print "StartTime = #"; CdoAppointmentItem.StartTime; "#"
      Debug.Print "EndTime = #"; CdoAppointmentItem.EndTime; "#"
   Next CdoAppointmentItem

   ' Clean up.
   Set CdoAppointmentItem = Nothing
   Set CdoField = Nothing
```

Example 8-1. Filtering a Collection of AppointmentItem Objects (continued)

```
    Set CdoFields = Nothing
    Set CdoMessageFilter = Nothing
    Set CdoMessages = Nothing
    Set CdoFolder = Nothing

End Sub ' ShowAppointments
```

```
Immediate
dtStartOnOrBefore = #6-Sep-1999 11:59:59 PM #
dtEndOnOrAfter = #6-Sep-1999 #

----------
Subject = "Monday Meeting"
StartTime = #6-Sep-1999 10:00:00 AM #
EndTime = #6-Sep-1999 10:15:00 AM #
----------
Subject = "Client Meeting"
StartTime = #6-Sep-1999 11:00:00 AM #
EndTime = #6-Sep-1999 12:00:00 PM #
----------
Subject = "Cake Day"
StartTime = #6-Sep-1999 1:00:00 PM #
EndTime = #6-Sep-1999 1:15:00 PM #
```

Figure 8-2. Sample output from the code in Example 8-1

Take another look at these lines from Example 8-1:

```
    ' Get the filter object's Fields collection, and add two fields.
    Set CdoFields = CdoMessageFilter.Fields
    Set CdoField = CdoFields.Add(CdoPR_START_DATE, dtStartOnOrBefore)
    Set CdoField = CdoFields.Add(CdoPR_END_DATE, dtEndOnOrAfter)
```

When writing code that sets these fields, make sure you understand how CDO uses these values. CDO limits the Messages collection such that it contains AppointmentItem objects that have a StartTime value on *or before* the value that you set for the `CdoPR_START_DATE` property, and that have an EndTime value on *or after* the value that you set for the `CdoPR_END_DATE` property. This can seem a little counterintuitive when you first work with it, because it amounts to setting the `CdoPR_START_DATE` property to be the end of the time period for which to filter, and setting the `CdoPR_END_DATE` property to be the start of the time period for which to filter.

Creating an Appointment

Creating an appointment is much like creating a message, which we did in Chapter 6, *An Email Client Application*. To create an appointment, get a reference to the folder in which you'd like to create the appointment, then call the Add method of the folder's Messages collection. The syntax of the Add method is the same here as it is when creating an email message. (See the "Sending Mail" section in Chapter 6.) Once the item is created, set its appointment-specific properties as desired and call the AppointmentItem object's Update method to save the appointment in the message store. Example 8-2 demonstrates creating an appointment that begins at 10:00 on the morning of April 5, 2001, and ends that same morning at 10:30. Note in the example that the user's time is being marked as busy, and also that the user will be reminded of the appointment 15 minutes prior to its start time.

Example 8-2. Creating an Appointment

```
' gCdoSession previously Dim'ed, Set, and loggon on with valid profile.
Dim CdoFolder As MAPI.Folder
Dim CdoMessages As MAPI.Messages
Dim CdoAppointmentItem As MAPI.AppointmentItem

' Get the user's Calendar folder.
Set CdoFolder = gCdoSession.GetDefaultFolder(CdoDefaultFolderCalendar)

' Get the folder's Messages collection.
Set CdoMessages = CdoFolder.Messages

' Add a new item to the Messages collection.
Set CdoAppointmentItem = CdoMessages.Add

' Set the appointment's properties.
With CdoAppointmentItem
    .Subject = "XYZ Company Proposal"
    .Text = "XYZ is coming to demonstrate their widgets."
    .StartTime = #4/5/2001 10:00:00 AM# ' 5-Apr-2001
    .EndTime = #4/5/2001 10:30:00 AM#
    .BusyStatus = CdoBusy
    .ReminderSet = True
    .ReminderMinutesBeforeStart = 15
End With

' Save the appointment.
CdoAppointmentItem.Update

' Cleanup
Set CdoAppointmentItem = Nothing
Set CdoMessages = Nothing
Set CdoFolder = Nothing
```

Note that nothing prohibits creating appointments that occur at the same time as existing appointments. A user may wish to have multiple appointments scheduled concurrently, so it's not a good idea to prohibit it. However, you may want to have your application alert the user to such conflicts. To do so, read the free/busy data for the user prior to saving the appointment. (Reading free/busy data is discussed later in this chapter, in the section "Getting Free/Busy Information.") If the user is shown to be busy during the time of the appointment, allow the user to choose how to handle it. From this discussion, it also follows that if you are writing an application that displays calendar information, you must be prepared to display appointments that happen concurrently. Outlook does a nice job of this, as shown in Figure 8-3.

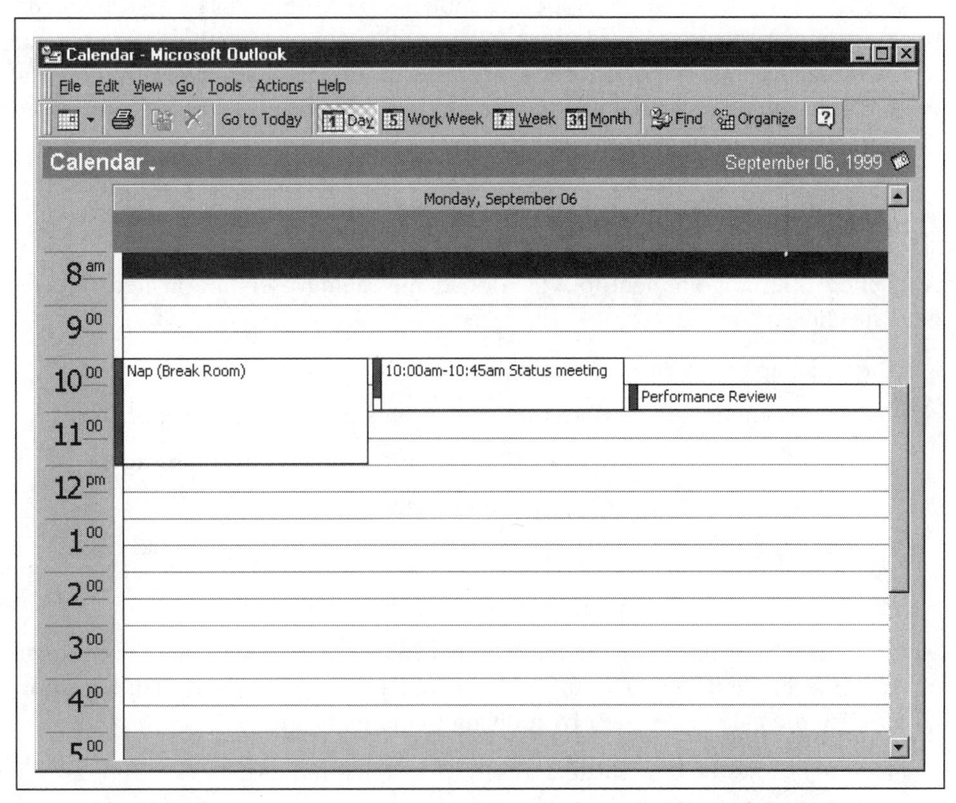

Figure 8-3. Multiple concurrent appointment items, as shown in Microsoft Outlook

To move an appointment to a different time of day, or even to a different date, simply set its StartTime and EndTime properties to the new desired values.

Deleting an Appointment

To delete an appointment, call the AppointmentItem object's Delete method, as shown here:

```
CdoAppointmentItem.Delete
```

If you want the appointment to be moved to the "Deleted Items" folder, rather than being deleted, supply the Delete method's optional argument:

```
CdoAppointmentItem.Delete DeletedItems:=True
```

If the appointment is recurring, the result depends on whether the AppointmentItem object represents the original appointment or a specific recurrence. If the AppointmentItem object represents the original appointment, the Delete method deletes the entire series. If the AppointmentItem object represents a specific recurrence, only that recurrence is deleted. Whether the AppointmentItem object refers to the original appointment or to a specific recurrence is determined by how the object is obtained, as described later in this chapter, in the section titled "Recurrence."

Creating a Meeting

A meeting is an appointment to which other messaging users are invited. To create a meeting:

1. Create an appointment as already described.
2. Set the AppointmentItem object's MeetingStatus property to `CdoMeeting`.
3. Add recipients in the same way as is done for standard email messages.
4. Call the AppointmentItem object's Send method.

This process does two things:

- It creates an appointment in the user's own calendar folder.
- It sends a message to the identified recipients. The recipients see the message as a MeetingItem object in their Inbox folders. Recipients can then accept or decline the meeting request by replying to the message.

Example 8-3 shows how to create and send a meeting request.

Example 8-3. Creating and Sending a Meeting Request

```
' gCdoSession previously Dim'ed, Set, and logged on with valid profile.

Dim CdoFolder As MAPI.Folder
Dim CdoMessages As MAPI.Messages
Dim CdoAppointmentItem As MAPI.AppointmentItem
Dim CdoRecipients As MAPI.Recipients
Dim CdoRecipient As MAPI.Recipient

' Get the user's calendar folder.
Set CdoFolder = gCdoSession.GetDefaultFolder(CdoDefaultFolderCalendar)

' Get the folder's collection of appointments.
Set CdoMessages = CdoFolder.Messages
```

Example 8-3. Creating and Sending a Meeting Request (continued)

```
' Create an appointment.
Set CdoAppointmentItem = CdoMessages.Add

' Set the appointment's properties.
CdoAppointmentItem.Subject = "Let's have lunch"
CdoAppointmentItem.StartTime = #7/1/2000 12:00:00 PM#
CdoAppointmentItem.EndTime = #7/1/2000 1:00:00 PM#

' Turn the appointment into a meeting.
CdoAppointmentItem.MeetingStatus = CdoMeeting

' Invite someone.
Set CdoRecipients = CdoAppointmentItem.Recipients
Set CdoRecipient = CdoRecipients.Add("Annemarie")
CdoRecipient.Resolve

' Send the request.
CdoAppointmentItem.Send

' Clean up.
Set CdoRecipient = Nothing
Set CdoRecipients = Nothing
Set CdoAppointmentItem = Nothing
Set CdoMessages = Nothing
Set CdoFolder = Nothing
```

Getting Free/Busy Information

It's not necessary to know another user's schedule in order to send her a meeting request. If the other user is busy, she is perfectly free to decline the request. However, it is clearly more efficient if the meeting organizer is able to check for mutually free times before sending a meeting request.

Free/busy information is retrieved via the Recipient object's GetFreeBusy method. The syntax is:

```
strFreeBusy = CdoRecipient.GetFreeBusy(StartTime, EndTime, Interval)
```

The method returns a string that is encoded to represent the messaging user's free/busy status during the specified period. Each character in the returned string represents one time slot, where the duration of a time slot is given by the *`Interval`* parameter. The parameters are used as follows:

`StartTime`
: This is a Variant/Date that specifies the start date and time of the block of time for which to check free/busy status.

`EndTime`
: This is a Variant/Date that specifies the end date and time of the block of time for which to check free/busy status.

Interval
This is the duration, in minutes, of each time slot for which to check free/busy status.

For example, to check a user's availability on January 1, 2001, using a time slot duration of 30 minutes, first obtain a Recipient object representing the user (more on that in a minute), then invoke the Recipient object's GetFreeBusy method, like this:

```
strFreeBusy = CdoRecipient.GetFreeBusy( _
   StartTime:=#1/1/2001#, _
   EndTime:=#1/1/2001 11:59:59 PM#, _
   Interval:=30)
```

This call returns a 48-character string because there are 48 30-minute time slots in the period specified. The first character represents the time slot from 12:00 A.M. to 12:30 A.M., the second from 12:30 A.M. to 1:00 A.M., and so on. The reason it starts at 12:00 A.M. is that I specified 12:00 A.M. in the ***StartTime*** parameter in the code fragment. (Actually, I didn't specify a time at all, which is the same as specifying 12:00 A.M.) I could just as easily have specified a different start time. The returned string looks something like this:

```
"000000000000000000010023000003210000000000000000"
```

To interpret the value at a particular character location, convert the digit at that location to a number, and compare the number to the following constants:

`CdoFree`
This value indicates that the user has no schedule commitments during the time slot.

`CdoTentative`
This value indicates that the user has at least one tentative commitment during the time slot.

`CdoBusy`
This value indicates that the user has at least one confirmed commitment during the time slot.

`CdoOutOfOffice`
This value indicates that the user has at least one out-of-office commitment during the time slot.

The code in Example 8-4 prompts the user to select a messaging user from the Address Book, then retrieves the selected user's free/busy information and prints it to Visual Basic's immediate window. A portion of the output is shown in Figure 8-4. As you can see in the figure, this user is busy for at least part of the half-hour time slot that starts at 10:00 A.M. All this assumes, of course, that the messaging system has access to the user's free/busy information in order to provide it to your program. In general, this means that the target user must exist on the same mail server as the logged-in user, but the specifics are dependent on the mail server software and associated service providers being used. If free/busy information is not available, a **CdoE_NO_SUPPORT** error is raised when the GetFreeBusy method is called. Example 8-4 handles this circumstance.

Example 8-4. Retrieving a Messaging User's Free/Busy Information

```
Private Sub ShowFreeBusy(ByVal CdoRecipient As MAPI.Recipient, _
   dt As Date, nInterval As Long)

   Dim dtFrom As Date
   Dim dtTo As Date
   Dim strFreeBusy As String
   Dim i As Integer
   Dim nFreeBusy As MAPI.CdoBusyStatus
   Dim dtCurrent As Date

   ' Calculate the start and end times from the given date.
   dtFrom = CDate(Format(dt, "dd-mmm-yyyy") & " 12:00:00AM")
   dtTo = CDate(Format(dt, "dd-mmm-yyyy") & " 11:59:59PM")

   ' Get the free/busy information.
   On Error Resume Next
   strFreeBusy = CdoRecipient.GetFreeBusy(dtFrom, dtTo, nInterval)
   If Err.Number = CdoE_NO_SUPPORT Then
      Debug.Print "Free/Busy information not available."
      Exit Sub
   End If
   On Error GoTo 0

   ' Display the information.

   ' First show the raw string.
   Debug.Print
   Debug.Print "Free/Busy string = """; strFreeBusy; """"
   Debug.Print

   ' Now loop for each time slot, printing time and availability
   ' information.
   dtCurrent = dtFrom
   For i = 1 To Len(strFreeBusy)
      ' Print the time.
      Debug.Print Format(dtCurrent, "d-mmm-yyyy hh:mm:ss "),
      ' Get the availability code for this time slot.
      nFreeBusy = CLng(Mid(strFreeBusy, i, 1))
      ' Branch based on the user's availability in this time slot.
      Select Case nFreeBusy
      Case CdoFree
         Debug.Print "Free"
      Case CdoTentative
         Debug.Print "Tentative"
      Case CdoBusy
```

Example 8-4. Retrieving a Messaging User's Free/Busy Information (continued)

```
            Debug.Print "Busy"
         Case CdoOutOfOffice
            Debug.Print "Out of Office"
         End Select
         ' Set up for next time slot.
         dtCurrent = DateAdd("n", nInterval, dtCurrent)
      Next i

End Sub ' ShowFreeBusy
```

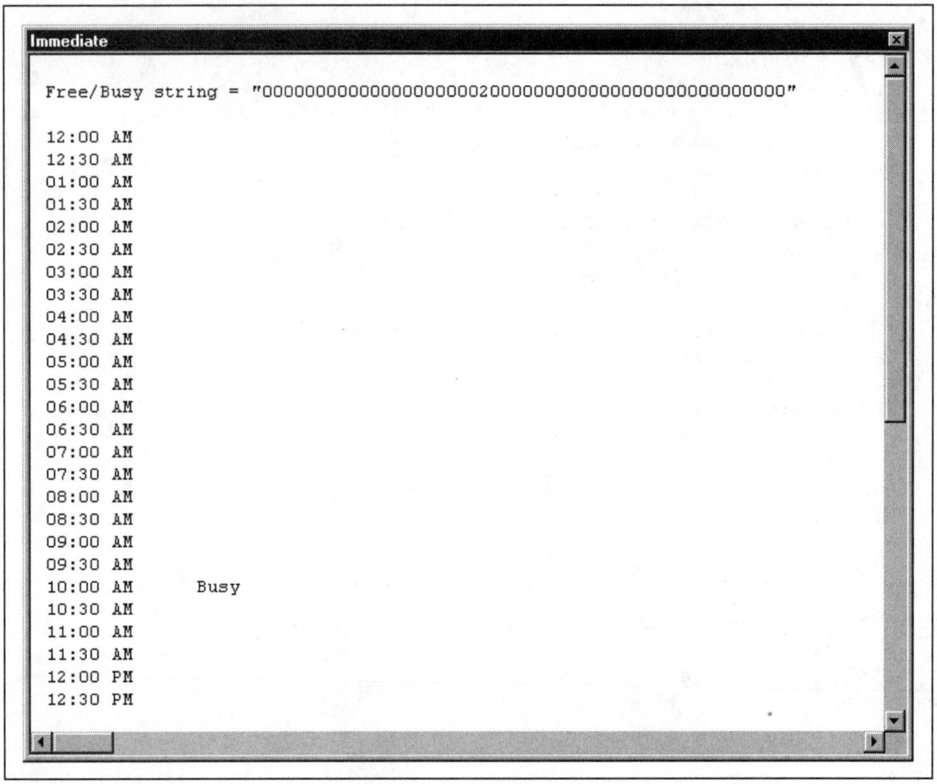

```
Immediate

Free/Busy string = "000000000000000000002000000000000000000000000000"

12:00 AM
12:30 AM
01:00 AM
01:30 AM
02:00 AM
02:30 AM
03:00 AM
03:30 AM
04:00 AM
04:30 AM
05:00 AM
05:30 AM
06:00 AM
06:30 AM
07:00 AM
07:30 AM
08:00 AM
08:30 AM
09:00 AM
09:30 AM
10:00 AM      Busy
10:30 AM
11:00 AM
11:30 AM
12:00 PM
12:30 PM
```

Figure 8-4. Typical output from the code in Example 8-4

Recurrence

An appointment is made recurring by calling the AppointmentItem object's Get-RecurrencePattern method. This method returns a RecurrencePattern object, which is used to set recurrence information for the appointment. Calling GetRecurrence-Pattern also sets the AppointmentItem object's IsRecurring property to `True`. Changes made to a RecurrencePattern object take effect when a call is made to the underlying AppointmentItem object's Send or Update method.

An appointment can recur daily, weekly, monthly, or yearly. This is the *recurrence unit.* The default recurrence unit is weekly, but you can change this by setting the RecurrencePattern object's RecurrenceType property to one of the following values:

`CdoRecurTypeDaily`
: The appointment recurs daily.

`CdoRecurTypeWeekly`
: The appointment recurs weekly (the default).

`CdoRecurTypeMonthly`
: The appointment recurs monthly.

`CdoRecurTypeMonthlyNth`
: The appointment recurs monthly, on the *n*th occurrence of a specific day of the week—for example, on the third Wednesday of each month.

`CdoRecurTypeYearly`
: The appointment recurs yearly.

`CdoRecurTypeYearlyNth`
: The appointment recurs yearly, on the *n*th occurrence of a specific day of the week in a specific month—for example, on the third Wednesday in April.

The RecurrenceType property is used in conjunction with other properties of the RecurrencePattern object to achieve a wide variety of recurrence patterns. The other properties used, and their meanings, vary depending on the value set in RecurrenceType. I'll address each recurrence unit, and the properties related to each recurrence unit, one at a time.

Daily Recurrence

This is the simplest recurrence pattern. For appointments that occur every day, or every *n* days, the RecurrenceType property of the RecurrencePattern object should be set to `CdoRecurTypeDaily`. The Interval property is then set to indicate how often the meeting should recur (in days), the default being 1. The following code fragment causes an appointment to recur daily.

```
Dim CdoRecurPattern As MAPI.RecurrencePattern
' Assume CdoAppointmentItem already created.

' Make the appointment recurring and get the recurrence pattern.
Set CdoRecurPattern = CdoAppointmentItem.GetRecurrencePattern
CdoRecurPattern.RecurrenceType = CdoRecurTypeDaily

' Save the recurrence pattern changes.
CdoAppointmentItem.Update
```

The maximum Interval value for daily recurrence is 999.

Weekly Recurrence

This is the default that CDO uses for newly created appointments. For appointments that occur every week, or every *n* weeks, the RecurrencePattern object is set to `CdoRecurTypeWeekly`. The Interval property is then set to indicate how often the meeting should recur (in weeks), the default again being 1. In addition, the day of the week upon which the meeting recurs can be set via the DayOfWeekMask property of the RecurrencePattern object. The DayOfWeekMask property can be set to any of the following values:

`CdoSunday`
: The appointment recurs on Sundays.

`CdoMonday`
: The appointment recurs on Mondays.

`CdoTuesday`
: The appointment recurs on Tuesdays.

`CdoWednesday`
: The appointment recurs on Wednesdays.

`CdoThursday`
: The appointment recurs on Thursdays.

`CdoFriday`
: The appointment recurs on Fridays.

`CdoSaturday`
: The appointment recurs on Saturdays.

In addition, these values can be added or logically `Or`ed together to indicate that the appointment recurs on more than one day each week.

The following code fragment sets an appointment to recur on Tuesdays and Fridays, every three weeks:

```
Dim CdoRecurPattern As MAPI.RecurrencePattern
' Assume CdoAppointmentItem already created.

' Make the appointment recurring and get the recurrence pattern.
Set CdoRecurPattern = CdoAppointmentItem.GetRecurrencePattern
CdoRecurPattern.RecurrenceType = CdoRecurTypeWeekly
CdoRecurPattern.Interval = 3 ' every third week
CdoRecurPattern.DayOfWeekMask = CdoTuesday + CdoFriday

' Save the recurrence pattern changes.
CdoAppointmentItem.Update
```

The maximum Interval value for weekly recurrence is 99.

Monthly Recurrence

There are two types of monthly recurrence. In the first type, an appointment must recur on a given day of the month, the 10th for example. In the second type, an appointment must recur on the month's *n*th occurrence of a given day of the week, the third Monday for example.

To cause an appointment to recur on a given day of the month, set the RecurrencePattern object's RecurrenceType property to **`CdoRecurTypeMonthly`**, and set the DayOfMonth property to the day of the month on which the appointment should recur (the default is the current day of the month).

The maximum value for the DayOfMonth property is 31. If the DayOfMonth property is greater than the number of days in a given month, the appointment occurs on the last day of that month.

If desired, the Interval property can be set to indicate how often the appointment should recur (in months), the default being 1. For example, set the Interval property to 3 for an appointment that recurs quarterly. Here's a snippet that sets an appointment to recur on the 10th of every month:

```
Dim CdoRecurPattern As MAPI.RecurrencePattern
' Assume CdoAppointmentItem already created.

' Make the appointment recurring and get the recurrence pattern.
Set CdoRecurPattern = CdoAppointmentItem.GetRecurrencePattern
CdoRecurPattern.RecurrenceType = CdoRecurTypeMonthly
CdoRecurPattern.Interval = 1 ' every month
CdoRecurPattern.DayOfMonth = 10 ' on the 10th

' Save the recurrence pattern changes.
CdoAppointmentItem.Update
```

For recurrence on a given day in a given week each month, set the RecurrencePattern object's RecurrenceType property to **`CdoRecurTypeMonthlyNth`**. Set the Instance property to indicate the week in which the appointment should recur, and set the DayOfWeekMask property to indicate the day or days of the week on which the appointment should recur. As with **`CdoRecurTypeMonthly`**, the Interval property controls the number of months between recurrences, the default being 1. This example sets an appointment to recur on the third Monday of each month:

```
Dim CdoRecurPattern As MAPI.RecurrencePattern
' Assume CdoAppointmentItem already created.

' Make the appointment recurring and get the recurrence pattern.
```

```
Set CdoRecurPattern = CdoAppointmentItem.GetRecurrencePattern
CdoRecurPattern.RecurrenceType = CdoRecurTypeMonthlyNth
CdoRecurPattern.Instance = 3 ' 3rd week of the month
CdoRecurPattern.DayOfWeekMask = CdoMonday ' on Monday

' Save the recurrence pattern changes.
CdoAppointmentItem.Update
```

When the RecurrencePattern object's RecurrenceType property is set to `CdoRecurTypeMonthlyNth`, the Instance property can take any value from 1 through 5. If the Instance property is set to 5, the appointment recurs on the *last* occurrence of the given day each month, which is sometimes the fifth occurrence and sometimes the fourth.

Yearly Recurrence

An appointment can be made to recur yearly by setting its RecurrencePattern object's RecurrenceType property to `CdoRecurTypeYearly`. Unlike the other RecurrenceType values, `CdoRecurTypeYearly` doesn't permit the Interval property to be anything other than 1. If your application needs to create appointments that recur less frequently than every year, use a RecurrenceType of `CdoRecurTypeMonthly`, and set the Interval property to the appropriate number of months, which can be greater than 12.

When setting yearly recurrence, set the MonthOfYear property of the Recurrence-Pattern object to indicate the month in which the appointment should recur (for example, 3 for March), and set the DayOfMonth property to indicate the appropriate day of the month (any value from 1 through 31). This example sets an appointment to recur every April 15th:

```
Dim CdoRecurPattern As MAPI.RecurrencePattern
' Assume CdoAppointmentItem already created.

' Make the appointment recurring and get the recurrence pattern.
Set CdoRecurPattern = CdoAppointmentItem.GetRecurrencePattern
CdoRecurPattern.RecurrenceType = CdoRecurTypeYearly
CdoRecurPattern.MonthOfYear = 4 ' in April
CdoRecurPattern.DayOfMonth = 15 ' on the 15th of the month

' Save the recurrence pattern changes.
CdoAppointmentItem.Update
```

The last type of recurrence is `CdoRecurTypeYearlyNth`. This setting, in conjunction with the MonthOfYear, DayOfWeekMask, and Instance properties, allows for setting appointments to recur on a given month's *n*th occurrence of a given day of the week, once a year. For example, this code sets an appointment to recur on the first Sunday in October:

```
Dim CdoRecurPattern As MAPI.RecurrencePattern
' Assume CdoAppointmentItem already created.

' Make the appointment recurring and get the recurrence pattern.
Set CdoRecurPattern = CdoAppointmentItem.GetRecurrencePattern
CdoRecurPattern.RecurrenceType = CdoRecurTypeYearlyNth
CdoRecurPattern.MonthOfYear = 10 ' in October
CdoRecurPattern.DayOfWeekMask = CdoSunday ' on Sunday
CdoRecurPattern.Instance = 1 ' 1st Sunday of the month

' Save the recurrence pattern changes.
CdoAppointmentItem.Update
```

Properties that Depend on RecurrenceType

Table 8-1 summarizes the properties that are used in association with the RecurrenceType property to set the recurrence pattern of an appointment. Use this table as a quick reference to determine which additional properties must be set when using a particular recurrence type.

Table 8-1. Properties Used in Association with the RecurrenceType Property

RecurrenceType	Associated Properties
`CdoRecurTypeDaily`	Interval
`CdoRecurTypeWeekly`	DayOfWeekMask Interval
`CdoRecurTypeMonthly`	DayOfMonth Interval
`CdoRecurTypeMonthlyNth`	DayOfWeekMask Instance Interval
`CdoRecurTypeYearly`	DayOfMonth Interval MonthOfYear
`CdoRecurTypeYearlyNth`	DayOfWeekMask Instance Interval MonthOfYear

Limiting the Number of Recurrences

The number of recurrences can be limited by setting the PatternStartDate, PatternEndDate, or Occurrences properties. The PatternStartDate property indicates the first date on which a recurring appointment will occur, the PatternEndDate property indicates the last date on which a recurring appointment will occur, and the

Occurrences property indicates the number of occurrences of the appointment. These properties are interrelated: if the value of one of the properties is changed, CDO will adjust the values of the others automatically to keep the properties consistent with each other. By default, recurring appointments recur without end.

When an appointment is made to be recurring, CDO does not store appointment objects for every recurrence of the appointment. Rather, a single appointment object represents the entire series of appointments. You can verify this by writing a short loop to dump the contents of the user's Calendar folder. Example 8-5 shows such a loop, and its output is shown in Figure 8-5.

Example 8-5. Dumping the Contents of the User's Calendar Folder

```
Private Sub DumpDefaultCalendar()

   ' gCdoSession already Dim'ed, Set, and logged on.

   Const ComE_INVALIDARG As Long = -2147024809

   Dim CdoFolder As MAPI.Folder
   Dim CdoMessages As MAPI.Messages
   Dim CdoAppointmentItem As MAPI.AppointmentItem
   Dim CdoRecurPattern As MAPI.RecurrencePattern

   ' Get the user's default calendar folder.
   Set CdoFolder = gCdoSession.GetDefaultFolder(CdoDefaultFolderCalendar)

   ' Get the collection of appointments.
   Set CdoMessages = CdoFolder.Messages

   ' Loop for each appointment.
   For Each CdoAppointmentItem In CdoMessages

      ' Dump some information about the appointment.
      Debug.Print "----------"
      Debug.Print "StartTime : "; CdoAppointmentItem.StartTime
      Debug.Print "EndTime : "; CdoAppointmentItem.EndTime
      Debug.Print "IsRecurring : "; CdoAppointmentItem.IsRecurring

      ' If the appointment is recurring, then get the RecurrencePattern
      ' object and dump its properties.
      If CdoAppointmentItem.IsRecurring Then
         Set CdoRecurPattern = CdoAppointmentItem.GetRecurrencePattern
         On Error GoTo ErrorInvalidArg
         Debug.Print "   Class : ";
         Debug.Print CdoRecurPattern.Class
         Debug.Print "   DayOfMonth : ";
         Debug.Print CdoRecurPattern.DayOfMonth
         Debug.Print "   DayOfWeekMask : ";
         Debug.Print CdoRecurPattern.DayOfWeekMask
         Debug.Print "   Duration : ";
         Debug.Print CdoRecurPattern.Duration
```

Example 8-5. Dumping the Contents of the User's Calendar Folder (continued)

```
            Debug.Print "   EndTime : ";
            Debug.Print CdoRecurPattern.EndTime
            Debug.Print "   Instance : ";
            Debug.Print CdoRecurPattern.Instance
            Debug.Print "   Interval : ";
            Debug.Print CdoRecurPattern.Interval
            Debug.Print "   MonthOfYear : ";
            Debug.Print CdoRecurPattern.MonthOfYear
            Debug.Print "   NoEndDate : ";
            Debug.Print CdoRecurPattern.NoEndDate
            Debug.Print "   Occurrence : ";
            Debug.Print CdoRecurPattern.Occurrences
            Debug.Print "   PatternEndDate : ";
            Debug.Print CdoRecurPattern.PatternEndDate
            Debug.Print "   PatternStartDate : ";
            Debug.Print CdoRecurPattern.PatternStartDate
            Debug.Print "   RecurrenceType : ";
            Debug.Print CdoRecurPattern.RecurrenceType
            Debug.Print "   StartTime : ";
            Debug.Print CdoRecurPattern.StartTime
            On Error GoTo 0
         End If

         ' More AppointmentItem properties.
         Debug.Print "Subject : "; CdoAppointmentItem.Subject
         Debug.Print "Location : "; CdoAppointmentItem.Location
         Debug.Print "Type : "; CdoAppointmentItem.Type
         Debug.Print "Class : "; CdoAppointmentItem.Class

      Next CdoAppointmentItem

      ' Clean up.
      Set CdoRecurPattern = Nothing
      Set CdoAppointmentItem = Nothing
      Set CdoMessages = Nothing
      Set CdoFolder = Nothing

      Exit Sub

ErrorInvalidArg:

      ' Some of the RecurrencePattern object's properties are valid
      ' only for certain settings of the RecurrenceType property.
      ' This error handler catches the error of trying to access
      ' a property that is not currently valid.

      If Err.Number = ComE_INVALIDARG Then
         Debug.Print "<invalid>"
         Resume Next
      Else
         Err.Raise Err.Number
      End If

End Sub ' DumpDefaultCalendar
```

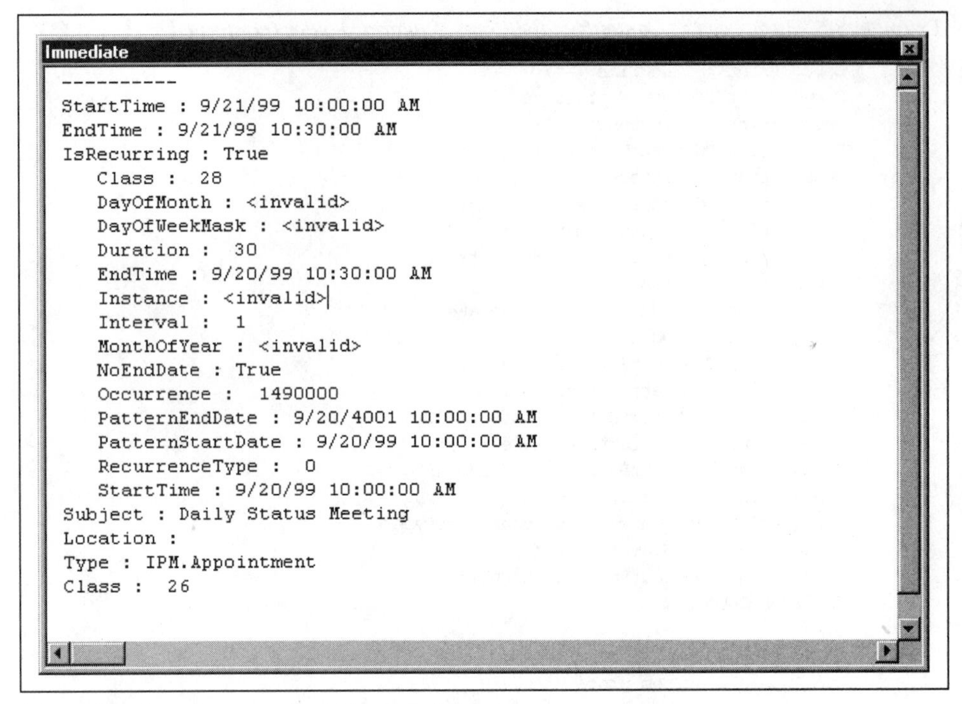

Immediate

StartTime : 9/21/99 10:00:00 AM
EndTime : 9/21/99 10:30:00 AM
IsRecurring : True
Class : 28
DayOfMonth : <invalid>
DayOfWeekMask : <invalid>
Duration : 30
EndTime : 9/20/99 10:30:00 AM
Instance : <invalid>
Interval : 1
MonthOfYear : <invalid>
NoEndDate : True
Occurrence : 1490000
PatternEndDate : 9/20/4001 10:00:00 AM
PatternStartDate : 9/20/99 10:00:00 AM
RecurrenceType : 0
StartTime : 9/20/99 10:00:00 AM
Subject : Daily Status Meeting
Location :
Type : IPM.Appointment
Class : 26

Figure 8-5. Sample output from Example 8-5

Figure 8-5 shows that the user has exactly one appointment in her Calendar folder, and that the appointment happens to be recurring. The RecurrenceType property is 0, which is the value of the constant `CdoRecurTypeDaily`, so this is an appointment that recurs daily.

Given a specific date and the information in the RecurrencePattern object, it's possible to calculate whether the appointment falls on the date in question. Fortunately, however, we don't have to perform such calculations ourselves—CDO can do it for us. When a filter is applied to a Messages collection, CDO adjusts the Messages collection so that it contains a unique AppointmentItem object for each and every appointment recurrence that falls within the filtered timeframe. Example 8-6 shows a loop with such a filter applied, and Figure 8-6 shows the resulting output. (The `Debug.Print` statements aren't shown in Example 8-6 so as to focus attention on the remaining code.) Note in Figure 8-6 that the appointment is shown to occur on 10/25/99, even though the code in Example 8-6 was run against the same calendar folder as the code in Example 8-5. If the filter had specified a range of 10/25/99 through 10/26/99, two AppointmentItem objects would have been in the Messages collection—one for each day.

Example 8-6. Filtering the Contents of the User's Calendar Folder

```
Private Sub DumpFilteredDefaultCalendar ()

   ' gCdoSession previously Dim'ed, Set, and logged on.

   Dim CdoFolder As MAPI.Folder
   Dim CdoMessages As MAPI.Messages
   Dim CdoMessageFilter As MAPI.MessageFilter
   Dim CdoFields As MAPI.Fields
   Dim CdoField As MAPI.Field
   Dim CdoAppointmentItem As MAPI.AppointmentItem

   ' Get the user's calendar folder.
   Set CdoFolder = gCdoSession.GetDefaultFolder(CdoDefaultFolderCalendar)

   ' Get the folder's collection of appointments.
   Set CdoMessages = CdoFolder.Messages

   ' Get the collection's MessageFilter object.
   Set CdoMessageFilter = CdoMessages.Filter

   ' Get the filter object's Fields collection, and add two fields.
   Set CdoFields = CdoMessageFilter.Fields
   Set CdoField = CdoFields.Add(CdoPR_START_DATE, #10/25/1999 11:59:59 PM#)
   Set CdoField = CdoFields.Add(CdoPR_END_DATE, #10/25/1999#)

   ' Dump the information for each appointment item.
   For Each CdoAppointmentItem In CdoMessages
      '
      ' Debug.Print statements and associated error handling
      ' removed for brevity.
      '
   Next CdoAppointmentItem

   ' Clean up.
   Set CdoAppointmentItem = Nothing
   Set CdoField = Nothing
   Set CdoFields = Nothing
   Set CdoMessageFilter = Nothing
   Set CdoMessages = Nothing
   Set CdoFolder = Nothing

End Sub ' DumpFilteredDefaultCalendar
```

An AppointmentItem object obtained from a filtered Messages collection refers to a specific appointment instance, rather than to the entire series of recurrences. Changes made to properties of an AppointmentItem object thus attained affect only that specific recurrence. To affect the entire series of recurrences, it is necessary to update the original AppointmentItem object or its RecurrencePattern object. The original appointment's RecurrencePattern object can be obtained by calling the GetRecurrencePattern method of any AppointmentItem object instance,

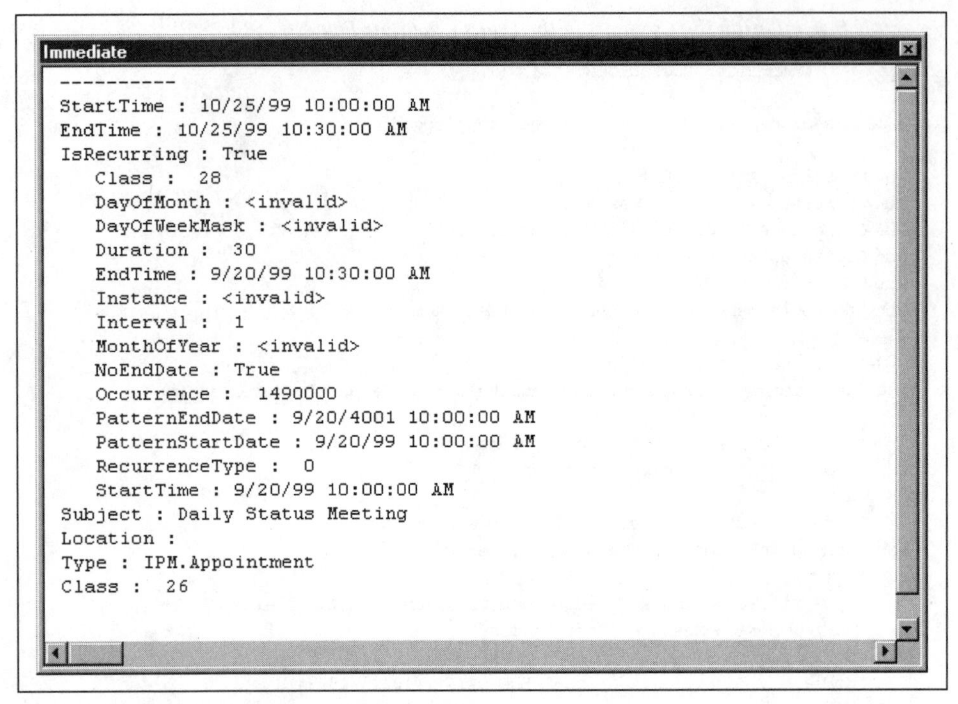

Immediate

StartTime : 10/25/99 10:00:00 AM
EndTime : 10/25/99 10:30:00 AM
IsRecurring : True
Class : 28
DayOfMonth : <invalid>
DayOfWeekMask : <invalid>
Duration : 30
EndTime : 9/20/99 10:30:00 AM
Instance : <invalid>
Interval : 1
MonthOfYear : <invalid>
NoEndDate : True
Occurrence : 1490000
PatternEndDate : 9/20/4001 10:00:00 AM
PatternStartDate : 9/20/99 10:00:00 AM
RecurrenceType : 0
StartTime : 9/20/99 10:00:00 AM
Subject : Daily Status Meeting
Location :
Type : IPM.Appointment
Class : 26

Figure 8-6. Sample output from Example 8-6

because all AppointmentItem objects in the series use the same RecurrencePattern object. Furthermore, the Parent property of the RecurrencePattern object contains a reference to the original AppointmentItem object. This makes it easy to get a reference to the original AppointmentItem object, given an AppointmentItem object that represents a specific recurrence, as shown in Example 8-7.

Example 8-7. Obtaining the Original Appointment from a Specific Recurrence

```
Private Function GetOriginalAppointment( _
   ByVal CdoAppointmentItem As MAPI.AppointmentItem _
) As MAPI.AppointmentItem

   Dim CdoRecurPattern As MAPI.RecurrencePattern

   ' Get series-wide recurrence pattern.
   Set CdoRecurPattern = CdoAppointmentItem.GetRecurrencePattern

   ' Return orginal appointment.
   Set GetOriginalAppointment = CdoRecurPattern.Parent

End Function ' GetOriginalAppointment
```

When changes are made to individual appointment recurrences, the system still stores only a single appointment that represents all recurrences, albeit in a way that retains the changes made. Because only the base appointment item appears in the calendar folder's Messages collection, it is not possible to search or filter for the recurrences based on their modified properties, unless also filtering by date. For example, say that the subject text of a particular recurrence was changed, and later CDO code is executed that iterates through the unfiltered Messages collection looking for appointments having the modified subject text. The appointment will not be found. To find the appointment, it is necessary to filter the Messages collection for a date range containing the modified appointment recurrence. When this is done, the appointment is found with modifications intact.

To modify an appointment so that it is no longer recurring, call the ClearRecurrencePattern method on the original AppointmentItem object.

Summary

CDO gives easy access to calendar data. Through the AppointmentItem and MeetingItem objects, it is possible to create calendar entries and meeting requests programmatically. Appointments and meetings can be made to recur in a variety of simple or complex patterns.

In the next chapter we'll have a look at tasks and task folders.

9

Task Folders

If you use Microsoft Outlook, you are familiar with *task items.* As the name implies, task items store information about tasks—things that you might find on a "to-do" list. Stored information about each task includes the task description and may include other values, such as due date, start date, status, priority, percent complete, date completed, total work, actual work, assigned to, and others. A task may also have rich text and attachments associated with it, just like messages, making it possible to store associated documents within the task itself.

However, now that I've built you up, I have to let you down a little. CDO doesn't provide much support for working with tasks. In fact, the only task-specific functionality that CDO provides is the ability to retrieve the user's default task folder. In addition, although CDO can create task items, it has no way to create task requests. If you're writing an application that requires detailed control over task items, think about using the Outlook object model instead of CDO. The Outlook object model is introduced in Appendix B, *Programming the Outlook Object Model.* Having said that, I'll note that CDO can handle simple processing of task items. Tasks are stored as message items in the message store. Some of the task's information is stored in standard message properties, which means that CDO's ability to manipulate message items can be applied to task items.

In this chapter I'll show you how to create, save, send, move, and delete task items. I'll identify the standard message properties that are used by task items, and I'll show you how the task-specific properties are stored (and why it's difficult to access them).

Finding the Default Task Folder

A user is permitted to have any number of task folders, but one of them (the one created first) is considered to be the default task folder. CDO provides a simple way to get access to the default task folder. To do so, use the Session object's GetDefaultFolder method, with an argument of **CdoDefaultFolderTasks**, as shown here:

```
' gCdoSession previously Dim'ed, Set, and logged on.
Dim CdoFolderTasks As MAPI.Folder

Set CdoFolderTasks = _
   gCdoSession.GetDefaultFolder(CdoDefaultFolderTasks)
```

When I refer to the Tasks folder (with a capital "T"), I mean the user's default task folder.

Reading Tasks

From CDO's point of view, tasks are stored as Message objects. It's easy to tell when a Message object represents a task: its Type property is set to "**IPM.Task**". It is this value that signifies to Microsoft Outlook, for example, to display an item using the Task form rather than the Message form.

Some points about accessing task items through CDO:

- A task's description is found in the Message object's Subject property.
- Unlike message items, the Text property of a Message object representing a task item is typically left empty, though it doesn't have to be.
- Task items can accommodate rich text. To do this through CDO, use the CdoHelper component introduced in Chapter 6, *An Email Client Application.*
- Task items can accommodate attachments. This is done in the same way as it is with email message items, as discussed in Chapter 6.
- Most of the really useful task information is stored in named properties, and Microsoft doesn't document the names (argh!). This is discussed in more detail later in this chapter.

The code in Example 9-1 loads a list box with the task descriptions from the user's Tasks folder. Sample output is shown in Figure 9-1.

Example 9-1. Loading a List Box with Tasks

```
Private Sub ShowTasks()

   ' gCdoSession previously Dim'ed, Set, and logged on.

   Dim CdoFolder As MAPI.Folder
   Dim CdoMessages As MAPI.Messages
   Dim CdoMessage As MAPI.Message

   ' Get the Tasks folder.
   Set CdoFolder = gCdoSession.GetDefaultFolder(CdoDefaultFolderTasks)
```

Example 9-1. Loading a List Box with Tasks (continued)

```
    ' Get the collection of tasks.
    Set CdoMessages = CdoFolder.Messages

    ' Loop for each task.
    For Each CdoMessage In CdoMessages
       ' This If statement is just for extra protection.
       If CdoMessage.Type = "IPM.Task" Then
          ' Add the task description to the list box.
          lstTasks.AddItem CdoMessage.Subject
       End If
    Next CdoMessage

    ' Cleanup
    Set CdoMessage = Nothing
    Set CdoMessages = Nothing
    Set CdoFolder = Nothing

End Sub ' ShowTasks
```

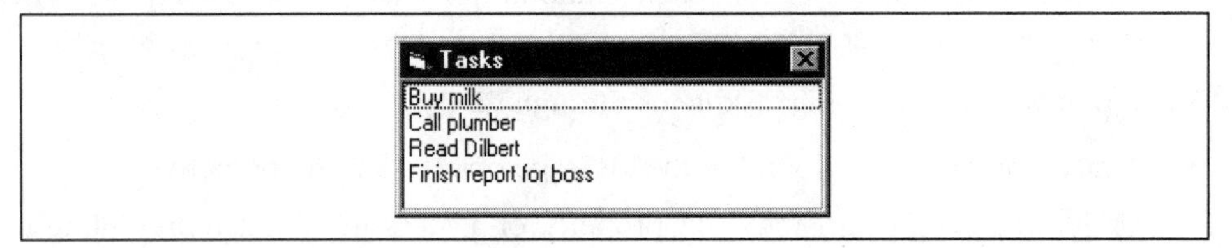

Figure 9-1. Sample output from Example 9-1

Creating a Task

To create a task, add a Message object to a folder's Messages collection, setting the Type property of the Message object to "`IPM.Task`". A task can be created in any folder, but the most logical choice is the user's Tasks folder, as shown here:

```
' gCdoSession previously Dim'ed, Set, and logged on.

Dim CdoFolder As MAPI.Folder
Dim CdoMessages As MAPI.Messages
Dim CdoMessage As MAPI.Message

' Get the Tasks folder.
Set CdoFolder = gCdoSession.GetDefaultFolder(CdoDefaultFolderTasks)

' Get the collection of tasks.
Set CdoMessages = CdoFolder.Messages

' Add a new task.
Set CdoMessage = CdoMessages.Add(Subject:="Buy milk", Type:="IPM.Task")

' Save the new item.
CdoMessage.Update
```

The body text can be set, if desired, by passing a string in the Text parameter of the Messages collection's Add method, or by setting the Text property of the Message object itself.

Copying, Moving, and Deleting

Because CDO represents tasks as Message objects, all of the methods available to messages are also available to tasks. For example, a task can be copied to another folder using the Message object's Copy method, as shown here:

```
Set CdoMessage2 = CdoMessage.CopyTo(CdoFolder2.ID, CdoFolder2.StoreID)
CdoMessage2.Update
```

or moved to a different folder, as shown here:

```
Set CdoMessage2 = CdoMessage.MoveTo(CdoFolder2.ID, CdoFolder2.StoreID)
```

or deleted, as shown here:

```
CdoMessage.Delete DeletedItems:=True
```

For detailed discussion of these and other Message object methods, refer to Chapter 6 and Chapter 7, *Enhancing the Email Client.*

Using Message Filters with Task Folders

Recall from Chapter 7 that Messages collections can be filtered using the MessageFilter object. The same technique can be applied to limit the set of tasks returned in a task folder's Messages collection. Although the MessageFilter object can't filter on task item-specific properties, such as due date, some of the properties that can be filtered are nevertheless useful when working with tasks. The properties of the MessageFilter object that can be applied to tasks are:

Conversation
: Setting the Conversation property causes the associated Messages collection to contain only Message objects having their ConversationTopic properties equal to this value. The datatype is String.

Fields
: By adding Field objects to the MessageFilter object's Fields collection, it is possible to filter on properties that are not directly accessible through the MessageFilter object. For example, this code restricts a Messages collection to items having attachments:

```
' CdoMessages already Dim'ed and Set.
Dim CdoMessageFilter As MAPI.MessageFilter
Dim CdoFields As MAPI.Fields

Set CdoMessageFilter = CdoMessages.Filter
```

```
Set CdoFields = CdoMessageFilter.Fields
CdoFields.Add CdoPR_HASATTACH, True

' At this point, CdoMessages only returns items that have attachments.
```

Importance

Setting the Importance property causes the associated Messages collection to contain only Message objects having their Importance properties equal to this value. It is a Long that can be set to `CdoLow`, `CdoNormal`, or `CdoHigh`.

Recipients

Setting the Recipients property causes the associated Messages collection to contain only Message objects having at least one recipient whose Name property contains this value as a substring. That is, if any portion of a recipient's name matches the value in this property, the task is matched. Note that only tasks that have been assigned have recipients. The datatype is String. Case is not significant.

Sender

Setting the Sender property causes the associated Messages collection to contain only Message objects whose sender's name contains this value as a substring. That is, if any portion of the sender's name matches the value in this property, the task is matched. Tasks always have a sender, even if they haven't been assigned. The datatype is String. Case is not significant.

Size

Setting the Size property causes the associated Messages collection to contain only Message objects having their approximate sizes greater than this value. The datatype is Long. (The size of a message represents all of the data in all of the message's properties, including attachments.)

Subject

Setting the Subject property causes the associated Messages collection to contain only Message objects whose subject contains this value as a substring. That is, if any portion of the subject matches the value in this property, the task is matched. The datatype is String. Case is not significant.

Text

Setting the Text property causes the associated Messages collection to contain only Message objects where the body text contains this value as a substring. The datatype is String.

TimeFirst

Setting the TimeFirst property causes the associated Messages collection to contain only Message objects having their TimeReceived properties equal to or greater than this value. When a user creates a task for herself (i.e., no task request is involved), the TimeReceived property of the task's Message object indicates the time at which the task was saved to the message store. The datatype is Date.

TimeLast

Setting the TimeLast property causes the associated Messages collection to contain only Message objects having their TimeReceived properties less than or equal to this value. The datatype is Date.

Type

Setting the Type property causes the associated Messages collection to contain only Message objects having their Type properties equal to this value. The datatype is String.

The default message type for task items is "`IPM.Task`". However, a custom client application is permitted to set the Type property of a Message object to any string. The MessageFilter object can subsequently be used to find these items. A precaution is necessary, however. Client applications, including Microsoft Outlook, typically use the message type to determine what form to use for displaying the message item. If a task's message type is changed from "`IPM.Task`" to "`Dave`", for example, Outlook will not know how to display the item. If you plan to create custom message types for certain tasks, create custom types that start with "`IPM.Task.`"—for example, "`IPM.Task.Dave`". Outlook will continue to recognize such an item as a task, yet the message type is different from the norm and can be used for filtering.

Unread

Setting the Unread property causes the associated Messages collection to contain only Message objects having their Unread properties equal to this value. The datatype is Boolean.

This code fragment shows how to filter for high-importance tasks, ignoring everything else:

```
' gCdoSession previously Dim'ed, Set, and logged on.

Dim CdoFolder As MAPI.Folder
Dim CdoMessages As MAPI.Messages
Dim CdoMessage As MAPI.Message
Dim CdoMessageFilter As MAPI.MessageFilter

' Get the Tasks folder and its Messages collection.
Set CdoFolder = gCdoSession.GetDefaultFolder(CdoDefaultFolderTasks)
Set CdoMessages = CdoFolder.Messages

' Get the Messages collection's filter.
Set CdoMessageFilter = CdoMessages.Filter
```

```
' We only want tasks, and only of high importance.
CdoMessageFilter.Type = "IPM.Task"
CdoMessageFilter.Importance = CdoHigh

' Loop for each such task.
For Each CdoMessage In CdoMessages
    '
    ' Process each task.
    '
Next CdoMessage
```

Task Item-Specific Properties and the Fields Collection

I've already said that CDO doesn't support any task item-specific properties. In such cases, it is often possible to use a CDO object's Fields collection to access the underlying MAPI properties that aren't directly exposed. Indeed, that's what the Fields collection is for. The following paragraphs discuss the Fields collection, specifically of Message objects that represent task items. You'll see how to discover all of the properties exposed by a MAPI object. Ultimately, the task item-specific properties will remain (almost) out of our reach, but along the way you'll learn some good reusable techniques. Finally, if you don't mind taking some risk, you'll learn how to access the task item-specific properties anyway.

The designers of CDO knew that it would be impractical to expose every underlying property that a MAPI object could have. More importantly, MAPI applications are permitted to add custom properties to MAPI objects dynamically. Clearly, CDO's designers couldn't know in advance what custom properties application developers would add. By providing a mechanism to access such properties in a generic way, CDO's designers provided a great deal of flexibility.

Consider an example. Folders in the Microsoft Exchange Server information store expose a property that indicates whether there are rules configured for that folder. CDO knows nothing of this property, so it's not exposed by CDO's Folder object. It can nevertheless be accessed through CDO using the Fields collection. Example 9-2 shows a function that does just that. The function accepts a reference to a Folder object as a parameter and returns a Boolean that indicates whether that folder is configured to have rules.

Example 9-2. Accessing a Custom Property Exposed by the Microsoft Exchange Server Information Store

```
Public Function FolderHasRules(ByVal CdoFolder As MAPI.Folder) As Boolean

   ' This function is used to determine whether a folder residing in a
   ' Microsoft Exchange Server information store has rules. If so, True
   ' is returned. If not, or if the folder doesn't reside in Exchange
   ' Server, then False is returned.
```

Example 9-2. Accessing a Custom Property Exposed by the Microsoft Exchange Server Information Store (continued)

```
   ' This value comes from Exchange Server documentation.
   Const PR_HAS_RULES As Long = &H663A000B

   Dim CdoFields As MAPI.Fields
   Dim CdoField As MAPI.Field
   Dim nErrNumber As Long

   ' Get the folder's Fields collection.
   Set CdoFields = CdoFolder.Fields

   ' Get the specific field we want.
   ' Here is where a CdoE_NOT_FOUND error will occur if the folder is not
   ' located in a Microsoft Exchange Server information store. To catch
   ' this error, "On Error Resume Next" is used, and the value of
   ' Err.Number is read immediately after the call.
   On Error Resume Next
   Set CdoField = CdoFields.Item(PR_HAS_RULES)
   nErrNumber = Err.Number
   On Error GoTo 0

   ' If no error, then return the value retrieved.
   If nErrNumber = 0 Then
      FolderHasRules = CdoField.Value
   ' Else if CdoE_NOT_FOUND, then the folder is not located in a
   ' Microsoft Exchange Server information store. Return False in
   ' this case.
   ElseIf nErrNumber = CdoE_NOT_FOUND Then
      FolderHasRules = False
   ' Else there was an unexpected error. Raise it to the caller.
   Else
      Err.Raise nErrNumber
   End If

   ' Cleanup
   Set CdoField = Nothing
   Set CdoFields = Nothing

End Function ' FolderHasRules
```

Notice in Example 9-2 that the Fields collection is indexed by the numeric identifier of the desired MAPI property. For this particular example, I was able to find this folder-related property in the Microsoft Exchange Server documentation. Another way to determine what properties are exposed by a specific object is to examine the items in that object's Fields collection. Example 9-3 shows a subroutine that dumps the Fields collection of a Message object.

Example 9-3. Dumping the Fields Collection of a Message Object

```
Private Sub DumpFields(ByVal CdoObject As Object)

   Dim Fields As MAPI.Fields
```

Example 9-3. Dumping the Fields Collection of a Message Object (continued)

```
   Dim Field As MAPI.Field
   Dim strIDHex As String
   Dim strIDSymbolic As String

   ' Get the object's Fields collection.
   Set Fields = CdoObject.Fields

   ' Loop for each Field in the collection.
   For Each Field In Fields

      ' Get hex and symbolic versions of the ID property.
      strIDHex = "&H" & Left("00000000", 8 - Len(Hex(Field.ID))) _
         & Hex(Field.ID)
      strIDSymbolic = CdoPrTextFromCode(Field.ID)
      If strIDSymbolic = "" Then
         strIDSymbolic = "<no symbolic constant>"
      End If

      ' Print the information.
      Debug.Print "----------"
      Debug.Print "ID = "; Trim(CStr(Field.ID)); " ("; strIDHex; _
         ", "; strIDSymbolic; ")"
      Debug.Print "Type = "; Field.Type
      Debug.Print "Value = "; Field.Value
   Next Field

   ' Cleanup
   Set Field = Nothing
   Set Fields = Nothing

End Sub ' DumpFields
```

Because many CDO classes contain Fields collections, the parameter to the *DumpFields* subroutine in Example 9-3 is declared as Object, rather than as a specific type of object. This allows us to pass any object that has a Fields collection to the subroutine. The subroutine obtains a reference to the object's Fields collection, then iterates through each item, printing information about each Field object to the Visual Basic IDE Immediate window. The ID property of each Field object is printed in three forms: (1) the decimal value, (2) the hexadecimal value, and (3) the CDO symbolic constant having that value (if there is one). The symbolic constant is obtained by calling the *CdoPrTextFromCode* function included in this book's downloadable sample code and shown in part in Chapter 7, in the section "Hidden Messages." The Field object's datatype and value are also printed. The datatype is given in the Field object's Type property, which is a Long. The *DumpFields* function prints the numeric value, then calls the *FieldTypeNameFromValue* function to print the name of the datatype for easy reading. The *FieldTypeNameFromValue* function is shown in Example 9-4. The values permitted in the Type property are shown in Table 9-1.

Example 9-4. The FieldTypeNameFromValue Function

```
Public Function FieldTypeNameFromValue(ByVal nFieldType As Long) As String

   ' Return the name of the datatype whose value is given in nFieldType.
   ' Note that this function is specifically for use with the MAPI.Field.Type
   ' property, not Visual Basic's vbVarType enumeration.

   Dim bIsArray As Boolean
   Dim strBaseType As String

   bIsArray = (nFieldType > vbArray)
   If bIsArray Then
      nFieldType = nFieldType - vbArray
   End If

   Select Case nFieldType
   Case vbBlob
      strBaseType = "vbBlob"
   Case vbBoolean
      strBaseType = "vbBoolean"
   Case vbCurrency
      strBaseType = "vbCurrency"
   Case vbDate
      strBaseType = "vbDate"
   Case vbDouble
      strBaseType = "vbDouble"
   Case vbInteger
      strBaseType = "vbInteger"
   Case vbLong
      strBaseType = "vbLong"
   Case vbSingle
      strBaseType = "vbSingle"
   Case vbString
      strBaseType = "vbString"
   Case vbVariant
      strBaseType = "vbVariant"
   End Select

   If bIsArray Then
      FieldTypeNameFromValue = "vbArray + " & strBaseType
   Else
      FieldTypeNameFromValue = strBaseType
   End If

End Function ' FieldTypeNameFromValue
```

Table 9-1. The Meanings of Values Found in the Field Object's Type Property

Type	Numeric Value	Meaning
vbArray	8192	The Field object represents a multivalue property
vbBlob	65	Binary (a binary large object)
vbBoolean	11	Boolean

Table 9-1. The Meanings of Values Found in the Field Object's Type Property (continued)

Type	Numeric Value	Meaning
vbCurrency	6	Currency
vbDate	7	Date
vbDouble	5	Double
vbInteger	2	Integer
vbLong	3	Long
vbSingle	4	Single
vbString	8	String
vbVariant	12	Variant

When the `vbArray` datatype appears, it signifies that the Field object represents an array (or, in MAPI terminology, a *multivalue property*). The appearance of `vbArray` is always in addition to one of the other type values. For example, a Field object that represents an integer array would have its Type property equal to `vbArray + vbInteger`.

Typical output from Example 9-3 is shown in Example 9-5. The output was generated by passing to the *DumpFields* subroutine a Message object representing a task item. The output is lengthy, but it's worth including here because it shows the variety and amount of information available through the Fields collection. As you peruse the list, keep in mind that not all of these properties are available on all Message objects. Some properties may only be available when using a certain message store (as we saw with the `PR_HAS_RULES` property), and some properties may be available only on certain messages. Your code should always be ready to deal gracefully with the absence of any particular property.

Example 9-5. Sample Output from the DumpFields Routine (Example 9-3)

```
----------
ID = 131083 (&H0002000B, CdoPR_ALTERNATE_RECIPIENT_ALLOWED)
Type =  11  (vbBoolean)
Value = True
----------
ID = 1507331 (&H00170003, CdoPR_IMPORTANCE)
Type =  3  (vbLong)
Value =  1
----------
ID = 1703966 (&H001A001E, CdoPR_MESSAGE_CLASS)
Type =  8  (vbString)
Value = IPM.Task
----------
ID = 2293771 (&H0023000B, CdoPR_ORIGINATOR_DELIVERY_REPORT_REQUESTED)
Type =  11  (vbBoolean)
Value = False
----------
```

Example 9-5. Sample Output from the DumpFields Routine (Example 9-3) (continued)

```
ID = 2490371 (&H00260003, CdoPR_PRIORITY)
Type =  3  (vbLong)
Value =  0
----------
ID = 2686987 (&H0029000B, CdoPR_READ_RECEIPT_REQUESTED)
Type =  11  (vbBoolean)
Value = False
----------
ID = 3538947 (&H00360003, CdoPR_SENSITIVITY)
Type =  3  (vbLong)
Value =  0
----------
ID = 3604510 (&H0037001E, CdoPR_SUBJECT)
Type =  8  (vbString)
Value = Develop 3-year technology plan
----------
ID = 3735616 (&H00390040, CdoPR_CLIENT_SUBMIT_TIME)
Type =  7  (vbDate)
Value = 10/5/99 9:39:30 AM
----------
ID = 3866882 (&H003B0102, CdoPR_SENT_REPRESENTING_SEARCH_KEY)
Type =  65  (vbBlob)
Value = 534D54503A444740455845435043 2E434F4D00
----------
ID = 4260098 (&H00410102, CdoPR_SENT_REPRESENTING_ENTRYID)
Type =  65  (vbBlob)
Value =
00000000812B1FA4BEA310199D6E00DD010F54020000000044617665204772756E6467656967657200534D
54500064674065786563706 32E636F6D00
----------
ID = 4325406 (&H0042001E, CdoPR_SENT_REPRESENTING_NAME)
Type =  8  (vbString)
Value = Dave Grundgeiger
----------
ID = 6553630 (&H0064001E, CdoPR_SENT_REPRESENTING_ADDRTYPE)
Type =  8  (vbString)
Value = SMTP
----------
ID = 6619166 (&H0065001E, CdoPR_SENT_REPRESENTING_EMAIL_ADDRESS)
Type =  8  (vbString)
Value = dg@execpc.com
----------
ID = 7340062 (&H0070001E, CdoPR_CONVERSATION_TOPIC)
Type =  8  (vbString)
Value = Develop 3-year technology plan
----------
ID = 7405826 (&H00710102, CdoPR_CONVERSATION_INDEX)
Type =  65  (vbBlob)
Value = 01BF0F3F6EA9740E16BEE337450D84BDECB2E167D32E
----------
ID = 202965250 (&H0C190102, CdoPR_SENDER_ENTRYID)
Type =  65  (vbBlob)
```

Example 9-5. Sample Output from the DumpFields Routine (Example 9-3) (continued)

```
Value =
00000000812B1FA4BEA310199D6E00DD010F5402000000004461766520477275 6E646765696765720053 4D
5450006467406578656370632E636F6D00
----------
ID = 203030558 (&H0C1A001E, CdoPR_SENDER_NAME)
Type =  8  (vbString)
Value = Dave Grundgeiger
----------
ID = 203227394 (&H0C1D0102, CdoPR_SENDER_SEARCH_KEY)
Type =  65  (vbBlob)
Value = 534D54503A444740455845435043 2E434F4D00
----------
ID = 203292702 (&H0C1E001E, CdoPR_SENDER_ADDRTYPE)
Type =  8  (vbString)
Value = SMTP
----------
ID = 203358238 (&H0C1F001E, CdoPR_SENDER_EMAIL_ADDRESS)
Type =  8  (vbString)
Value = dg@execpc.com
----------
ID = 234946571 (&H0E01000B, CdoPR_DELETE_AFTER_SUBMIT)
Type =  11  (vbBoolean)
Value = False
----------
ID = 235274304 (&H0E060040, CdoPR_MESSAGE_DELIVERY_TIME)
Type =  7  (vbDate)
Value = 10/5/99 9:39:30 AM
----------
ID = 235339779 (&H0E070003, CdoPR_MESSAGE_FLAGS)
Type =  3  (vbLong)
Value =  1
----------
ID = 235405315 (&H0E080003, CdoPR_MESSAGE_SIZE)
Type =  3  (vbLong)
Value =  867
----------
ID = 236912651 (&H0E1F000B, CdoPR_RTF_IN_SYNC)
Type =  11  (vbBoolean)
Value = True
----------
ID = 268435486 (&H1000001E, CdoPR_BODY)
Type =  8  (vbString)
Value = Include synergistic realignment of resources into multifunctional action pods.
----------
ID = 268828675 (&H10060003, CdoPR_RTF_SYNC_BODY_CRC)
Type =  3  (vbLong)
Value = -169416192
----------
ID = 268894211 (&H10070003, CdoPR_RTF_SYNC_BODY_COUNT)
Type =  3  (vbLong)
Value =  69
----------
```

Example 9-5. Sample Output from the DumpFields Routine (Example 9-3) (continued)

```
ID = 268959774 (&H1008001E, CdoPR_RTF_SYNC_BODY_TAG)
Type =  8  (vbString)
Value = INCLUDESYNERGISTICREALIGNMENTOFRESOURCESINTOMULTIFUNCTIONALACTIONPODS
----------
ID = 269025538 (&H10090102, CdoPR_RTF_COMPRESSED)
Type =  65  (vbBlob)
Value =
A8000000C40000004C5A46753B58733503000A00726370673132351632 00F80B606E0E103033339D01F720
02A403E3020063680AC06073657430200713028 07D190A81756300500B03756C6E850220650BA620496E63
0A40910100207379130072670400 1A740DE02009700740696 76EA307800230206F6614E173086186630791
0B80746F206D12C07914B0667513C014B0022007402093 00D0176220700470732E0AA20B0A8011F1001930
----------
ID = 269484035 (&H10100003, CdoPR_RTF_SYNC_PREFIX_COUNT)
Type =  3  (vbLong)
Value =  0
----------
ID = 269549571 (&H10110003, CdoPR_RTF_SYNC_TRAILING_COUNT)
Type =  3  (vbLong)
Value =  1
----------
ID = 276824067 (&H10800003, <no symbolic constant>)
Type =  3  (vbLong)
Value =  1280
----------
ID = 805765184 (&H30070040, CdoPR_CREATION_TIME)
Type =  7  (vbDate)
Value = 10/5/99 9:39:27 AM
----------
ID = 805830720 (&H30080040, CdoPR_LAST_MODIFICATION_TIME)
Type =  7  (vbDate)
Value = 10/5/99 9:44:10 AM
----------
ID = 806027522 (&H300B0102, CdoPR_SEARCH_KEY)
Type =  65  (vbBlob)
Value = 97AB0B830747F9478994134F28B673DA
----------
ID = 1071513603 (&H3FDE0003, <no symbolic constant>)
Type =  3  (vbLong)
Value =  28591
----------
ID = -2147483637 (&H8000000B, <no symbolic constant>)
Type =  11  (vbBoolean)
Value = True
----------
ID = -2147352573 (&H80020003, <no symbolic constant>)
Type =  3  (vbLong)
Value =  272
----------
ID = -2147024832 (&H80070040, <no symbolic constant>)
Type =  7  (vbDate)
Value = 8/24/00 8:00:00 AM
----------
```

Example 9-5. Sample Output from the DumpFields Routine (Example 9-3) (continued)

```
ID = -2146959357 (&H80080003, <no symbolic constant>)
Type =  3  (vbLong)
Value =  0
----------
ID = -2146893760 (&H80090040, <no symbolic constant>)
Type =  7  (vbDate)
Value = 8/24/00 8:00:00 AM
----------
ID = -2144862205 (&H80280003, <no symbolic constant>)
Type =  3  (vbLong)
Value =  5104
----------
ID = -2144796642 (&H8029001E, <no symbolic constant>)
Type =  8  (vbString)
Value = 8.5
----------
ID = -2144731125 (&H802A000B, <no symbolic constant>)
Type =  11  (vbBoolean)
Value = False
----------
ID = -2144665536 (&H802B0040, <no symbolic constant>)
Type =  7  (vbDate)
Value = 8/1/00
----------
ID = -2144600000 (&H802C0040, <no symbolic constant>)
Type =  7  (vbDate)
Value = 8/24/00
----------
ID = -2144534517 (&H802D000B, <no symbolic constant>)
Type =  11  (vbBoolean)
Value = False
----------
ID = -2144468989 (&H802E0003, <no symbolic constant>)
Type =  3  (vbLong)
Value =  0
----------
ID = -2144403453 (&H802F0003, <no symbolic constant>)
Type =  3  (vbLong)
Value =  0
----------
ID = -2137194432 (&H809D0040, <no symbolic constant>)
Type =  7  (vbDate)
Value = 8/23/00 7:00:00 PM
----------
ID = -2137128896 (&H809E0040, <no symbolic constant>)
Type =  7  (vbDate)
Value = 7/31/00 7:00:00 PM
----------
ID = -2137063421 (&H809F0003, <no symbolic constant>)
Type =  3  (vbLong)
Value =  0
----------
```

Example 9-5. Sample Output from the DumpFields Routine (Example 9-3) (continued)

```
ID = -2136932349 (&H80A10003, <no symbolic constant>)
Type =  3  (vbLong)
Value =  1
----------
ID = -2136801269 (&H80A3000B, <no symbolic constant>)
Type =  11  (vbBoolean)
Value = False
----------
ID = -2136735741 (&H80A40003, <no symbolic constant>)
Type =  3  (vbLong)
Value = -10000
----------
ID = -2134769659 (&H80C20005, <no symbolic constant>)
Type =  5  (vbDouble)
Value =  0
----------
ID = -2134704125 (&H80C30003, <no symbolic constant>)
Type =  3  (vbLong)
Value =  0
----------
ID = -2134638589 (&H80C40003, <no symbolic constant>)
Type =  3  (vbLong)
Value =  0
----------
ID = -2134245365 (&H80CA000B, <no symbolic constant>)
Type =  11  (vbBoolean)
Value = False
----------
ID = -2134179829 (&H80CB000B, <no symbolic constant>)
Type =  11  (vbBoolean)
Value = False
----------
ID = -2134114301 (&H80CC0003, <no symbolic constant>)
Type =  3  (vbLong)
Value =  0
----------
ID = -2134048765 (&H80CD0003, <no symbolic constant>)
Type =  3  (vbLong)
Value =  0
----------
ID = -2133721058 (&H80D2001E, <no symbolic constant>)
Type =  8  (vbString)
Value =
----------
ID = -2133524477 (&H80D50003, <no symbolic constant>)
Type =  3  (vbLong)
Value =  3
----------
ID = -2133262306 (&H80D9001E, <no symbolic constant>)
Type =  8  (vbString)
Value =
----------
```

Example 9-5. Sample Output from the DumpFields Routine (Example 9-3) (continued)

```
ID = -2133196770 (&H80DA001E, <no symbolic constant>)
Type =  8  (vbString)
Value = Dave Grundgeiger
----------
ID = -2133065717 (&H80DC000B, <no symbolic constant>)
Type =  11  (vbBoolean)
Value = False
----------
ID = -2133000181 (&H80DD000B, <no symbolic constant>)
Type =  11  (vbBoolean)
Value = False
----------
ID = 3997726 (&H003D001E, CdoPR_SUBJECT_PREFIX)
Type =  8  (vbString)
Value =
----------
ID = 235012126 (&H0E02001E, CdoPR_DISPLAY_BCC)
Type =  8  (vbString)
Value =
----------
ID = 235077662 (&H0E03001E, CdoPR_DISPLAY_CC)
Type =  8  (vbString)
Value =
----------
ID = 235143198 (&H0E04001E, CdoPR_DISPLAY_TO)
Type =  8  (vbString)
Value =
----------
ID = 235471106 (&H0E090102, CdoPR_PARENT_ENTRYID)
Type =  65  (vbBlob)
Value = 0000000061D29510DD2B314E869888857E191E65A2810000
----------
ID = 236650507 (&H0E1B000B, CdoPR_HASATTACH)
Type =  11  (vbBoolean)
Value = False
----------
ID = 236781598 (&H0E1D001E, CdoPR_NORMALIZED_SUBJECT)
Type =  8  (vbString)
Value = Develop 3-year technology plan
----------
ID = 267649027 (&H0FF40003, CdoPR_ACCESS)
Type =  3  (vbLong)
Value =  3
----------
ID = 267845635 (&H0FF70003, CdoPR_ACCESS_LEVEL)
Type =  3  (vbLong)
Value =  1
----------
ID = 267911426 (&H0FF80102, CdoPR_MAPPING_SIGNATURE)
Type =  65  (vbBlob)
Value = 61D29510DD2B314E869888857E191E65
----------
```

Example 9-5. Sample Output from the DumpFields Routine (Example 9-3) (continued)

```
ID = 267976962 (&H0FF90102, CdoPR_RECORD_KEY)
Type =  65  (vbBlob)
Value = 24342000
----------
ID = 268042498 (&H0FFA0102, CdoPR_STORE_RECORD_KEY)
Type =  65  (vbBlob)
Value = 61D29510DD2B314E869888857E191E65
----------
ID = 268108034 (&H0FFB0102, CdoPR_STORE_ENTRYID)
Type =  65  (vbBlob)
Value =
0000000038A1BB1005E5101AA1BB08002B2A56C200006D737073742E646C6C00000000004E495441F9BFB8
0100AA0037D96E000000433A5C57494E444F57535C50726F66696C65735C64617665675C4170706C696361
74696F6E20446174615C4D6963726F736F66745C4F75746C6F6F6B5C6D61696C2E70737400
----------
ID = 268304387 (&H0FFE0003, CdoPR_OBJECT_TYPE)
Type =  3  (vbLong)
Value =  5
----------
ID = 268370178 (&H0FFF0102, CdoPR_ENTRYID)
Type =  65  (vbBlob)
Value = 0000000061D29510DD2B314E869888857E191E6524342000
----------
ID = 873267203 (&H340D0003, CdoPR_STORE_SUPPORT_MASK)
Type =  3  (vbLong)
Value =  14333
----------
ID = 267780354 (&H0FF60102, CdoPR_INSTANCE_KEY)
Type =  65  (vbBlob)
Value = 00203424
```

Notice in Example 9-5 that not all of the property IDs have corresponding CDO symbolic constants. Those that don't represent custom properties exposed by a service provider. Furthermore, property IDs that have their high-order bit set to 1 represent *named properties*. (These are the properties in Example 9-5 whose property IDs are negative.) Named properties were discussed in Chapter 2, *MAPI*. Their relevant feature for the purpose of the current discussion is that their property IDs are permitted to change from one MAPI session to the next. There lies the rub. While it is certainly possible to dump the Fields collection—as I have done here—to find property IDs of interest, it's not safe for your commercial application to rely on those property IDs remaining unchanged. However, for the purpose of experimentation, and even for the purpose of writing non-critical applications, the techniques presented here can be useful.

Finally, for the sake of completeness I'll mention that if you can find the name of a named property documented, CDO allows that name to be used as the index to the Fields collection in order to retrieve the corresponding Field object. At the time of this writing (late 1999), Microsoft has not documented the named properties related to task items.

Summary

Tasks are a useful tool for keeping track of activities and potentially even relationships between activities. Today, CDO provides basic support for creating and manipulating task items. Using the Fields collection, it's possible to go deeper and directly manipulate task item-specific data, but only for experimentation or for writing non-critical, non-commercial applications.

Chapter 10, *Contacts Folders*, is about accessing Outlook Contacts folders through CDO.

10

Contacts Folders

Contacts folders are an abstraction provided not by MAPI or CDO, but by Microsoft Outlook. To MAPI and CDO, a contact is just a message that happens to have certain properties useful for storing contact-related information. Because CDO doesn't provide a class that exposes contact properties, it's difficult to get at all of the contact information. This is the same problem that we had with tasks folders in the previous chapter. However, unlike with tasks, MAPI does define many standard property tags for storing and accessing contact information. These MAPI property tags can be used in conjunction with a CDO Field object to store and retrieve contact data. Just as with task items, however, some contact item properties can't be accessed reliably through CDO because they are exposed as named properties. You learned why this is a problem in the previous chapter.

This chapter discusses the basic contact information that is available through a Message object and shows how to get additional contact information by going through a Field object. Also discussed is using the MessageFilter object to search for specific contacts.

Finding the Default Contacts Folder

A user can have any number of contacts folders, but one of them (the one created first) is considered to be the default contacts folder. CDO provides a simple way to get access to the default contacts folder. To do so, use the Session object's GetDefaultFolder method, with an argument of `CdoDefaultFolderContacts`, as shown here:

```
' gCdoSession previously Dim'ed, Set, and logged on.
Dim CdoFolderContacts As MAPI.Folder

Set CdoFolderContacts = _
   gCdoSession.GetDefaultFolder(CdoDefaultFolderContacts)
```

When I refer to the Contacts folder (with a capital "C"), I mean the user's default contacts folder.

Reading Contact Information

Reading basic information from a contact item is just like reading a message. Contact items are represented by Message objects, which reside in Messages collections contained in Folder objects. The code in Example 10-1 shows how to iterate through the contact items found in the user's Contacts folder.

Example 10-1. Iterating Contacts

```
' gCdoSession previously Dim'ed, Set, and logged on.

Dim CdoFolder As MAPI.Folder
Dim CdoMessages As MAPI.Messages
Dim CdoMessage As MAPI.Message

' Get the collection of contact items from the Contacts folder.
Set CdoFolder = gCdoSession.GetDefaultFolder(CdoDefaultFolderContacts)
Set CdoMessages = CdoFolder.Messages

' Loop for each contact.
For Each CdoMessage In CdoMessages
    '
    ' Process the contact item.
    '
Next CdoMessage

' Cleanup
Set CdoMessage = Nothing
Set CdoMessages = Nothing
Set CdoFolder = Nothing
```

All of the standard Message object properties can be used with contact items. Note that the Subject property of the Message object is set to the name of the contact, and the Type property of the Message object is set to "`IPM.Contact`".

In addition to the properties exposed by the Message object, standard MAPI contact item-related properties can be accessed through the Message object's Fields collection.

The process for getting or setting a MAPI property using the Fields collection is:

1. Obtain a reference to the Fields collection of the CDO object whose property is to be read or written.
2. From the Fields collection, obtain the Field object that represents the specific property to be read or written.
3. Read or write the value, using the Field object's Value property.

For example, the function shown in Example 10-2 returns the business telephone number of a contact item passed to the function as a parameter:

Example 10-2. Getting a Contact's Business Telephone Number

```
Public Function GetBusinessTelephoneNumber( _
   ByVal CdoMessage As MAPI.Message _
) As String

   ' The GetBusinessTelephoneNumber function returns the business
   ' telephone number for the contact represented by the given
   ' CdoMessage object.

   Dim CdoFields As MAPI.Fields
   Dim CdoField As MAPI.Field

   ' Get the Message object's Fields collection.
   Set CdoFields = CdoMessage.Fields

   ' Get the Field object that represents the business telephone number.
   Set CdoField = CdoFields.Item(CdoPR_BUSINESS_TELEPHONE_NUMBER)

   ' Return the value of this property.
   GetBusinessTelephoneNumber = CdoField.Value

   ' Cleanup
   Set CdoField = Nothing
   Set CdoFields = Nothing

End Function ' GetBusinessTelephoneNumber
```

The *GetBusinessTelephoneNumber* function shown in Example 10-2 is called like this:

```
' Assume that CdoMessage represents a contact item.
Dim strBusinessTelephoneNumber

strBusinessTelephoneNumber = GetBusinessTelephoneNumber(CdoMessage)
```

Similarly, Example 10-3 shows a subroutine that assigns a new value to the business telephone number of the given contact item.

Example 10-3. Assigning a Contact's Business Telephone Number

```
Private Sub LetBusinessTelephoneNumber( _
   ByVal CdoMessage As MAPI.Message, _
   ByVal strNewValue As String _
)

   ' The LetBusinessTelephoneNumber function sets the business
   ' telephone number for the contact represented by the given
   ' CdoMessage object.

   Dim CdoFields As MAPI.Fields
```

Example 10-3. Assigning a Contact's Business Telephone Number (continued)

```
    Dim CdoField As MAPI.Field
    Dim nError As Long

    ' Get the Message object's Fields collection.
    Set CdoFields = CdoMessage.Fields

    ' Get the Field object that represents the business telephone number.
    ' If it's found, then set its value. If it's not found, then add it,
    ' setting its value at the same time.
    On Error Resume Next
    Set CdoField = CdoFields.Item(CdoPR_BUSINESS_TELEPHONE_NUMBER)
    nError = Err.Number
    On Error GoTo 0
    If nError = 0 Then
       ' The Field object was found. Now set its value.
       CdoField.Value = strNewValue
    ElseIf nError = CdoE_NOT_FOUND Then
       ' The Field object was not found. Add it and set its value.
       Set CdoField = CdoFields.Add(CdoPR_BUSINESS_TELEPHONE_NUMBER, _
          strNewValue)
    Else
       ' Else an error occurred.
       Err.Raise nError
    End If

    ' Cleanup
    Set CdoField = Nothing
    Set CdoFields = Nothing

End Sub ' LetBusinessTelephoneNumber
```

Notice in Example 10-3 that the code accounts for the possibility that a `CdoE_NOT_FOUND` error may occur when executing this statement:

```
Set CdoField = CdoFields.Item(CdoPR_BUSINESS_TELEPHONE_NUMBER)
```

Specifically, an error will occur if the contact item currently has no value for the `CdoPR_BUSINESS_TELEPHONE_NUMBER` property. You see, MAPI and CDO both endeavor to be as efficient as possible. Therefore, CDO Fields collections don't carry around Field objects for properties that have never been set. If there is a Field object for the `CdoPR_BUSINESS_TELEPHONE_NUMBER` property, the code assigns it a new value. If not, the code in Example 10-3 traps the resulting error and creates the Field object, using this statement:

```
Set CdoField = CdoFields.Add(CdoPR_BUSINESS_TELEPHONE_NUMBER, _
      strNewValue)
```

Your code must remain aware that if a value has not been assigned for a particular property, there will likely be no Field object to represent it.

The *LetBusinessTelephoneNumber* subroutine shown in Example 10-3 is called like this:

```
' Assume that CdoMessage represents a contact item.

LetBusinessTelephoneNumber CdoMessage, "(800) 555-1212"
CdoMessage.Update
```

Notice the call to the Message object's Update method in this code fragment. Without it, the change is not saved to the message store.

When using Microsoft Outlook to enter a telephone number for a contact, Outlook normalizes the telephone number. That is, Outlook modifies the string entered by the user so that it is saved in the form "`(nnn) nnn-nnnn`". This is a function of Outlook, not MAPI or CDO. The underlying MAPI property for a telephone number is just a string. When you write code that assigns a value to a telephone number property, be aware that MAPI stores the value exactly the way your code assigned it. If you want the string to be normalized, you'll have to do the normalization within your own code.

Both Example 10-2 and Example 10-3 use the predefined constant `CdoPR_BUSINESS_TELEPHONE_NUMBER`. CDO defines many constants that correspond to standard MAPI properties. These constants can be used as the index to a Fields collection to obtain a reference to the Field object that represents the MAPI property, assuming that the MAPI object being referenced exposes that property. In addition to `CdoPR_BUSINESS_TELEPHONE_NUMBER`, here are the CDO constants that represent contact-related properties:

`CdoPR_ASSISTANT`
: The name of the contact's administrative assistant.

`CdoPR_ASSISTANT_TELEPHONE_NUMBER`
: The phone number of the contact's administrative assistant.

`CdoPR_BUSINESS_FAX_NUMBER`
: The telephone number of the contact's fax machine.

`CdoPR_BUSINESS2_TELEPHONE_NUMBER`
: A secondary business telephone number for the contact.

`CdoPR_CALLBACK_TELEPHONE_NUMBER`
: A telephone number at which the contact can be reached.

`CdoPR_CAR_TELEPHONE_NUMBER`
: The contact's car telephone number.

`CdoPR_COMPANY_NAME`
: The contact's company name.

CdoPR_COUNTRY
: The name of the contact's country.

CdoPR_DEPARTMENT_NAME
: The name of the contact's department at the contact's company.

CdoPR_DISPLAY_NAME
: The full name of the contact.

CdoPR_GENERATION
: An abbreviation that follows the contact's name and indicates the contact's generation, such as "Jr.", "Sr.", or "III".

CdoPR_GIVEN_NAME
: The contact's first name.

CdoPR_GOVERNMENT_ID_NUMBER
: A government identification number for the contact.

CdoPR_HOME_FAX_NUMBER
: The contact's home fax machine telephone number.

CdoPR_HOME_TELEPHONE_NUMBER
: The contact's home telephone number.

CdoPR_HOME2_TELEPHONE_NUMBER
: A secondary home telephone number for the contact.

CdoPR_INITIALS
: The contact's initials.

CdoPR_ISDN_NUMBER
: The telephone number for the contact's ISDN telephone line.

CdoPR_LOCALITY
: The name of the contact's city or town.

CdoPR_LOCATION
: Additional location information for the contact, such as "Building 7, 3rd floor".

CdoPR_MANAGER_NAME
: The name of the contact's manager.

CdoPR_MOBILE_TELEPHONE_NUMBER
: The telephone number of the contact's mobile telephone.

CdoPR_OFFICE_LOCATION
: The contact's office location, in whatever format is meaningful for this contact.

CdoPR_ORGANIZATIONAL_ID_NUMBER
: The contact's ID number, as used within the contact's company.

CdoPR_OTHER_TELEPHONE_NUMBER
: An additional telephone number for the contact.

`CdoPR_PAGER_TELEPHONE_NUMBER`
: The telephone number for the contact's pager.

`CdoPR_POST_OFFICE_BOX`
: A string identifying the post office box of the contact—for example, "PO Box 10000".

`CdoPR_POSTAL_ADDRESS`
: The contact's postal address. The postal address consists of the street address, city or town, state or province, and postal code. The string returned by this property may contain carriage return characters (ASCII 13) to break the string into multiple lines.

`CdoPR_POSTAL_CODE`
: The contact's postal code (ZIP code in the United States).

`CdoPR_PRIMARY_FAX_NUMBER`
: The telephone number of the contact's primary fax machine.

`CdoPR_PRIMARY_TELEPHONE_NUMBER`
: The contact's primary telephone number.

`CdoPR_RADIO_TELEPHONE_NUMBER`
: The contact's radio telephone number.

`CdoPR_STATE_OR_PROVINCE`
: The name of the contact's state or province.

`CdoPR_STREET_ADDRESS`
: The contact's street address. The string returned by this property may contain carriage return characters (ASCII 13) to separate the street address into multiple lines.

`CdoPR_SURNAME`
: The contact's family name.

`CdoPR_TELEX_NUMBER`
: The contact's telex number.

`CdoPR_TITLE`
: The contact's job title.

Any of these properties can be accessed using the same technique shown in Example 10-2 and Example 10-3. To avoid writing dozens of accessor procedures, you may want to write two general-purpose procedures that can read and write any property, given the property tag. Example 10-4 provides these two general-purpose procedures. The *GetMAPIProperty* function takes as parameters a CDO object and a property tag, and returns the value of the given property. The *LetMAPIProperty* subroutine takes as parameters a CDO object, a property tag, and a value to be assigned to the property, and does the assignment. As with the

LetBusinessTelephoneNumber subroutine shown in Example 10-3, the caller must invoke the CDO object's Update method after calling *LetMAPIProperty*. The `CdoObject` parameter of each procedure is declared as Object, rather than as MAPI.Message, because many CDO classes expose a Fields collection, and by declaring the parameter as Object, the procedures can be used with any of them.

Example 10-4. Generic CDO Code for Reading and Writing MAPI Properties

```
Public Function GetMAPIProperty( _
   ByVal CdoObject As Object, _
   ByVal CdoPropTag As MAPI.CdoPropTags _
) As Variant

   ' The GetMAPIProperty function returns the value of the given
   ' MAPI property on the given CDO object.

   Dim CdoFields As MAPI.Fields
   Dim CdoField As MAPI.Field

   ' Get the CDO object's Fields collection.
   Set CdoFields = CdoObject.Fields

   ' Get the Field object that represents given property tag.
   Set CdoField = CdoFields.Item(CdoPropTag)

   ' Return the value of this property.
   GetMAPIProperty = CdoField.Value

   ' Cleanup
   Set CdoField = Nothing
   Set CdoFields = Nothing

End Function ' GetMAPIProperty

Public Sub LetMAPIProperty( _
   ByVal CdoObject As Object, _
   ByVal CdoPropTag As MAPI.CdoPropTags, _
   ByVal vntNewValue As Variant _
)

   ' The LetMAPIProperty function sets a new value for the given
   ' property on the given CDO object.

   Dim CdoFields As MAPI.Fields
   Dim CdoField As MAPI.Field
   Dim nError As Long

   ' Get the CDO object's Fields collection.
   Set CdoFields = CdoObject.Fields

   ' Get the Field object that represents the given property.
   ' If it's found, then set its value. If it's not found, then
   ' add it, setting its value at the same time.
```

Example 10-4. Generic CDO Code for Reading and Writing MAPI Properties (continued)

```
    On Error Resume Next
    Set CdoField = CdoFields.Item(CdoPropTag)
    nError = Err.Number
    On Error GoTo 0
    If nError = 0 Then
       ' The Field object was found. Now set its value.
       CdoField.Value = vntNewValue
    ElseIf nError = CdoE_NOT_FOUND Then
       ' The Field object was not found. Add it and set its value.
       Set CdoField = CdoFields.Add(CdoPropTag, vntNewValue)
    Else
       ' Else an error occurred.
       Err.Raise nError
    End If

    ' Cleanup
    Set CdoField = Nothing
    Set CdoFields = Nothing

End Sub ' LetMAPIProperty
```

For example, the *GetMAPIProperty* function shown in Example 10-4 can be used to retrieve the contact's job title like this:

```
' Assume that CdoMessage represents a contact item.
Dim strTitle As String

strTitle = GetMAPIProperty(CdoMessage, CdoPR_TITLE)
```

Similarly, the *LetMAPIProperty* function can be used to set a new job title (in this case, to "CEO") like this:

```
' Assume that CdoMessage represents a contact item.

LetMAPIProperty CdoMessage, CdoPR_TITLE, "CEO"
```

Filtering Contacts

By default, a contacts folder object's Messages collection contains a Message object for each contact in the folder. To limit the contacts that are returned to the client, use the MessageFilter object returned by the Filter property of the Messages collection. MessageFilter objects were introduced in Chapter 7, *Enhancing the Email Client*, and they are used here in the same way. In addition to the standard filtering that can be achieved by using the MessageFilter object's properties, it is also possible to filter on contact-specific properties through the use of the MessageFilter object's Fields collection. The general steps are:

1. Obtain a reference to the Messages collection of a contacts folder.
2. Obtain a reference to the MessageFilter object returned by the Filter property of the Messages collection.

3. Obtain a reference to the MessageFilter object's Fields collection.
4. Using the Fields collection's Add method, add a Field object that represents the specific property on which to filter.
5. Set the Value property of the Field object to the desired value.
6. If desired, add additional Field objects and set their Value properties.
7. Iterate through the Message objects in the Messages collection obtained in Step 1. Only Message objects that match the filter criteria will be seen.

These steps are illustrated in Example 10-5, which shows a segment of code that filters the Contacts folder for contacts having an address in Honolulu, Hawaii, USA. Notice the use of the *LetMAPIProperty* subroutine from Example 10-4.

Example 10-5. Filtering Contacts Based on Locality

```
' gCdoSession previously Dim'ed, Set, and logged on.

Dim CdoFolder As MAPI.Folder
Dim CdoMessages As MAPI.Messages
Dim CdoMessage As MAPI.Message
Dim CdoMessageFilter As MAPI.MessageFilter

' Get the Contacts folder and its Messages collection.
Set CdoFolder = gCdoSession.GetDefaultFolder(CdoDefaultFolderContacts)
Set CdoMessages = CdoFolder.Messages

' Get the MessageFilter object from the Messages collection.
Set CdoMessageFilter = CdoMessages.Filter

' We only want contacts, and only those contacts with an address in
' Honolulu, Hawaii, USA.
LetMAPIProperty CdoMessageFilter, CdoPR_MESSAGE_CLASS, "IPM.Contact"
LetMAPIProperty CdoMessageFilter, CdoPR_LOCALITY, "Honolulu"
LetMAPIProperty CdoMessageFilter, CdoPR_STATE_OR_PROVINCE, "HI"
LetMAPIProperty CdoMessageFilter, CdoPR_COUNTRY, "United States of America"

' Loop for each such Contact.
For Each CdoMessage In CdoMessages
    '
    ' Process each Contact.
    '
Next CdoMessage
```

Creating a Contact

Because contacts are stored as message items in the MAPI system, creating a contact is just like creating a new message. The steps to create a new contact are:

1. Obtain a reference to the Messages collection of a contacts folder.

2. Invoke the Messages collection's Add method to create a new contact item as a Message object.
3. (Optional) Set properties of the new contact item.
4. Invoke the Message object's Update method to save the contact in the message store.

Example 10-6 shows how to create a new contact, setting some additional properties at the same time. This code makes use of the *LetMAPIProperty* subroutine shown in Example 10-4. Figure 10-1 shows the newly created contact, as displayed by Microsoft Outlook 98.

As was the case with task items, some contact item properties are inaccessible. One of these properties is the "file as" setting in Outlook. This is the setting that labels each contact in Outlook's Address Card view. Therefore, contacts created programmatically appear to have no name when looked at in this view. CDO does not provide a workaround for this.

Example 10-6. Creating a Contact

```
' gCdoSession previously Dim'ed, Set, and logged on.

Dim CdoFolder As MAPI.Folder
Dim CdoMessages As MAPI.Messages
Dim CdoMessage As MAPI.Message

' Get the Contacts folder.
Set CdoFolder = gCdoSession.GetDefaultFolder(CdoDefaultFolderContacts)

' Get the collection of Contacts.
Set CdoMessages = CdoFolder.Messages

' Add a new Contact.
Set CdoMessage = CdoMessages.Add(Subject:="Jane Doe", Type:="IPM.Contact")
LetMAPIProperty CdoMessage, CdoPR_DISPLAY_NAME, "Jane Doe"
LetMAPIProperty CdoMessage, CdoPR_GIVEN_NAME, "Jane"
LetMAPIProperty CdoMessage, CdoPR_SURNAME, "Doe"
LetMAPIProperty CdoMessage, CdoPR_BUSINESS_TELEPHONE_NUMBER, _
   "(800) 555-1212"

' Save the new item.
CdoMessage.Update
```

Embedding a Contact in an Email

As you saw in Chapter 6, *An Email Client Application*, a MAPI message can be embedded inside another MAPI message. Because a contact is just a MAPI

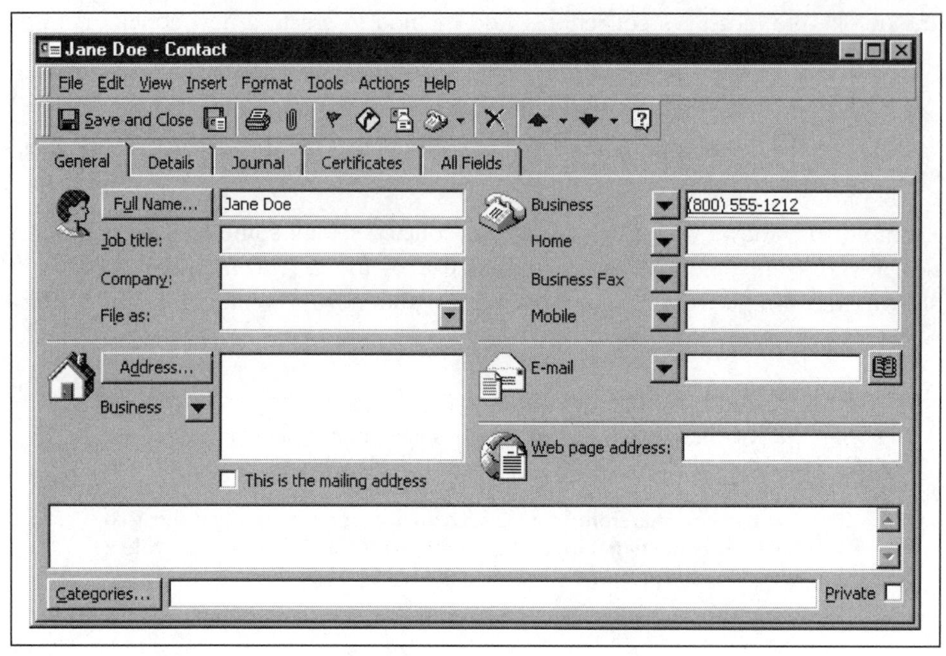

Figure 10-1. The contact created by the code in Example 10-6

message, contacts can be embedded inside other MAPI messages. This allows, for example, emailing a contact to a friend. Example 10-7 shows how this is done.

Example 10-7. Sending a Contact to a Friend

```
' gCdoSession previously Dim'ed, Set, and logged on.

' These are for the contact.
Dim CdoFolderContacts As MAPI.Folder
Dim CdoContacts As MAPI.Messages
Dim CdoContact As MAPI.Message
Dim CdoMessageFilter As MAPI.MessageFilter

' These are for the outgoing message.
Dim CdoFolderOutbox As MAPI.Folder
Dim CdoMessages As MAPI.Messages
Dim CdoMessage As MAPI.Message
Dim CdoAttachments As MAPI.Attachments
Dim CdoRecipients As MAPI.Recipients
Dim CdoRecipient As MAPI.Recipient

' Find a contact of interest.
Set CdoFolderContacts = _
   gCdoSession.GetDefaultFolder(CdoDefaultFolderContacts)
Set CdoContacts = CdoFolderContacts.Messages
Set CdoMessageFilter = CdoContacts.Filter
CdoMessageFilter.Subject = "Albert Einstein"
Set CdoContact = CdoContacts.Item(1) ' Will fail if no Albert Einstein.
```

Example 10-7. Sending a Contact to a Friend (continued)

```
' Create a new outgoing message.
Set CdoFolderOutbox = gCdoSession.Outbox
Set CdoMessages = CdoFolderOutbox.Messages
Set CdoMessage = CdoMessages.Add(Subject:="Here's a contact for Albert")

' Embed the contact.
Set CdoAttachments = CdoMessage.Attachments
Call CdoAttachments.Add( _
   Name:="Albert Einstein", _
   Position:=1, _
   Type:=CdoEmbeddedMessage, _
   Source:=CdoContact.ID)

' Address the outgoing message.
Set CdoRecipients = CdoMessage.Recipients
Set CdoRecipient = CdoRecipients.Add(Name:="Annemarie")
CdoRecipient.Resolve

' Send the message on its way.
CdoMessage.Send
```

Example 10-8 shows how to extract an embedded contact on the receiving end, adding it to the Contacts folder.

Example 10-8. Copying an Embedded Contact to the Contacts Folder

```
' gCdoSession previously Dim'ed, Set, and logged on.
' Assume that CdoMessage represents that email that contains the
' embedded contact item.

' These are for the incoming message.
Dim CdoAttachments As MAPI.Attachments
Dim CdoAttachment As MAPI.Attachment

' These are for the contact.
Dim CdoFolderContacts As MAPI.Folder
Dim CdoContacts As MAPI.Messages
Dim CdoContact As MAPI.Message
Dim CdoContactCopy As MAPI.Message

' Get contact from the email. Assume that the incoming email has only
' one attachment, and that its type is CdoEmbeddedMessage.
Set CdoAttachments = CdoMessage.Attachments
Set CdoAttachment = CdoAttachments.Item(1)
Set CdoContact = CdoAttachment.Source

' Get the Contacts folder
Set CdoFolderContacts = _
   gCdoSession.GetDefaultFolder(CdoDefaultFolderContacts)

' Move the contact to the Contacts folder.
Set CdoContactCopy = CdoContact.CopyTo(CdoFolderContacts.ID, _
```

Example 10-8. Copying an Embedded Contact to the Contacts Folder (continued)

```
    CdoFolderContacts.StoreID)

' Must do this.
CdoContactCopy.Update
```

Summary

In this chapter you learned how to work with contact items through CDO. Contacts, like tasks, are not directly exposed by CDO, but it's possible to work with them as messages and through the Fields collection. MAPI provides many standard properties for storing contact information, a bonus we didn't get with task items.

In Chapter 11, *Web Applications*, you'll learn how to take what you've learned about CDO and apply it to applications written for the Web.

11

Web Applications

If you're not yet familiar with Microsoft Internet Information Server (IIS) and Active Server Pages (ASP), it's time to learn. IIS is web server software that runs on Windows NT. ASP is a technology built into IIS that executes *embedded scripts* (short programs) in web pages prior to the pages being transmitted to the web browser. The general goal of running ASP script is to create HTML content dynamically to be sent to the browser. Because script is executed entirely on the server, and because only HTML is sent to the browser, this technology supports all browsers.

ASP interests us here because it can create and manipulate CDO objects. This opens the door to creating web pages that allow the user to manipulate email, contacts, calendars, etc.—in short, anything that can be done in a standard application using CDO. In addition, Microsoft has provided the CDO Rendering Library, an object model specifically designed for reading data from CDO objects and generating HTML for displaying the data. While the CDO Rendering Library doesn't do anything that can't be done using ASP script, it's nice not to have to write that script. (Note that occasionally in this chapter, and especially in code, I refer to the CDO Rendering Library as "CDORL" in the interest of brevity. This is not a Microsoft acronym.)

This chapter teaches you how to use CDO and the CDO Rendering Library on web pages using IIS and ASP. The CDO Rendering Library is rich. To fully explore it would require a book in itself. This chapter does cover all of the information you will need in order to display CDO information on web pages. What is not covered in detail are the many settings that can be adjusted to modify the default appearance of information. I will, however, try to provide enough information on these settings to point you in the right direction.

The scripts in this chapter are written in VBScript, which is generally similar to, and for the most part is a subset of, Visual Basic. To understand the content of this chapter, you must be familiar with basic web concepts, such as what a browser is and what HTML is, and with the CDO information presented thus far in the book. Although not strictly necessary, it will be tremendously helpful if you're already familiar with IIS and ASP. For further reading on these technologies, I recommend the O'Reilly books *ASP in a Nutshell*, by A. Keyton Weissinger, and *Developing ASP Components*, by Shelley Powers. For an HTML reference I recommend O'Reilly's *HTML: The Definitive Guide*, by Chuck Musciano and Bill Kennedy.

The Development Environment

Writing web pages is easy—all you need is a text editor. Deploying and testing the pages is another matter. If you're writing straight HTML, it's enough to save the file and then open it with a web browser to see how it looks. However, web pages that contain ASP script are meant to be interpreted by a web server, not by a browser. Therefore, it is necessary to deploy your pages on a web server in order to test them. In addition, for our purposes, the web server must have MAPI, CDO, and the CDO Rendering Library installed, as well as MAPI service providers for one or more message stores and message transports. To use the samples presented in this chapter, therefore, you must have the following:

1. A server computer running IIS version 4.0 or later, with a *virtual directory* set up for your application. See IIS documentation for information on setting up virtual directories and mapping them to file system folders. If you prefer, a Windows 9x machine running Personal Web Server can be used for development and testing.
2. A server computer running Microsoft Exchange Server version 5.5 or later. This will serve as the message store and transport provider. Security issues are easier if Exchange is installed on the same server as is IIS, but it's OK to have Exchange and IIS on different servers. These security issues are discussed later in this chapter.
3. Exchange Server comes with an ASP application called Outlook Web Access. This application must be installed on the server that runs IIS. Doing so installs MAPI, CDO, and the CDO Rendering Library, as well as the service providers needed for accessing Exchange. The Outlook Web Access application itself will not be used.

The development and testing process generally proceeds like this:

1. Write a web page using the editor of your choice.
2. Save the web page to the folder that you created on the IIS server. All web pages that contain ASP script must have a filename extension of *.asp*.
3. Use a web browser to open the web page from the virtual directory that you created on the IIS server.

Before beginning serious development, try creating a simple web page that has script. This ensures that your ASP environment is in working order. Example 11-1 shows the code for a simple web page that displays the date and time on which the page was read by the browser. Note that the page consists of a mixture of HTML and VBScript. HTML is passed verbatim to the browser, but script is interpreted by the server. Such interpretation may result in additional HTML being created and sent to the browser on the fly. In the case of Example 11-1, the string "`<%= Now %>`" (shown in bold in the example) is replaced by a string representing the current date and time. The actual text sent to the browser should resemble that shown in Example 11-2, and its appearance in a browser window should be similar to Figure 11-1.

Example 11-1. A Simple ASP Page

```
<html>
<head>
<title>Test ASP Page</title>
</head>
<body>
<h1>Test ASP Page</h1>
<p>This page was last refreshed on <%= Now %>.</p>
</body>
</html>
```

Example 11-2. The HTML Rendering of the Script in Example 11-1

```
<html>
<head>
<title>Test ASP Page</title>
</head>
<body>
<h1>Test ASP Page</h1>
<p>This page was last refreshed on 2/21/00 10:25:46 AM.</p>
</body>
</html>
```

The Server Environment

When a user runs a program on her computer, that program runs with the rights associated with that particular user. If the program attempts to access network resources, such as network folders or an Exchange server, the access succeeds only if the user who ran the program has the rights to do so. This is more complicated in web applications because the web server is not running under the end user's login name. To access a message store on a web user's behalf requires an understanding of the Windows NT authentication process. This process and its relation to IIS are explained in this section.

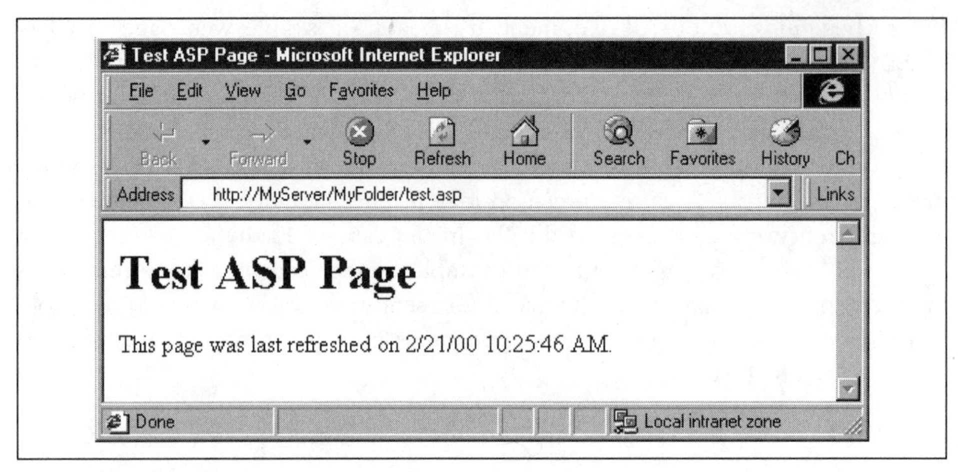

Figure 11-1. The display resulting from the script in Example 11-1

When IIS is installed on a computer, the installation process creates a username on that computer called "IUSR_*ComputerName*", where *ComputerName* is the name of the computer on which IIS is installed. For example, if IIS is installed on a computer named "MyServer", the username "IUSR_MyServer" is created on that computer. IIS keeps track of the password for this username. When script on a web page attempts to access a protected resource, IIS tries to gain access to that resource in two ways. First, IIS tries to access the resource as the IUSR_*ComputerName* username. If an administrator has granted access rights to that user, the access succeeds. If not, IIS attempts to communicate with the web user's browser in order to determine the identity of the web user. If it can be reliably determined who the web user is, IIS can impersonate the web user for the purpose of gaining access to the protected resource. Each method of gaining access to resources has its advantages.

IUSR_ComputerName

As already mentioned, the IUSR_*ComputerName* username is set up by default during IIS installation. However, it can be changed to any existing username, including a domain username. In addition, this can be configured differently for each virtual directory on a web site, or even for each individual page. If you're writing a web application that accesses network resources but doesn't depend on the identity of the web user for rights to those resources, set up a domain username that has rights to the resources and configure IIS to use that username. To change the username associated with a virtual directory:

1. In IIS's Internet Service Manager, right-click the virtual directory and choose Properties. The Properties dialog box appears, as shown in Figure 11-2.

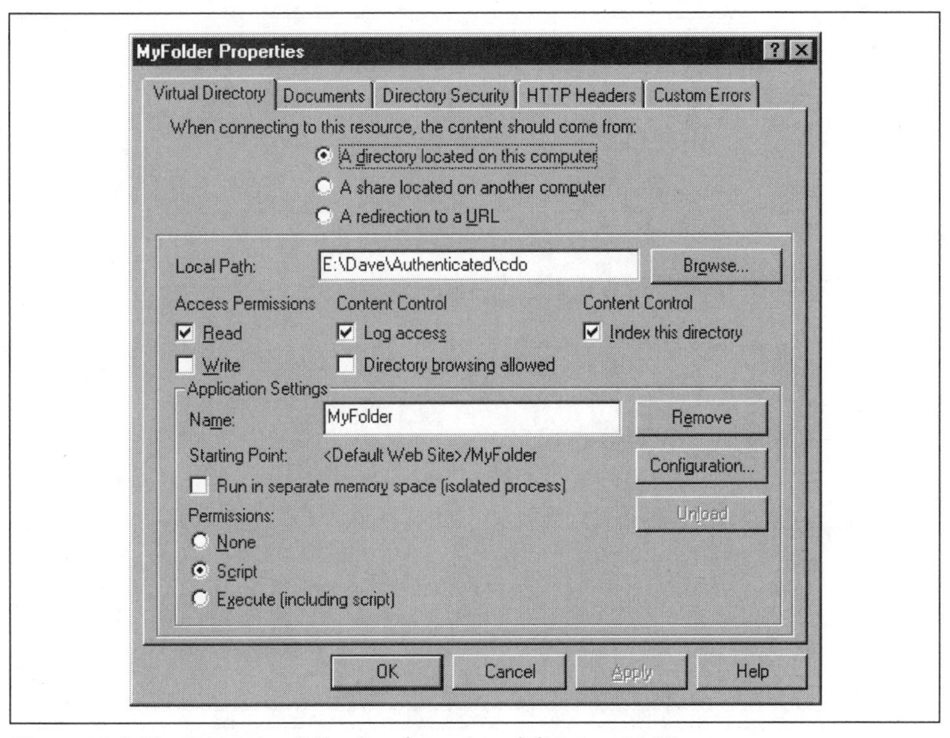

Figure 11-2. The Properties dialog box for a virtual directory in IIS

2. Click the Directory Security tab. The Properties dialog box now appears as shown in Figure 11-3.
3. In the Anonymous Access and Authentication Control frame, click the Edit button. The Authentication Methods dialog box appears, as shown in Figure 11-4.
4. As shown in Figure 11-4, ensure that only the Allow Anonymous Access checkbox is checked.
5. Click the Edit button. The Anonymous User Account dialog box appears, as shown in Figure 11-5.
6. Enter a username or click the Browse button to select a username from a list.
7. After selecting a username, uncheck the Enable Automatic Password Synchronization checkbox to enable the Password textbox. (Note that it may already be unchecked.)
8. Enter the correct password for the given username.
9. Click the OK button. The Confirm Password dialog box appears, as shown in Figure 11-6.
10. Enter the password again, and click the OK button.

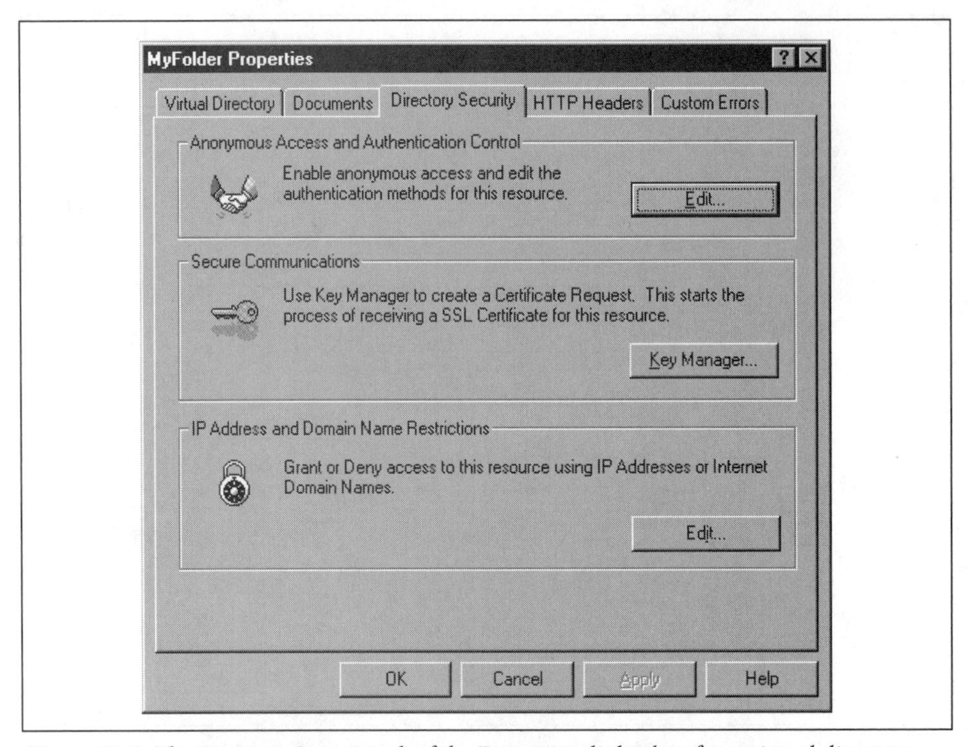

Figure 11-3. The Directory Security tab of the Properties dialog box for a virtual directory

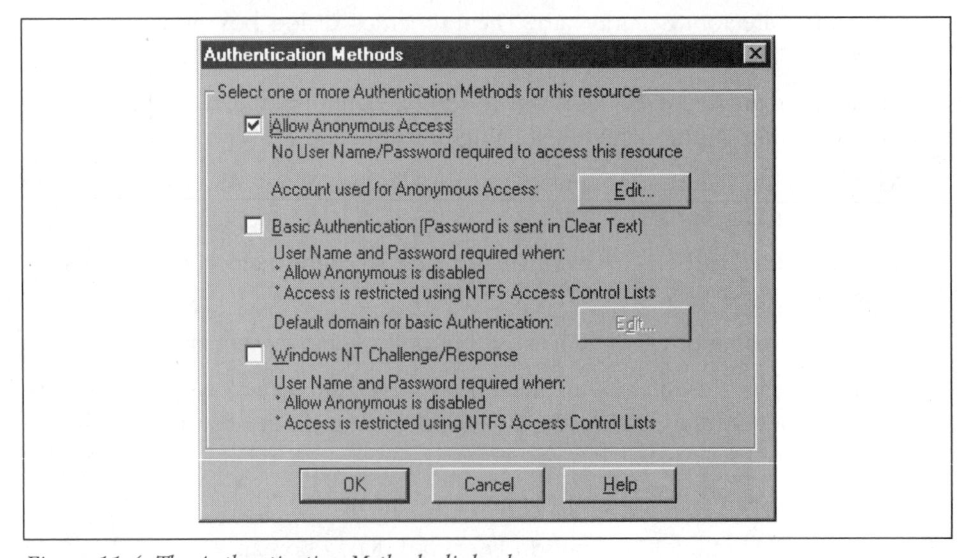

Figure 11-4. The Authentication Methods dialog box

To change the username associated with a specific web page:

1. In IIS's Internet Service Manager, right-click the file and choose Properties. The Properties dialog box appears, as shown in Figure 11-7.

Figure 11-5. The Anonymous User Account dialog box

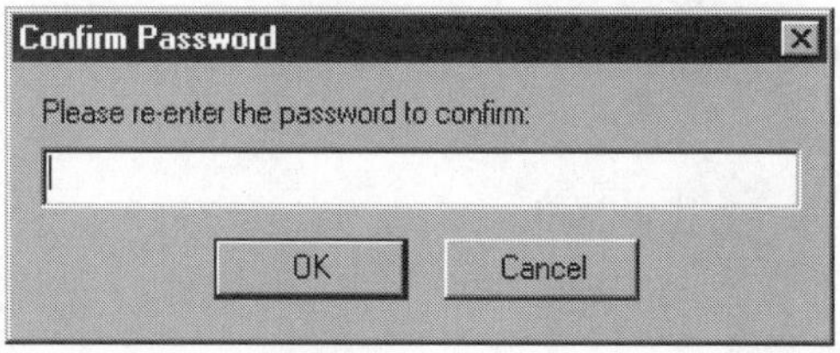

Figure 11-6. The Confirm Password dialog box

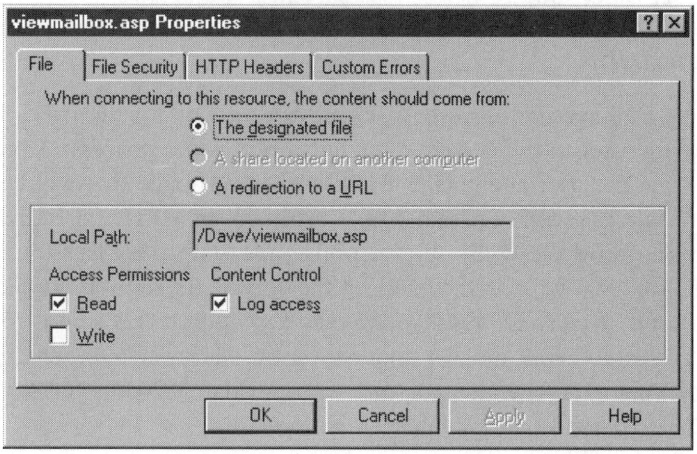

Figure 11-7. The Properties dialog box for a file in IIS

2. Click the File Security tab. The Properties dialog box now appears as shown in Figure 11-8.
3. Continue from Step 3 in the previous set of instructions.

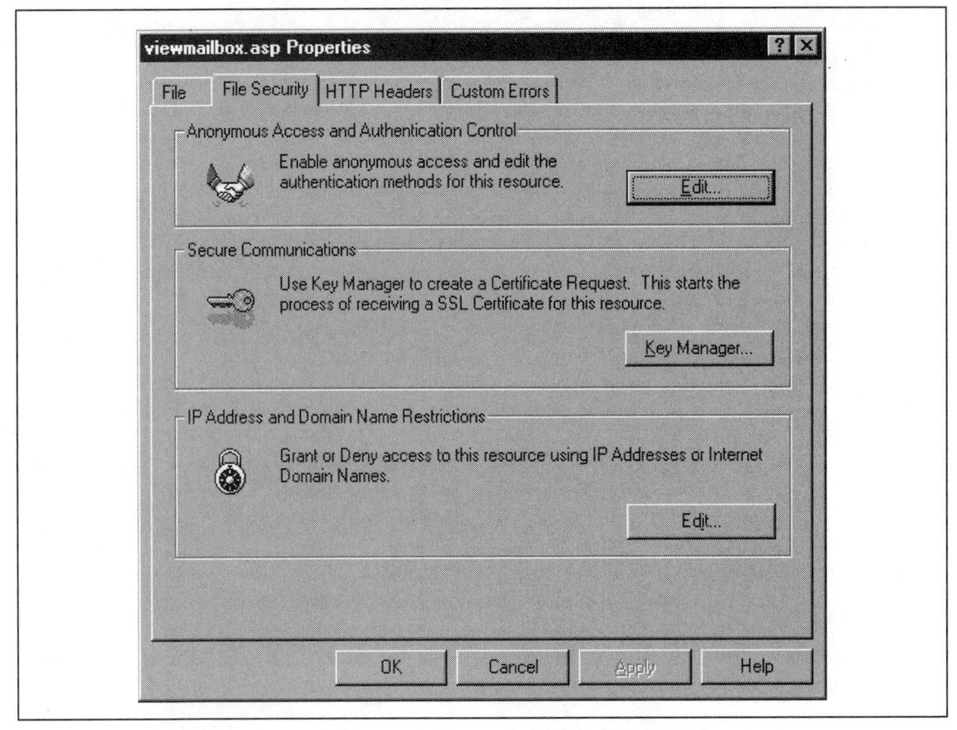

Figure 11-8. The File Security tab of the Properties dialog box for a file

Authentication

For accessing user-specific resources, IIS provides a way for the user's browser to authenticate the user to the server. (*Authentication* is the process of proving who you are.) When the user attempts to browse to a web page that will be accessing protected resources, script on that page can send an HTTP "401 Unauthorized" response to the browser. Within the response, the script also lists the authentication mechanisms that will be accepted by the server. IIS supports two authentication mechanisms: *Basic* and *NTLM Challenge/Response*. (NTLM stands for "NT LAN Manager.") Basic authentication is understood by Microsoft Internet Explorer and Netscape Navigator. At the time of this writing (March 2000), NTLM Challenge/Response is understood only by Internet Explorer.

Basic authentication

When the browser receives the "401 Unauthorized" response, it pops up a message box to the user asking for a username and password, as shown in Figure 11-9. The server uses the supplied username and password for accessing protected resources.

Basic authentication sends the user's username and password to the server in clear text. If Basic authentication is used, it is prudent to use an additional security protocol, such as Secure Socket Layer (SSL), to encrypt the transmission.

In addition, ASP script has access to the username and password entered by the user. In security-sensitive environments (such as banking, government, and e-commerce), code from development teams should be reviewed to ensure that username and password information is not used inappropriately. Developers should not have the ability to deploy their own code on a production server in such environments.

Figure 11-9. Dialog box presented to the user for Basic authentication

Because of Basic authentication's inherent security risk, IIS has it disabled by default. To turn this capability on, check the appropriate checkbox in the Authentication Methods dialog box, already shown in Figure 11-4. IIS warns you of the security risk, as shown in Figure 11-10.

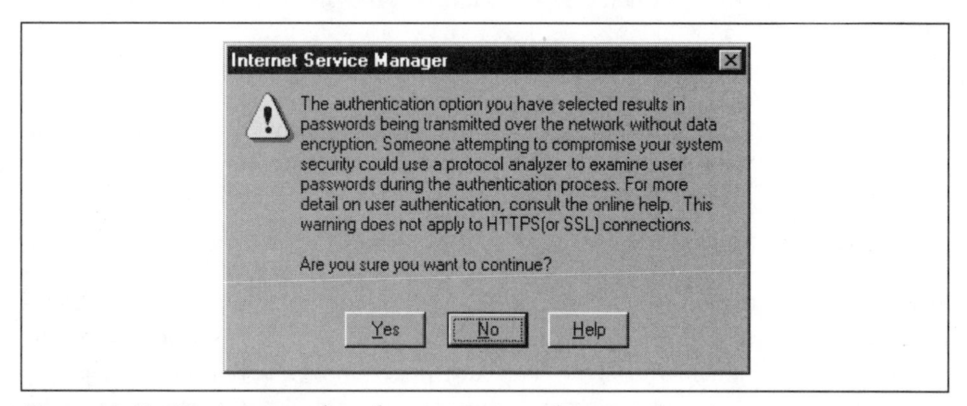

Figure 11-10. IIS's warning when choosing Basic authentication

NTLM Challenge/Response authentication

This authentication mechanism is appropriate only on intranets, because it requires the end user to be on a domain that is accessible and trusted by the IIS server. When the browser receives the "401 Unauthorized" response, it requests the page from the server again. The server again sends the "401 Unauthorized" response, and includes a random value (the *challenge*). The client computer encrypts the random value using a hash of the user's password. The encrypted value is then sent back to the server, which forwards it and the original challenge to the user's domain controller. The domain controller encrypts the original challenge using its locally stored copy of the user's password hash. If this encrypted value matches the value supplied by the user, the user is authenticated. Note that the web page script is responsible only for sending the first "401 Unauthorized" response. The subsequent challenge/response communication is handled by the server. Code examples are shown later in this chapter.

When a user is authenticated to the IIS server using NTLM Challenge/Response, the server is able to access server resources on the user's behalf. However, attempts by IIS to access resources on other servers fail, even though IIS is impersonating the user and the user has been granted rights to the resources. This is a side-effect of the current NT security mechanism. When the IIS server attempts to access resources on another machine, that machine tries to authenticate the request using the same challenge/response mechanism just described. However, because the IIS server doesn't possess the user's password hash, it is unable to encrypt the challenge, so the request fails.

If you wish to use NTLM Challenge/Response to authenticate access to Microsoft Exchange, Exchange must be installed on the same computer as is IIS. Basic authentication doesn't have this constraint because with Basic authentication, IIS does possess the user's password. This limitation is reported to have gone away under Windows 2000.

The examples in this chapter use Basic authentication and were tested in an environment where IIS and Exchange did not reside on the same machine.

ASP Applications and Sessions

From the perspective of ASP, a *web application* is made up of all of the web pages contained in a virtual directory and its subdirectories. A *session* is a period of time during which a particular user is accessing pages in the application. A session begins when a user accesses a page in the application and ends when script on a page explicitly terminates the session or after a period of time has elapsed with no new page access. The default period of time is 20 minutes. The application is said to begin when the first session begins and to end when the last session ends.

Application and session startup and shutdown are ideal times to perform initialization and cleanup activities. For the application to be notified of these events, a file called *global.asa* must be in the application's root folder, and in this file must be script to handle these events. Example 11-3 shows a skeleton *global.asa* file.

Example 11-3. Skeleton global.asa File

```
<script language="VBScript" runat="Server">

Sub Application_OnStart
   ' Application-wide initialization goes here.
End Sub

Sub Application_OnEnd
   ' Application-wide cleanup goes here.
End Sub

Sub Session_OnStart
   ' Per-session initialization goes here.
End Sub

Sub Session_OnEnd
   ' Per-session cleanup goes here.
End Sub

</script>
```

Note the use of the `<SCRIPT>` tag to identify the enclosed text as VBScript that is to be run by the server. VBScript is the default scripting language in IIS unless an administrator changes this setting, so usually a script will work if the `LANGUAGE` attribute is omitted. However, a frequent cause of an annoying error is to omit the `RUNAT` attribute, which causes the script to be transmitted to and executed on the browser.

A *global.asa* file suitable for a CDO application is shown in Example 11-4.

Example 11-4. A global.asa File to Support CDO Applications

```
<SCRIPT LANGUAGE="VBScript" RUNAT="Server">

Sub Application_OnStart

   ' Instantiate a CDORL Application object and save it in the
   ' ASP Application object.
   Set Application.Contents("CdorlApplication") = _
      Server.CreateObject("AMHTML.Application")
```

Example 11-4. A global.asa File to Support CDO Applications (continued)

```
End Sub ' Application_OnStart

Sub Application_OnEnd

   ' Release the CDORL Application object.
   Set Application.Contents("CdorlApplication") = Nothing

End Sub ' Application_OnEnd

Sub Session_OnStart

   ' Initialize the CDO Session object.
   Set Session.Contents("CdoSession") = Nothing

   ' Initialize the security context handle.
   Session.Contents("hImp") = 0

End Sub ' Session_OnStart

Sub Session_OnEnd

   Dim CdorlApplication
   Dim CdoSession
   Dim hImp

   ' Get the CDO Rendering Application object.
   Set CdorlApplication = _
      Application.Contents("CdorlApplication")

   ' Use the right security context for releasing the CDO Session object.
   hImp = Session.Contents("hImp")
   CdorlApplication.Impersonate(hImp)

   ' Release the CDO Session object if there is one.
   Set CdoSession = Session.Contents("CdoSession")
   If Not (CdoSession Is Nothing) Then
      CdoSession.Logoff
      Set Session.Contents("CdoSession") = Nothing
      Set CdoSession = Nothing
   End If

   Set CdorlApplication = Nothing

End Sub ' Session_OnEnd

</SCRIPT>
```

The *Application_OnStart* subroutine is called once when the first user accesses the web site. It is not called again until all sessions have ended and a new one has begun. This is the place to initialize state that is common to all users of a web site. The *Application_OnStart* subroutine in Example 11-4 creates a CDORL Application object and saves it in the ASP Application object. Only one CDORL Application object is needed by the entire application, which is why it's being created here. It is accessed by script on web pages through the ASP Application object.

The *Application_OnEnd* subroutine is called after the last web session ends and is the place to put application-wide cleanup. The *Application_OnEnd* subroutine in Example 11-4 releases the CDORL Application object that was created in the *Application_OnStart* subroutine.

The *Session_OnStart* subroutine is called at the start of each user's session. This is the place to initialize user-specific state that is to be maintained throughout the user's session. The *Session_OnStart* subroutine in Example 11-4 initializes two values in the ASP Session object that will be filled in later. Although this might seem like a good place to create a CDO Session object, a MAPI session can't be established until authorization credentials are gathered from the user.

The *Session_OnEnd* subroutine is called at the end of each user's session and is the place to put session-specific cleanup code. The *Session_OnEnd* subroutine in Example 11-4 releases the session's CDO Session object. Note that before doing so, it makes a call to the CDORL Application object's Impersonate method. This method is explained later in this chapter. For now, just be aware that the Impersonate method is a critical factor in ensuring that CDO calls are made in the right security context.

Establishing a MAPI Session

Example 11-5 shows a complete ASP page for creating a CDO Session object and logging on to Exchange Server. Note that this and subsequent examples assume the existence of the *global.asa* file shown in Example 11-4.

Example 11-5. Establishing a MAPI Session

```
<!-- #include file="lib.inc" -->
<%
   ' ---------------------------------------------------------------
   ' logon.asp
   ' This page establishes a MAPI session.
   ' ---------------------------------------------------------------

   Dim strUsername
   Dim strProfileInfo
   Dim CdoSession
   Dim CdoFolder
   Dim CdorlApplication

   ' Make sure that the user is authenticated.
   If Request.ServerVariables("AUTH_USER") = "" Then
      Response.Status = "401 Unauthorized"
```

Example 11-5. Establishing a MAPI Session (continued)

```
      Response.AddHeader "WWW-Authenticate", "Basic"
      Response.End
   End If

   ' Get the username.
   strUsername = Request.ServerVariables("AUTH_USER")

   ' Get the CDORL Application object. This will be used for obtaining
   ' the security context after logging on to MAPI.
   Set CdorlApplication = Application.Contents("CdorlApplication")

   ' Create a CDO Session object.
   Set CdoSession = Server.CreateObject("MAPI.Session")

   ' Save the CDO Session object for later use.
   Set Session.Contents("CdoSession") = CdoSession

   ' Log on to MAPI.
   strProfileInfo = "MyExchangeServer" & vbLf & strUsername
   CdoSession.Logon , , False, True, , , strProfileInfo

   ' Save the security context.
   Session.Contents("hImp") = CdorlApplication.ImpID

   ' The Logon method always succeeds, so try to access something to
   ' ensure that a connection was made.
   Set CdoFolder = CdoSession.GetDefaultFolder(CdoDefaultFolderInbox)

   ' Clean up.
   Set CdorlApplication = Nothing
   Set CdoFolder = Nothing
   Set CdoSesion = Nothing

   ' Display the user's information stores.
   Response.Redirect "viewinfostores.asp"

%>
```

Note the following in Example 11-5:

- The `#include` directive tells IIS to include the text from the file *lib.inc* just as though it had been typed into this page. *lib.inc* is a file I created to hold procedures and constants that may be used from many pages in the application. The procedures will be shown in this chapter as they are discussed. The constants are defined as follows:

  ```
  ' MAPI properties
  Const CdoPR_DISPLAY_NAME = &H3001001F
  Const CdoPR_SUBJECT = &H0037001F
  Const CdoPR_BODY = &H1000001F
  Const CdoPR_START_DATE = &H00600040
  Const CdoPR_END_DATE = &H00610040
  Const CdoPR_LOCATION = &H3A0D001F
  ```

```
Const CdoPR_MESSAGE_CLASS = &H001A001F
Const CdoPR_EMAIL_ADDRESS = &H3003001F
Const PR_IPM_PUBLIC_FOLDERS_ENTRYID = &H66310102

' Constants that represent the various CDORL classes.
Const CdoClass_Application = 1
Const CdoClass_ObjectRenderer = 2
Const CdoClass_ContainerRenderer = 3
Const CdoClass_Format = 4
Const CdoClass_Formats = 5
Const CdoClass_Patterns = 6
Const CdoClass_Pattern = 7
Const CdoClass_Views = 8
Const CdoClass_TableView = 9
Const CdoClass_Columns = 10
Const CdoClass_Column = 11
Const CdoClass_CalendarView = 12

' Constants used by the Render method of
' the CDORL ContainerRenderer object.
Const CdoFolderContents = 1
Const CdoFolderHierarchy = 2

' Constants used by the GetDefaultFolder method of
' the CDO Session object.
Const CdoDefaultFolderCalendar = 0
Const CdoDefaultFolderInbox = 1
Const CdoDefaultFolderOutbox = 2
Const CdoDefaultFolderSentItems = 3
Const CdoDefaultFolderDeletedItems = 4
Const CdoDefaultFolderContacts = 5
Const CdoDefaultFolderJournal = 6
Const CdoDefaultFolderNotes = 7
Const CdoDefaultFolderTasks = 8

' Constants used by the GetAddressList method of
' the CDO Session object.
Const CdoAddressListGAL = 0
Const CdoAddressListPAB = 1
```

Some texts use the numeric values in code samples. However, real-world programs should define the symbolic constants because they make code more readable as well as more maintainable.

- The script checks the value of the AUTH_USER server variable in ASP's Request object to see if it is an empty string. If so, the user has not yet been authenticated, so the script initiates authentication by returning a "401 Unauthorized" response and including a header line that indicates the type of authentication supported. The `Response.End` statement causes the response to be sent immediately, discarding the rest of the page. The handshaking described earlier in the chapter then ensues, but this is handled by IIS, not by the script. When authentication completes successfully, the page is accessed again. This time the **AUTH_USER** server variable contains the username of the authenticated user, causing the `If` block to be skipped.

Example 11-5 uses Basic authentication. To use NTLM Challenge/Response authentication, change the code to the following (note the bolded text):

```
' Make sure that the user is authenticated.
If Request.ServerVariables("AUTH_USER") = "" Then
   Response.Status = "401 Unauthorized"
   Response.AddHeader "WWW-Authenticate", "NTLM"
   Response.End
End If
```

Remember to check that IIS is configured to support the authentication mechanism you want to use. This is done in the Authentication Methods dialog box, shown earlier in Figure 11-4. Consider also whether your users will have a browser that supports the chosen authentication method.

- After the user has been authenticated, the user's username is read from the **AUTH_USER** server variable. This is used later in the script to log on to the user's Exchange mailbox.
- The CDORL Application object is obtained from the ASP Application object. This is the CDORL Application object that was created in the *Application_OnStart* subroutine in *global.asa*. The CDORL Application object is used later in the script to obtain a security context handle. As will be explained, the security context handle helps to ensure that IIS impersonates the authenticated user at appropriate times.
- A CDO Session object is created and stored in the ASP Session object. By storing the CDO Session object in the ASP Session object, the CDO Session object is made available to all script pages that are accessed during the user's ASP session.
- The CDO Session object's Logon method is called to log onto the user's Exchange Server mailbox. The syntax of the Logon method is:

```
CdoSession.Logon([ProfileName][,ProfilePassword][,ShowDialog][,NewSession]
                 [,ParentWindow][,NoMail][,ProfileInfo])
```

Because this application is intended to be able to access the mailbox of any user, it uses the Logon method's ***ProfileInfo*** parameter to specify the Exchange Server name and mailbox alias of the user. The script also assumes that the user's username is the same as the user's Exchange Server mailbox alias, as is commonly the case. The parameters of the Logon method were described in detail in Chapter 6, *An Email Client Application*.

- After logging on through the CDO Session object, the ImpID property of the CDORL Application object contains a security context handle. This handle is saved in the ASP Session object and is used later with the CDORL Application object's Impersonate method to ensure that IIS is placed in the proper security context before performing certain actions on behalf of the user.

- When logging on from a web page, the CDO Session object's Logon method succeeds even if the user is not successfully logged on to Exchange. The script therefore attempts to access an object in the user's mailbox to verify that logon was successful. If this fails, the user is redirected to a page explaining the failure. If it succeeds, the user is redirected to a page that displays the user's information stores (shown later in this chapter).
- As shown here, it is not necessary for an ASP page to send any visible content to the user. Some pages exist simply for their effect.

Displaying CDO Data

From previous chapters, you already know how to traverse the CDO object model. For a review of the CDO object model, refer back to Chapter 5, *Collaboration Data Objects*. In the current chapter, I won't spend time on the structure of CDO. Rather, I'll focus on explaining how to display CDO's various objects on a web page.

To display CDO data on a web page, it is necessary to generate HTML that represents the data, and to send that HTML to the user's browser. There are two ways to generate the HTML. One is to execute script that reads CDO object properties and constructs HTML strings based on property values, and the other is to pass CDO objects to CDO Rendering Library objects and to ask the CDO Rendering Library objects to create the HTML.

Generating HTML in Script

Example 11-6 shows a function that takes as an argument a CDO InfoStores collection object and returns an HTML string representing the list of InfoStore objects in the collection. In this example I chose to build a one-column HTML table, with one row per information store. The names of the information stores are displayed in the cells of the table. I have also used line breaks (`vbCrLf`) and white space to make the generated HTML more readable to anyone viewing the raw HTML. This is for aesthetic reasons only, and has no effect on the browser's display. Example 11-7 shows an example of the HTML this function might generate for an InfoStores collection having two items.

Example 11-6. Rendering an InfoStores Collection

```
Public Function RenderInfoStores(CdoInfoStores)

   ' This procedure returns an HTML string representing a list of the
   ' information stores in the given InfoStores collection.

   Dim strRetVal
   Dim CdoInfoStore

   ' Start the table.
```

Example 11-6. Rendering an InfoStores Collection (continued)

```
   strRetVal = "<table border=""1"">" & vbCrLf

   ' Loop through each InfoStore object.
   For Each CdoInfoStore In CdoInfoStores

      ' Write a table row for this InfoStore.
      strRetVal = strRetVal & "   <tr><td>" & CdoInfoStore.Name _
         & "</td></tr>" & vbCrLf

   Next ' CdoInfoStore

   ' Finish off the table.
   strRetVal = strRetVal & "</table>" & vbCrLf

   RenderInfoStores = strRetVal

   ' Clean up.
   Set CdoInfoStore = Nothing

End Function ' RenderInfoStores
```

Example 11-7. Sample Output from the RenderInfoStores Function in Example 11-6

```
<table border="1">
   <tr><td>Public Folders</td></tr>
   <tr><td>Mailbox - Dave Grundgeiger</td></tr>
</table>
```

In order to call the *RenderInfoStores* function, it is necessary to have an InfoStores object to pass to it. This can be obtained from the CDO Session object stored in the ASP Session object. Example 11-8 shows a function, *RenderUserInfoStores*, that wraps up this task and the call to *RenderInfoStores*. Example 11-9 shows a web page that calls the *RenderUserInfoStores* function and sends the result to the user's browser. The resulting display is shown in Figure 11-11.

Example 11-8. Rendering the InfoStores Collection of the Logged-On User

```
Public Function RenderUserInfoStores

   ' This procedure returns an HTML string representing a list of the
   ' currently logged-on user's message stores.

   Dim CdoSession
   Dim CdoInfoStores

   ' Get the current CDO Session object.
   Set CdoSession = Session.Contents("CdoSession")

   ' Get the user's InfoStores collection object.
   Set CdoInfoStores = CdoSession.InfoStores

   ' Create the HTML.
```

Example 11-8. Rendering the InfoStores Collection of the Logged-On User (continued)

```
   RenderUserInfoStores = RenderInfoStores(CdoInfoStores)

   ' Clean up.
   Set CdoInfoStores = Nothing
   Set CdoSession = Nothing

End Function ' RenderUserInfoStores
```

Example 11-9. Calling the RenderUserInfoStores Function from a Web Page

```
<!-- #include file="lib.inc" -->
<%
   ' ------------------------------------------------------------------
   ' yourinfostores.asp
   ' This page displays the user's list of information stores.
   ' ------------------------------------------------------------------
%>
<html>
<head>
<title>Your Information Stores</title>
</head>
<body>
<h1>Your Information Stores</h1>

<%
   Response.Write RenderUserInfoStores
%>

</body>
</html>
```

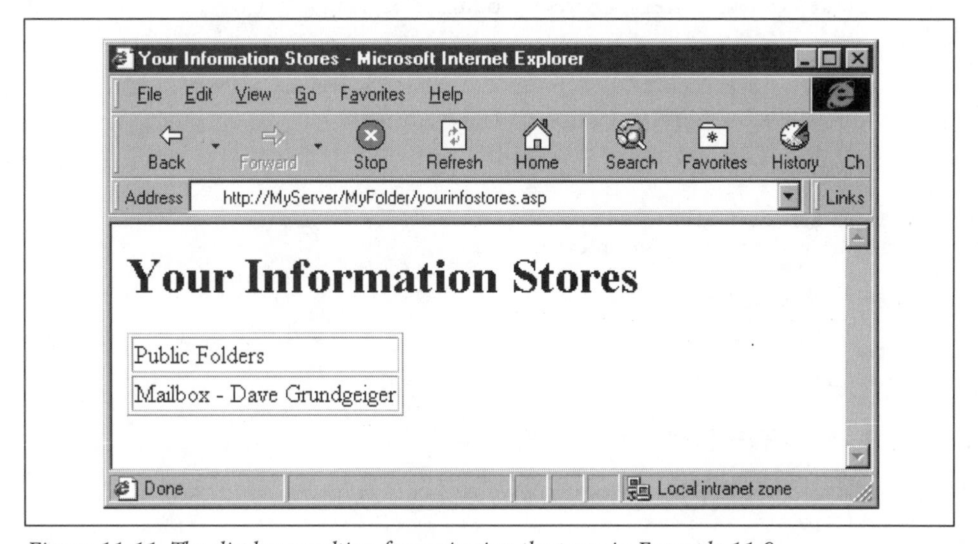

Figure 11-11. The display resulting from viewing the page in Example 11-9

Having displayed the list of information stores to the user, it would be nice to allow the user to click an information store name to see what it contains. To provide this ability, it is necessary to modify the code in the *RenderInfoStores* function of Example 11-6 such that it creates link elements in the HTML. These links will point to a page that is capable of listing a specific information stores folder, given the ID of the information store that is to be displayed. Example 11-10 shows the suitably modified *RenderInfoStores* function. The additions to the code are in boldface. A sample of the HTML produced by this new function is shown in Example 11-11.

Example 11-10. Modifying the RenderInfoStores Function to Produce HTML That Has Link Elements

```
Public Function RenderInfoStores(CdoInfoStores)

   ' This procedure returns an HTML string representing a list of the
   ' information stores in the given InfoStores collection.

   Dim strRetVal
   Dim CdoInfoStore
   Dim strLink

   ' Start the table.
   strRetVal = "<table border=""1"">" & vbCrLf

   ' Loop through each InfoStore object.
   For Each CdoInfoStore In CdoInfoStores

      ' Construct a link for viewing this InfoStore.
      strLink = "viewinfostore.asp?ID=" & CdoInfoStore.ID

      ' Write a table row for this InfoStore.
      strRetVal = strRetVal & "   <tr><td><a href=""" & strLink & """>" _
         & CdoInfoStore.Name & "</a></td></tr>" & vbCrLf

   Next ' CdoInfoStore

   ' Finish off the table.
   strRetVal = strRetVal & "</table>" & vbCrLf

   RenderInfoStores = strRetVal

   ' Clean up.
   Set CdoInfoStore = Nothing

End Function ' RenderInfoStores
```

Example 11-11. Sample Output from the Modified RenderInfoStores Function in Example 11-10

```
<table border="1">
   <tr><td><a href="viewinfostore.asp?ID=C30">Public Folders</a></td></tr>
```

Example 11-11. Sample Output from the Modified RenderInfoStores Function in Example 11-10 (continued)

```
   <tr><td><a href="viewinfostore.asp?ID=4B7">Mailbox - Dave Grundgeiger</a></td></tr>
</table>
```

The ID values in Example 11-11 have been shortened for clarity. In practice, information store IDs are much longer.

Having thus modified the *RenderInfoStores* function, the web page of Example 11-9 produces a display with a hyperlink for each information store name. Each hyperlink points to the same place—a file named *viewinfostore.asp*—but each has a different value for the *ID* parameter. The *ID* parameter has a value equal to the ID of the selected information store. This parameter value can be retrieved by the script in *viewinfostore.asp* and passed to the CDO Session object's GetInfoStore method to retrieve the correct InfoStore object. A possible implementation of the *viewinfostore.asp* page is shown in Example 11-12.

Example 11-12. Rendering a Specific InfoStore Based on an HTTP Parameter

```
<!-- #include file="lib.inc" -->
<%
   ' ----------------------------------------------------------------
   ' viewinfostore.asp
   ' This page displays the list of folders in the information store
   ' specified by the ID parameter.
   ' ----------------------------------------------------------------
%>
<html>
<head>
<title>InfoStore--CDO Web Demonstration</title>
</head>
<body>
<h1>CDO Web Demonstration</h1>

<%
   Response.Write RenderInfoStore(Request.QueryString("ID"))
%>

</body>
</html>
```

The script in Example 11-12 uses the ASP Request object's QueryString method to retrieve the value of the *ID* parameter and pass it to a hypothetical *RenderInfoStore* function. The *RenderInfoStore* function could use the techniques presented so far in this chapter to build a list of folders contained in the information store. Similarly, additional functions could be written to render each type of CDO object.

Generating HTML with the CDO Rendering Library

The CDO Rendering Library was created to take over much of the drudgery of generating HTML from CDO data. The general process is to instantiate a *renderer*, then assign a CDO object to the renderer's DataSource property, and then call a method on the renderer to generate HTML. In practice this can be either simple or complex, depending on whether the CDO Rendering Library's default settings are suitable for the CDO objects you wish to render, and for the visual effect you're trying to achieve. In addition, some CDO objects can't be rendered by the CDO Rendering Library, in which case you can use the techniques presented in the preceding section.

The CDO Rendering Library object model

Figure 11-12 shows the CDO Rendering Library's object model diagram.

Here is a brief description of each object. Don't worry if the concepts of views, columns, formats, and patterns aren't clear right now. They are explained more fully later in the chapter:

The RenderingApplication object
: This object is also known as the CDO Rendering Library Application object. It provides methods for creating and managing other objects in the hierarchy. It is not itself used for rendering CDO data.

The ContainerRenderer object
: This object reads data from a CDO collection object and generates a string representing the collection as an HTML table. The CDO objects that can be rendered by a ContainerRenderer object are the AddressEntries collection, the Folders collection, the Messages collection, and the Recipients collection. Code examples for each are given later in this chapter.

The ObjectRenderer object
: This object reads data from a CDO object and generates a string representing one specific property of the CDO object.

The Views collection
: This collection holds TableView and CalendarView objects that can be applied to the ContainerRenderer object (via its CurrentView property). Views control the appearance of a rendered CDO collection object.

The TableView object
: This object controls the appearance of rendered AddressEntries, Folders, Messages, and Recipients collections. Views are discussed later in this section.

The CalendarView object
: This object controls the appearance of rendered Messages collections that contain AppointmentItem objects. Rendering calendars is not discussed in this chapter.

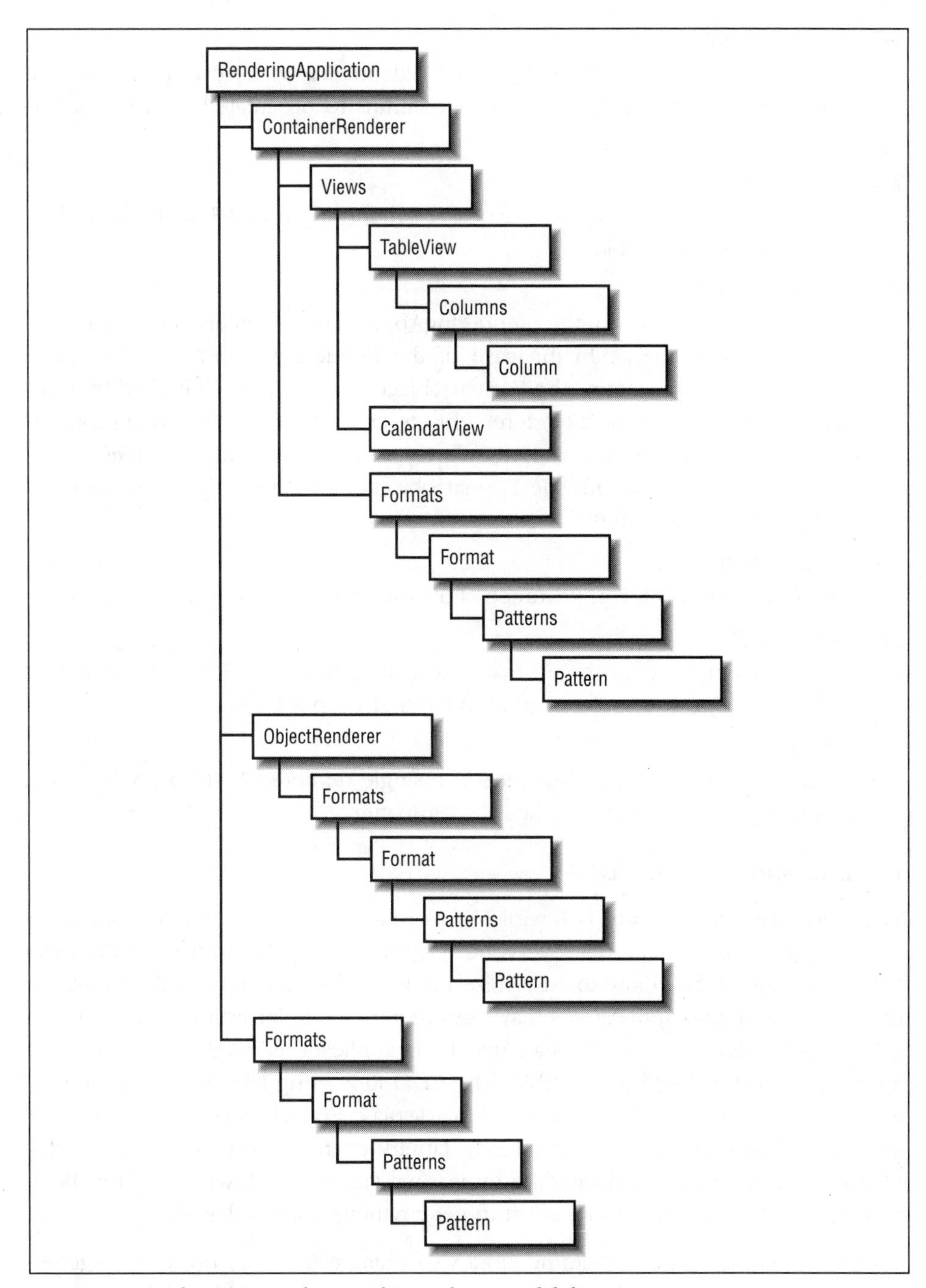

Figure 11-12. The CDO Rendering Library object model diagram

The Columns collection
: This collection exists in TableView and CalendarView objects. It contains the Column objects that define the HTML columns to be created by a Container-Renderer object.

The Column object
: This object controls the appearance of a column in an HTML table created by a ContainerRenderer object.

The Formats collection
: This collection exists in the RenderingApplication, ContainerRenderer, and ObjectRenderer objects. In the case of the RenderingApplication object, the Formats collection contains the Format objects that are to be inherited by ContainerRenderer and ObjectRenderer objects created by the RenderingApplication object. For the ContainerRenderer and ObjectRenderer objects, the Formats collection contains the Format objects that control the appearance of rendered MAPI properties.

The Format object
: This object controls the appearance of a single rendered MAPI property.

The Patterns collection
: This collection exists in the Format object. It contains the Pattern objects that control the appearance of a single rendered MAPI property.

The Pattern object
: This object controls the appearance of a single rendered MAPI property when the value of the property matches a given pattern.

Views, formats, and patterns

The CDO Rendering Library is flexible in its rendering of data. Rather than have just one visual appearance that everyone must live with, Microsoft gave the CDO Rendering Library the ability to customize the look of generated HTML. For example, just because two applications may both require a tabular listing of the items in a Messages collection doesn't mean that both applications need the same set of message properties listed in the table. The CDO Rendering Library allows the programmer to determine which properties to display, and even how each property looks on the screen. The CDO Rendering Library even supports the ability to display a property differently depending on its own value. The downside of this flexibility is that it takes a little more effort to get anything displayed at all.

The purpose of the CDO Rendering Library's ContainerRenderer object is to generate HTML tables from CDO collection objects. For example, a Messages collection is rendered as an HTML table where each row is one message, and each column is one MAPI property that applies to a Message object. In order for the CDO Rendering Library to know which MAPI properties to include in the table, it is necessary to define a view and assign that view to the ContainerRenderer object's CurrentView property. There are two kinds of view objects: the CalendarView object, for controlling the appearance of Messages collections containing calendar data, and the TableView object, for controlling the appearance of all other collections. Both objects contain a Columns collection, which determines the number of columns in the rendered table as well as the MAPI properties displayed in each column.

For finer control, the Column object has the RenderUsing property. This property is a string that controls the appearance of the MAPI property being rendered. If the RenderUsing property is left blank, the CDO Rendering Library displays the value of the MAPI property in a default way appropriate to its datatype. However, by setting the RenderUsing property to a combination of literal text and *substitution tokens*, it is possible to achieve more complex HTML output, such as table cells that contain links to other pages. An example of creating a view, adding columns, and setting the RenderUsing property is given later, in the discussion of rendering a Folders collection.

The purpose of the CDO Rendering Library's ObjectRenderer object is to generate non-tabular HTML output from individual MAPI properties. This is done by passing a MAPI property ID to the ObjectRenderer object's RenderProperty method. Generally, the RenderProperty method renders MAPI properties in a default way appropriate to their datatype. However, to allow fine-grained control of the appearance of rendered MAPI properties, Format objects can be added to the ObjectRenderer object's Formats collection. Each Format object in the collection represents a MAPI property that should get special treatment during rendering. The property of the Format object determines to which MAPI property the Format object applies. If the RenderProperty method is asked to render a MAPI property for which a Format object exists, the Format object's Patterns collection is consulted to determine how the MAPI property is to be rendered. Each Pattern object in the collection corresponds to a particular value or range of values that the MAPI property may take on. When the value of the MAPI property is equal to the value or is within the range of values identified by the Pattern object, it is rendered using the Pattern object's RenderUsing property (similar to the use of the RenderUsing property of the Column object previously described). A single Format object's Patterns collection can hold many Pattern objects, thereby providing different rendering based on the value of the MAPI property. An example of using the ObjectRenderer object's Formats collection is given later in this chapter, in the section "Rendering individual MAPI properties."

Lastly, the RenderingApplication object itself has a Formats collection. The structure of this collection is the same as that described inpd the previous paragraph. If one of the rendering objects is rendering a MAPI property for which there is no associated rendering information, the CDO Rendering Library looks to the RenderingApplication object's Formats collection for information on how to render the property.

Rendering a folders collection

Example 11-12 included a call to a hypothetical function, *RenderInfoStore*, that would take an information store ID and render the list of folders contained by the store. We are now ready to develop this function. Example 11-13 shows the *RenderInfoStore* function.

Example 11-13. The RenderInfoStore Function

```
Public Function RenderInfoStore(strID)

   ' This procedure returns an HTML string representing a list of the
   ' folders in the InfoStore whose ID is given by strID.

   Dim CdoSession
   Dim CdoInfoStore
   Dim CdoFolder
   Dim CdoFolders
   Dim CdorlApplication
   Dim CdorlRenderer
   Dim CdorlViews
   Dim CdorlView
   Dim CdorlColumns
   Dim CdorlColumn
   Dim strLink
   Dim nErr

   ' Get the CDORL Application object.
   Set CdorlApplication = Application.Contents("CdorlApplication")

   ' Set the correct security context.
   CdorlApplication.Impersonate(Session.Contents("hImp"))

   ' Get the CDO Session object.
   Set CdoSession = Session.Contents("CdoSession")

   ' Get the InfoStore given by strID.
   Set CdoInfoStore = CdoSession.GetInfoStore(strID)

   ' Get the collection of folders contained in this InfoStore.
   Set CdoFolder = CdoInfoStore.RootFolder
   On Error Resume Next
   Set CdoFolders = CdoFolder.Folders
   nErr = Err.Number
   On Error Goto 0
   If nErr <> 0 Then
      ' An error occurs when attempting to access the root folder of
      ' the Microsoft Exchange Public Folders. The following Set
      ' statement obtains the root folder using a different method.
      Set CdoFolder = _
         CdoSession.GetFolder( _
            CdoInfoStore.Fields(PR_IPM_PUBLIC_FOLDERS_ENTRYID), _
            CdoInfoStore.ID)
```

Example 11-13. The RenderInfoStore Function (continued)

```
      Set CdoFolders = CdoFolder.Folders
   End If

   ' Create a ContainerRenderer object for rendering the Folders collection.
   Set CdorlRenderer = _
      CdorlApplication.CreateRenderer(CdoClass_ContainerRenderer)

   ' Set the data source. Note that the "Set" keyword is not used.
   CdorlRenderer.DataSource = CdoFolders

   ' Add a custom view for viewing this collection.
   '
   ' Get the Views collection and add a View.
   Set CdorlViews = CdorlRenderer.Views
   Set CdorlView = CdorlViews.Add("MyView")
   '
   ' Get the Columns collection and add the column that we want displayed.
   Set CdorlColumns = CdorlView.Columns
   Set CdorlColumn = CdorlColumns.Add("Folder", CdoPR_DISPLAY_NAME, _
      30, 0, 0)
   '
   ' Set the RenderUsing property such that each item in the list is
   ' rendered as a link.
   CdorlColumn.RenderUsing = "<a href=""viewfolder.asp?ID=%obj%&StoreID=" _
      & CdoInfoStore.ID & """>%value%</a>"
   '
   ' Make this the current View.
   CdorlRenderer.CurrentView = CdorlView

   ' Create the HTML.
   RenderInfoStore = CdorlRenderer.Render(CdoFolderContents)

   ' Clean up.
   Set CdorlColumn = Nothing
   Set CdorlColumns = Nothing
   Set CdorlView = Nothing
   Set CdorlViews = Nothing
   Set CdorlRenderer = Nothing
   Set CdorlApplication = Nothing
   Set CdoFolders = Nothing
   Set CdoFolder = Nothing
   Set CdoInfoStore = Nothing
   Set CdoSession = Nothing

End Function ' RenderInfoStore
```

The *RenderInfoStore* function in Example 11-13 assumes the existence of the *global.asa* file shown in Example 11-4.

The core functionality of the *RenderInfoStore* function is embodied in these steps:

1. Obtain a RenderingApplication object.
2. Obtain the CDO object that is to be rendered. In this case, it is a Folders collection.
3. Create a ContainerRenderer object for rendering the Folders collection.
4. Assign the Folders collection to the ContainerRenderer object's DataSource property.
5. Create a TableView object and assign it to the ContainerRenderer object's CurrentView property.
6. Call the ContainerRenderer object's Render method to generate the HTML table.

The HTML produced by the *RenderInfoStore* function is shown in Example 11-14, and the browser display is shown in Figure 11-13. (Note again that the ID values shown in the example have been shortened for readability.)

Example 11-14. Sample HTML Produced by the RenderInfoStore Function of Example 11-13

```
<table border=0 cellspacing=0 cellpadding=1 WIDTH=240>
<tr bgcolor=CCCC99 valign="top">
<th ALIGN="left" WIDTH=240><FONT COLOR=000000 SIZE=2>Folder</font></th>
</tr>
<tr bgcolor=FFFFFF valign="top" align="left">
<td><a href="viewfolder.asp?ID=A1&StoreID=FF">Calendar</a></td>
</tr>
<tr bgcolor=FFFFFF valign="top" align="left">
<td><a href="viewfolder.asp?ID=A2&StoreID=FF">Contacts</a></td>
</tr>
<tr bgcolor=FFFFFF valign="top" align="left">
<td><a href="viewfolder.asp?ID=A3&StoreID=FF">Deleted Items</a></td>
</tr>
<tr bgcolor=FFFFFF valign="top" align="left">
<td><a href="viewfolder.asp?ID=A4&StoreID=FF">Drafts</a></td>
</tr>
<tr bgcolor=FFFFFF valign="top" align="left">
<td><a href="viewfolder.asp?ID=A5&StoreID=FF">Inbox</a></td>
</tr>
<tr bgcolor=FFFFFF valign="top" align="left">
<td><a href="viewfolder.asp?ID=A6&StoreID=FF">Journal</a></td>
</tr>
<tr bgcolor=FFFFFF valign="top" align="left">
<td><a href="viewfolder.asp?ID=A7&StoreID=FF">Notes</a></td>
</tr>
<tr bgcolor=FFFFFF valign="top" align="left">
<td><a href="viewfolder.asp?ID=A8&StoreID=FF">Outbox</a></td>
</tr>
<tr bgcolor=FFFFFF valign="top" align="left">
<td><a href="viewfolder.asp?ID=A9&StoreID=FF">Sent Items</a></td>
```

Example 11-14. Sample HTML Produced by the RenderInfoStore Function of Example 11-13

```
</tr>
<tr bgcolor=FFFFFF valign="top" align="left">
<td><a href="viewfolder.asp?ID=AA&StoreID=FF">Tasks</a></td>
</tr>
</table>
```

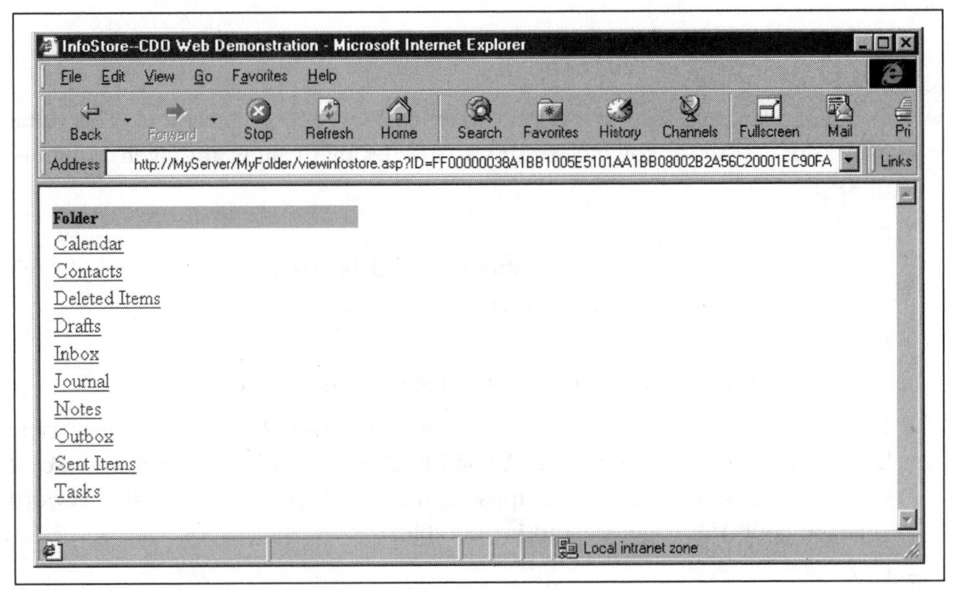

Figure 11-13. Sample browser display produced by the RenderInfoStore function of Example 11-13

Have a closer look at the code that creates the view:

```
' Add a custom view for viewing this collection.
'
' Get the Views collection and add a View.
Set CdorlViews = CdorlRenderer.Views
Set CdorlView = CdorlViews.Add("MyView")
'
' Get the Columns collection and add the column that we want displayed.
Set CdorlColumns = CdorlView.Columns
Set CdorlColumn = CdorlColumns.Add("Folder", CdoPR_DISPLAY_NAME, _
   30, 0, 0)
'
' Set the RenderUsing property such that each item in the list is
' rendered as a link.
CdorlColumn.RenderUsing = "<a href=""viewfolder.asp?ID=%obj%&StoreID=" _
  & CdoInfoStore.ID & """>%value%</a>"
'
' Make this the current View.
CdorlRenderer.CurrentView = CdorlView
```

A view is created by calling the Add method of the ContainerRenderer object's Views collection. The syntax for the Add method is:

```
Set CdorlView = CdorlViews.Add(Name[, Class][, SortBy][, SortAscending])
```

The parameters of the Add method are:

Name
A unique name by which the view can be referenced in code.

Class
Controls whether a TableView or a CalendarView object is created. The value can be one of the following constants (the decimal values are given in parentheses):

`CdoClassTableView` *(9)*
Indicates that a TableView object should be created. This is the default value if the argument is omitted.

`CdoClassCalendarView` *(12)*
Indicates that a CalendarView object should be created.

These symbolic constants are defined in the CDO Rendering Library type library (*cdohtml.dll*). However, VBScript doesn't read type libraries, so if you're going to use them, you must define them using the `Const` keyword either in your ASP page or in an include file.

SortBy
This is the MAPI property on which to sort the items in the table. The default is `CdoPR_MESSAGE_DELIVERY_TIME` (`&HE060040`), but only if that property exists as a column in the table. If it doesn't, there is no default sort order.

SortAscending
This controls the sort order of the table. Set to `True` for ascending, `False` for descending. The default is `False`.

The Columns collection of a newly created view is empty, so the work doesn't end here. A column must be added to the collection for each desired column in the table. The syntax of the Columns collection's Add method is:

```
Set CdorlColumn = CdorlColumns.Add(DisplayName, Property, Width, _
   Flags, InsertAfter[, Type])
```

The parameters of the Add method are:

DisplayName
A unique name by which the Column object can be referenced in code.

Property
The MAPI property that is to be rendered in the column.

`Width`

The width of the displayed column. The width is expressed in characters unless the `CdoColumnBitmap` flag is set in the ***`Flags`*** parameter. If it is, the width is expressed in pixels.

`Flags`

Controls certain display attributes for the column. The value is the sum of zero or more of the following constants (the decimal values are given in parentheses):

`CdoColumnBitmap` *(8)*

Indicates that the property in this column is displayed using a bitmap.

`CdoColumnNotSortable` *(32)*

Indicates that the property can't be used for sorting the display.

These symbolic constants are defined in the CDO Rendering Library type library (*cdohtml.dll*). However, VBScript doesn't read type libraries, so if you're going to use them, you must define them using the **`Const`** keyword either in your ASP page or in an include file.

`InsertAfter`

The index of the Column object after which the new Column object is to be added. To add the Column object at the beginning of the collection, pass 0 in this parameter. The display order of the columns is determined by the order of the Column objects in the Columns collection.

`Type`

Identifies the datatype of the property and can take any value that would be returned by Visual Basic's *VarType* function, except **`vbNull`** and **`vbDataObject`**. This parameter is required only if the property to be rendered is a custom property.

Example 11-13 also sets the Column object's RenderUsing property, shown again here:

```
' Set the RenderUsing property such that each item in the list is
' rendered as a link.
CdorlColumn.RenderUsing = "<a href=""viewfolder.asp?ID=%obj%&StoreID=" _
   & CdoInfoStore.ID & """>%value%</a>"
```

This is not necessary if all that is desired is to display the folder names. However, this example shows how to create links that allow the user to click a folder name to be directed to a page that shows that folder's contents. Text in the RenderUsing property is rendered verbatim, unless it is a substitution token. Substitution tokens are replaced during rendering by the values for which they stand. This example uses the "`%obj%`" and "`%value%`" substitution tokens. Table 11-1 shows valid substitution tokens and their replacement values.

Table 11-1. Substitution Tokens for the RenderUsing Property

Substitution Token	Replaced by
`%apptlength%`	The number of rows spanned by an appointment or free block. (This is only for AppointmentItem objects being viewed in `CdoModeCalendarDaily` mode.)
`%apptwidth%`	The number of columns spanned by an appointment or free block. (This is only for AppointmentItem objects being viewed in `CdoModeCalendarDaily` mode.)
`%classpath%`	The class of a message, in lowercase (for example, "`ipm.note`").
`%columns%`	The number of columns in the view. (This is only for AppointmentItem objects being viewed in `CdoModeCalendarDaily` mode.)
`%date%`	A string containing the date for which appointments are being rendered. (This is only for AppointmentItem objects.)
`%kvalue%`	The value of the property, expressed in kilobytes (i.e., the value divided by 1024). (This is only for numeric properties.)
`%obj%`	The message store identifier for the object whose property is being rendered. This identifier can later be used to retrieve the object again from the message store. The `%obj%` substitution token is used in this chapter to pass object identifiers to ASP pages that have code that renders the object whose identifier is passed.
`%parentobj%`	The message store identifier for the Message object's parent folder. (This is only for Message objects.)
`%rowid%`	The row number in the table. (This is only for objects rendered by the ContainerRenderer object.)
`%tablewidth%`	The width of the table, expressed in pixels. (This is only for properties rendered in a calendar view.)
`%time%`	A string containing the time of the time slot being rendered. (This is only for AppointmentItem objects being viewed in `CdoModeCalendarDaily` mode.)
`%value%`	The value of the property.

After the view is created and assigned to the ContainerRenderer object's CurrentView property, the HTML table is generated by calling the ContainerRenderer object's Render method. The syntax of the Render method is:

```
strHTML = CdorlContainerRenderer.Render(Style[, PageNo][, Raw]_
   [, ResponseObject])
```

The parameters are:

Style

Set this parameter to `CdoFolderContents (1)`.

PageNo

This parameter works in association with the ContainerRenderer object's RowsPerPage property. Each call to the Render method returns at most the number of rows specified in the RowsPerPage property. The *PageNo* parameter of the Render method indicates which page is desired. This allows very large collections to be broken easily into a series of HTML pages. The default value for the RowsPerPage property is 25. The default value for the *PageNo* parameter is 1.

Raw
This parameter is reserved and must not be used.

ResponseObject
If desired, the ASP Response object can be passed in this parameter. If it is, the generated HTML is written to it rather than being returned from the function. In that case, the return value is an empty string.

Rendering a messages collection

Example 11-15 shows *RenderMessages*, a function for rendering a CDO Messages collection.

Example 11-15. Rendering a Messages Collection

```
Public Function RenderMessages(CdoMessages)

   ' This procedure returns an HTML string representing a list of the
   ' messages in the given Messages collection.

   Dim CdorlApplication
   Dim CdorlRenderer

   ' Get the CDORL Application object.
   Set CdorlApplication = Application.Contents("CdorlApplication")

   ' Set the correct security context.
   CdorlApplication.Impersonate(Session.Contents("hImp"))

   ' Create a ContainerRenderer object to render this collection.
   Set CdorlRenderer = _
      CdorlApplication.CreateRenderer(CdoClass_ContainertRenderer)

   ' Set the link pattern.
   CdorlRenderer.LinkPattern = "<a href = ""viewmessage.asp?ID=%obj%" _
         & """>%value%</a>"

   ' Set the data source. Note that the "Set" keyword is not used.
   CdorlRenderer.DataSource = CdoMessages

   ' Render the messages.
   RenderMessages = CdorlRenderer.Render(CdoFolderContents)

   ' Clean up.
   Set CdorlRenderer = Nothing
```

Example 11-15. Rendering a Messages Collection (continued)

```
    Set CdorlApplication = Nothing

End Function ' RenderMessages
```

There are two major differences between the *RenderMessages* function shown in Example 11-15 and the *RenderInfoStore* function that was shown in Example 11-13. One is that the *RenderMessages* function doesn't go to the trouble of creating a custom view. This is because Microsoft Exchange Server provides default views for rendering Messages collections. The second difference is the use of the ContainerRenderer object's LinkPattern property to create a hyperlinked column in the generated table. Example 11-13 created a hyperlink by setting the RenderUsing property of a Column object. That could have been done here as well. The procedure would be:

1. Get the TableView object from the ContainerRenderer object's CurrentView property.
2. In the TableView object's Columns collection, iterate through the Column object to find the column that is to be hyperlinked.
3. Set the RenderUsing property of the Column object.

In this case using the LinkPattern property is clearly more straightforward. It is set in a manner similar to setting the RenderUsing property. When using the LinkPattern property, the CDO Rendering Library chooses which column to use for the hyperlink. The first column that represents a non-empty string property (other than the message class) is used for the link. If there is no such column, the last column in the table is used.

Rendering a Recipients collection

Rendering a Recipients collection is just like rendering a Folders collection: assign the collection to the ContainerRenderer object's DataSource property, create a view, and call the ContainerRenderer object's Render method. Example 11-16 shows a function, *RenderRecipients*, that does just this.

Example 11-16. Rendering a Recipients Collection

```
Public Function RenderRecipients(CdoRecipients)

    ' This procedure returns an HTML string representing a list of the
    ' recipients in the given Recipients collection.

    Dim CdorlApplication
    Dim CdorlRenderer
    Dim CdorlViews
    Dim CdorlView
    Dim CdorlColumns
```

Example 11-16. Rendering a Recipients Collection (continued)

```
    Dim CdorlColumn

    ' Get the CDORL Application object.
    Set CdorlApplication = Application.Contents("CdorlApplication")

    ' Set the correct security context.
    CdorlApplication.Impersonate(Session.Contents("hImp"))

    ' Create a ContainerRenderer object to render this collection.
    Set CdorlRenderer = _
       CdorlApplication.CreateRenderer(CdoClass_ContainerRenderer)

    ' Set the link pattern.
    CdorlRenderer.LinkPattern = _
       "<a href = ""viewrecipient.asp?ID=%obj%"">%value%</a>"

    ' Set the data source. Note that the "Set" keyword is not used.
    CdorlRenderer.DataSource = CdoRecipients

    ' Add a custom view for viewing this collection.
    '
    ' Get the Views collection and add a View.
    Set CdorlViews = CdorlRenderer.Views
    Set CdorlView = CdorlViews.Add("MyView")
    '
    ' Get the Columns collection and add the column that we want displayed.
    Set CdorlColumns = CdorlView.Columns
    Set CdorlColumn = CdorlColumns.Add("Display Name", _
       CdoPR_DISPLAY_NAME, 30, 0, 0)
    Set CdorlColumn = CdorlColumns.Add("Email Address", _
       CdoPR_EMAIL_ADDRESS, 30, 0, 1)
    '
    ' Make this the current View.
    CdorlRenderer.CurrentView = CdorlView

    ' Render the recipients.
    RenderRecipients = CdorlRenderer.Render(CdoFolderContents)

    ' Clean up.
    Set CdorlColumn = Nothing
    Set CdorlColumns = Nothing
    Set CdorlView = Nothing
    Set CdorlViews = Nothing
    Set CdorlRenderer = Nothing
    Set CdorlApplication = Nothing

End Function ' RenderRecipients
```

Note the code that sets the LinkPattern property of the ContainerRenderer object:

```
' Set the link pattern.
CdorlRenderer.LinkPattern = _
   "<a href = ""viewrecipient.asp?ID=%obj%"">%value%</a>"
```

The substitution token "%obj%" is replaced by a string containing the ID value of the AddressEntry object underlying the recipient being displayed. This ID can be used elsewhere to retrieve the AddressEntry object through the CDO Session object's GetAddressEntry method, as shown here:

```
' This could be code in viewrecipient.asp.

Dim strID

' Retrieve the address entry identifier being passed in.
strID = Request.QueryString("ID")

' Get the requested address entry.
' Assume CdoSession has already been set.
Set CdoAddressEntry = CdoSession.GetAddressEntry(strID)

' Use the AddressEntry object...
```

Rendering an AddressEntries collection

Example 11-17 shows a function that renders any given AddressEntries collection. The code is very similar to that shown in Example 11-16 for rendering a Recipients collection. The ContainerRenderer object's LinkPattern property is set to point to a hypothetical page, *viewaddressentry.asp*, that would display properties of the address entry. As in Example 11-16, the "%obj%" substitution token is replaced by the unique identifier of the address entry being rendered.

Example 11-17. Rendering an AddressEntries Collection

```
Public Function RenderAddressEntries(CdoAddressEntries)

   ' This procedure returns an HTML string representing a list of the
   ' address entries in the given AddressEntries collection.

   Dim CdorlApplication
   Dim CdorlRenderer
   Dim CdorlViews
   Dim CdorlView
   Dim CdorlColumns
   Dim CdorlColumn

   ' Get the CDORL Application object.
   Set CdorlApplication = Application.Contents("CdorlApplication")

   ' Set the correct security context.
   CdorlApplication.Impersonate(Session.Contents("hImp"))

   ' Create a ContainerRenderer object to render this collection.
   Set CdorlRenderer = _
      CdorlApplication.CreateRenderer(CdoClass_ContainerRenderer)

   ' Set the link pattern.
```

Example 11-17. Rendering an AddressEntries Collection (continued)

```
    CdorlRenderer.LinkPattern = _
       "<a href = ""viewaddressentry.asp?ID=%obj%"">%value%</a>"

    ' Set the data source. Note that the "Set" keyword is not used.
    CdorlRenderer.DataSource = CdoAddressEntries

    ' Add a custom view for viewing this collection.
    '
    ' Get the Views collection and add a View.
    Set CdorlViews = CdorlRenderer.Views
    Set CdorlView = CdorlViews.Add("MyView")
    '
    ' Get the Columns collection and add the column that we want displayed.
    Set CdorlColumns = CdorlView.Columns
    Set CdorlColumn = CdorlColumns.Add("Display Name", _
       CdoPR_DISPLAY_NAME, 30, 0, 0)
    Set CdorlColumn = CdorlColumns.Add("Email Address", _
       CdoPR_EMAIL_ADDRESS, 30, 0, 1)
    '
    ' Make this the current View.
    CdorlRenderer.CurrentView = CdorlView

    ' Render the address entries.
    RenderAddressEntries = CdorlRenderer.Render(CdoFolderContents)

    ' Clean up.
    Set CdorlColumn = Nothing
    Set CdorlColumns = Nothing
    Set CdorlView = Nothing
    Set CdorlViews = Nothing
    Set CdorlRenderer = Nothing
    Set CdorlApplication = Nothing

End Function ' RenderAddressEntries
```

Example 11-18 shows how the *RenderAddressEntries* function might be used. The example shows a function *RenderGAL*, which renders the Global Address List.

Example 11-18. Rendering the Global Address List

```
Public Function RenderGAL

    ' This procedure returns an HTML string representing a list of the
    ' addresses in the Global Address List.

    Dim CdorlApplication
    Dim CdoSession
    Dim CdoAddressList
    Dim CdoAddressEntries

    ' Get the CDORL Application object.
    Set CdorlApplication = Application.Contents("CdorlApplication")
```

Example 11-18. Rendering the Global Address List (continued)

```
    ' Set the correct security context.
    CdorlApplication.Impersonate(Session.Contents("hImp"))

    ' Get the CDO Session object.
    Set CdoSession = Session.Contents("CdoSession")

    ' Get AddressEntries collection from the Global Address List.
    Set CdoAddressList = CdoSession.GetAddressList(CdoAddressListGAL)
    Set CdoAddressEntries = CdoAddressList.AddressEntries

    ' Render the HTML.
    RenderGAL = RenderAddressEntries(CdoAddressEntries)

    ' Clean up.
    Set CdoAddressEntries = Nothing
    Set CdoAddressList = Nothing
    Set CdoSession = Nothing
    Set CdorlApplication = Nothing

End Function ' RenderGAL
```

Rendering individual MAPI properties

In addition to rendering CDO collections, the CDO Rendering Library has the ability to render individual properties of CDO objects. The code in Example 11-19 renders the `PR_SUBJECT`, `PR_IMPORTANCE`, and `PR_BODY` properties of a Message object. The display of the resulting HTML is shown in Figure 11-14.

Example 11-19. Rendering Individual MAPI Properties

```
' CdorlApplication and CdoMessage already Dim'ed and Set.

Dim CdorlRenderer
Dim strHTML

' Create an ObjectRenderer object for rendering the message.
Set CdorlRenderer = _
    CdorlApplication.CreateRenderer(CdoClass_ObjectRenderer)

' Set the data source. Note that the "Set" keyword is not used.
CdorlRenderer.DataSource = CdoMessage

' Render the message subject.
strHTML = "Subject: " _
    & CdorlRenderer.RenderProperty(CdoPR_SUBJECT) & "<br>"

' Render the message importance.
strHTML = strHTML & "Importance: " _
    & CdorlRenderer.RenderProperty(CdoPR_IMPORTANCE) & "<br><hr>"

' Render the message body.
strHTML = strHTML & CdorlRenderer.RenderProperty(CdoPR_BODY)
```

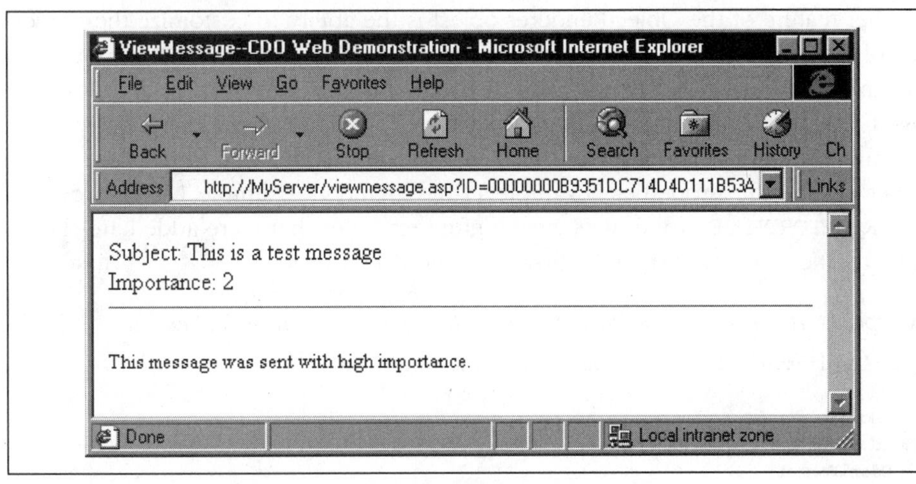

Figure 11-14. The display resulting from Example 11-19

The RenderingApplication object's CreateRenderer method is called with an argument of `CdoClass_ObjectRenderer` to create an ObjectRenderer object. The desired property is rendered by calling the ObjectRenderer object's RenderProperty method. The syntax of the RenderProperty method is:

```
strHTML = objObjectRend.RenderProperty(Property[, Raw][, ResponseObject])
```

The parameters are:

`Property`
The MAPI property that is to be rendered.

`Raw`
This parameter is reserved and must not be used.

`ResponseObject`
If desired, the ASP Response object can be passed in this parameter. If it is, the generated HTML is written to it rather than being returned from the function. In that case, the return value is an empty string.

It may not be immediately clear why this:

```
strHTML = CdorlRenderer.RenderProperty(CdoPR_BODY)
```

is preferable to this:

```
strHTML = CdoMessage.Text
```

The reason is that the message body text doesn't necessarily make good HTML. For example, browsers ignore carriage returns within the body of a web page, so just sending the message text to the browser causes all line breaks in the text to be lost. In contrast, the ObjectRenderer object's RenderProperty method inserts appropriate tags to maintain formatting, such as `<p>...</p>` and `<br>`. It also detects strings that represent web addresses and turns them into clickable links.

Another feature of the ObjectRenderer object is the ability to customize the rendering of properties. Consider the rendering of the PR_IMPORTANCE property in Example 11-19. The user is not likely to know that the values 0, 1, and 2 signify low, normal, and high importance, respectively. The CDO Rendering Library's Format and Pattern objects provide a way to indicate exactly how to display specific values of specific properties. Example 11-20 augments Example 11-19 to display the PR_IMPORTANCE property as meaningful text. Lines that were added are shown in bold. The resulting display is shown in Figure 11-15.

Example 11-20. Rendering the PR_IMPORTANCE Property as Meaningful Text

```
' CdorlApplication and CdoMessage already Dim'ed and Set.

Dim CdorlRenderer
Dim CdorlFormats
Dim CdorlFormat
Dim CdorlPatterns
Dim CdorlPattern
Dim strHTML

' Create an ObjectRenderer object for rendering the message.
Set CdorlRenderer = _
   CdorlApplication.CreateRenderer(CdoClass_ObjectRenderer)

' Set the data source. Note that the "Set" keyword is not used.
CdorlRenderer.DataSource = CdoMessage

Set CdorlFormats = CdorlRenderer.Formats
Set CdorlFormat = CdorlFormats.Add(CdoPR_IMPORTANCE)
Set CdorlPatterns = CdorlFormat.Patterns
Set CdorlPattern = CdorlPatterns.Add(0, "Low")
Set CdorlPattern = CdorlPatterns.Add(1, "Normal")
Set CdorlPattern = CdorlPatterns.Add(2, "High")

' Render the message subject.
strHTML = "Subject: " _
   & CdorlRenderer.RenderProperty(CdoPR_SUBJECT) & "<br>"

' Render the message importance.
strHTML = strHTML & "Importance: " _
   & CdorlRenderer.RenderProperty(CdoPR_IMPORTANCE) & "<br><hr>"

' Render the message body.
strHTML = strHTML & CdorlRenderer.RenderProperty(CdoPR_BODY)
```

The code in Example 11-20 follows these steps to customize the display of the PR_IMPORTANCE property:

1. Add a Format object to the ObjectRenderer object's Formats collection using the Formats collection's Add method. The syntax being used here is:

   ```
   Set CdorlFormat = CdorlFormats.Add(varProperty)
   ```

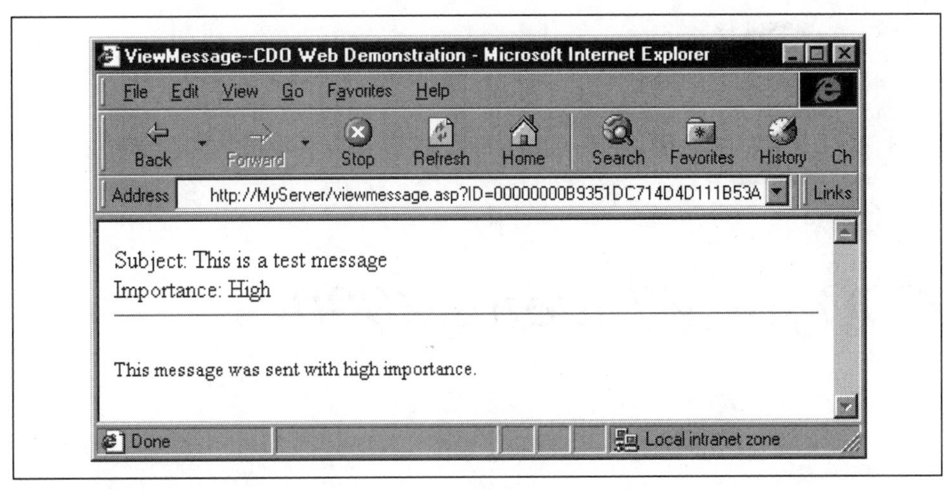

Figure 11-15. The display resulting from Example 11-20

The parameter is a Variant that specifies the MAPI property for which a format is being added.

2. For each potential value of the property, add a Pattern object to the new Format object's Patterns collection using the collection's Add method. The syntax used in Example 11-20 is:

   ```
   Set CdoPattern = CdoPatterns.Add(varValue, varRenderUsing)
   ```

   The *varValue* parameter indicates a value that the property might have, and the *varRenderUsing* parameter is a string that indicates what to display instead of the value. In addition to plain text, substitution tokens (already shown in Table 11-1) and HTML codes can be used in the *varRenderUsing* parameter.

3. Render the property with the ObjectRenderer object.

Summary

In this chapter you learned how to write CDO applications for the Web. The IIS environment was discussed, including the security hurdles involved with getting IIS and Microsoft Exchange server to talk nicely with each other. Several examples showed how to program CDO objects from web pages and how to leverage the CDO Rendering Library to do the work of generating HTML output from CDO object properties.

Chapter 12, *CDO for Windows 2000*, gives a brief overview of this new technology and shows how to take advantage of its features.

12

CDO for Windows 2000

CDO for Windows 2000 shares its name with CDO 1.21, and that's unfortunate. It gives the impression that CDO for Windows 2000 is the latest, greatest, updated version of CDO. Unfortunately, that isn't so. CDO for Windows 2000 and CDO 1.21 are different products altogether. The purpose of CDO 1.21 is to give Automation clients easy access to MAPI. In contrast, CDO for Windows 2000 is oriented toward server-side programs that need to send and receive Internet email and newsgroup postings. Visual Basic developers who wish to access MAPI's powerful features will continue to use CDO 1.21.

Because CDO for Windows 2000 is not MAPI-based, this book doesn't go deeply into its features. Rather, this chapter gives an overview of what those features are and provides samples of sending and receiving plain-text email. Posting to and reading from newsgroups are not discussed.

Before going further, you might wish to turn to Appendix A, *Programming Internet Email Protocols*, and read the first two sections to get an overview of how Internet email works. This chapter uses certain terms (such as *Simple Mail Transport Protocol [SMTP]*) defined in those sections.

Getting Started

All versions of the Windows 2000 operating system include CDO for Windows 2000, so there is no need to obtain and deploy this component separately. However, some features of CDO for Windows 2000 require the use of Microsoft's SMTP service. This system service is included only in server versions of Windows 2000 and in Internet Information Server (IIS). Without this service, Internet emails cannot be received, and they can be sent only if the client machine is able to communicate with some other SMTP email server. For example, a client machine that can dial in to an Internet service provider (ISP) fits this description (assuming that the ISP provides email services, as most do). Note that some of the examples in this chapter assume the presence of the SMTP service.

CDO for Windows 2000 is made available to a Visual Basic project by setting a reference to it in the References dialog box. To set a reference, choose Project → References from the Visual Basic menu. The References dialog box appears, as shown in Figure 12-1.

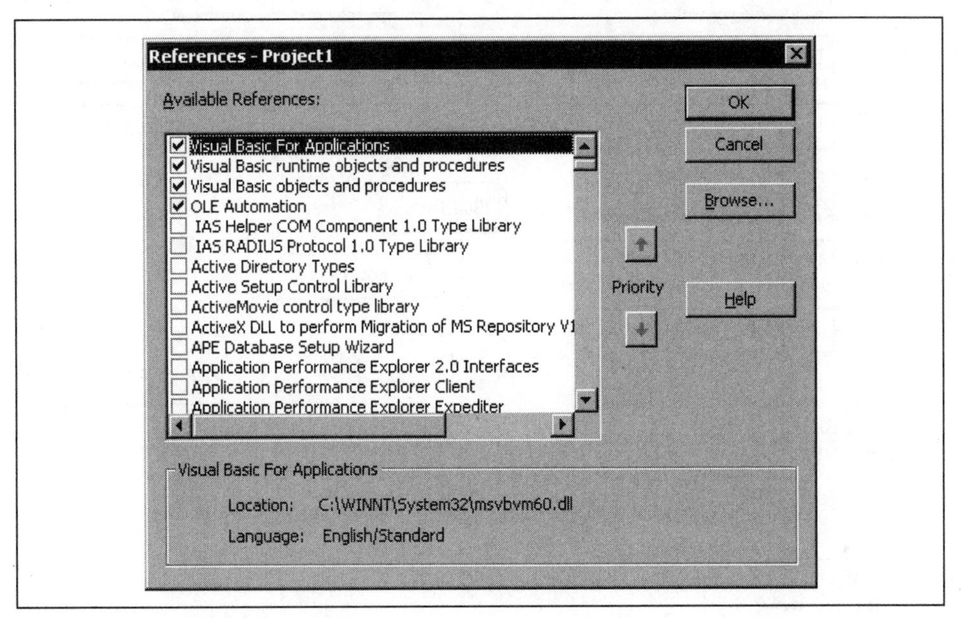

Figure 12-1. The References dialog box

Scroll down the list of available references until you find "Microsoft CDO for Windows 2000 Library" and "Microsoft ActiveX Data Objects 2.5 Library." Select these items if they're not already selected, and click OK. The reference to ActiveX Data Objects (ADO) is needed because CDO for Windows 2000 uses ADO Field and Stream objects.

The CDO for Windows 2000 Object Model

Figure 12-2 shows the object model diagram for CDO for Windows 2000.

The format of the CDO for Windows 2000 object model diagram is a little different from the format of other object model diagrams in this book. Whereas typical object model diagrams focus on expressing relationships among classes, the CDO

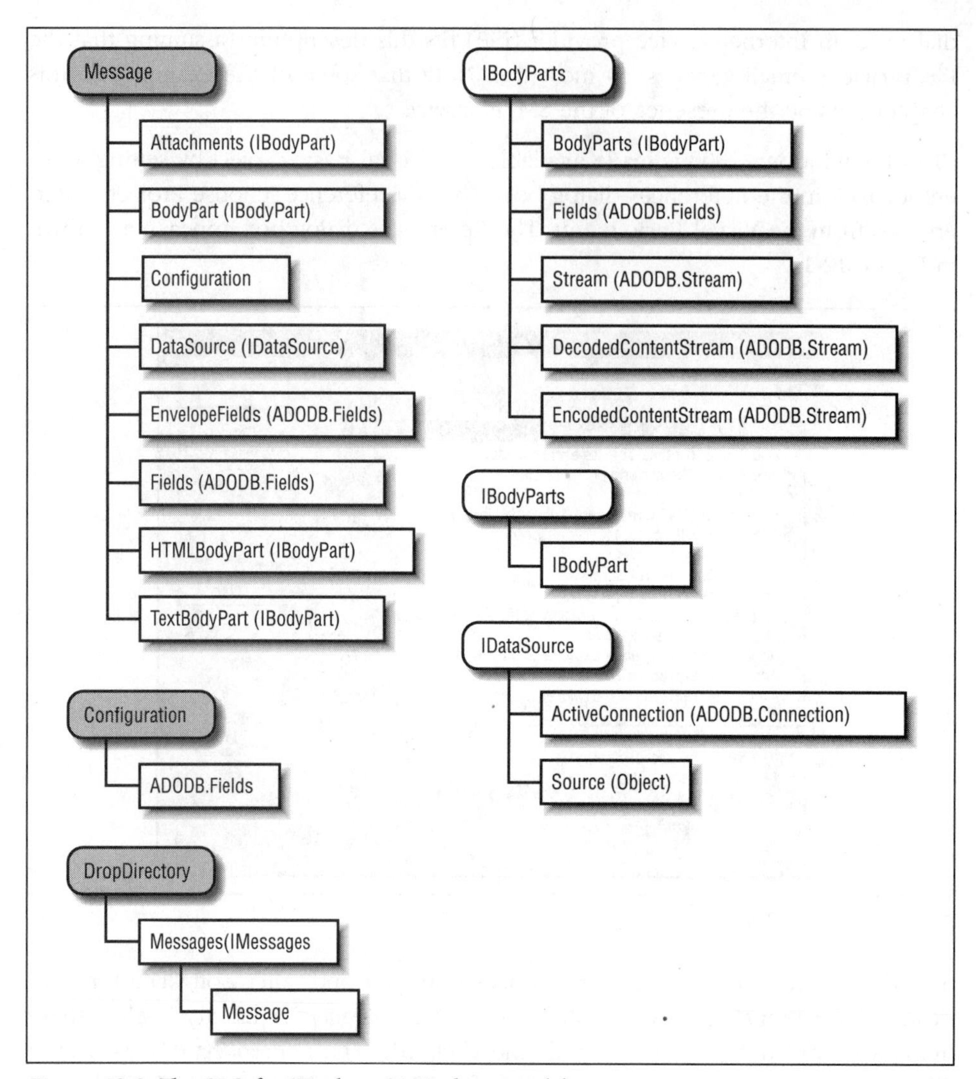

Figure 12-2. The CDO for Windows 2000 object model

for Windows 2000 object model diagram also must express relationships among interfaces, because in this object model, interfaces play an important role.

An *interface* is the set of methods and properties exposed by a class. A developer using a class written by another developer needs to know the class's interface in order to call methods and use properties appropriately. This is simple so far, but it gets complicated. COM classes can expose more than one interface. It's up to the caller to ask for the interface that it wants to use before calling a method or accessing a property that is part of that interface. If the caller then wants to call a method that's part of a different interface, it must ask the object for that different interface before making the call. A class can designate one of its interfaces to be its *default interface*. The default interface is used when an object is instantiated and used without explicitly specifying an interface. This is the typical usage in Visual Basic.

Historically, Visual Basic has blurred the distinction between classes and interfaces. In the past, each Visual Basic class had just one interface, and each interface was associated with just one class. The introduction of the `Implements` keyword has changed that, although the Visual Basic IDE still lacks explicit support for creating interface definitions. (The only way to define an interface in Visual Basic is to create a class.)

The three gray rounded rectangular boxes in Figure 12-2 represent classes and their associated default interfaces. The three white rounded rectangular boxes represent interfaces that are not associated with specific classes. These interfaces cannot be instantiated directly, because they are not themselves classes. Certain methods return objects that expose certain of these interfaces. An object obtained in this way can be used in accordance with the definition of the associated interface, even though the caller doesn't have any idea what the class of the object is. A couple of examples will demonstrate this.

The Message class is a true class, so it can be instantiated like this:

```
Dim Cdo2Message As CDO.Message
Set Cdo2Message = New CDO.Message
```

After execution of the `Set` statement in this fragment, methods and properties of the `CDO.Message` class can be used, as shown here:

```
Cdo2Message.Subject = "This is the subject"
```

Technically speaking, the Subject property is defined by the class's default interface, not by the class itself. The distinction is usually of little importance.

In contrast, interfaces cannot be instantiated. To get a reference to one of the interfaces shown in Figure 12-2, it's necessary to call a method that returns a reference to some object that exposes the desired interface. Here's an example of using the `IBodyPart` interface:

```
' Cdo2Message already Dim'ed and set.
Dim Cdo2BodyPart As CDO.IBodyPart
Set Cdo2BodyPart = Cdo2Message.BodyPart
```

To satisfy the request to read the BodyPart property of the Message object, CDO for Windows 2000 instantiates an object that exposes the `IBodyPart` interface. The class of the object is unknown (to the caller) and doesn't matter. What matters is that the caller can access the object through the methods and properties defined by the `IBodyPart` interface.

The Message Class

The Message class represents a message item. To send an email, instantiate a Message object, set its properties, and invoke the Send method (demonstrated later in this chapter). Here are the Message class's properties. The usage of many of these properties is beyond the scope of this chapter and won't be discussed further. Some of these properties apply only to newsgroup postings, which are not discussed in this book.

Attachments

(Read only) An `IBodyParts` collection that represents the attachments to the message. On outgoing messages, use the Message object's AddAttachment method to add attachments to the message.

AutoGenerateTextBody

A Boolean value that indicates whether the TextBody property of a message should be set automatically based on the value in the HTMLBody property of the message. This property is forced to `False` when the MimeFormatted property is `False`. The default value for AutoGenerateTextBody is `True` on new messages and `False` on existing messages.

BCC

A string that contains blind copy recipients of the message, separated by commas. Each recipient must be in the form:

```
"DisplayName" <MailAddress@Network.Domain>
```

or:

```
MailAddress@Network.Domain
```

For example, this code fragment sets two blind copy recipients:

```
' Cdo2Message previously Dim'ed and Set.
Cdo2Message.BCC = """Bill Gates"" <billg@microsoft.com>, " _
    & """Bill Clinton"" <president@whitehouse.gov>"
```

The default value of this property is an empty string. This property is always an empty string on received messages.

BodyPart

(Read only) An `IBodyPart` reference that is the root body part of a multipart message. This property is not used for messages with a single text body part.

CC

A string that contains the copy recipients of the message. The format of the string is the same as that of the BCC property described earlier. The default value of this property is an empty string.

Configuration

Returns the Configuration object that contains the configuration settings for this message. All messages have a default configuration. To modify the configuration, either obtain a reference to the Message object's Configuration object and make changes to it, or else instantiate a Configuration object, make changes to it, and assign it to the Message object's Configuration property. If you will be sending many messages with the same configuration, the latter method is more efficient. The Configuration object is discussed in detail later in this section.

DataSource

(Read only) An `IDataSource` reference that is used for storing and retrieving message content in other objects. Although this facility won't be discussed in this book, CDO for Windows 2000 has the ability to embed messages either within other messages or within ADO streams. The `IDataSource` interface is used for this purpose.

DSNOptions

Specifies the Delivery Status Notification (DSN) options for the message. Set this property to request delivery status notification from message transfer agents handling the message. This property is of type `CdoDSNOptions` and can take the following values:

`cdoDSNDefault`
: No notifications are requested.

`cdoDSNNever`
: No notifications are requested.

`cdoDSNFailure`
: Return a notification if delivery fails.

`cdoDSNSuccess`
: Return a notification if delivery succeeds.

`cdoDSNDelay`
: Return a notification if delivery is delayed.

`cdoDSNSuccessFailOrDelay`
: Return a notification if delivery fails, succeeds, or is delayed.

The default value is `cdoDSNDefault`.

EnvelopeFields

(Read only) This property is used only in conjunction with transport event sinks. Transport event sinks allow a transport mechanism to notify a client of certain events. Transport event sinks are not discussed in this chapter.

Fields

(Read only) The Fields collection for the Message object. ADO Field objects in the collection store values related to the message, many of which are duplicated in the Message object's properties.

FollowUpTo

A string containing the names of the newsgroups to which any responses to this message should be posted.

From

A string that contains the authors of the message. The format of the string is the same as that of the BCC property described earlier. If this property is set to contain multiple authors, the Sender property also should be set. The Sender property identifies the person actually sending the message. If the From property is not set, the value of the Sender property is used. If neither property is set, an error is raised.

HTMLBody

A string that contains the HTML version of the message, if there is one. The default value is an empty string.

HTMLBodyPart

(Read only) An `IBodyPart` reference that represents the HTML version of the message, if there is one. This property is not used for messages with a single text body part.

Keywords

A string that contains a list of keywords, separated by commas. Keywords can be used by message recipients to help determine if a message is of interest. The default value is an empty string.

MDNRequested

A Boolean value that indicates whether a Message Disposition Notification is requested on this message. The default value is `False`.

MimeFormatted

A Boolean value that indicates whether the message is to be formatted using Multipurpose Internet Mail Extensions (MIME). This must be set to `True` in order to have a multipart message (for example, in order to have both a plain text and an HTML version of the message).

Newsgroups

A string that contains the names of the newsgroup recipients of this message, separated by commas. The default value is an empty string.

Organization

A string that contains the name of the sender's organization, to appear on newsgroup posts. The default value is an empty string.

ReceivedTime

(Read only) The date and time the message was received at the mail server. The date and time are in coordinated universal time (UTC) unless the message's Configuration object has been set with a time zone. If a time zone is specified, the date and time returned are offset by the time zone. If the date and time can't be read from the message headers, attempting to read this property causes a `CDO_E_PROP_NOT_FOUND` error to be raised. Because you can't control the condition of the headers on incoming messages, you must be prepared to handle this error.

ReplyTo

A string containing the addresses to which replies should be sent. The format of the string is the same as that of the BCC property described earlier. The default value is an empty string.

Sender

A string containing the address of the sender of the message, if different from the From property or if there are multiple addresses in the From property. The default value is an empty string.

SentOn

(Read only) The date and time the message was sent. The date and time are in UTC unless the message's Configuration object has been set with a time zone. If a time zone is specified, the date and time returned are offset by the time zone.

Subject

A string containing the message subject. The default value is an empty string.

TextBody

A string containing the plain text version of the message. The default value is an empty string.

TextBodyPart

(Read only) An `IBodyPart` reference that represents the plain text version of the message. This property is not used for messages with a single text body part.

To

A string containing the principal recipients of the message. The format of the string is the same as that of the BCC property described earlier. The default value is an empty string.

The methods of the Message class are:

AddAttachment

Adds an attachment to the message. The syntax is:

```
Set Cdo2BodyPart = Cdo2Message.AddAttachment(URL, [UserName], [Password])
```

The return value is of type `IBodyPart` and is a reference to the newly attached object.

The parameters are:

URL

A string that identifies the location of the file to be attached. It is in the form of a Uniform Resource Locator (URL). The URL prefixes supported are `file://`, `ftp://`, `http://`, and `https://`. The default prefix is `file://`, which means that standard file paths are also legal in this parameter.

UserName

An optional string that specifies a username that is to be used for authentication when accessing the resource given in the *URL* parameter via Hypertext Transport Protocol (HTTP). Both Basic and NTLM authentication are supported. (See Chapter 11, *Web Applications*, for an explanation of these authentication mechanisms.)

Password

An optional string that specifies a password to be used in association with the *UserName* parameter.

AddRelatedBodyPart

Adds a body part representing a resource that is referenced by a link in the HTML part of the message. For example, the HTML part of the message may have a link to a file called *MyImage.gif*. This file can be made part of the message itself and transported with it by calling AddRelatedBodyPart. The syntax is:

```
Set Cdo2BodyPart = Cdo2Message.AddRelatedBodyPart(URL, Reference, _
   ReferenceType, [UserName], [Password])
```

The return value is of type `IBodyPart` and is a reference to the newly added body part. The parameters are:

URL

A string that identifies the location of the resource to be added, in the form of a URL. The URL prefixes supported are `file://`, `ftp://`, `http://`, and `https://`. The default prefix is `file://`, which means that standard file paths are also legal in this parameter.

Reference

A string that names the resource for the purpose of linking to it from the HTML part of the message. This name is either a *Content-ID* or *Content-Location*, as defined in the MIME and MHTML protocols.

ReferenceType

A value from the enumerated datatype `CdoReferenceType`. The value passed in this parameter indicates what kind of reference is passed in the *Reference* parameter. The values that can be passed are `cdoRefTypeId`, which indicates a *`Content-ID`* reference, and `cdoRefTypeLocation`, which indicates a *`Content-Location`* reference.

`UserName`

An optional string that specifies a username that is to be used for authentication when accessing the resource given in the *`URL`* parameter via HTTP. Both Basic and NTLM authentication are supported. (See Chapter 11 for an explanation of these authentication mechanisms.)

`Password`

An optional string that specifies a password to be used in association with the *`UserName`* parameter.

CreateMHTMLBody

Converts the contents of a web page into a multipart message. Graphics and other linked resources are included as body parts within the message. The function is not recursive—if linked resources have links to additional resources, the additional resources are not included in the message. The syntax is:

```
Cdo2Message.CreateMHTMLBody URL, [Flags], [UserName], [Password]
```

The parameters are:

`URL`

A URL that specifies the location of the web page to convert.

`Flags`

A set of values that determines how much data is included in the message. The *`Flags`* parameter can take one or more values from the enumerated data type `CdoMHTMLFlags`. The flags and their meanings are given in Table 12-1. Multiple flags can be specified by summing their values.

Table 12-1. The CdoMHTMLFlags Enumeration

Value	Description
`CdoSuppressAll`	Don't include any linked resources.
`CdoSuppressBGSounds`	Don't include resources from `<BGSOUND>` elements.
`CdoSuppressFrames`	Don't include resources from `<FRAME>` elements.
`CdoSuppressImages`	Don't include resources from `<IMG>` elements.
`CdoSuppressNone`	Include all linked resources.
`CdoSuppressObjects`	Don't include resources from `<OBJECT>` elements.
`CdoSuppressStyleSheets`	Don't include resources from `<LINK>` elements.

`UserName`

An optional string that specifies a username that is to be used for authentication when accessing the resource given in the *`URL`* parameter via HTTP.

Both Basic and NTLM authentication are supported. (See Chapter 11 for an explanation of these authentication mechanisms.)

Password

An optional string that specifies a password to be used in association with the *UserName* parameter.

Forward

Creates a new message object to be used for forwarding the message. The syntax is:

```
Set Cdo2Message2 = Cdo2Message.Forward
```

GetInterface

Provides an alternate means of obtaining the BodyPart and DataSource properties. The syntax is:

```
Set Cdo2Object = Cdo2Message.GetInterface(Interface)
```

The function's single parameter, *Interface*, is a string that specifies the interface that is to be returned. Specifying "IBodyPart" is the same as reading the Message object's BodyPart property. Specifying "IDataSource" is the same as reading the Message object's DataSource property.

GetStream

Returns the entire message serialized into an ADO Stream object. The syntax is:

```
Set AdoStream = Cdo2Message.GetStream
```

The value returned from the GetStream function is of type `ADODB.Stream`.

Post

Posts the message to the newsgroups specified in the Newsgroups property. The syntax is:

```
Cdo2Message.Post
```

PostReply

Creates a new Message object to be used for posting a reply to this newsgroup message. The syntax is:

```
Set Cdo2Message2 = Cdo2Message.PostReply
```

Reply

Creates a new Message object to be used for replying to the sender of this email message. The syntax is:

```
Set Cdo2Message2 = Cdo2Message.Reply
```

ReplyAll

Creates a new Message object to be used for replying to the sender and all "To" and "CC" recipients of this email message. The syntax is:

```
Set Cdo2Message2 = Cdo2Message.ReplyAll
```

Send

Sends the message. The syntax is:

```
Cdo2Message.Send
```

The Configuration Class

The Configuration class represents the configuration settings for a message. A Configuration object is obtained either through reading the Configuration property of a Message object or by instantiating a Configuration object directly. Configuration objects that are instantiated directly can be assigned to the Configuration property of one or more messages.

The Configuration object has only one property, the Fields property. This is a collection of type ADODB.Fields, where each Field object in the collection represents one setting in the configuration. A complete reference for all of the potential field values is beyond the scope of this chapter, but examples later in the chapter show typical usage.

The Configuration object has two methods:

Load

Loads the configuration object from settings available on the machine. If either Microsoft IIS or Microsoft Outlook Express is running on the local machine, CDO for Windows 2000 can load the Configuration object settings from the configuration settings of those programs. The syntax is:

```
Cdo2Configuration.Load LoadFrom, [URL]
```

The parameters are:

LoadFrom

A value from the enumerated datatype `CdoConfigSource`. The values and their meanings are given in Table 12-2. (Note that as of this writing the Microsoft Developer Network (MSDN) documentation gives the wrong names for these constants.)

URL

Do not use this parameter. It is reserved for future use.

GetInterface

Reserved for future use.

Table 12-2. The CdoConfigSource Enumeration

Value	Meaning
`cdoDefaults`	Load the configuration from both IIS and Outlook Express settings.
`cdoIIS`	Load the configuration from IIS settings.
`cdoOutlookExpress`	Load the configuration from Outlook Express settings.

The DropDirectory Class and the Interfaces

The DropDirectory class is used in conjunction with Microsoft's SMTP service and is discussed later in this chapter, under "Reading Email." The `IBodyPart` and `IBodyParts` interfaces support multipart messages and will not be discussed in this chapter. The `IDataSource` interface is an advanced feature that allows serializing message objects into other objects. It won't be discussed further in this chapter, either.

Sending Email

There are two ways to send email using CDO for Windows 2000. One method is to send messages to an email server using the SMTP protocol. The other method is to write messages to disk, where they are picked up by Microsoft's SMTP system service. This section describes each method.

Sending Email via SMTP

CDO for Windows 2000 is able to talk directly to an SMTP email server. This can be Microsoft's SMTP service or an email server located at your ISP. Example 12-1 shows a subroutine that sends a plain-text email message using this method.

Example 12-1. Sending Email Via SMTP

```
Private Sub SendMessage()

   Dim Cdo2Configuration As CDO.Configuration
   Dim Cdo2Fields As ADODB.Fields
   Dim Cdo2Message As CDO.Message

   ' Create a new Configuration object.
   Set Cdo2Configuration = New CDO.Configuration

   ' Get a reference to the Configuration object's Fields collection
   Set Cdo2Fields = Cdo2Configuration.Fields

   ' Set the Configuration object's properties through its Fields
   ' collection.
   With Cdo2Fields
      .Item(cdoSMTPServer) = "yourmailserver.com"
      .Item(cdoSendUsingMethod) = cdoSendUsingPort
      .Update ' Important
   End With

   ' Create a new message.
   Set Cdo2Message = New CDO.Message

   ' Set the message's configuration.
   Set Cdo2Message.Configuration = Cdo2Configuration
```

Example 12-1. Sending Email Via SMTP (continued)

```
   ' Set the message content.
   Cdo2Message.Subject = "This is the message subject."
   Cdo2Message.TextBody = "This is the message text."

   ' Address the message.
   Cdo2Message.From = "jane@mycompany.com"
   Cdo2Message.To = "john@yourcompany.com"

   ' Send the message.
   Cdo2Message.Send

   Set Cdo2Message = Nothing
   Set Cdo2Configuration = Nothing

End Sub ' SendMessage
```

Note how the message's configuration is set in Example 12-1:

```
' Set the Configuration object's properties through its Fields
' collection.
With Cdo2Fields
   .Item(cdoSMTPServer) = "yourmailserver.com"
   .Item(cdoSendUsingMethod) = cdoSendUsingPort
   .Update ' Important
End With
```

The constants in this code—`cdoSMTPServer` and `cdoSendUsingMethod`—are string constants defined by CDO for Windows 2000. The strings are used as indexes into the Fields collection in order to specify a particular Field object. The value of the Field object is then set appropriately. Many fields can be set, and many of them go beyond the scope of this brief discussion. The fields that are relevant to this discussion are:

`cdoSendEmailAddress`
: A string containing the Sender's email address. The From property of outgoing messages is set to this value if no other value is set in the Message object.

`cdoSendPassword`
: (Write only) A string containing the password for authenticating to the SMTP server, if needed.

`cdoSendUserName`
: A string containing the username for authenticating to the SMTP server, if needed.

`cdoSendUserReplyEmailAddress`
: A string containing the address to which email replies should be sent, if different from the "From" address.

`cdoSendUsingMethod`
: A value of type `CdoSendUsing` that indicates how messages are to be sent. The values this field can have are:

  `cdoSendUsingPickup`
  : Indicates that messages should be written to the SMTP service pickup directory to be sent by the SMTP service.

  `cdoSendUsingPort`
  : Indicates that messages should be sent directly to an SMTP email server using the SMTP protocol.

`cdoSMTPAuthenticate`
: A value of type `CdoProtocolsAuthentication` that indicates the authentication mechanism to use when sending messages directly to an SMTP email server. The values this field can have are:

  `cdoAnonymous`
  : No authentication. Use this setting when the email server does not require SMTP users to authenticate.

  `cdoBasic`
  : Basic authentication. This mechanism causes the username and password to be sent in clear text to the email server.

  `cdoNTLM`
  : NTLM ("NT LAN Manager") authentication. This is a challenge-response mechanism that does not involve sending the password across the network.

`cdoSMTPConnectionTimeout`
: A Long value indicating the number of seconds to wait while trying to establish a connection with an SMTP server. This value is ignored if the `cdoSendUsingMethod` field is not `cdoSendUsingPort`. The default value is 30.

`cdoSMTPServer`
: A string containing the name or IP address of the SMTP email server. This value is ignored if the `cdoSendUsingMethod` field is not `cdoSendUsingPort`.

`cdoSMTPServerPickupDirectory`
: A string containing the path of the pickup directory used by the SMTP service. This value is ignored if the `cdoSendUsingMethod` field is not `cdoSendUsingPickup`.

`cdoSMTPServerPort`
: A Long value indicating the IP port on which the email server is listening for new SMTP connections. The default is 25, which is the industry standard.

Sending Email via the SMTP Service Pickup Directory

In addition to being able to send email directly to an SMTP email server, CDO for Windows 2000 works with the Microsoft SMTP service *pickup directory*. A pickup directory is a folder that is continually scanned by the SMTP service for outgoing mail. When mail is found in this folder, the SMTP service forwards it using SMTP and then deletes the mail from the folder. Example 12-2 shows a subroutine that sends a message by writing it to the pickup directory, where it will be found and processed by the SMTP service.

Example 12-2. Sending Email Via the SMTP Service Pickup Directory

```
Private Sub SendMessageViaPickup()

   Dim Cdo2Configuration As CDO.Configuration
   Dim Cdo2Fields As ADODB.Fields
   Dim Cdo2Message As CDO.Message

   ' Create a new Configuration object.
   Set Cdo2Configuration = New CDO.Configuration

   ' Get a reference to the Configuration object's Fields collection
   Set Cdo2Fields = Cdo2Configuration.Fields

   ' Set the Configuration object's properties through its Fields
   ' collection.
   With Cdo2Fields
      .Item(cdoSendUsingMethod) = cdoSendUsingPickup
      .Item(cdoSMTPServerPickupDirectory) = _
         "\\MyServer\MyShare\Inetpub\Mailroot\Pickup"
      .Update ' Important
   End With

   ' Create a new message.
   Set Cdo2Message = New CDO.Message

   ' Set the message's configuration.
   Set Cdo2Message.Configuration = Cdo2Configuration

   ' Set the message content.
   Cdo2Message.Subject = "Sent using pickup folder."
   Cdo2Message.TextBody = "This is the message text."

   ' Address the message.
   Cdo2Message.From = """Jane Smith"" <jane@mycompany.com>"
   Cdo2Message.To = """John Doe"" <john@yourcompany.com>"

   ' Send the message.
   Cdo2Message.Send
```

Example 12-2. Sending Email Via the SMTP Service Pickup Directory (continued)

```
   Set Cdo2Message = Nothing
   Set Cdo2Configuration = Nothing

End Sub ' SendMessageViaPickup
```

The difference between this example and Example 12-1 is the way the Configuration object is set:

```
' Set the Configuration object's properties through its Fields
' collection.
With Cdo2Fields
   .Item(cdoSendUsingMethod) = cdoSendUsingPickup
   .Item(cdoSMTPServerPickupDirectory) = _
      "\\MyServer\MyShare\Inetpub\Mailroot\Pickup"
   .Update ' Important
End With
```

This code specifies that mail should be sent using a pickup directory, and then it sets the full path of the directory to use.

Receiving Email

The only way to read email with CDO for Windows 2000 is to use it in conjunction with Microsoft's SMTP service. The SMTP service receives all email messages targeted to a specific domain and writes them to a predetermined directory, known as the *drop directory*. After emails have been placed in the drop directory, they are available to your Visual Basic program via the DropDirectory class in CDO for Windows 2000.

The DropDirectory class represents the SMTP service's drop directory. The class has no properties and only a single method, the GetMessages method. The syntax of the GetMessages method is:

```
Function GetMessages([ByVal DirName As String]) As IMessages
```

The `DirName` parameter specifies the full path of the drop directory. If the parameter is omitted or passed as an empty string, CDO for Windows 2000 looks to IIS on the local machine, if present, to discover where the drop directory is. Neither the drop directory nor the SMTP service need be on the local machine. The only requirement is that the local machine has access to the drop directory.

The value returned by the GetMessages method is an `IMessages` collection of Message objects. Example 12-3 shows a subroutine that iterates through the messages found in the specified drop directory, printing each message's subject text to Visual Basic's Immediate window.

Example 12-3. Iterating Through the Messages Found in the Drop Directory

```
Private Sub ReceiveEmail()

   Const cstrDropDirectory As String = _
      "\\MyServer\MyShare\Inetpub\Mailroot\Drop\"

   Dim Cdo2DropDirectory As CDO.DropDirectory
   Dim Cdo2Messages As CDO.IMessages
   Dim Cdo2Message As CDO.Message

   ' Create a new drop directory object to represent the file system
   ' folder that contains the incoming emails.
   Set Cdo2DropDirectory = New CDO.DropDirectory

   ' Get the collection of messages in the drop directory.
   Set Cdo2Messages = Cdo2DropDirectory.GetMessages(cstrDropDirectory)

   ' Loop for each message.
   For Each Cdo2Message In Cdo2Messages
      ' Write the subject line to the immediate window.
      Debug.Print Cdo2Message.Subject
   Next Cdo2Message

   ' Cleanup
   Set Cdo2Message = Nothing
   Set Cdo2Messages = Nothing
   Set Cdo2DropDirectory = Nothing

End Sub ' ReceiveEmail
```

All emails received by the SMTP service are deposited in the drop directory, regardless of the user for whom they're destined. It's up to your software to read the properties of each message, determine who the message is for, and take appropriate action.

Summary

This chapter introduced you to CDO for Windows 2000. You learned that this is a different technology that does not supersede CDO version 1.21. You learned that CDO for Windows 2000 does not provide the folder-within-folder hierarchy available in MAPI-based technologies. Indeed, there isn't even an Inbox—all email destined to a specific domain is written to a common directory, and it's up to your program to sort out what is to be done with it. CDO for Windows 2000 is best suited to server-side email programming tasks.

Programming Internet Email Protocols

This book is primarily about Messaging Application Programming Interface (MAPI)—Microsoft's abstract interface to messaging systems. Throughout the book, you've seen that programming against MAPI allows the intricacies and peculiarities of specific storage and transport mechanisms to be hidden behind MAPI service providers. This is a powerful architecture that simplifies messaging application development. Without any knowledge of Internet protocols, for example, client applications can send and receive email via the Internet.

However, there is cost associated with this power. The computers on which MAPI client applications are to run must have MAPI installed on them, and they must have appropriate MAPI profiles set up. In addition, most of the code in this book requires CDO to be installed. If you have an application in which for some reason you do not wish to use MAPI, you might consider programming the Internet protocols directly. This appendix shows you how to do that using the Winsock custom control that is included with Visual Basic 6. (If you're writing an application to run under Windows 2000, you can use CDO for Windows 2000 instead. See Chapter 12, *CDO for Windows 2000*, for details.) Be aware that when you choose not to use MAPI, your application becomes intricately tied to the underlying storage and transport mechanisms, making it very expensive to add support for different storage and transport mechanisms in the future.

How Email Is Sent on the Internet

On the Internet, email clients communicate with email servers using four-letter textual commands. These commands are sent via the *Transmission Control Protocol (TCP)*, which is a *connection-oriented* protocol for communicating over a network. Connection-oriented means that certain steps are taken to establish communication between client and server, communication ensues, and then certain steps are taken to break communication. This is in contrast to a *connectionless* protocol, in which data is sent without first establishing a connection. Connection-oriented protocols are often likened to telephone calls, where the parties maintain an active connection during the conversation. In contrast, connectionless protocols are likened to postal communication, where there is no active connection between the communicating parties. (The postal analogy is not meant to imply that connectionless protocols are inherently slower. In fact, they are typically faster because connections impose overhead.)

To establish a connection with a server, an email client application must know the network address of the server computer. On the Internet, network addresses appear in either of two forms. One form is called the *IP address*, which is a sequence of four numbers separated by periods, each number being in the range 0 to 255. An example of an IP address is `10.199.13.200`. The other form of Internet address is intended to be more readable by human beings and is of the form *`computer.network.domain`*—for example, `mail.mycompany.com`. Either form is acceptable when specifying the address of a computer on the Internet. In practice, the latter is much more common.

TCP allows a computer to engage in many simultaneous conversations. For example, an email server may be running several processes, each conversing with a different client computer. The protocol must provide a way for the server to differentiate incoming data so that it knows which data should be handled by which process. TCP handles this requirement by introducing the concept of a *port*. When the client and server establish a TCP connection, they negotiate a port on which they will communicate. Note that a port is not a physical entity, it's just a number that the client and server use to identify a particular communication session.

The port has an additional purpose. When a client requests a connection to a server, the client must specify the port on which communication should take place. By agreement, certain port numbers are always used for certain types of communication. For example, a client wishing to send mail asks a server for a connection on port 25. This is a clue to the server that the client intends to use the Simple Mail Transport Protocol (SMTP), which is an Internet protocol for sending email. When such a request is received, the server computer routes the request to the server process that knows how to speak SMTP. Similarly, a client wishing to retrieve email from a server requests a connection on port 110, which is the port reserved for that purpose. Such ports are referred to as *well-known* ports. Well-known ports are used only to request connections. During the connection process, the server and client negotiate a different port number to be used for communication. This frees up the well-known port so that the server can receive requests from other clients.

In some circumstances, the topology of a network could necessitate using a port other than one of the well-known ports for communicating with an email server. Specifically, proxy servers are sometimes configured to manipulate traffic passing through them on certain ports. If you have trouble connecting to an email server that should be available, check with the network's administrator to determine whether there is a proxy server between the client and email server, and whether the proxy server's configuration could be affecting traffic on ports 25 and 110.

SMTP and POP3

After a connection is established, the client can begin sending commands to the server, and the server can respond to the commands. This back-and-forth communication is in the form of plain text that is readable to the human eye. Valid commands and responses are defined by Internet protocols. SMTP defines commands for sending email, and the *Post Office Protocol version 3 (POP3)* defines commands for retrieving email. There are other protocols, notably the *Internet Message Access Protocol (IMAP)*, a successor to POP. However, this chapter focuses on SMTP and POP3 because of their ubiquity.

Here's a sample SMTP conversation. The strings "`Server:` " and "`Client:` " are not part of the conversation but are inserted here to indicate the source of each command or response:

```
Client: MAIL FROM: dg@execpc.com
Server: 250 dg@execpc.com... Sender ok
Client: RCPT TO: dg@execpc.com
Server: 250 dg@execpc.com... Recipient ok
Client: DATA
Server: 354 Enter mail, end with "." on a line by itself
Client: From: dg@execpc.com
Client: To: dg@execpc.com
Client: Subject: This is a test message
Client:
Client: Here is the body of the message.
Client: Multiple lines can be entered.
Client: A period by itself signifies the end.
Client: .
Server: 250 IAA01968 Message accepted for delivery
```

Note the general format of the conversation. The client sends the server a four-letter command, possibly with arguments, and the server returns a numeric response code followed by a textual response. The text portion of the server response may vary from server to server, so client code should rely only on the numeric portion. The commands and responses shown here, as well as the commands and responses appropriate to POP3, will be discussed in detail later in this appendix, under "Sending Email" and "Retrieving Email." First, it's time to learn how to establish a connection with a mail server from your Visual Basic client application.

The Winsock Control

The Winsock ActiveX control provided in Visual Basic 6 handles the low-level work of setting up, maintaining, and tearing down TCP connections. Your Visual Basic code need only supply the address of a server to talk to and the port on which to request a connection. Typically you will obtain the email server address either from your company's network administrator or from your Internet service provider (ISP). As already mentioned, the port will be either 25 or 110, depending on whether you're sending email or retrieving it. For the ensuing discussion, I will assume that you are familiar with ActiveX controls in general—that is, you know how to add a control to a form, how to set and read properties in code and at design time, and how to call methods.

By default, the Winsock control doesn't appear in your Toolbox. To add it to the Toolbox for your project, from the Visual Basic menu choose Project → Components. The Components dialog box appears, as shown in Figure A-1.

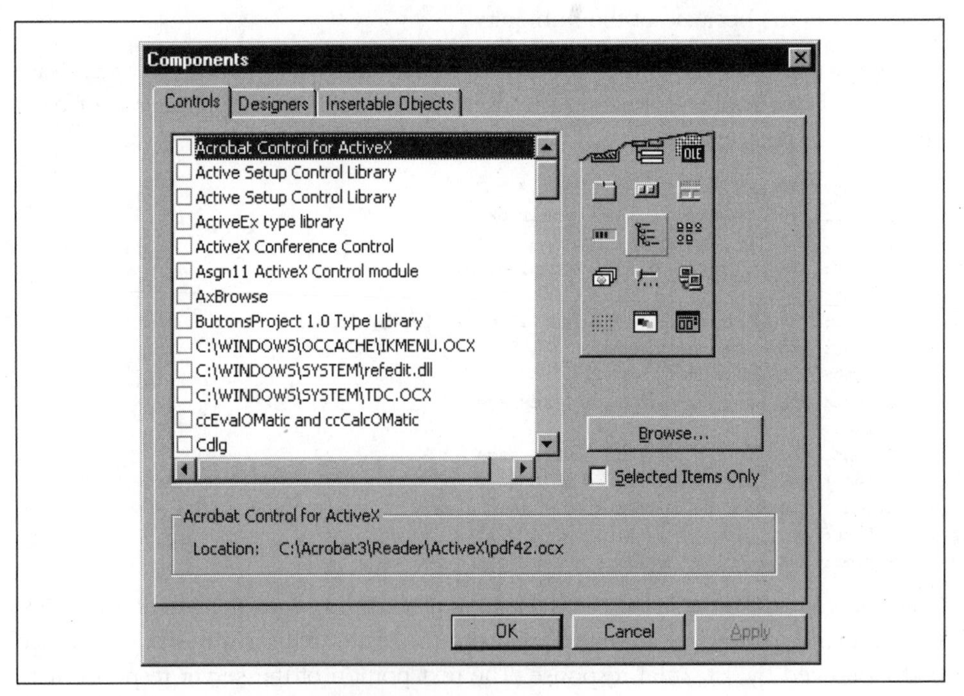

Figure A-1. The Components dialog box

Scroll down the list of components until you find "Microsoft Winsock Control 6.0". Select the checkbox if it's not selected already, then click OK. After doing so, you'll see the Winsock control in your Toolbox. (If you don't see the Toolbox at all, choose View → Toolbox from the Visual Basic menu.) The Toolbox with the Winsock control's icon is shown in Figure A-2.

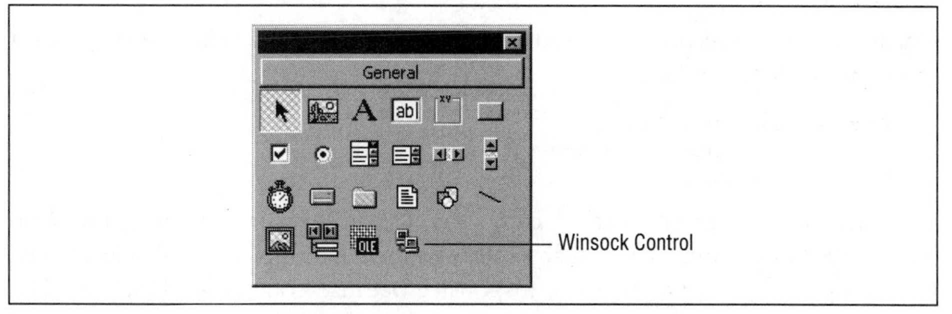

Figure A-2. A Toolbox with the Winsock control

Once the Toolbox has the Winsock control, the control can be added to a form. Typically, the control is added to only one form in the project, and that instance is used by all code in the project. The Winsock control is invisible at runtime, so it doesn't matter where it's placed. One good design is to have a form that is never shown; its only purpose is to provide a home for the control. Any helper procedures that you write for sending and retrieving email can be written as public procedures on the form and used by code throughout the project.

Establishing a Connection

Before mail can be sent or retrieved, a connection must be established with an email server. This is done using the Winsock control's Connect method, as shown here:

```
Winsock1.Connect "mail.execpc.com", 25
```

The arguments to this method are the address of the email server and the port on which to request connection. The fact that this code fragment requests connection on port 25 tells the server that the client is interested in using the SMTP protocol for sending email. A request to use the POP3 protocol to retrieve email uses port 110, as shown here:

```
Winsock1.Connect "mail.execpc.com", 110
```

The Connect method is asynchronous. That is, it returns control to the next line of Visual Basic code even before the connection is established. When the connection does become established, the Winsock control raises the Connect event and sets the value of the control's State property to sckConnected. It is an error to send SMTP or POP3 commands before the connection is established.

The TCP connection can be closed either by the client or by the server. To close it from the client side, call the Winsock control's Close method, as shown here:

```
Winsock1.Close
```

Finally, if the connection is closed by the server, the Winsock control raises a Close event, as shown here:

```
Private Sub Winsock1_Close()
   ' Place any cleanup code here.
End Sub ' Winsock1_Close
```

This asynchronous mechanism of communication makes programming the Winsock control more complicated than other email mechanisms, but it also lets Visual Basic programs appear to be more responsive because code is not blocked while waiting for a server's response.

Sending Commands and Receiving Responses

After a connection is established, commands can be sent to the email server via the Winsock control's SendData method. The SendData method takes as an argument the text that is to be sent. This line, for instance, sends the SMTP MAIL command:

```
Winsock1.SendData "MAIL FROM: dg@execpc.com" & vbCrLf
```

Note the vbCrLf appended to the end of the string. All data sent to SMTP and POP3 servers must be terminated by the carriage return plus linefeed character combination.

As with the Connect method, the SendData method is asynchronous—it returns control to the Visual Basic program even before it gets confirmation that the command was successfully received by the server. When confirmation does arrive, the Winsock control notifies your Visual Basic application via the DataArrival event. You will typically handle this event by calling the Winsock control's GetData event to retrieve the response and to act on it. This code fragment displays a message box whenever data is received from the server:

```
Private Sub Winsock1_DataArrival(ByVal bytesTotal As Long)
   Dim strData As String
   Winsock1.GetData strData, vbString
   MsgBox strData, vbOKOnly + vbInformation, "Data received from server"
End Sub ' Winsock1_DataArrival
```

The *bytesTotal* parameter of the DataArrival event procedure indicates the size of the data received from the server. The **vbString** constant passed to the GetData method requests that the data be given in string format rather than as an array of bytes. In this appendix we will deal only with string data.

It's clear that a lot of state management has to be done when using the Winsock control. Your program has to keep track of what command it sent last, whether it has received a success response from the server, and what command to send next. In a robust, real-world application, I recommend writing code to encapsulate this mechanism so that the rest of your program doesn't have to worry about it. Such code could take many forms. For the examples in this appendix, I've written helper procedures that send data and then block while waiting for a response from the server. Blocking is accomplished by performing a do-nothing loop until the DataArrival event sets a particular module-level variable to **True**. The module-level variable, the DataArrival event, and the helper procedures are shown in Example A-1.

Example A-1. Winsock Helper Procedures

```
' Declare these variables at module level.
Private mstrResponse As String
Private mbResponseReceived As Boolean

Private Sub Winsock1_DataArrival(ByVal bytesTotal As Long)

   Dim strData

   ' Retrieve the response string.
   Winsock1.GetData strData, vbString

   ' Strip the terminating CRLF.
   strData = Left(strData, Len(strData) - 2)

   ' Save the data.
   mstrResponse = strData
   Debug.Print "Server: " & strData
   mbResponseReceived = True

End Sub

Public Sub ConnectAndWait(strServer As String, nPort As Long)

   ' Request connection
   mbResponseReceived = False
   Debug.Print "Client: (Initiates connection on port "; Trim(nPort); ")"
   Winsock1.Connect strServer, nPort

   ' Wait for connection
   Do While Not mbResponseReceived
      DoEvents
```

Example A-1. Winsock Helper Procedures (continued)

```
    Loop

End Sub

Public Sub CloseConnection()

    Debug.Print "Client: (Closes connection)"
    Winsock1.SendData "QUIT" & vbCrLf
    Winsock1.Close

End Sub ' CloseConnection

Public Function SendAndWait(strData As String) As String

    ' Send data.
    SendDontWait strData

    ' Wait for response.
    Do While Not mbResponseReceived
        DoEvents
    Loop

    SendAndWait = mstrResponse

End Function ' SendAndWait

Public Sub SendDontWait(strData As String)

    Debug.Print "Client: " & strData
    mbResponseReceived = False
    Winsock1.SendData strData & vbCrLf

End Sub ' SendDontWait
```

Example A-1 contains these procedures:

Winsock1_DataArrival
: This event handler is called by the Winsock control when data arrives from the server. This event handler sets ***mbResponseReceived*** to **True** so that other procedures know that data has been received. The procedure then retrieves the data from the control and saves it in ***mstrResponse*** for use by the *SendAndWait* function. The data is also written to Visual Basic's Immediate window for debugging.

ConnectAndWait
: This subroutine establishes a connection with a given server over a given port. After requesting a connection, the procedure blocks until a response is received and handled by the DataArrival event procedure. A message is also written to Visual Basic's Immediate window for debugging.

CloseConnection

This subroutine closes the connection and writes a debug message to Visual Basic's Immediate window.

SendAndWait

This function sends a string to the server and blocks until a response is received. A message is written to Visual Basic's Immediate window for debugging, and the received response is returned to the caller.

SendDontWait

This subroutine sends a string to the server, writes a debug message to Visual Basic's Immediate window, and returns immediately. This subroutine is useful for sending strings when a response is not expected.

The procedures shown in Example A-1 are a minimal implementation, suitable for demonstration and experimentation. Production code should parse the return code in the data received from the server to ensure that the server's response is relevant to the last command sent, and that no errors have occurred. You may also wish to add a Timer control to the form so that you can take action if no response has been received in a preset amount of time.

Sending Email

With our helper procedures in hand, it's time to send some email. The code in Example A-2 does just that.

Example A-2. Sending an Email

```
Private Sub SendAnEmail()

   ' Connect to the email server.
   ConnectAndWait "mail.execpc.com", 25

   ' Initiate an email.
   SendAndWait "MAIL FROM: dg@execpc.com"

   ' Set the recipient.
   SendAndWait "RCPT TO: juser@company.com"

   ' Indicate that we're ready to send the email itself.
   SendAndWait "DATA"

   ' Send the email.
   SendDontWait "From: dg@execpc.com"
   SendDontWait "To: juser@company.com"
   SendDontWait "Subject: This is a test email."
   SendDontWait "" ' Required; separates header from body.
   SendDontWait "Here is the body of the email."
   SendDontWait "Insert as many lines as desired."
```

Example A-2. Sending an Email (continued)

```
    SendDontWait "End with a period on a line by itself."
    SendAndWait "."

    ' Close the connection.
    CloseConnection

End Sub ' SendAnEmail
```

This code connects to a server, issues the commands necessary to send an email, and then closes the connection. The resulting debug messages written to Visual Basic's Immediate window look like this:

```
Client: (Initiates connection on port 25)
Server: 220 pop00.execpc.com ESMTP Sendmail 8.8.8 ready at Sat, 27 Nov 1999 16:14:
01 -0600
Client: MAIL FROM: dg@execpc.com
Server: 250 dg@execpc.com... Sender ok
Client: RCPT TO: juser@company.com
Server: 250 juser@company.com... Recipient ok
Client: DATA
Server: 354 Enter mail, end with "." on a line by itself
Client: From: dg@execpc.com
Client: To: juser@company.com
Client: Subject: This is a test email.
Client:
Client: Here is the body of the email.
Client: Insert as many lines as desired.
Client: End with a period on a line by itself.
Client: .
Server: 250 QAA06621 Message accepted for delivery
Client: (Closes connection)
```

After connecting to the email server, the program sends the `MAIL` command to notify the server of the client's intent to send an email. The argument to the `MAIL` command identifies the sender of the email. Upon receiving a response from the server, the client specifies the recipient of the email by sending the `RCPT` command. After receiving the next response, the client could send additional `RCPT` commands if desired. In Example A-2, however, only one recipient is desired, so the client goes on to send the `DATA` command. This indicates that the client is ready to send the headers and body of the email. After receiving the next response, the client sends the headers and body. The server does not respond until the client terminates this mode by sending a period on a line by itself. Finally, if the client has no more work for the server, it closes the connection.

Note that the client is responsible for sending message headers that indicate the sender, recipient(s), and message subject. These headers are separated from the body of the message by a blank line. All email servers involved with the delivery of the email will append additional header information to the header section. The headers can be parsed on the receiving end to provide detailed originator and routing information for the email.

If the client needs to send a period on a line by itself as part of an email, it does so by sending two periods in that position. The email server converts the two periods back to a single period, which it saves as part of the email body.

Retrieving Email

To retrieve email from a server, the email client establishes a connection to the server on port 110 and then sends appropriate POP3 commands. Example A-3 shows how this is done, using the helper procedures introduced in Example A-1. This sample code logs onto a POP3 server and inquires whether any email is waiting. If there is, additional commands are sent to retrieve the first email, which is then displayed in a text box.

Example A-3. Retrieving an Email

```
Private Sub RetrieveAnEmail()

   Dim strResponse As String
   Dim nMsgCount As Long
   Dim nStart As Long
   Dim nLength As Long

   ' Connect to the email server.
   ConnectAndWait "mail.execpc.com", 110

   ' Log in.
   SendAndWait "USER dg"
   SendAndWait "PASS MyPassword"

   ' Find out how many emails there are.
   strResponse = SendAndWait("STAT")
   nStart = InStr(strResponse, " ") + 1
   nLength = InStr(nStart, strResponse, " ") - nStart
   nMsgCount = CLng(Mid(strResponse, nStart, nLength))

   ' If there are any emails at all, retrieve the first one.
   If nMsgCount > 0 Then
      SendAndWait "RETR 1"
      txtMsg.Text = SendAndWait("NOOP")
   Else
      txtMsg.Text = "(There are no messages on the server.)"
   End If

   ' Close the connection.
   CloseConnection

End Sub ' RetrieveAnEmail
```

The debug output generated by this example is shown in Example A-4.

Example A-4. A Sample POP3 Conversation

```
Client: (Initiates connection on port 110)
Server: +OK POPROX (version 1.0) at pop05.execpc.com starting.
Client: USER dg
Server: +OK Password required for dg.
Client: PASS MyPassword
Server: +OK dg has 6 messages (8355 octets).
Client: STAT
Server: +OK 6 8355
Client: RETR 1
Server: +OK 1347 octets
Client: NOOP
Server: Received: from a.mx.execpc.com (a.mx.execpc.com [169.207.1.102])
   by core0.mx.execpc.com (8.9.3) with ESMTP id KAA28326
   for <dg@execpc.com>; Sat, 27 Nov 1999 10:37:32 -0600 (CST)
Return-Path: <dg@execpc.com>
Received: from mailgw02.execpc.com (sendmail@mailgw02.execpc.com [169.207.3.78])
   by a.mx.execpc.com (8.8.8) with ESMTP id KAA25613
   for <dg@execpc.com>; Sat, 27 Nov 1999 10:37:25 -0600 (CST)
Received: from pop03.execpc.com (pop03.execpc.com [169.207.1.82])
   by mailgw02.execpc.com (8.9.1) id KAA04706
   for <dg@execpc.com>; Sat, 27 Nov 1999 10:37:12 -0600
Received: from daveg (lafra-2-99.mdm.mdx.execpc.com [169.207.192.227]) by pop03.
execpc.com (8.8.8) id KAA27574 for <dg@execpc.com>; Sat, 27 Nov 1999 10:36:39 -0600
Reply-To: <dg@execpc.com>
From: "Dave Grundgeiger" <dg@execpc.com>
To: <dg@execpc.com>
Subject: This is the subject.
Date: Sat, 27 Nov 1999 10:36:27 -0600
Message-ID: <000401bf38f5$92b8f0c0$74c1cfa9@daveg>
MIME-Version: 1.0
Content-Type: text/plain;
   charset="iso-8859-1"
Content-Transfer-Encoding: 7bit
X-Priority: 3 (Normal)
X-MSMail-Priority: Normal
X-Mailer: Microsoft Outlook 8.5, Build 4.71.2173.0
Importance: Normal
X-MimeOLE: Produced By Microsoft MimeOLE V4.72.3110.3
X-UIDL: f6a284799e6eeaa2207903fc3ac7de8a
Status: RO

This is the body.
This is the second line of the body.

.
Client: (Closes connection)
```

The steps to retrieve email are:

1. Establish a connection to port 110 on the POP3 server.
2. Log in to a valid POP3 account on the server. The server does not allow requests to retrieve email until a valid username and password have been supplied. Use the `USER` command to specify the username and the `PASS` command to specify the password.
3. Issue the `STAT` command to determine how many emails are waiting on the server for this user. A success response to the `STAT` command is of the form "`+OK` *`m n`*", where *`m`* is the number of emails waiting and *`n`* is the total size of the waiting emails, in bytes.
4. Issue the `RETR` command to retrieve a specific email. The argument to the `RETR` command is the message number of the email to be retrieved.

Note the use of the `NOOP` command in the *RetrieveAnEmail* subroutine of Example A-3. `NOOP` stands for "no operation" and is ignored by the server. It is used in this example in order to work around the fact that the helper procedures presented in Example A-1 don't account for multiple responses from a single command. That is, my *SendAndWait* function returns the first response that is received from the server after the command is sent. Look again at the code in *RetrieveAnEmail* that issues the `RETR` command:

```
SendAndWait "RETR 1"
txtMsg.Text = SendAndWait("NOOP")
```

In this code, the return value from the first call to the *SendAndWait* function is thrown away. That's because the first response received from the server after issuing the `RETR` command is simply a confirmation message, not the email itself. The email itself is sent immediately after, in a separate response. Given the simple architecture of the helper procedures, the easiest way to grab the next response is to issue another command. I don't want to send a command that actually does anything on the server, though, so `NOOP` is just right.

Emails retrieved from POP3 servers contain both the message headers and the message itself, as you can see by examining Example A-4. It is the responsibility of the client code to parse the headers and separate out the body, but doing so is beyond the scope of this brief appendix. I will point out, however, that the message headers and message body are separated by a blank line.

Finally, be aware that retrieving an email doesn't delete it from the server. To delete an email, issue the `DELE` command, with an argument indicating the message number of the email to be deleted. Using the *SendAndWait* function from Example A-1, it looks like this:

```
SendAndWait "DELE 1"
```

The resulting conversation fragment looks like this:

```
Client: DELE 1
Server: +OK Message 1 has been deleted.
```

Note that this action does not affect message numbering until the session is ended.

Summary

In this appendix you learned the basic techniques for sending and receiving plain text email using the SMTP and POP3 Internet email protocols. By programming these protocols directly, a Visual Basic application can dispense with MAPI and CDO *dll*s. However, Internet protocols are more difficult to program than is CDO, and doing so inextricably ties the Visual Basic application to the underlying email transport mechanism. Therefore, don't give up MAPI unless you have a compelling reason to do so.

If you have a need to delve deeper into Internet email programming, I recommend the O'Reilly book *Programming Internet Email*, by David Wood. It doesn't discuss Visual Basic at all. Rather, it explains Internet email protocols completely and profoundly. With the information in this appendix and David's book, you'll be all set to tackle complex Internet email programming tasks using Visual Basic.

B

Programming the Outlook Object Model

The Outlook object model is a collaboration-enabling technology similar to CDO. It is similar in that it provides Visual Basic a way to access MAPI and also exposes its features via Automation. Many programming tasks are well suited to either technology. The Outlook object model typically is used when writing VBScript or VBA (in Outlook 2000) inside Outlook itself, or when a program needs to access all of the properties of Outlook-specific items (such as tasks and contacts). Standalone messaging applications that aren't Outlook-specific use CDO. UI-less applications must use CDO.

The purpose of this appendix is to give you a brief introduction to the Outlook object model, but not to document the model in its entirety. This appendix shows how to use the Outlook object model to establish a MAPI session and to send and receive plain-text emails. Recall that Outlook Express is not the same as Outlook. Outlook Express does not expose the Outlook object model.

The Outlook Object Model Diagram

Figure B-1 shows the portion of the Outlook object model diagram that supports the functionality used in this appendix. (For a definition of object models and object model diagrams, see Chapter 5, *Collaboration Data Objects*.)

Similar to the CDO object model, the Outlook object model represents MAPI's folders-within-folders hierarchy using a Folders collection object containing MAPIFolder objects, each of which can contain a Folders collection object to represent subfolders, and so on. In addition, each Folder object contains an Items collection object, which in turn contains individual items of a particular type. The Outlook object model also defines individual classes that expose Outlook-specific messaging items (contacts, journal items, notes, posts to public folders, and tasks), whereas in CDO it is necessary to access these items through CDO's generic Message class.

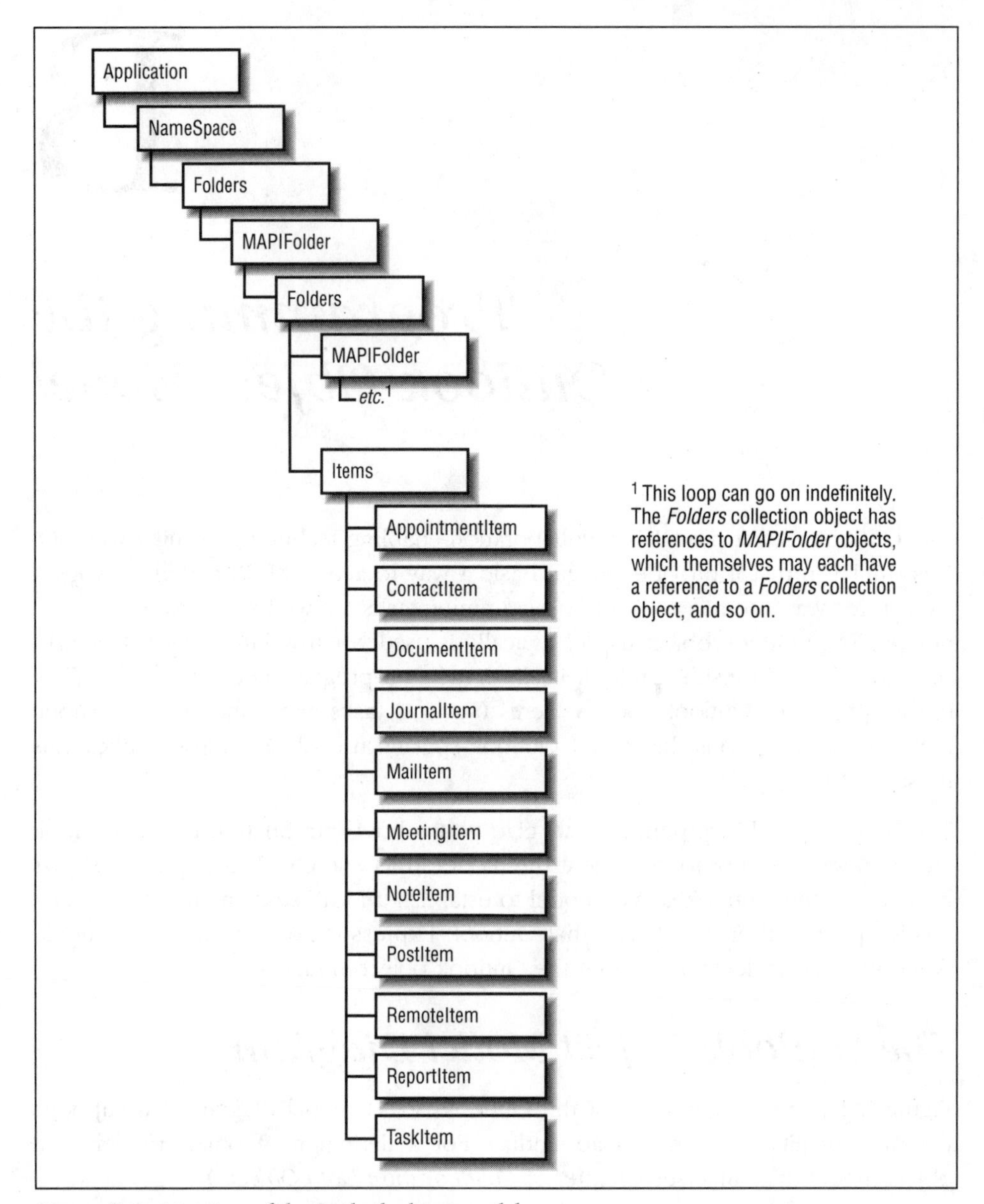

Figure B-1. A portion of the Outlook object model

The Outlook classes shown in Figure B-1 are:

Application
: Provides the main point of access for automating Outlook. All other objects are accessed through the Application object, and all Outlook objects have a reference back to this object.

NameSpace

Represents Outlook data stored in MAPI message stores. The NameSpace object has a Folders collection object, where each MAPIFolder object in the collection represents a single message store. Each MAPIFolder object has its own Folders collection to represent the folders in the message store.

Folders

Represents a collection of folders.

MAPIFolder

Represents a single MAPI folder. A MAPI folder can contain items and subfolders. Items are represented by a reference to an Items collection object, and subfolders are represented by a reference to a Folders collection object.

Items

Represents a collection of items in a folder.

AppointmentItem

Represents an appointment.

ContactItem

Represents a contact.

DocumentItem

Represents a document, such as a Microsoft Word document.

JournalItem

Represents a journal entry.

MailItem

Represents a mail message.

MeetingItem

Represents a meeting.

NoteItem

Represents a note.

PostItem

Represents an item posted to a public folder.

RemoteItem

Represents a mail message but contains only the subject, received date and time, sender, size, and the first 256 characters of the message text. This object gives a client running over a slow network connection enough information to decide whether to download the full MailItem.

ReportItem

Represents a mail-delivery report from a transport provider.

TaskItem

Represents a task.

Getting Started

The Outlook object model is made available to a Visual Basic project by setting a reference to the object model's type library. Type libraries and object models were explained in Chapter 5, in the context of accessing CDO from Visual Basic. To set a reference to the Outlook object model, choose Project → References from the Visual Basic menu. The References dialog box appears, as shown in Figure B-2.

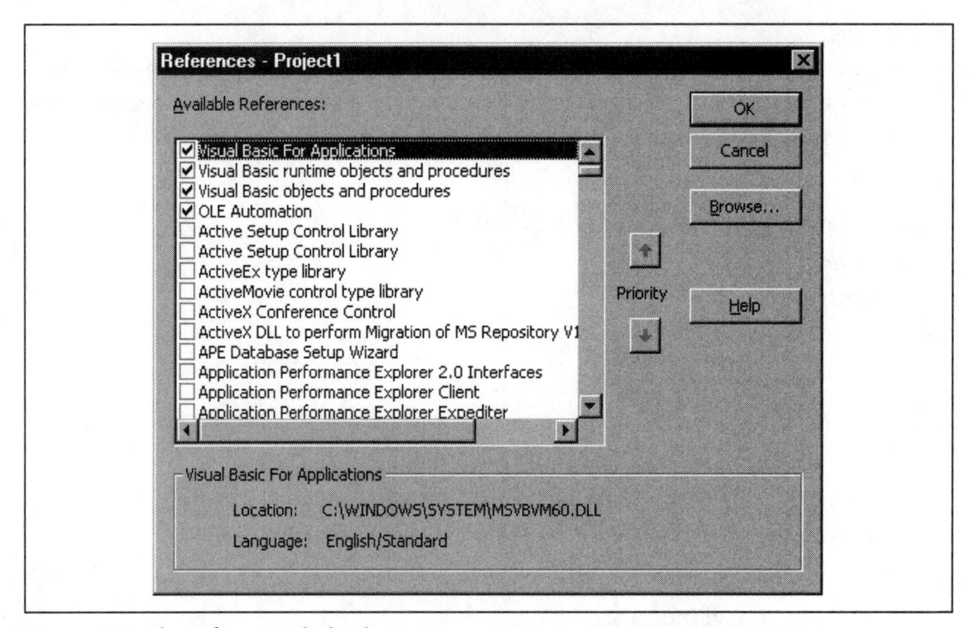

Figure B-2. The References dialog box

Scroll down the list of available references until you find "Microsoft Outlook 9.0 Object Library" (or the library appropriate to the version of Outlook you have installed). Select this item if it's not already selected, and click OK.

Connecting to Outlook and Establishing a MAPI Session

Before sending and reading email, it is necessary to obtain connections both to Outlook and to the MAPI subsystem. To connect to Outlook, instantiate an object of Outlook's Application class, as shown here:

```
Dim OutlookApplication As Outlook.Application
Set OutlookApplication = New Outlook.Application
```

The act of instantiating the Application object causes Outlook to load and run, if it's not running already. However, when Outlook is executed in this way, it does not appear in a window, nor is there a button for it in the task bar; instead, it runs as a hidden application.

The next order of business is to establish a MAPI session. The Application object doesn't have a method for doing this. Rather, it's necessary to obtain a NameSpace object from the Application object. This can be done in either of two ways. One way is to call the Application object's GetNamespace method, like this:

```
' OutlookApplication previously Dim'ed and Set.
Dim OutlookNameSpace As Outlook.NameSpace
Set OutlookNameSpace = Outlook.Application.GetNamespace("MAPI")
```

The argument to the GetNamespace method must always be the string "`MAPI`". The other way to get a NameSpace object from the Application object is to read the contents of the Application object's Session property, like this:

```
' OutlookApplication previously Dim'ed and Set.
Dim OutlookNameSpace As Outlook.NameSpace
Set OutlookNameSpace = Outlook.Application.Session
```

The NameSpace object is roughly analogous to CDO's Session object. Use the NameSpace object to establish a MAPI session, as shown here:

```
OutlookNameSpace.Logon , , ShowDialog:=True, NewSession:=True
```

The syntax of the Logon method is:

```
Logon([Profile],[Password],[ShowDialog],[NewSession])
```

The parameters to the Logon method are:

`Profile`
: This is the name of the profile that is to be used for the session. (MAPI profiles were explained in Chapter 2, *MAPI*.) To cause MAPI to prompt the user for a profile to use, pass an empty string in this parameter, and pass `True` in the *`NewSession`* parameter. This parameter is ignored if Outlook is already running.

`Password`
: Always pass an empty string in this parameter. If passwords are necessary, they can be specified as part of the configuration of the profile. The *`Password`* parameter is left over from earlier versions of MAPI and is now obsolete.

`ShowDialog`
: If MAPI is unable to log on because the *`Profile`* parameter is not supplied or is in error, this parameter controls whether a dialog box is displayed to allow the user to specify a profile name. If *`ShowDialog`* is `False`, an error is raised. This parameter is ignored if Outlook is already running.

`NewSession`
: Passing `True` in this parameter indicates that a new MAPI session should be established, even if an active session is already established on the computer.

Passing `False` indicates that MAPI should attempt to find and use an already-established MAPI session. If one is found, it is used for Outlook as well. If no existing session is found, a new one is created. This parameter is ignored if Outlook is already running.

Note well that all of these parameters are ignored if Outlook is already running. In that case, the session that is already in use by Outlook will continue to be used.

It's time-consuming to start up and shut down Outlook, so it's a good idea to perform this operation once in your application and maintain the connection to Outlook in a global variable. For example, the code in Example B-1 does this. Place this code in a *.bas* module in your project.

Example B-1. Procedures for Connecting to and Disconnecting from Outlook

```
' Global reference to Outlook Application object.
Public gOutlookApplication As Outlook.Application

Public Sub ConnectToOutlook()

   ' Run Outlook and establish a MAPI session.

   ' Proceed only if not already connected.
   If gOutlookApplication Is Nothing Then
      ' Start Outlook or get reference to currently running instance.
      Set gOutlookApplication = New Outlook.Application
      ' Log on to MAPI.
      gOutlookApplication.Session.Logon , , ShowDialog:=True, _
         NewSession:=True
   End If

End Sub ' ConnectToOutlook

Public Sub DisconnectFromOutlook()

   ' Log off of MAPI and release Outlook.

   If Not (gOutlookApplication Is Nothing) Then
      ' Log off first.
      gOutlookApplication.Session.Logoff
      ' Release Outlook.
      Set gOutlookApplication = Nothing
   End If

End Sub ' DisconnectFromOutlook
```

All classes in the Outlook object model have an Application property and a Session property, allowing the Application and NameSpace objects, respectively, to be obtained through any object.

Sending Email

After a MAPI session has been established, email messages can be sent and received. Example B-2 shows a subroutine that sends an email.

Example B-2. Sending Email

```
Private Sub SendMessage()

   Dim OutlookFolder As Outlook.MAPIFolder
   Dim OutlookMailItem As Outlook.MailItem
   Dim OutlookRecipient As Outlook.Recipient

   ' Run Outlook and establish a MAPI session.
   ConnectToOutlook

   ' Get a reference to the Outbox. (Messages must be created in
   ' some folder.)
   Set OutlookFolder = _
      gOutlookApplication.Session.GetDefaultFolder(olFolderOutbox)

   ' Create a new mail item.
   Set OutlookMailItem = OutlookFolder.Items.Add(olMailItem)
   OutlookMailItem.Subject = "This is the subject."
   OutlookMailItem.Body = "This is the body text."

   ' Add a recipient.
   Set OutlookRecipient = OutlookMailItem.Recipients.Add("dg")
   OutlookRecipient.Type = olTo

   ' Send the message.
   OutlookMailItem.Send

   ' Clean up.
   Set OutlookRecipient = Nothing
   Set OutlookMailItem = Nothing
   Set OutlookFolder = Nothing

   DisconnectFromOutlook

End Sub ' SendMessage
```

The *SendMessage* subroutine in Example B-2 performs the following steps:

1. Calls the *ConnectToOutlook* subroutine (already shown in Example B-1) to create an Application object and store a reference to it in the global variable *gOutlookApplication*.
2. Obtains a reference to the user's Outbox folder. This is done by calling the NameSpace object's GetDefaultFolder method. (The NameSpace object is referenced through the Application object's Session property.)

The GetDefaultFolder method returns a reference to a MAPIFolder object that represents the user's default folder of the requested type. (The default folders are set up automatically when Outlook is installed.) The GetDefaultFolder method takes one argument, which can be any of the following values:

`olFolderCalendar`
: The default Calendar folder

`olFolderContacts`
: The default Contacts folder

`olFolderDeletedItems`
: The default Deleted Items folder

`olFolderDrafts`
: The default Drafts folder

`olFolderInbox`
: The default Inbox folder

`olFolderJournal`
: The default Journal folder

`olFolderNotes`
: The default Notes folder

`olFolderOutbox`
: The default Outbox folder

`olFolderSentMail`
: The default Sent Mail folder

`olFolderTasks`
: The default Tasks folder

3. Creates a new message. The MAPIFolder object's Items collection represents the message items contained in the folder. To add an item to the folder, use the Items collection's Add method. The Add method returns a reference to a newly created MailItem object, which is then used to set properties of the new message. The Subject and Body properties are set in Example B-2. The MailItem class has a great many properties, many of which are outside of the scope of this appendix. Some of the most commonly used properties are:

Attachments
: Returns or sets a reference to the attachments associated with the message item. (Processing attachments with the Outlook object model is not discussed in this book.)

Body
: Returns or sets the body text of the message.

CreationTime
: Returns the date and time at which this message was created.

ReceivedTime
: Returns or sets the date and time at which this message was received.

Recipients
: Returns or sets a reference to the recipients associated with the message item. (Recipients are to be discussed shortly.)

Subject
: Returns or sets the subject text of the message.

4. Adds a recipient. The Recipients property of the MailItem object holds a reference to a Recipients collection, which is initially empty. To add a recipient, call the Recipients collection's Add method, passing either the display name of someone in the user's address book or the actual email address of the intended recipient. The Add method returns a reference to the newly created Recipient object, which can be used to set further properties of the recipient. Example B-2 sets the Recipient object's Type property to `olTo`, a constant indicating that the recipient is a primary recipient of the message. Set the Type property to `olCC` to make the recipient a copy recipient, or to `olBCC` to make it a blind copy recipient.
5. Sends the message using the MailItem object's Send method.

Reading Email

Example B-3 shows a subroutine that iterates through the user's Inbox folder, displaying each message's subject text to Visual Basic's Immediate window.

Example B-3. Reading Email

```
Private Sub IterateInbox()

   Dim OutlookFolder As Outlook.MAPIFolder
   Dim OutlookMailItem As Outlook.MailItem

   ' Run Outlook and establish a MAPI session.
   ConnectToOutlook

   ' Get a reference to the Inbox.
   Set OutlookFolder = _
      gOutlookApplication.Session.GetDefaultFolder(olFolderInbox)

   ' Loop for each message.
   For Each OutlookMailItem In OutlookFolder.Items
      ' Write the subject line to the immediate window.
      Debug.Print OutlookMailItem.Subject
   Next OutlookMailItem
```

Example B-3. Reading Email (continued)

```
   ' Clean up.
   Set OutlookMailItem = Nothing
   Set OutlookFolder = Nothing

   DisconnectFromOutlook

End Sub ' IterateInbox
```

The *IterateInbox* subroutine in Example B-3 performs the following steps:

1. Calls the *ConnectToOutlook* subroutine (already shown in Example B-1) to create an Application object and store a reference to it in the global variable *`gOutlookApplication`*.
2. Obtains a reference to the user's Inbox folder. This is done by calling the NameSpace object's GetDefaultFolder method, described in the previous section. (The NameSpace object is referenced through the Application object's Session property.)
3. Uses a `For Each` loop to cycle through each MailItem object in the Inbox folder's Items collection. Displays the MailItem object's Subject property in Visual Basic's immediate window.

After you familiarize yourself with the code in Example B-3, it's not difficult to modify it to suit your needs. For example, you may wish to write a subroutine that searches the user's Inbox for messages containing certain subject text, automatically deleting them. Example B-4 shows such a subroutine. This example also shows the use of the MailItem object's Delete method, which moves a mail item to the user's Deleted Items folder.

Example B-4. Deleting Messages that Meet a Certain Criterion

```
Private Sub DeleteUnwantedMessages()

   Const cstrCompareSubject As String = "MAKE MONEY FAST!"

   Dim OutlookFolder As Outlook.MAPIFolder
   Dim OutlookMailItem As Outlook.MailItem

   ' Run Outlook and establish a MAPI session.
   ConnectToOutlook

   ' Get a reference to the Inbox.
   Set OutlookFolder = _
      gOutlookApplication.Session.GetDefaultFolder(olFolderInbox)

   ' Loop for each message.
   For Each OutlookMailItem In OutlookFolder.Items
      If InStr(OutlookMailItem.Subject, cstrCompareSubject) > 0 Then
         OutlookMailItem.Delete
```

Example B-4. Deleting Messages that Meet a Certain Criterion (continued)

```
      End If
   Next OutlookMailItem

   ' Clean up.
   Set OutlookMailItem = Nothing
   Set OutlookFolder = Nothing

   DisconnectFromOutlook

End Sub ' DeleteUnwantedMessages
```

Summary

In this appendix, you learned that the Outlook object model is similar to CDO but not identical. It is the tool to use when you want client-side applications that integrate very closely with Outlook. You also learned how to send and receive plain-text email messages using the Outlook object model.

C

The Outlook E-mail Security Update

The Outlook E-mail Security Update is a downloadable patch from Microsoft that is intended to help protect users against most viruses that spread via attachments in email. The patch was released in the wake of the infamous ILOVEYOU virus. It works by limiting certain functionality within Outlook and within the Outlook object model. In particular, functionality related to attachments and to accessing email addresses programmatically is significantly restricted. Microsoft has announced that similar limitations will be placed on CDO, but as of press time did not have the CDO changes ready for distribution.

The update is available for both Outlook 98 and Outlook 2000. The version for Outlook 98 *disables CDO completely*. That's right—all CDO applications fail on any machine on which the Outlook E-mail Security Update for Outlook 98 is installed. The version for Outlook 2000 leaves CDO intact. Presumably Microsoft will announce a new update when changes to CDO have been completed. If changes are made to CDO that affect the information in this book, O'Reilly will note them on the book's web site. Go to *http://vb.oreilly.com/* and follow the link for this book.

The Outlook E-mail Security Update provides the following security features:

- Outlook users are prevented from accessing email attachments having filename extensions that indicate that the attachments contain executable code or a link to executable code.
- When a program attempts to use the Outlook object model to access the user's address book or to send email on behalf of the user, a dialog box prompts the user for permission to continue.
- Outlook's default security settings are altered to provide more security from viruses that are spread by means of scripting.

For detailed information (including links to several Knowledge Base articles) and to download the update, go to the Microsoft Office Update site at *http://officeupdate.microsoft.com/*, and follow the links for the Outlook E-mail Security Update.

D

Where Am I Running?

This appendix originally appeared in *Inside the Windows 95 Registry* (O'Reilly & Associates, Inc.), by Ron Petrusha. Because a couple of the registry settings discussed in Chapter 2, *MAPI*, depend on the operating system version, and because programmatically determining the operating system version is not as easy as it might seem, this excellent information is reproduced here. Many thanks to Ron and to O'Reilly for allowing me to do so.

Where Am I Running?

by Ron Petrusha

Originally published as Appendix A in *Inside the Windows 95 Registry*

Such a seemingly simple task as determining the version of the operating system on which an application is running has been surprisingly difficult for many programmers. In the past, the enormous prevalence of errors in version checking in both DOS and Windows applications led Microsoft to various forms of DOS and Windows version "spoofing" simply to compensate for the fact that developers didn't quite get it right.* The introduction of Microsoft's 32-bit platforms in many

* Under DOS, the version table that was activated by including the command `DEVICE=SETVER.EXE` in *CONFIG.SYS* listed applications that incorrectly queried the version number. Each entry in the table consisted of the application's filename and the version of DOS it thought it required in order to run. When the application queried the DOS version, it was given this number, rather than the actual DOS version number. Windows 3.1 supported *compatibility bits*, a variety of hexadecimal bit settings stored in the `[Compatibility]` section of *WIN.INI* that instructed Windows to provide special handling so that a Win30 application could run under Win31; the bulk of these settings were added to *WIN.INI* during installation.

Windows 95 continues to use these compatibility bits defined in the `[Compatibility]` section of *WIN.INI* (and not in the registry). But it goes a bit further, indicating the pervasiveness of these problems: Win95 includes a special utility, *MKCOMPAT.EXE*, that allows any user to modify the compatibility bits for a particular application. One of its standard options is to (in the program's own words) "lie about Windows' version number"! Surely it says something about the real world of software development when the two major operating systems must provide options to lie about something simple like the operating-system version number on an application-by-application basis.

ways has made a confusing situation even more confusing. In this appendix, we'll review how you determine the platform on which your application is running.

What does this have to do with the registry? Since the registry API—and, more important, the registries themselves—are so different in Windows 3.1, Windows 95, and Windows NT, it's important to know which platform your registry-enabled application is running on. Notice that the distinction here is Win31 vs. Win95 vs. WinNT, and not Win16 vs. Win32. The key is the operating system the application is running under, not what sort of application it is.

It would be nice, of course, if there were a single function that determined the platform and version of the operating system that worked uniformly and consistently across all of Microsoft's graphical systems software. This, unfortunately, isn't the case. The way that you determine the platform on which your application is running depends above all on whether your application was developed using the Win16 or the Win32 API.

32-Bit Applications

Of course, 32-bit applications can only run on 32-bit operating systems. This means, as you're no doubt aware, that your application may be running under Windows 95 or Windows NT. But it also means, remember, that your application may be running on Windows 3.1 under Win32s.

Traditionally, the *GetVersion* function is used to retrieve version information. The 16-bit version of *GetVersion* returns a long (4-byte) integer. Its lower-order word contains the version of Windows: the low-order byte contains the major version number, while the high-order byte contains the minor version number. The high-order word reports the MS-DOS version: its major version is stored in the high-order byte, and its minor version is in the low-order byte. This seems clear enough, but many developers still had difficulty with it. Two problems were particularly common:

- Confusing the major and minor version numbers. Probably because the bytes used to store the major and minor version numbers are the reverse of one another for DOS and Windows, it was very common to retrieve Windows' minor version number and treat it as the major version, and to retrieve the major version and interpret it as the minor version. When this happened, 3.10—the official version number reported by Win31—became transmogrified into Windows version 10.3.
- Testing for a particular version, rather than a baseline version. Almost all applications are written to take advantage of a particular API or some feature that is new to the underlying operating system. In these cases, the application

has to require that it run on the new version of that operating system, and not on earlier versions. One would think that developers would remember, though, that particularly in the software industry, nothing is immutable, and new versions inevitably give rise to even newer versions. In numerous instances, however, someone forgot this, and checked the version in a way similar to the following code fragment:

```
if (!(nMajorVersion == 3) && (nMinorVersion == 10))
   {
   MessageBox(NULL, "You might think about upgrading!",
              "Wrong O/S", MB_OK) ;
   return FALSE ;
   }
```

Except in the rare case that the programmer's intention was really to run only under Windows 3.1, the program should check for version 3.1 or greater; instead, it checks for version 3.1 and refuses to run if it finds anything else.

GetVersion is still present under Win32. However, in large measure to prevent silly mistakes like this, the Win32 API includes a new function, *GetVersionEx*, that also happens to provide the best way to determine the platform and version of the entire family of Microsoft's 32-bit systems software. Its syntax is:

```
BOOL GetVersionEx( LPOSVERSIONINFO lpVersionInformation ) ;
```

The function returns `True` if it succeeds and `False` if it fails. Its single parameter is an OSVERSIONINFO data structure that is defined as shown in Table D-1. The only requirement in calling the function is that the `OSVERSIONINFO`'s *`dwOSVersionInfoSize`* member be assigned an accurate value beforehand.

Table D-1. The OSVERSIONINFO Structure

Member	Type	Description
dwOSVersionInfoSize	DWORD	The size of the `OSVERSIONINFO` structure. It should be set to *`sizeof(OSVERSIONINFO)`* before the *GetVersionEx* function is called.
dwMajorVersion	DWORD	The major version of the operating system.
dwMinorVersion	DWORD	The minor version of the operating system.
dwBuildNumber	DWORD	The low-order word contains the operating system's build number; the high-order word identifies the operating system's major and minor versions.

dwPlatformId	DWORD	The platform supported by the operating system. It can have any of the following values:
		`VER_PLATFORM_WIN32S = 0`
		`VER_PLATFORM_WIN32_WINDOWS = 1`
		`VER_PLATFORM_WIN32_NT = 2`

szCSDVersion[128]	TCHAR	A zero-terminated string containing additional information about the operating system.

GetVersion and the Win32 API

Although we prefer *GetVersionEx*, you can, if you like, continue to use *GetVersion*. If you want to do this because you're developing both 16- and 32-bit applications and want to minimize platform differences, you should note that the Win32 version differs from the Win16 version. Both variations of the function return the version number of Windows in the same way. They differ in their use of the high-order word. In the 16-bit version, it is used to hold the major and minor version of MS-DOS. The 32-bit version, on the other hand, uses the high-order bit of the high-order byte to indicate the platform: if the bit is on, the platform is either Windows 95 or Win32s; if it is off, the platform is Windows NT. For platforms other than Windows 95 (where it is not supported), the remaining bits of the high-order byte indicate the build.

Since they both set the high-order bit of the high-order byte on, you have to also examine the major version number to differentiate between Windows 95 and Win32s. Windows 95 has a version number of 4 (and presumably forthcoming versions of 32-bit Windows will have a version number of greater than 4); Win32s has a version number of 3. So you could define a Boolean variable to indicate the presence or absence of each operating system as follows:

```
dwVer = GetVersion() ;
fWin95 = (dwVer && 0x80000000) && (LOBYTE(LOWORD(dwVer)) == 4) ;
fWin32s = (dwVer && 0x80000000) && (LOBYTE(LOWORD(dwVer)) == 3) ;
```

This makes it very easy to determine the platform on which your application is running. The *GetPlatform* function in Example D-1, for example, returns the value of the `OSVERSIONINFO` structure's `dwPlatformId` member. You can then use it at run-time to define a flag that determines if a particular version is present.

Example D-1. The GetPlatform Function

```
BOOL fWin95 = (VER_PLATFORM_WIN32_WINDOWS == GetPlatform()) ;
#include <windows.h>

DWORD GetPlatform(VOID)
{
   OSVERSIONINFO osVer ;
   osVer.dwOSVersionInfoSize = sizeof(osVer) ;
   return (GetVersionEx(&osVer)) ? osVer.dwPlatformId : 0;
}
```

If you're using Visual Basic, you first have to declare the *GetVersionEx* function and define its constants and data structure, as shown in Example D-2. Note that the `lpVersionInformation` data structure is passed by reference to the function, and that its `szCSDVersion` member is defined as a fixed-length string. The *GetPlatform* function is shown in Example D-3.

Example D-2. The Visual Basic Code Module Defining GetVersionEx

```
Public Declare Function GetVersionEx Lib "kernel32" _
      Alias "GetVersionExA" _
      (lpVersionInformation As OSVERSIONINFO) As Boolean

Type OSVERSIONINFO
   dwOSVersionInfoSize As Long
   dwMajorVersion As Long
   dwMinorVersion As Long
   dwBuildNumber As Long
   dwPlatformId As Long
   szCSDVersion As String * 128
End Type

Public Const VER_PLATFORM_WIN32s = 0
Public Const VER_PLATFORM_WIN32_WINDOWS = 1
Public Const VER_PLATFORM_WIN32_NT = 2
```

Example D-3. The Visual Basic GetPlatform Function

```
Public Function GetPlatform() As Long

Dim udtVer As OSVERSIONINFO

udtVer.dwOSVersionInfoSize = Len(udtVer)

If (GetVersionEx(udtVer)) Then
   GetPlatform = udtVer.dwPlatformId
Else
   GetPlatform = 0   ' returns Win32 as lowest common denominator
End If

End Function
```

GetVersionEx does have one relatively small limitation as far as determining the operating system platform is concerned: it doesn't allow you to distinguish between Windows NT Workstation and Windows NT Server, the two varieties of Windows NT. If you want to do that, you'll have to check the Windows NT registry; one of the string values shown in Table D-2 that indicates the type of Windows NT is stored as the default value of `HKLM\SYSTEM\CurrentControlSet\Control\ProductOptions`.

Table D-2. Values of the ProductOptions Subkey

REG_SZ String	Description	Windows NT Versions
WINNT	Windows NT Workstation	all
SERVERNT	Windows NT Server	3.5+
LANMANNT	Windows NT Advanced Server	3.1

In addition to making it easy to determine the platform on which your application is running, *GetVersionEx* makes determining the operating system's version number very simple: you just have to evaluate the OSVERSIONINFO's `dwMajorVersion` and `dwMinorVersion` members. Table D-3 indicates the version number returned by calling *GetVersionEx* under existing 32-bit Windows operating systems. Note that, when reporting the version number of Win32s, *GetVersionEx* returns the version number of Win32s itself; *GetVersion*, on the other hand, returns 3.10 as the Windows version.

Table D-3. Version Numbers of 32-bit Operating Systems Reported by GetVersionEx

Operating System	Major Version	Minor Version
Win32s	1	0
	1	10
	1	15
	1	20
	1	25
	1	30
Windows 95	4	0
Windows NT	3	10
	3	50
	3	51

If you do need to retrieve the version number to make sure that your application is running on an operating system with the appropriate feature set, it's important, unless there's a pressing reason to do otherwise (like the feature that you need is present in one release but discontinued in later releases), to make sure that the operating system version is greater than or equal to some base version. In the case of Windows 95 (or the x.0 release of any operating system), you don't even have to bother with the minor version:

```
if (osVer.dwMajorVersion >= 4)
// version is OK
```

In other cases—for example, if you require that your program run under Windows NT 3.51 or greater—you do have to look at the minor version:

```
if (osVer.dwMajorVersion == 3 && osVer.dwMinorVersion >= 51) ||
            (osVer.dwMajorVersion >= 4))
// version is OK
```

16-Bit Applications

For the most part, retrieving version and platform information for 16-bit applications relies almost completely on the *GetVersion* function. The sole possible exception is a 16-bit application running under Windows 95, which can still use *GetVersionEx*; like the registry API, it is an undocumented function exported by *KRNL386.EXE*.* This makes determining the platform or operating system on which an application is running somewhat more complicated, since 16-bit applications can run not only on 16-bit operating systems (Windows 3.x and Windows for Workgroups), but on 32-bit ones as well.

Once again, *GetVersion* returns a DWORD value in which the low-order byte of the low-order word contains the major version of the operating system, while the high-order byte of the low-order word contains the operating system's minor version. So you can retrieve the major and minor version as follows:

```
dwVersion = GetVersion() ;
dwMajorVersion = LOBYTE(LOWORD(dwVersion)) ;
dwMinorVersion = HIBYTE(LOWORD(dwVersion)) ;
```

Relying on the *GetVersion* function to identify a platform means that you have to be able to determine the platform on which your application is running based on its version number. Table D-4 lists the current and past versions of Microsoft's major graphical operating systems, environments, and operating system extensions.

Table D-4. Major and Minor Versions Returned by GetVersion

Operating System	Type	Versions
Windows	16-bit	3.0, 3.10[a]
Windows for Workgroups	16-bit	3.10[a]
Win32s	32-bit	3.10
Windows	32-bit	3.95
Windows NT	32-bit	3.10, 3.50, 3.51

[a] Although Microsoft released version 3.11 of both Windows for Workgroups and plain-vanilla Windows, both operating systems return 3.10 as their major and minor version. We might conjecture that one of the considerations involved in the decision to use the same version number for two different versions of the operating system was the reluctance to deal with all of the broken applications caused by developers thinking that their applications would be forever running happily under Win31.

This introduces a complication. Notice that the *GetVersion* function returns the same version for a variety of 16-bit (Windows and Windows for Workgroups) and 32-bit (Win32s and Windows NT) operating systems. In addition, the major and

* This raises a chicken and egg problem: On the one hand, to successfully call the API, you need to know the version number, since *GetVersionEx* is implemented on 16-bit platforms only under Win95. On the other hand, you're calling the function in the first place because you don't know the version. So how do you check the platform or version using a function that presupposes a particular platform (Windows 95) and version (Windows 4.0)? The solution is *GetProcAddress*, which returns a function's address if it is present and NULL if it is not.

minor version numbers reported by future versions of Windows and Windows NT may also be identical. So *GetVersion* alone is unable to indicate the platform whose version it reports.

The Two Faces of Windows 95

Windows 95 reports two different version numbers to applications, depending on whether they are 16-bit or 32-bit. If a 16-bit application uses *GetVersion* to determine the version number of Windows 95, the major version is reported as 3 and the minor version as 95. But if a 32-bit application uses *GetVersion* or *GetVersionEx* to retrieve the version number, the major version is reported as 4 and the minor version as 0.

From the viewpoint of accessing the registry API from 16-bit code, there are really just two distinct cases in which it may be difficult to deduce the underlying platform from its version number:

- Windows NT 3.1 versus Windows 3.1, Windows for Workgroups 3.1, and Win32s. Although it may be important for other reasons to determine whether your 16-bit application is running under Windows 3.1, Windows for Workgroups 3.1, or Win32s, all use the same limited registration database. Windows 3.1 and Windows for Workgroups 3.1 both support the "compatibility functions" in the registry API, while Win32s supports a number of Win32 functions as well,* although these can only operate on the limited registration database. So practically, you don't really need to distinguish between them. You do, however, have to differentiate these three platforms from Windows NT 3.1.
- Future versions of Windows NT and Windows. Since they haven't been released yet, we of course don't know what version numbers future versions of these two 32-bit operating systems will report to 16-bit applications.

In both cases, what is really important to detect is the presence of Windows NT. To do this, you just have to call the *GetWinFlags* function and test for the *WF_WINNT* flag; if it's set, your application is running under Windows NT; if not, it's running under Windows 3.x, Windows for Workgroups, Win32s, or Windows 95. Before calling the function, you'll also have to define the flag's value, since it's not included in the Win16 SDK:

```
#define WF_WINNT(0x4000)
```

* Win32s also supports *RegCreateKeyEx*, *RegEnumValue*, *RegOpenKeyEx*, *RegQueryValueEx*, *RegSetValueEx*, and *RegUnloadKey*.

For example, the *IsWinNT* function shown in Example D-4 returns a **True** if the platform at run-time is Windows NT, and returns **False** if it is anything else. Its Visual Basic equivalent is shown in Example D-5.

Example D-4. The IsWinNT Function

```
#include <windows.h>

#define WF_WINNT        (0x4000)

BOOL IsWinNT(VOID)
{
   return (WF_WINNT & GetWinFlags()) ;
}
```

Example D-5. The Visual Basic Version of IsWinNt, Including Its Code Module

```
Public Declare Function GetWinFlags Lib "kernel" _
        () As Long

Public Const WF_WINNT = &H4000

Public Function IsWinNT() As Boolean

#If Win16 Then
    IsWinNT = False
    If GetWinFlags() And WF_WINNT Then IsWinNT = True
#End If

End Function
```

You can then distinguish between 32-bit Windows and Windows NT with a code snippet like the following:

```
if (dwVerMajor > 3 || (dwVerMajor == 3 && dwVerMinor >= 50)))
//  32-bit O/S version 3.5 or greater is present
   if IsWinNT()
//  Windows NT 3.50+ is present
   else
//  Windows 3.95+ is present
```

The point may seem silly, but it's worth emphasizing that this fragment avoids a common error. If we simply checked the version with the code fragment:

```
if (dwVerMajor == 3 && dwVerMinor >= 50)
```

our `if` statement would be true only for versions with numbers between 3.5 and 3.99. Instead, we want to check for versions greater than or equal to 3.5, and then differentiate Win95 (and future versions of the Windows platform) from WinNT.

E

Resources for Messaging Developers

This appendix lists Internet sites that can help you if you get stuck. Links to the latest versions of MAPI and CDO are shown here, as well as links to discussion lists, newsgroups, and other sites with abundant MAPI, CDO, and Visual Basic information.

Although the links shown here were verified to be live at the time of printing, there is no guarantee that they will remain so. Visit O'Reilly's Visual Basic web site for the most current list of links. Start at *http://vb.oreilly.com* and click the link for this book.

MAPI and CDO Downloads

These are the official sites from which to download the current versions of MAPI and CDO and get current licensing information:

MAPI

http://www.microsoft.com/exchange/downloads/intro.htm

CDO

http://www.microsoft.com/exchange/downloads/CDO.htm

Discussion Lists

Discussion lists are one of the greatest treasures of the Internet. Here you have the opportunity to ask questions of a group of tens, hundreds, or thousands of people who are in your field of interest. The web URLs listed here link to pages that provide instructions for subscribing to the lists.

MAPI Developers Forum

The members of this list discuss MAPI and related topics, including CDO, Outlook, and Exchange Server. Subscribers include C, C++, and Visual Basic developers of all skill levels. There are approximately 500 subscribers.

http://peach.ease.lsoft.com/archives/mapi-l.html

Visual Basic List

The members of this list discuss everything related to Visual Basic, including how to use CDO from Visual Basic. This is a large, very active list with developers of all skill levels. There are plenty of advanced Visual Basic developers on this list who are ready to lend a hand when they can. There are approximately 4600 subscribers.

http://peach.ease.lsoft.com/archives/visbas-l.html

Visual Basic Beginner's List

For beginners who don't feel comfortable posting to the Visual Basic List, there is the Visual Basic Beginner's List. There are approximately 1100 subscribers.

http://peach.ease.lsoft.com/archives/visbas-beginners.html

If you've never before been a member of a discussion list, take care to note the concept of *netiquette*. This term refers to the rules of behavior expected from people who post messages to discussion lists. You will receive or be directed to a list of such expectations when you subscribe to a list, but they can be summed up as follows:

1. Monitor the discussion list a while before posting messages.
2. If available, search the list archives before posting a question.
3. Don't post questions that are outside of the list's discussion topic.
4. Be nice.
5. Answer the questions that you can.
6. Maximize your *signal-to-noise ratio*. (That means you should post more helpful answers than witty remarks.)

Newsgroups

Similar to discussion lists, Internet newsgroups provide a way for groups of people to post messages for all to see. Unlike discussion lists, newsgroups don't maintain a member list. Everyone is free to post and read messages.

Microsoft Newsgroups

Microsoft maintains about three dozen newsgroups specifically about Exchange, Outlook, and Exchange 2000. There is also one newsgroup devoted to messaging in general. Links to these newsgroups can be found at *http://www.microsoft.com/exchange/support/Newsgroups.htm.*

Other Newsgroups

The following newsgroups aren't listed on the Microsoft site; nevertheless, they host discussions of interest to messaging developers:

- *microsoft.public.win32.programmer.messaging*
- *microsoft.public.platformsdk.messaging*
- *microsoft.public.mail.misc*

Deja.com's Usenet Discussion Service

This web site allows searching newsgroup archives for particular key words or phrases. This is an awesome site if you don't know precisely which newsgroup you want: *http://www.deja.com/usenet/.*

Messaging-Related Web Sites

There are many excellent web sites providing information on messaging technologies. Here are just a few:

MSDN Online

This is the mother of all online help. The site has Microsoft's official documentation for developers, including documentation for MAPI and CDO. Just enter a search phrase and go. It includes:

General Microsoft Technical Documentation

http://msdn.microsoft.com

MAPI Documentation

http://msdn.microsoft.com/library/default.asp?URL=/library/psdk/mapi/book_9jqc.htm

CDO Documentation

http://msdn.microsoft.com/library/default.asp?URL=/library/psdk/cdo/kluaover_34a7.htm

CDOLive

This is a rich site devoted to CDO and related technology. There are articles, programming samples, links, training and book recommendations, and more.

http://www.cdolive.com

The Outlook and Exchange Developer Resource Center

This is a site with articles and sample code relating to Outlook and Exchange.

http://www.outlookexchange.com

Electronic Messaging Association

EMA is a non-profit trade association for the e-business and messaging industries. They are the publishers of *Messaging Magazine*. The site has news, information, book recommendations, and more.

http://www.ema.org

O'Reilly & Associates, Inc.

In addition to offering many outstanding books on Visual Basic programming, O'Reilly hosts a question-and-answer forum called *Ron's VB Forum*. In it, O'Reilly Visual Basic editor Ron Petrusha writes a bi-monthly column answering particularly interesting VB questions. Start at *http://vb.oreilly.com* and follow the link to *Ron's VB Forum*.

F

Obtaining the Sample Code

The sample applications discussed in Chapter 6, *An Email Client Application*, and Chapter 7, *Enhancing the Email Client*, can be downloaded directly from the O'Reilly & Associates web site. This appendix explains how to obtain these applications and how to register the CdoHelper component presented in Chapter 6.

The sample code is provided for instruction and demonstration purposes only. While O'Reilly & Associates, Inc., and the author believe the code to work correctly as described herein, neither can warrant that it is free of defects nor that it is suitable for any particular use.

Downloading the Code

Follow these steps to download the sample code:

1. Point your browser to *http://vb.oreilly.com*, O'Reilly's Visual Basic–specific web site and follow the link on that page for this book.
2. Review any late-breaking news presented on the site. If there is any news that alters the download instructions in this appendix, such will be stated clearly on the site. If not, continue with the steps below.
3. Click the link to download *SampleCode.zip*. The file size is approximately 170 KB.
4. After downloading, use a *.zip* file extraction utility, such as WinZip, to extract the files from *SampleCode.zip*. This creates a folder tree beginning with a folder named *vbmsg*. For example, if *SampleCode.zip* is extracted to the *C:*

drive root folder, all of the extracted files will reside within folders underneath *C:\vbmsg*.

5. Read the text in *C:\vbmsg\readme.txt* for any additional information.

When this book refers to specific file locations, they are given in the form *\vbmsg\foldername\filename.ext*. These are to be interpreted as relative to the folder into which the *.zip* file is extracted. For example, if the *.zip* file is extracted to the *C:* drive root folder, the above relative path refers to *C:\vbmsg\foldername\filename.ext*.

What's in the Download

All of the sample code is located in *\vbmsg\Samples*. In that folder are three subfolders:

Chapter 6
: This folder contains a single subfolder, *Messenger*, which in turn contains the Visual Basic files for the Messenger 2000 application presented in Chapter 6. To load the project in Visual Basic, open *\vbmsg\Samples\Chapter 6\Messenger\Messenger.vbp*.

Chapter 7
: This folder contains a Visual Basic *.bas* module with the code for converting MAPI property IDs to their textual descriptions, as explained in Chapter 7. The *.bas* module is located at *\vbmsg\Samples\Chapter 7\basCdoPrTextFromCode.bas*.

CdoHelper
: This folder contains a Visual C++ project that implements the CdoHelper component. This component can be used by Visual Basic applications to add RTF-encoded text to messages being sent through CDO and to read RTF-encoded text from such messages. (CDO itself doesn't support this feature.) The component can be used without knowing anything about C++, but the complete source code and project files are included for those who are interested. To use the component in Visual Basic, register it as described in the next section, then see Chapter 6 for instructions on its use. If you're interested in loading the C++ project in Visual Studio, open *\vbmsg\Samples\CdoHelper\CdoHelper.dsw*.

Registering the CdoHelper Component

As with all ActiveX components, the CdoHelper component must be registered before it is used. *Registering* means adding information about the component to the Windows Registry so that client applications know where the component is.

This step is often performed by an automated installation process, but for the CdoHelper component it must be done manually. To do so, choose Run from the Start menu, and enter:

```
regsvr32 path\CdoHelper.dll
```

where `path` is the full path of the folder containing *CdoHelper.dll*. For example, if the sample code was extracted to the *C:* drive root folder, the command is:

```
regsvr32 C:\vbmsg\Samples\CdoHelper\CdoHelper.dll
```

After the component is registered, it can be used in Visual Basic by setting a reference to *O'Reilly CDO Helper 1.0*. See Chapter 6 for further information.

If desired, the CdoHelper component can be unregistered by running the *regsvr32* program again, this time specifying the `-u` switch (for "unregister"). A typical command would look like this:

```
regsvr32 -u C:\vbmsg\Samples\CdoHelper\CdoHelper.dll
```

Your computer should already have the *regsvr32* program on it, but if it doesn't, you can download it from Microsoft by following these steps:

1. Go to *http://support.microsoft.com/support/downloads/dp2439.asp*.
2. Click the link to download *regsv32a.exe*. This is a self-extracting executable file that contains *regsvr32.exe*.
3. Download the file to your computer's *System* folder (on Windows 9x systems) or to the *System32* folder (on Windows NT or Windows 2000 systems).
4. Run the *regsv32a* program. This extracts *regsvr32.exe* into the folder from which you ran *regsv32a*.

Index

A

B

C

I

J

K

L

M

N

O

Q

R

S

T

U

V

W

About the Author

Dave Grundgeiger is a consultant at Tara Software, Inc., in Madison, Wisconsin, where he spends his days immersed in Microsoft DNA technologies. He is a proficient C++ and Visual Basic designer/developer, specializing in multi-tier vertical market business solutions using Visual Basic, IIS, MTS/COM+, and SQL Server. Dave's research interests include Artificial Intelligence, with emphasis on Natural Language Processing. He is particularly interested in applying AI techniques in real-world business applications. Dave has written for *MSDN Magazine* and *C/C++ Users Journal.*

Colophon

Our look is the result of reader comments, our own experimentation, and feedback from distribution channels. Distinctive covers complement our distinctive approach to technical topics, breathing personality and life into potentially dry subjects.

The animal on the cover of *CDO & MAPI Programming with Visual Basic* is a dove. Doves belong to the class Aves (birds) and the order Columbiformes (doves and pigeons), to which the now-extinct dodo bird, *Raphus cucullatus,* also belongs. Their family, Columbidae, includes over 300 species of pigeons and doves, including the common rock dove or feral pigeon (*Columba livia*).

Leanne Soylemez was the production editor for *CDO & MAPI Programming with Visual Basic.* Audrey Doyle was the copyeditor. Nancy Wolfe Kotary and Sarah Jane Shangraw provided quality control. Nancy Crumpton wrote the index, and Brenda Miller edited it.

Ellie Volckhausen designed the cover of this book, based on a series design by Edie Freedman. The cover image is an original illustration created by Susan Hart. Emma Colby produced the cover layout with QuarkXPress 4.1 using Adobe's ITC Garamond font.

Alicia Cech and David Futato designed the interior layout based on a series design by Nancy Priest. Mike Sierra implemented the design in FrameMaker 5.5.6. The text and heading fonts are ITC Garamond Light and Garamond Book. The illustrations that appear in the book were produced by Robert Romano using Macromedia FreeHand 8 and Adobe Photoshop 5. This colophon was written by Leanne Soylemez.

Whenever possible, our books use a durable and flexible lay-flat binding. If the page count exceeds this binding's limit, perfect binding is used.

More Titles from O'Reilly

Visual Basic Programming

Developing Visual Basic Add-ins

By Steven Roman
1st Edition December 1998
186 pages, ISBN 1-56592-527-0

A tutorial and reference guide in one, this short book covers all the basics of creating customized VB add-ins to extend the IDE, allowing developers to work more productively with Visual Basic. Readers with even a modest acquaintance with VB will be developing add-ins in no time. Includes numerous simple code examples.

VB & VBA in a Nutshell: The Language

By Paul Lomax
1st Edition October 1998
656 pages, ISBN 1-56592-358-8

For Visual Basic and VBA programmers, this book boils down the essentials of the VB and VBA languages into a single volume, including undocumented and little-documented areas essential to everyday programming. The convenient alphabetical reference to all functions, procedures, statements, and keywords allows programmers to use this book both as a standard reference guide and as a tool for troubleshooting and identifying programming problems.

Access Database Design & Programming, 2nd Edition

By Steven Roman
2nd Edition July 1999
432 pages, ISBN 1-56592-626-9

This second edition of the bestselling *Access Database Design & Programming* covers Access' new VBA Integrated Development Environment used by Word, Excel, and PowerPoint; the VBA language itself; Microsoft's latest data access technology, Active Data Objects (ADO); plus Open Database Connectivity (ODBC).

Visual Basic Controls in a Nutshell

By Evan S. Dictor
1st Edition July 1999
762 pages, ISBN 1-56592-294-8

To create professional applications, developers need extensive knowledge of Visual Basic controls and their numerous properties, methods, and events. This quick reference documents the steps involved in using each major VB control, the order in which their events are fired, and the unexpected ways in which their properties, methods, and events interact.

Learning VBScript

By Paul Lomax
1st Edition July 1997
616 pages, Includes CD-ROM
ISBN 1-56592-247-6

This definitive guide shows Web developers how to take full advantage of client-side scripting with the VBScript language. In addition to basic language features, it covers the Internet Explorer object model and discusses techniques for client-side scripting, like adding ActiveX controls to a Web page or validating data before sending it to the server. Includes CD-ROM with over 170 code samples.

Writing Word Macros

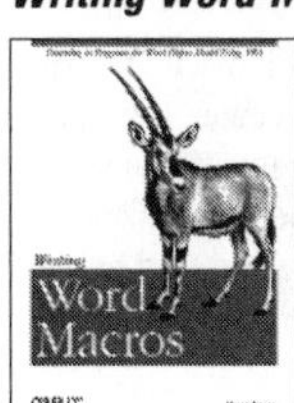

By Steven Roman
2nd Edition October 1999
410 pages, ISBN 1-56592-725-7

This no-nonsense book delves into VBA programming and tells how you can use VBA to automate all the tedious, repetitive jobs you never thought you could do in Microsoft Word. It takes the reader step-by-step through writing VBA macros and programs.

How to stay in touch with O'Reilly

1. Visit Our Award-Winning Web Site

http://www.oreilly.com/

★"Top 100 Sites on the Web" —*PC Magazine*
★"Top 5% Web sites" —*Point Communications*
★"3-Star site" —*The McKinley Group*

Our web site contains a library of comprehensive product information (including book excerpts and tables of contents), downloadable software, background articles, interviews with technology leaders, links to relevant sites, book cover art, and more. File us in your Bookmarks or Hotlist!

2. Join Our Email Mailing Lists

New Product Releases

To receive automatic email with brief descriptions of all new O'Reilly products as they are released, send email to:
listproc@online.oreilly.com
Put the following information in the first line of your message (*not* in the Subject field):
subscribe oreilly-news

O'Reilly Events

If you'd also like us to send information about trade show events, special promotions, and other O'Reilly events, send email to:
listproc@online.oreilly.com
Put the following information in the first line of your message (*not* in the Subject field):
subscribe oreilly-events

3. Get Examples from Our Books via FTP

There are two ways to access an archive of example files from our books:

Regular FTP

- ftp to:
  ftp.oreilly.com
  (login: anonymous
  password: your email address)
- Point your web browser to:
  ftp://ftp.oreilly.com/

FTPMAIL

- Send an email message to:
  ftpmail@online.oreilly.com
  (Write "help" in the message body)

4. Contact Us via Email

order@oreilly.com
To place a book or software order online. Good for North American and international customers.

subscriptions@oreilly.com
To place an order for any of our newsletters or periodicals.

books@oreilly.com
General questions about any of our books.

software@oreilly.com
For general questions and product information about our software. Check out O'Reilly Software Online at **http://software.oreilly.com/** for software and technical support information. Registered O'Reilly software users send your questions to: **website-support@oreilly.com**

cs@oreilly.com
For answers to problems regarding your order or our products.

booktech@oreilly.com
For book content technical questions or corrections.

proposals@oreilly.com
To submit new book or software proposals to our editors and product managers.

international@oreilly.com
For information about our international distributors or translation queries. For a list of our distributors outside of North America check out:
http://www.oreilly.com/www/order/country.html

5. Work with Us

Check out our website for current employment opportunites:
www.jobs@oreilly.com
Click on "Work with Us"

O'Reilly & Associates, Inc.
101 Morris Street, Sebastopol, CA 95472 USA
TEL 707-829-0515 or 800-998-9938
(6am to 5pm PST)
FAX 707-829-0104

International Distributors

UK, Europe, Middle East and Africa (except France, Germany, Austria, Switzerland, Luxembourg, Liechtenstein, and Eastern Europe)

INQUIRIES

O'Reilly UK Limited
4 Castle Street
Farnham
Surrey, GU9 7HS
United Kingdom
Telephone: 44-1252-711776
Fax: 44-1252-734211
Email: information@oreilly.co.uk

ORDERS

Wiley Distribution Services Ltd.
1 Oldlands Way
Bognor Regis
West Sussex PO22 9SA
United Kingdom
Telephone: 44-1243-779777
Fax: 44-1243-820250
Email: cs-books@wiley.co.uk

France

INQUIRIES

Éditions O'Reilly
18 rue Séguier
75006 Paris, France
Tel: 33-1-40-51-52-30
Fax: 33-1-40-51-52-31
Email: france@editions-oreilly.fr

ORDERS

GEODIF
61, Bd Saint-Germain
75240 Paris Cedex 05, France
Tel: 33-1-44-41-46-16 (French books)
Tel: 33-1-44-41-11-87 (English books)
Fax: 33-1-44-41-11-44
Email: distribution@eyrolles.com

Germany, Switzerland, Austria, Eastern Europe, Luxembourg, and Liechtenstein

INQUIRIES & ORDERS

O'Reilly Verlag
Balthasarstr. 81
D-50670 Köln
Germany
Telephone: 49-221-973160-91
Fax: 49-221-973160-8
Email: anfragen@oreilly.de (inquiries)
Email: order@oreilly.de (orders)

Canada (French language books)

Les Éditions Flammarion ltée
375, Avenue Laurier Ouest
Montréal (Québec) H2V 2K3
Tel: 00-1-514-277-8807
Fax: 00-1-514-278-2085
Email: info@flammarion.qc.ca

Hong Kong

City Discount Subscription Service, Ltd.
Unit D, 3rd Floor, Yan's Tower
27 Wong Chuk Hang Road
Aberdeen, Hong Kong
Tel: 852-2580-3539
Fax: 852-2580-6463
Email: citydis@ppn.com.hk

Korea

Hanbit Media, Inc.
Chungmu Bldg. 201
Yonnam-dong 568-33
Mapo-gu
Seoul, Korea
Tel: 822-325-0397
Fax: 822-325-9697
Email: hant93@chollian.dacom.co.kr

Philippines

Global Publishing
G/F Benavides Garden
1186 Benavides Street
Manila, Philippines
Tel: 632-254-8949/637-252-2582
Fax: 632-734-5060/632-252-2733
Email: globalp@pacific.net.ph

Taiwan

O'Reilly Taiwan
No. 3, Lane 131
Hang-Chow South Road
Section 1, Taipei, Taiwan
Tel: 886-2-23968990
Fax: 886-2-23968916
Email: taiwan@oreilly.com

China

O'Reilly Beijing
Room 2410
160, FuXingMenNeiDaJie
XiCheng District
Beijing, China PR 100031
Tel: 86-10-66412305
Fax: 86-10-86631007
Email: beijing@oreilly.com

India

Computer Bookshop (India) Pvt. Ltd.
190 Dr. D.N. Road, Fort
Bombay 400 001 India
Tel: 91-22-207-0989
Fax: 91-22-262-3551
Email: cbsbom@giasbm01.vsnl.net.in

Japan

O'Reilly Japan, Inc.
Yotsuya Y's Building
7 Banch 6, Honshio-cho
Shinjuku-ku
Tokyo 160-0003 Japan
Tel: 81-3-3356-5227
Fax: 81-3-3356-5261
Email: japan@oreilly.com

All Other Asian Countries

O'Reilly & Associates, Inc.
101 Morris Street
Sebastopol, CA 95472 USA
Tel: 707-829-0515
Fax: 707-829-0104
Email: order@oreilly.com

Australia

Woodslane Pty., Ltd.
7/5 Vuko Place
Warriewood NSW 2102
Australia
Tel: 61-2-9970-5111
Fax: 61-2-9970-5002
Email: info@woodslane.com.au

New Zealand

Woodslane New Zealand, Ltd.
21 Cooks Street (P.O. Box 575)
Waganui, New Zealand
Tel: 64-6-347-6543
Fax: 64-6-345-4840
Email: info@woodslane.com.au

Latin America

McGraw-Hill Interamericana
Editores, S.A. de C.V.
Cedro No. 512
Col. Atlampa
06450, Mexico, D.F.
Tel: 52-5-547-6777
Fax: 52-5-547-3336
Email: mcgraw-hill@infosel.net.mx

O'REILLY®

O'Reilly & Associates, Inc.
101 Morris Street
Sebastopol, CA 95472-9902
1-800-998-9938

Visit us online at:
www.oreilly.com
order@oreilly.com

O'REILLY WOULD LIKE TO HEAR FROM YOU

Which book did this card come from?

____

Where did you buy this book?

- ❑ Bookstore
- ❑ Computer Store
- ❑ Direct from O'Reilly
- ❑ Class/seminar
- ❑ Bundled with hardware/software
- ❑ Other ________________

What operating system do you use?

- ❑ UNIX
- ❑ Macintosh
- ❑ Windows NT
- ❑ PC(Windows/DOS)
- ❑ Other ________________

What is your job description?

- ❑ System Administrator
- ❑ Programmer
- ❑ Network Administrator
- ❑ Educator/Teacher
- ❑ Web Developer
- ❑ Other ________________

❑ Please send me O'Reilly's catalog, containing a complete listing of O'Reilly books and software.

Name ________________ Company/Organization ________________

Address ________________

City ________ State ________ Zip/Postal Code ________ Country ________

Telephone ________________ Internet or other email address (specify network) ________________

Nineteenth century wood engraving of a bear from the O'Reilly & Associates Nutshell Handbook® *Using & Managing UUCP.*

PLACE STAMP HERE

NO POSTAGE NECESSARY IF MAILED IN THE UNITED STATES

BUSINESS REPLY MAIL

FIRST CLASS MAIL PERMIT NO. 80 SEBASTOPOL, CA

Postage will be paid by addressee

O'Reilly & Associates, Inc.
101 Morris Street
Sebastopol, CA 95472-9902